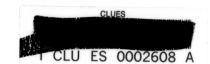

Dying Gods
in
Twentieth-Century Fiction

Dying Gods
in
Twentieth-Century
Fiction

K. J. Phillips

Lewisburg
Bucknell University Press
London and Toronto: Associated University Presses

91-117

© 1990 by Associated University Presses, Inc.

Associated University Presses
440 Forsgate Drive
Cranbury, NJ 08512

Associated University Presses
25 Sicilian Avenue
London WC1A 2QH, England

Associated University Presses
P.O. Box 488, Port Credit
Mississauga, Ontario
Canada L5G 4M2

Library of Congress Cataloging-in-Publication Data

Phillips, K. J., 1950–
    Dying gods in twentieth-century fiction / K. J. Phillips.
        p.   cm.
    Bibliography: p.
    Includes index.
    ISBN 0-8387-5161-X (alk. paper)
    1. Fiction—20th century—History and criticism.   2. Dying and rising gods in literature.   I. Title.
    PN3503.P47   1990
    809.3'938—dc20   88-48036
                                                                                  CIP

Contents

Acknowledgments

I would like to thank Professors Charlene Avallone, Joseph Chadwick, Mark Heberle, Michael Kline, Richard Lessa, Alan MacGregor, Deborah Ross, Roger Whitlock, and Rob Wilson for generously reading and commenting on sections of the manuscript. I would especially like to thank Professor Todd Sammons for patiently teaching me word processing on a computer.

Small portions of the book appeared previously as essays and are reprinted by permission: "Persephone and the Pigs in William Faulkner's *The Sound and the Fury*," *International Fiction Review* 14 (Winter 1987): 14–17, and "Hindu Avatars, Moslem Martyrs, and Primitive Dying Gods in E. M. Forster's *A Passage to India*," *Journal of Modern Literature* 15 (Summer 1989).

The poem "Adonis, Dying" is reprinted by permission of the translator, John Dillon, of Trinity College, Dublin. Lines from *Three Novels by Samuel Beckett: Molloy, Malone Dies, The Unnamable*, copyright 1955, 1956, 1958, are reprinted by permission of Grove Press, Inc. Lines from Virginia Woolf, *To the Lighthouse*, copyright 1955; Virginia Woolf, *The Waves*, copyright 1959; and Eudora Welty, *The Collected Stories*, copyright 1980, are reprinted by permission of Harcourt, Brace, Jovanovich, Inc. Lines from Joseph Conrad, *Nostromo*, copyright 1951, Modern Library, are reprinted by permission of Harper & Row. Lines from "Two Songs from a Play" in *The Poems of W. B. Yeats: A New Edition*, edited by Richard J. Finneran, copyright 1928 by Macmillan Publishing Company, renewed 1956 by Georgie Yeats, are reprinted by permission of Macmillan Publishing Company.

1
Introduction

Adonis, Dying
$\qquad$ by Praxilla (Greece, ca. 450 B.C.)

Loveliest of what I leave
$\qquad$ is the sun himself
Next to that the bright stars
$\qquad$ and the face of mother moon
Oh yes, and cucumbers in season,
$\qquad$ and apples, and pears.[1]

Surely a god like Adonis, along with his equally famous partner, Aphrodite, has long since died from the modern world, with no further possibility of recall. But in the seventy-five hundred or so years since planting cultures first imagined dying/reviving deities, Adonis has emerged as nimbly from periodic eclipses in prestige as he did from natural decay in sympathy with the seasons.[2] After Sir James Frazer popularized the dying gods and their eternal goddesses in *The Golden Bough*, such vegetation deities exercised an enormous fascination on modern writers.[3] Dying/reviving gods actually flourish in twentieth-century fiction.

Dying Gods in Myth

The always violent myths of the vegetation deities basically tell of a god who dies when the plants wither in the cold months or in a dry season. One or more catastrophes have befallen him: a boar wounds him fatally in the groin, a rival dismembers him, an enemy pins him to a stake or tree or cross, or an antagonist throws his body into water. A goddess, mourning, searches for him and may descend to the underworld to obtain his release. Before the god's death, god and goddess celebrate their annual "sacred marriage," imitated by priest and priestess. Women lament the god's death, throwing their scarcely sprouted "gardens of Adonis" into the water to commemorate his brief life, and rejoice at his rebirth, modulating their plaintive ululations into exultant alleluias.

11

After telling about a series of dying gods, Frazer also recounts the story of Persephone, a dying goddess linked to the changing seasons. The god Hades abducts her into the underworld; her mother, Demeter, pursues them and finally wrangles a deal with Zeus whereby Persephone returns for part of each year. Archaeological discoveries after Frazer's time have revealed other dying goddesses: the Sumerian Inanna, for example, who chooses to risk the underworld for her own sake, to seek knowledge rather than a spouse.[4] Hung on a stake, she herself undergoes the three-day death more familiarly assigned to a god. (Dumuzi, the shepherd whom she has made king, remains at home during her adventure. He later endures his own season of death.)

Stories of dying deities vary in motivation and event, as well as in male or female central players. John Vickery contrasts Adonis's "dreamy voluptuousness" with Attis's "puritanical sacrifice" (castration).[5] Some stories present a goddess who connives in her god's downfall, whereas others feature an innocent mother-consort or sister-consort who restores the dead deity. Sometimes a brother, not a goddess, plans the god's death; because a "good" brother periodically defeats an "evil" one, the latter may also become a type of dying god. Despite these important differences, to which I will return according to the version favored by each author, usually I treat the myths as basically cognate; all versions include a deity who dies periodically, a power that attacks him or her, and a companion who searches for the body (see table 1).

Table 1

Origin	Searcher	Dying Deity	Attacker
Sumerian	Attendants	Inanna	—
Babylonian	Ishtar	Tammuz	—
Ugaritic	Anat	Baal	Mot and Yamm
Phrygian	Cybele	Attis	Boar
Syrian-Greek	Aphrodite	Adonis	Boar
Roman	Venus	Adonis	Boar
Roman	Ceres	Proserpine	Pluto
Greek	Demeter	Persephone	Hades
Greek	Athene	Dionysus	Titans
Egyptian	Isis	Osiris	Set
Toltec-Aztec	Coatlicue	Quetzalcoatl	Tezcatlipoca
Scandinavian	Hermod	Balder	Loki
Greek-Aramaic	The Marys	Jesus	Judas

In Melanesia the cult of the dying deity Hainuwele was, at least until recently, still observed in an equatorial culture.[6] After Hainuwele is born from a coconut stuck on the tusk of a dying boar, she dances in a nine-spiraled labyrinth, handing out gifts at each turn. The people delightedly accept her beads, plates, and betel nuts; however, finally overcome by jealousy that she can produce such treasures, they kill this wondrous creature. From her fallen body grow tuberous plants (the principal Melanesian foodstuff), and sexual organs appear on human bodies for the first time.

Hainuwele's story registers the sad fact that new life depends on death: the pig and the coconut (which would otherwise have grown into a tree) die for the nourishment of humans. Although we do not imagine the lopped coconut suffering, varying degrees of pain compound the other sacrifices for a future. Hainuwele, though she recognizes and teaches these sacrifices, does not commit suicide. She does not seek suffering as an end in itself, and she would not have left life, if others had not killed her. Circumstances constrain her to leave, as everybody dies.

The Melanesians commemorate this deity with a nine-day dance in a labyrinth, representing their path through life, to death, and into rebirth. The women distribute betel nuts as Hainuwele did. But for all the compassion that has so far characterized their homage to the goddess, the community has instituted a brutal episode in their rites, repeating the original hostility to Hainuwele. Two young people copulate under a log structure; a ritual executioner looses the logs, which fall on the couple and crush them. The cannibal tribe then eat their sacrifice.

Joseph Campbell cautions us not to misinterpret: "These are not gifts, bribes, or dues rendered to God, but fresh enactments here and now, of the god's own sacrifice in the beginning, through which he, she, or it became incarnate in the world process."[7] We all become food soon enough, for worms; why hasten the process? Nevertheless, the grimly generous lovers seem to acknowledge that the individual goes down, the race survives. Though the couple accept the necessity of death, they do not deny themselves. They make love. They try to imitate Hainuwele, who, consciously facing death, still dances: she takes joy in this life and leaves her personal dancing long enough to give gifts to others.

Hainuwele is not known widely enough to have influenced the writers in this study. Her story, however, inspires a combination of admiration, for a lucid and generous deity, and horror, at brutal rites, that epitomizes the ambivalent response of modern authors to dying deities in general.

Dying Gods in Twentieth-Century Fiction

My purpose in this study is to investigate how modern fiction writers transform the dying/reviving deities, how extensively they mine the myths, and why the stories proved so attractive in the first place.

Modern authors have transformed the myths either ironically or "programmatically." An ironic author has a character go through the motions of a dying god or a grieving goddess, but unfortunately these ordeals no longer serve any purpose. Suffering occurs according to the old patterns of boar hunt, death by water, or dismemberment, but it fails to bring any benefit, either personal or communal. Characters who are "just folks" are cast into the role of a dying deity, unasked, undeserving—and unaware—since it is the authors and readers, generally not the characters, who perceive the parallels. The character is neither good enough to support a god's stature nor bad enough to deserve such affliction, yet the character receives the god's fate anyway. The authors may imply that a whole society has sunk into the underworld in the god's place, but the cycle is stuck. The god stays dead and the goddess keeps grieving. Authors using irony resort to the myth of dying gods to expose the hellish quality of modern life (its purposelessness, anonymity, or refined brutality—the sterility corresponding to the god's time below) or even of all life, in any age, if the author's metaphysical despair extends far enough. Samuel Beckett, for example, compassionately laments the human fate from this bleak limit.

One might suspect that most modern authors, if not so somber as Beckett, would still recast the myth of the dying god ironically, especially if the "sense of historical apocalypse coupled with spiritual abyss" is "recognisably modernist."[8] Nevertheless, the irony that would convert eternal renewal into abysmal monotony does not, after all, infect all modern authors who try to apply the myths to their world. A sizable group borrows from the old stories programmatically: that is, the authors have some program to bring the divine back into life. Such authors expect the reappearance not so much of a literal god as of a "god-in-us" or of a fuller life, like the season when the gods inhabited the earth. The return of the god or goddess hinges on some set of changes, in politics, economics, or psychological attitudes, which the author recommends. D. H. Lawrence, for instance, would invite Quetzalcoatl back from "behind the sun" by practicing spiritual sexuality as the lure.

How do these modern transformations of myth, to show the god permanently mired in the underworld or else almost ready to come back, affect fictional form? First, dying gods reside with equal ease in realistic or in fantastic narratives. Second, in twentieth-century fiction dying gods do not just decorate a passing simile or two but contribute to a connected series of references.[9] Furthermore, the authors usually bury references discreetly. The only writers here who renarrate old stories outright, naming dying gods explicitly, are Thomas Mann in *Joseph and His Brothers*, D. H. Lawrence in *The Plumed Serpent* and *The Man Who Died*, and Saul Bellow in his essayistic short story "A Sermon by Doctor Pep."

As for the extent of borrowing, the dying gods have to be reckoned a major modern motif. In fact, most of the principal modernists know and elaborately adapt the stories of these gods. I will look at several European and American authors: Conrad, Kafka, Forster, Lawrence, Hemingway, Woolf, Faulkner, Mann, and Welty. Even after the modernists, when the first flush of enthusiasm for Frazer had faded, allusions to dying deities do not slacken off. Authors after 1950 are as steeped in such myths as their elders: Beckett, O'Connor, Bellow, Malamud, García Márquez, Konwicki, and Oates.

For a few of these authors, critics have already noted pertinent allusions. In this case, my task will be to place the modern works in the context of the whole return to the dying gods: to determine why so many authors plundered the myths, how modern use of the motif departs from ancient attitudes, and how the modern authors differ from each other. For despite common mythological sources, the authors are far from writing the same book over and over. Even in instances of an already suspected familiarity with myths, however, I will frequently disagree with the current view of how the author refashions them. In *To the Lighthouse*, for example, Virginia Woolf traces the triangle connecting Demeter, Persephone, and Hades more insistently than has been thought; in an unexpected twist, Woolf's Demeter actually acquiesces in all abductions, whereas Hades turns benign.

I also point to several works whose mythological roots have completely escaped attention so far. I have not seen any study that acknowledges Joseph Conrad's real debt in *Nostromo* to a specific Aztec ritual for a dying god. Nor have Beckett's critics yet plumbed the reasons why the dying god should be such a pervasive presence in Beckett's trilogy, especially the middle volume, *Malone Dies*. In similarly ignored borrowings, Forster underlines vestiges of pagan rites in Hindu and Moslem ceremonies for *A Passage to India*, William Faulkner reworks the legend of Isis and Osiris in *Pylon*, and Welty mocks a gaggle of ironically willing Persephones in "Asphodel."

I should warn from the outset that I am not searching for psychological "archetypes." If Virginia Woolf, Ernest Hemingway, and William Butler Yeats all mention black pigs (as they do in *To the Lighthouse*, *A Farewell to Arms*, and "The Valley of the Black Pig"), I am not claiming that they herd these pigs up from a collectively owned, unconscious dark drove. Instead, I am suggesting that they read the same sources in mythology and folklore, or they read each other. I assume influence, not archetypes. In fact, I avoid the word "archetypes," either in Carl Jung's sense of "inborn possibilities for ideas" or in Northrop Frye's sense of "conventions" (because Frye's term is too easily confused with Jung's). As much as possible I try to determine the original sources in which these authors encountered the myths. Usually they picked up *The Golden Bough*, part of the multivolume set or the popular 1922 abridged edition, either studying it or just browsing. Some (such as Lawrence) tackled the works of additional anthropologists like Edward Tylor or Jane Harrison, whereas others (e.g., Forster) reviewed scholars of Indian mythology who pointedly drew comparisons with vegetation rites. Still others (e.g., Conrad) scavenged from historians, such as William Prescott, for Aztec lore. If no source is recorded, but internal evidence in the fiction hints at knowledge of a myth, I assume at the very least that the author heard anthropological talk from friends and has not reverted spontaneously to primordial images. Nor am I collecting vague seasonal references. The clues I am following as pointers to vegetation myths are simply too specific to be common unconscious property: Yeats's black pig, or Forster's "ten-day baskets of corn," or Welty's character made bald. These images connect, respectively, to the dying god's enemy, to gardens of Adonis, and to the goddess's priestess who may offer her hair as an alternative to participating in ritual prostitution.

Just as I do not try to prove that the authors are all rooted in the same unconscious images, I do not try to show the modern works growing out of a historical fact, a ritual regicide. Frazer, of course, insisted that, historically, people did imitate the dying god either voluntarily or involuntarily. Other anthropologists have disputed Frazer's claims, finding "No record, clear or obscure, of an annual or periodic sacrifice of divine kings."[10] (As we have seen, however, Hainuwele's worshipers do sacrifice human victims.) Richard Hardin complains that if no King of the Wood ever stalked through a sacred grove, then critics should stop relying on a discredited *Golden Bough*. Writers, as opposed to critics, have never much cared whether Frazer had all his facts straight, because the obviously fictional, not literal myths have most appealed to artists. Isis, for example, in the improbable form of a huge bird conceiving from the corpse of Osiris, appears in scenes created by Mann, Woolf, and Faulkner.

Why then are modern authors so attracted to the dying gods? They gravitate to these myths in particular because of the gods' sacred marriage and because of the violence that the gods endure. While the first component of the myths expresses a joy in living and sexuality, the second corresponds to the violence that has in reality pervaded the twentieth century. Although most myths feature pleasure and pain, these stories include the most intense joy and the most intense suffering—and, uniquely, the death—of deities. Dying gods, unlike remote, complacent Olympians, reflect human experience in more than its frivolity. The stories are meaningful because of what they say about human trials and choices.

Myth-minded authors have taken two tacks in interpreting the violence hounding the dying gods. One is to say that the gods recognize the pain already inherent in life. The other is to assert that the gods or their rites add to the amount of pain in the world. If the deity simply recognizes the existence of suffering and agrees to accept his or her share, then modern authors usually admire that deity. They adopt the myth because, far from being an escapist fantasy, it bluntly registers *what the world is*. Such authors hold up the myth as a way of confronting and questioning, in the manner of the naturalist Annie Dillard, "What kind of world is this, anyway? Why not make fewer barnacle larvae and give them a decent chance? . . . I have to acknowledge that the sea is a cup of death and the land is a stained altar stone. . . . If an aphid lays a million eggs, several might survive. . . . It's a wretched system."[11] The puzzlement and even anguish of this statement also characterize the attitude of authors attracted to the dying gods. Modern authors may view the Greek Adonis pierced by his boar, or the Egyptian Osiris torn by his brother, as an apt reflection of a wretched system that actually exists in nature and in society. Animals do feed on animals. Men do kill their brothers. People die. The authors may be horrified by the suffering, but they do not want to pretend that it is not there. They contemplate the dying god to remind themselves of the extra larvae profligately exposed, the little fish crunched by the big, the massacres and pogroms. Because the dying deities know about this destruction too, because they *are* the world, immanent in it, one group of authors accepts such myths for their austere lucidity: admitting, through an imaginative projection, that death overcomes everyone.

On the other hand, if the rites that accompanied a particular myth ever required a person to duplicate the dying god's sacrifice, then the dying god may be said to add to the stock of pain. The usually politically or socially minded authors who interpret the myth in this light condemn it. They appropriate aspects of a dying god's story to represent stupid and brutal societies or governments, forcing their citizens onto the altar stone of racial prejudice, totalitarianism, or useless wars.

In the chapters that follow I distinguish three ways (with some overlap) in which myths of dying gods have served modern authors: to make reflexive statements about art (chapters 2 and 3), to question the metaphysical nature of the world (chapters 3 and 4), and to explore political and social issues (chapters 4–9). Here I would like to set out areas of dispute in the interpretation of authors' use of dying deities. I will indicate what these areas of dispute are and suggest what my polemical stance will be when I return to these topics in chapter 10.

REFLEXIVITY

Although authors have probably always imbedded self-conscious questions about the purpose and means of art within literary works, it is generally assumed that modern authors lay special claim to such self-consciousness.[12] And though a *topos* proclaiming the inadequacy of art or the artist also has a long history, twentieth-century authors again place their doubts in the foreground. In fact, they often simultaneously elevate art to a sacrament and denigrate it as "lies," with a seriousness, an exaggerated pride, and an exacerbated despair that seem characteristically modern. If the penchant of modern authors for both reflexivity and ambivalence is well known, I would like to add the surprising extent to which the dying god has served the twentieth century as a kind of "objective correlative" for reflexive ambivalence. I will show how authors have drawn analogies from dying god to art work, artist, and any fictive lens (including social codes) for seeing the world.

HISTORY

Several critics accuse myth users of trying to hide from history, of refusing to take responsibility for changing real political and social conditions, from a refuge of "timeless truths." On the contrary, I will argue that most authors studied here allude to myths of dying deities precisely as a means to face the particular horrors of twentieth-century history. Moreover, the effect of their works is not to encourage a passive withdrawal into mythic models. Rather than seeking through myth an escape into mindless "blood and guts," these authors pursue a mindful, conscious examination of the myths and their continued application or dangers.[13]

GENDER

The presence of goddesses in myths of dying deities played an important part in drawing modern authors to those stories. I will offer a two-part argument about attitudes toward the goddesses. First, I will argue that authors who claim to praise "feminine traits" through the myths do not always imagine for women a social role in any way corresponding to their power in mythology. Some feminists conclude that because such misogyny exists in the interpretation of dying deities (particularly by Jungians), we should throw out the vegetation myths altogether.[14] Nevertheless, I will try to show how the dying deities need not be thrown out but can be reinterpreted, without just reinforcing stereotypes.

SPIRITUALITY

It is often taken as axiomatic that the twentieth century has thoroughly secularized itself.[15] Certainly belief in the Judeo-Christian god has declined since 1882, when Nietzsche pronounced "god is dead" in the famous passage from *The Gay Science*:

> We have killed him. . . . How were we able to drink up the sea? Who gave us the sponge to wipe away the whole horizon? What did we do when we loosened this earth from its sun? Wither does it now move? Wither do we move? Away from all suns? . . . Do we not stray, as

through infinite nothingness?. . . Has it not become colder? Does not night come on continually, darker and darker?. . . What lustrums, what sacred games shall we have to devise? Is not the magnitude of this deed too great for us? Shall we not ourselves have to become Gods, merely to seem worthy of it?[16]

No sooner had Nietzsche—in a mood characterized by some hopefulness and much anguish—hauled out Jehovah (whom he discovered already enfeebled) than he ushered in another god, Dionysus (one of the dying gods, in fact), as a model for humans. Why was Nietzsche so attracted to Dionysus, Lawrence to Quetzalcoatl, Woolf to Isis, Hemingway to Attis and Cybele, and so on? Critics usually read any obvious allusions to dying gods as an ironic statement, as if the author were turning over shards of broken beliefs to show how shattered all beliefs have become. Critics may conclude that these authors, including Eliot in *The Waste Land*, want to borrow only formal elements from the myths, while they find the meaning uninteresting or irrelevant.[17] On the contrary, I will argue that many twentieth-century authors, although changing the import of the old stories, did want the myths to stimulate a new spirituality (not a new orthodoxy), so that some "meaning" exists rather than just an exposure of bankruptcy.

Dying Gods in Earlier Literature

Although the popularity of the dying gods surged in the twentieth century after Frazer's work, interest in their myths has not lapsed between neolithic times and the present. To show the vitality of this tradition, I will sketch some variants on the myths from Gilgamesh to twentieth-century poetry. Obviously a view of such an enormous time must be selective. I want, however, to mention at least a few of the intervening inheritors from primitive mythology because the most famous versions—the Bible, Ovid's *Metamorphoses*, Shakespeare's "Venus and Adonis," Shelley's "Adonais"—may have colored my authors' understanding of the deities, about whom they nevertheless learned most from anthropologists, either directly or indirectly. For example, Venus as a dangerous floozy (in the works of Ovid and Shakespeare) has competed in the twentieth century with a more dignified persona for the ancient goddess.

PREBIBLICAL AND BIBLICAL PERIODS

The twentieth century has no monopoly on ironic reinterpretations of the deities' stories. The transmitter of the Mesopotamian *Epic of Gilgamesh*, recorded in the second millennium B.C., knows a myth of the dying god but purposely alters it. The storyteller models King Gilgamesh's descent to the underworld, to find his dead friend Enkidu, on Inanna's and Ishtar's descents to the "great below" to gain knowledge or to fetch Tammuz. Ishtar even appears in the epic to declare her love for Gilgamesh, as if he were a divinely invested king who should be ready to mate with a priestess in the role of the goddess, to bless the natural world. But Gilgamesh rejects Ishtar's advances, accusing her of deceiving her lovers, and he cannot bring Enkidu back from death. The king locates the precious plant that confers immortality but loses it when he falls asleep and a snake steals it. The ancient storyteller opens a myth of renewal only to make the ironic point that humans, unlike snakes, cannot slough their skins to rejuvenate themselves. Instead, they die, once and for all.

The biblical Book of Jonah also uses myth in an ironic mood. The author expertly sets up conventions for the dying god, then demolishes our readied expectations. Stanley Edgar Hyman points to the "archetypal experience" behind the story: the belly of the fish is a womb, which satisfies our need to be reborn.[18] But the story of the fish belly touches us not just because Jonah fits the pattern of a dying/reviving god but rather because he fails to fit at crucial points. The smooth hum of the traditional plot hits a wonderfully humorous clinker: Jonah experiences his radical incubation only to emerge as the same old Jonah. Reborn but not transformed, he complains as much as ever. If the grumpy prophet now goes to Nineveh, he complies for purely pragmatic reasons—disgruntled aversion to further fish innards.

The author of Jonah can imitate even small details of the myth of the dying god for comic effect. When the narrator reports that the Nineveh in which Jonah is belatedly setting foot takes exactly three days to cross, that time period would immediately be familiar to an audience long accustomed to deities who went to the underworld for three days and three nights: Inanna hung on a stake, Tammuz sunk to the pit. Indeed, the ungodlike Jonah also ruminates for three days in the fish. When the narrator stretches Nineveh to a crossing of three days, however, he wryly insinuates Jonah's private opinion that the city too is an "underworld": a hellish, unattractive place, not worth all the trudging, hoarseness, and heat prostration it will require of him. Jonah, tramping slowly across the metropolis, as when he mulled in the belly, again resembles Tammuz traversing the underworld. Yet Jonah, unlike Tammuz, does not care about reviving any community. To a man afraid of being called a liar if the city does not blow up as predicted, Nineveh is a hell to his ego just as much after it repents as it was a hell for its sins before he grudgingly converted its citizens.

Myths of vegetation deities have left their mark on other parts of the Old Testament. The Song of Songs probably preserves some of the erotic chants used by worshipers enacting the deities' sacred marriage.[19] In particular, the bride's recurrent lament for her absent lover recalls the goddess's difficult search for the dead god. The daughters of Jerusalem backing up the bride may derive from the chorus of women who keened each year with the goddess.

Apparently the worship of fertility gods and goddesses under several names survived in Canaan into biblical times, because the prophets repeatedly bristle up at reports of images and orgies in "high places" (sacred groves). Although Deuteronomy prohibits bringing the "hire of a harlot" or the "wages of a dog" (male prostitute) into the temple, suggesting Frazer's cultic sexuality, King Josiah in 621 B.C. finds that this same scroll of Deuteronomy has only accumulated dust and that sacred poles (asherim) in honor of the fertility goddess Asherah have sprung up everywhere.[20] Isaiah turns the people's continued faith in gardens of Adonis, "pleasant plants. . . slips of an alien god. . . which blossom in the morning that you sow," into a metaphor predicting a bitter harvest for such observances.[21] Jeremiah castigates the women for imprinting their cakes with the likeness of the "queen of heaven," and Ezekiel even hears "women weeping for Tammuz" at the north gate of the Hebrew temple.[22] But if King Josiah knocks down the asherim, he still affirms his own covenants next to a pillar, turning the prestige of the phallic markers accompanying the goddess to the account of Yahweh.[23]

One of the most interesting ways the vegetation deities influence the Old Testament is through the important metaphor comparing the Lord's love for Israel to the love of a bridegroom for his bride. Hosea, who introduces this metaphor to all the prophets, in effect joins the cult that he cannot beat down, or at least joins the language of the Canaanite humanized gods whom he abhors, to the language now evoking the "unpicturable" Yahweh.[24] The prophets' moving portraits of the Lord's humanlike longing, jealousy, and vacillation whether to punish or forgive his wayward bride, plus his concern for flowing grain, wine, and oil, owe much to the Canaanite concepts of Baal mating with Anat and the two of them pouring out the fruits of the earth.

As for the New Testament, when Jesus takes care to act "as it is written," he not only follows the Old Testament but also the familiar "script" of vegetation gods. The imagery of good shepherd, fisher of men, savior hung on a tree, sojourner for three days in hell, son of a "star of the sea," victim lanced in the side, and lord of bread and wine who is himself consumed by his worshipers, all mimic aspects of earlier dying gods.[25] Although Christianity underlines that Christ died and resurrected once and for all, historically, whereas the mythical gods die and revive every year with the seasons, the proselytizing early church in fact emphasized similarities rather than differences between the new religion and various fertility cults, so that rabbits and eggs and solstitial evergreens could work their way comfortably into Easter and Christmas.

CLASSICAL PERIOD

Vegetation myths apparently influenced classical epic, dramatic, and pastoral traditions. W. F. Jackson Knight speculates that the form of the *Odyssey* may derive from eastern poems like *The Journey of Ishtar* and *The Epic of Gilgamesh*.[26] The prerogative and daring to go out on the quest pass from Ishtar to the male protagonists of Western epic; Odysseus, Aeneas, and Dante descend to the underworld, while the women in those poems, Penelope, Dido, and Beatrice, unlike Ishtar, sit out the excitement at home or in heaven. The *Odyssey* may owe other motifs, along with the search for underworldly knowledge, to vegetation deities. Like Adonis and Attis, Odysseus suffers a thigh wound from a boar; like the shepherd Tammuz, he spends three days in his loyal herdsman's hut before coming back into his own, "between the waxing and the waning of the moon."[27] The monthly dying/reviving moon typically presides over vegetation deities.

Classical drama as well as the epic may gain some impetus from myths of periodic renewal. Following Gilbert Murray, Joseph Campbell compares tragic *katharsis* to earlier ritual *katharsis*, "which was the function of the festival and mystery play of the dismembered bull-god, Dionysos."[28] Scholars now dispute the claim of Murray's Cambridge school that Greek drama develops directly out of ritual, pointing to dramatists' sources in epic plots rather than in the life of Dionysus.[29] Nevertheless, if crediting Dionysus's cults with all Greek drama is too broad, a play like Euripides' *The Bacchae*, in which a flamboyant and vengeful Dionysus appears as a character, certainly draws on his myth with ironic intent. Whereas the author of Jonah twists "rebirth" for comic effect, here Euripides savages the notion. Although we can chuckle at the petty tyrant Jonah and perhaps admire the gutsiness of his selfish complaints against God, we can only cringe at Pentheus's tyranny and pity his cruel punishment from Dionysus. A supercilious Dionysus can reassemble his scattered limbs, but the mortal Pentheus torn to pieces by frenzied women dies irrevocably. As in *The Epic of Gilgamesh*, the contrast between renewable gods and unrecoverable humans forms the main, sobering point.

With an attribution almost as sweeping as the Cambridge school linking Greek drama to ritual, Northrop Frye traces the whole pastoral tradition, stretching from Theocritus's elegies through Milton's "Lycidas," to the form of the lament for Adonis.[30] Frye claims that even Walt Whitman, as much as he urged poets to forget the matter of Troy and invent new themes, himself remembered, in his own pastoral elegy, "When Lilacs Last in the Dooryard Bloomed," such specific trappings of the dying god as "purple flowers thrown on coffins, a great star drooping in the west, imagery of 'ever-returning spring,' and all the rest of it."[31]

The Greek vegetation deities—Adonis and Aphrodite, Dionysus, Persephone and Demeter—mainly influenced later writers who flocked to the classics for imagery. Most of the other ancient Middle Eastern or primitive versions had to wait for nineteenth- and twentieth-century anthropologists to advertise them. Isis, however, did enjoy a vogue in classical literature, appearing in Apuleius's *Golden Ass* and other works. Apuleius's majestic Isis instructs her initiate, "I am Nature, the universal Mother, mistress of all the elements, primordial child of time, sovereign of all things spiritual, queen of the dead, queen also of the immortals, the single manifestation of all gods and goddesses that are."[32]

When the Latin Ovid retells the stories of Isis, Adonis and Venus, Attis and Cybele, he focuses on piquant, cynically observed human foibles. Although Venus claims to have warned Adonis about boars, she interrupts her reminiscences of him to confide how ruthlessly she punished another young man's infraction, leaving a glimmer of suspicion that she may have secretly engineered Adonis's death too. Elsewhere Ovid blames her for devising Proserpine's rape, as if to take the chortling, lecherous Pluto and Jupiter off the hook.

MIDDLE AGES

Jessie Weston, in her influential *From Ritual to Romance*, derives the medieval Fisher King and Waste Land from the dying gods and their eclipse. Medieval legend and ancient vegetation myths share several motifs: a wound in the groin, sterility of the land, and focus on sexuality, as in the possibly female and male symbols of grail cup and lance.[33] Departing from mythical precedent, the medieval land blights during the sick king's presence, rather than during the god's absence. This change leaves the way open to assume guilt for king and community—Malory's condemnation of selfish individualism, for example—whereas the god was always innocent. Other scholars have objected to Weston's reading of the grail legends as the confused record of earlier fertility rites.[34] Nevertheless, such squabbles have not prevented authors from easily combining grail legend and myth of dying god. For example, Woolf's young dying "God" Percival bears a medieval quester's name; and Malamud's dying/reviving baseball player belongs to the Knights team.

RENAISSANCE

In Book 4, Chapter 28, of Rabelais's *Gargantua and Pantagruel*, Pantagruel narrates how a voice hails a becalmed ship, commanding its captain, Thamous, to announce the news that "the great god Pan was dead." The name Thamous is probably drawn from Tammuz, another name for the god said to be dead, not the name of the captain. The same garbled anecdote appears in Plutarch, who does not seem to realize that a syncretic religion is apparently coalescing Pan and Tammuz, nor that the god's death is only temporary.[35] Rabelais, though, does his own synthesizing of dying gods, because Pantagruel concludes that the mourners on the shore are really shrieking for Christ: "I do not consider my reading of the story far-fetched. For he [Christ] can rightfully be called, in the Greek tongue, Pan; seeing that he is our All."[36]

Spenser's famous "Gardin of Adonis" in *The Faerie Queene* (Book 3, Canto 6) offers an earthly paradise of perpetual spring and unending harvest. Sounding more like a pagan than a Christian, Spenser insists that what transforms earth into a paradise is sexual love, because "Franckly each paramour his leman knowes / Each bird his mate." Yet if Venus can enjoy Adonis in an arbor, periodic grief still interrupts their embraces: "All [although] be he subiect to mortalitie, / Yet is eterne in mutabilitie, / And by succession made perpetuall, / Transformed oft, and chaunged diuerslie: / For him the Father of all formes they call."[37] Although the boar of time charges out of its cave to decay matter, eternal forms—available to Nature and presumably to Art—shape the raw substances again.

In "Venus and Adonis" Shakespeare turns the myth to farce. He pictures Venus as a tireless, middle-aged nymphomaniac, grappling her frail, reasonable young man to the mattress, "Like a wild bird being tam'd with too much handling." When Adonis's horse breaks away from him to mate with a jennet, Venus looks by implication like an ass, though Adonis does not entirely escape ridicule as a callow, stubborn mule. Venus regains some sympathy when, "Like a milch doe, whose swelling dugs do ache, / Hasting to feed her fawn," she tries to protect a heedless Adonis. Although Shakespeare injects a serious note that love always painfully induces "a life in death," he blames Venus more than the nature of things—more than the vulnerability attendant on strong attachments. Venus describes the thrusting of the boar in sexual terms, but it is female sexuality, not passion in general, that destroys people: "by a kiss [the boar] thought to persuade him there; / And nuzzling in his flank the loving swine / Sheath'd, unaware, the tusk in his soft groin. / Had I been tooth'd like him, I must confess, / With kissing him I should have killed him first."[38]

ROMANTIC PERIOD

The romantic poets adapt the god's plunge into the underworld as an image for the way genius taps into dangerous yet rich veins of art, buried in imagination and in nature. Tracing a history of the "garden of Adonis" trope in poetry, Frye believes that

> visions of descent in medieval and Renaissance poetry are usually infernal visions, based on Virgil but ignoring his interest in rebirth. Only with Romantic poetry do we begin to get once more the oracular or quest descent, where the hero gets something more for his descent than a tragic tale or an inspection of torments. In Keats's *Endymion* there are adventures in both upward and downward directions, the upward ones

being mainly quests for beauty and the downward ones quests for truth. The Gardens of Adonis in this poem seem to be down rather than up, as they do at the conclusion of Blake's *Book of Thel*.[39]

Shelley, who began his "Adonais" to mourn the death of Keats, modifies conventions of pastoral elegy and of laments for dying gods. He shifts the tone at the end of his poem from loss to rejoicing by asserting that the dead poet is immortal through the poetry he has left behind.[40] This equation of the dying god with Keats recalls an earlier curious merging of myth and biography: Sir Philip Sidney's "fatal thigh-wound made him a favorite historical embodiment of Adonis."[41] Whereas Shelley's subjective identification of the dying god may seem particularly characteristic of the romantic age, in all periods a myth of the dying god often gains urgency for an author only after a personal or actual loss. Milton grieved for a friend, Edward King, in "Lycidas," as Whitman remembered the slain Lincoln in "When Lilacs Last in the Dooryard Bloomed." Even in the twentieth century, when many authors supposedly keep their private personalities on the sidelines, Woolf identifies the dying "God" Percival in *The Waves* with her late brother, Thoby Stephen; Eliot, describing the god's purple flowers in *The Waste Land*, may be haunted by a lilac-carrying friend, Jean Verdenal, who was killed in World War I.[42]

OTHER NINETEENTH-CENTURY LITERATURE

Despite the renewed respect for myth in romantic poets, several voices in the mid-nineteenth century begin to complain that the old stories have overstayed their welcome. Karl Marx, for example, though he admires Greek mythology and wonders how this product of "the childhood of mankind" could have attained such sophistication, demands, "Where does Vulcan come in as against Roberts & Co.; Jupiter, as against the lightning rod?"[43] Presumably, Adonis and the boar would contend even more feebly beside astronaut and laser beam. Walt Whitman also advises, "Cross out please those immensely overpaid accounts" to Troy and Athens and Jerusalem. Yet if he is ready to ban mythology entirely in "Song of the Exposition," in "Song of Myself" he is still introducing it. Although he boasts that he can replace the old gods and find their equal on the street corner in the "mechanic's wife" or the "snag-toothed hostler," he has apparently just studied a whole sheaf of myths and, in fact, parades the gods with gusto:

Buying drafts of Osiris and Isis and Belus and Brahma and Adonai,
In my portfolio placing Manito loose, and Allah on a leaf, and the crucifix engraved,
With Odin, and the hideous-faced Mexitli, and all idols and images,
Honestly taking them all for what they are worth, and not a cent more,

Admitting they were alive and did the work of their day,
Admitting they bore mites as for unfledged birds who have now to rise
and fly and sing for themselves,
   Accepting the rough deific sketches to fill out better in myself
   . . . bestowing them freely on each man and woman I see.[44]

Whitman relies, in fact, on the prototypical god and goddess to teach him
his social and artistic mission. Like Isis embracing Osiris, Whitman will
link his arm around all creatures to infuse healing into them and even new
life: "To any one dying [. . .] I raise him with resistless will [. . .] I am he
bringing help for the sick as they pant on their backs, / And for strong
upright men I bring yet more needed help [. . .] becoming already a
creator! / Putting myself here and now to the ambushed womb of the
shadows!"[45] Imagining that he is making love to both seen and unseen, to
the prostitute, the hostler, and the stars, Whitman claims he can breathe
new life into the world as Isis did—by touching real people and perhaps by
conjuring them in song, when he names and brings to our attention even
the lowest creatures.

TWENTIETH-CENTURY EXAMPLES (OTHER THAN FICTION)

   This century did not "cross out" its accounts from old legends but traded
on them vigorously. Writers heeded Whitman's example in "Song of Myself" to transform the dying gods more than his advice in "Song of the
Exposition" to dismiss them. Twentieth-century writers belied Marx's
prediction that myths would decay into irrelevance, bearing out instead
Friedrich Nietzsche's shrewder prophecy that people would rummage in
old stories through personal need, not academic fussiness: "Man today,
stripped of myth, stands famished amongst all his pasts and must dig fran-
tically for roots, be it among the most remote antiquities."[46]
   In 1923 T. S. Eliot issued his famous call for a "mythical method" as "a
way of controlling, of ordering, of giving a shape and a significance to the
immense panorama of futility and anarchy which is contemporary
history."[47] Although he implies that authors such as Joyce may pillage
myths for aesthetic reasons, leaving meaning behind but taking the more
portable plots to provide undergirding for the real interest, word play,
Eliot hopes that myths will supply "significance" for society as well as
"shape" for the page. In fact, the historical chaos that Eliot wants to contain by means of myth, and the religious longings that he and Nietzsche
detect among artists, both contribute strongly to the modern fascination
with dying gods.
   After Eliot's call for a mythical method, vegetation deities indeed stirred
and awakened throughout modern plays and poetry, not just in fiction. In
Tennessee Williams's play *Sweet Bird of Youth*, for example, a character
named Chance Wayne (the god waning, not waxing) hides in the Royal

Palms Hotel, on Easter Sunday, from an Attis-type threatened castration, and the neglected film actress Princess Kosmonopolis uses up all possible rebirths in "the greatest come-back in the history of the industry." Beckett's short play *Pas* bases many details and its brief action—repeated pacing in nine steps—on Demeter's restless search during nine days. The dying gods have even worked their way into modern films. Although my topic is fiction, I have included a few pages in chapter 6 on Francis Ford Coppola's movie *Apocalypse Now*, which relies heavily on literary sources.

Among poets, I will briefly mention Eliot and Yeats, because these influential writers probably first introduced a few of my fiction authors to vegetation myths. In *The Waste Land* Eliot alludes to several rites for dying gods mentioned by Frazer: effigies or humans substituted for hanged or burned gods, a floating puppet retrieved on a distant shore and declared reborn, a buried Osiris made of straw from which plants germinate. In Eliot's poem, however, all these gestures to imitate the god are tentative or locked in the stage of suffering. The Phoenician Sailor has drowned, but his eyes have not verifiably transmuted into pearls. Soldiers "plant" a corpse, but who knows if a "Dog" will dig it up before it has sprouted and bloomed. April comes back, the "cruellest month," but spiritual renewal does not accompany the seasons, automatically "breeding / Lilacs out of the dead land." Despite ubiquitous references to dying gods, the gods' cycles of giving all, with sympathy and control, and retaking all, with joy, remain remote from Eliot's twentieth-century automatons, "neither / Living nor dead."

Yeats's poems influenced by myths of dying gods include "The Second Coming," "The Valley of the Black Pig," "Her Vision in the Wood," "Two Songs from a Play," "A Dialogue of Self and Soul," and "Vacillation." In "Two Songs from a Play," Yeats shows Dionysus and Athene, Spica and Astraea, and Christ and Mary succeeding each other in historical cycles.[48] In a haunting stanza from "Two Songs," the poet sees "a staring virgin stand / Where holy Dionysus died, / And tear the heart out of his side, / And lay the heart upon her hand / And bear that beating heart away; / . . . As though god's death were but a play." This last line suggests mystery rites, which brought hope to worshipers of dying gods. Nevertheless, the line also ominously implies that humanity forgets that anyone— whether god, soldier, poet, or woman mourning—really suffers. Nations keep enacting the same scenes of wars and executions stupidly, to "feed the crow" and to "Drive to a flashier bauble." Civilizations—Greek, Roman, and Christian—grow out of one another, but neither rabble nor elite learn very much from the dying gods whom they claim to revere, except how to crucify new victims.

Yeats's foreboding that people will play at a dangerous game of life and death, casting fellow human beings as dying gods through more and more painful incarnations as the centuries go by, echoes eerily in contemporary news. In 1981, Israel, fearing that its Arab neighbors were trying to develop nuclear weapons to destroy it, attacked the Tammuz Nuclear Reactor in Iraq.[49] Ordinary citizens in the Middle East probably do not recognize an ancient dying god in the name of the nuclear installation, just as Westerners who mark "Thursday" on their calendars are unlikely to remember the god Thor. Tammuz is now the neutral month of July, though the managers who labeled the reactor must have known the god behind the month. To name a nuclear reactor after a dying god may be just learned display: a comparison of Tammuz, dissolved to give energy to the crops, with the atom, split to create power. Yet, as Mircea Eliade outlines, myths of deities, murdered to form life, easily shade into myths of whole worlds periodically destroyed.[50] Yeats's predictions include, I hope, no new stanza to his historical series in "Two Songs": a truly concluding stanza, in which a Tammuz nuclear weapon explodes once and for all, and a staring morning star watches as the earth's heart finally ceases to beat.

2

Tracing and Erasing the World: Tammuz as Artist

For Woolf in *The Waves* and Mann in *Joseph and His Brothers*, the dying god becomes an occasion to meditate the value of art. Although both authors fiercely defend literature, they also finally mistrust its adequacy to resurrect the past. Just as they know that the god rises and then falls, they create and then undercut a "divine" work. Keeping reverence and doubt in uneasy conjunction, they deride and boast of, by turns, their artistic calling. They contradict former statements as their books proceed and cause the "death" of each pridefully offered story in irony and a kind of internal palinode.

Woolf

To help her portray the mysterious Percival, who compels the devotion of the six speaking characters in *The Waves* (1931), Virginia Woolf borrows specific attributes of the dying/reviving god. Percival fits the pattern of vegetation deity most obviously because he dies young but also because he quickens the rest of his world. He infuses the physical world with a unifying order, and he promises to correct social injustice. The fact that Woolf undermines all claims to "godhead" in homey or humorous comparisons does not diminish the real reverence that Percival inspires. Like a mythological figure who sums up human possibilities on a larger scale, Percival reflects the others' experience: each of the six friends takes on some aspect of the dying god too. When Percival dies, the others invoke him with a stylized chorus of "Come," as women keen for the buried god. Finally, Woolf converts the friends' impossible desire that Percival revive into the urgent modernist question whether art can restore the past to us or grant to our loves perhaps their only chance for immortality.

Woolf consciously prepares us to see Percival as a primitive god. Bernard, the artist, asserts outright that Percival is a "God."[1] He tempers his enthusiasm, however, by admitting that Percival's most godlike act would be to get a stalled bullock cart moving again by means of violent language. Even this humorous example of setting a little world in motion occurs in the conditional tense; we don't know if Percival, riding the roads in India, had time even to urge on the cows before his horse threw him.

So that we don't confuse this "God" with Christ, Neville introduces Percival to us as a "pagan." Neville has just "gibe[d] and mock[ed]" at an Easter procession, where the figurines, practically senile, are "borne niddle–noddling along the streets" (35–36). Unlike Christ isolated "in a glass case," Percival merges much more closely with nature: "Not a thread, not a piece of paper lies between him and the sun, between him and the rain, between him and the moon as he lies naked, tumbled, hot, on his bed" (48). Louis makes the death of this man who, like a vegetation god, displays such affinity for the physical world represent all other deaths, claiming, "he died in Egypt; he died in Greece; all deaths are one death" (170). Although Louis insists that he himself hails from ancient civilizations, using the names "Egypt" and "Greece" to bolster his sense of superiority to the local English, here he conjures with geography new identities for the "God" Percival: Osiris, Attis, and Adonis, who died yearly in Egypt and Greece.

The clearest hint that Woolf is indeed associating Percival with these Mediterranean gods occurs when Rhoda mourns for him: "Now I will relinquish; now I will let loose. Now I will at last free the checked, the jerked back desire to be spent, to be consumed. We will gallop together over desert hills where the swallow dips her wings in dark pools and the pillars stand entire. Into the wave that dashes upon the shore, into the wave that flings its white foam to the uttermost corners of the earth I throw my violets, my offering to Percival" (164). Woolf alludes to dying gods three times in this passage, with specific details suggesting Attis, Adonis, and Osiris.

First, violets belong to Attis. Wreaths of violets decorated trees in honor of Attis, since the flowers were said to have sprung from his blood.[2] Rhoda and Louis have, in fact , already evoked Attis, at the going-away party for Percival, by imagining that "savages" throw violets and "deck the beloved with garlands" (140). They also imagine horns, a procession, and "bleeding limbs which they have torn from the living body"(140). These details recall Frazer's description of celebrations for Attis: flower-swathed effigy, flutes, procession, and self-mutilating priests.[3] The phrase "bleeding limbs" refers to the jealous sparring in which the friends often indulge (215), and blood also presages at this early communal meal Percival's later death.

In the scene of Rhoda's mourning, she throws her violets into the river, a second allusion to dying gods, since women tossed "gardens of Adonis" into a body of water.[4] Third, Isis "in the likeness of a swallow fluttered round the pillar that contained her dead brother [Osiris], twittering mournfully."[5] This image may have struck Woolf with particular force, because her own favorite brother, Thoby, died as a young man. When she finished *The Waves*, she wanted to scrawl Thoby's name across it.[6] The pillar that Rhoda seeks encloses *her* Osiris, Percival, now inaccessible. Rhoda's very specific assortment of violets, water, swallow, and pillar all occur in Frazer's chapter on the dying gods. Woolf refers to *The Golden Bough* in *A Room of One's Own* (1929), and it seems likely from her imagery in *The Waves* that she is recalling details about the dying gods to express Rhoda's grief.[7]

Pillars accumulate several related meanings for Rhoda. They represent stately and distant cleanness, as opposed to the muck and confusion she perceives closer to hand; a place to hide; and the stability of art, in contrast to painfully unstable nature. In fact, by choosing the artfully wrought marble of pillars—safe but also dead—Rhoda finally denies the associations with fertility cults created by her reference to violets: "after Percival died . . . I prayed that I might thunder for ever on the verge of the world where there is no vegetation, but here and there a marble pillar. I threw my bunch into the spreading wave" (205). Rhoda would rather root out the vegetation than submit to its painful cycles.

Although Rhoda assumes in her mind the same form as Isis, a swallow, she cannot revive her Osiris. Moreover, despite the fact that Bernard says Percival will at least briefly remain an "arbiter," Rhoda cannot make him a judge in the underworld (155). Nor will she let him live on in a son, as Isis bears Horus and as Susan and Bernard's wife each has a son soon after Percival dies. The only way Rhoda and Percival could "gallop together" would be if she herself were to die. Instead of accepting death, as in fertility cults, Rhoda relinquishes her violets to express an actual desire for death. In fact, we later hear that she commits suicide "seeking some pillar" (281); she flings not only her violets but herself to oblivion.

In addition to attracting this imagery of reviving god in violets and swallows, Percival resembles a deity by giving order to all the other characters. Rhoda says they swarm around him like previously aimless minnows around a stone (136). To Louis, Percival dissolves their defensive assertions of separateness and difference (137). Jinny calls their reunion at dinner "this globe whose walls are made of Percival," and Bernard cherishes "the swelling and splendid moment created by us from Percival" (145–46). These last two images make Percival coexistent with a whole world. Emphasizing the purpose and very substance that Percival lends to them, Neville fears that "without Percival there is no solidity. We are silhouettes, hollow phantoms moving mistily without a background" (122).

Beyond informing the physical world with meaning and matter, as an immanent god, Percival can also right the social world, as a grail knight—or

so the others expect. Grail knight and dying god may be related: Weston
derives the infertile waste land and impotent Fisher King from the period in
the dying god's cycle when he is castrated or absent.[8] In any case, Woolf
combines the two figures of grail quester and dying god easily.[9] She chooses
to name the beloved Percival after the medieval Parzival, bumbler and
lover, rather than after Galahad, for example, the coldly perfect and chaste
knight. Percival, like his namesake, is thoroughly down-to-earth and "conventional" (123): he guffaws, snores, plays games, and loves Susan. We don't
know much about him except that he hates insincerity; and while he despises weakness, he shows kindness. Yet he works no personal miracles.
He fails to win Susan and even to persuade Bernard to accompany him on
an outing to Hampton Court. But if he experiences the usual disappoint-
ments, he displays an unusual zest and an equanimity approaching indifference (156). His name from the grail stories helps explain the others' conviction, totally unproved, that as an official in India he would have "done
justice" and "denounced some monstrous tyranny," that he would have
"protected" people and "shocked the authorities" (152, 243).

Percival as a knight riding against a dragon becomes a paradigm for human beings fighting against death (or against its minions and harbingers,
sadness and dullness). One way of fighting death is through loving, through
sex, as the dying god defies his imminent death with his sacred marriage.
An aging Jinny, for instance, still signaling to men—even if just to a cab
driver—poignantly becomes a knight by "riding" against the day, in the
style of Percival (195, 275). Louis objects that Jinny's scarf and Susan's
teakettle, accoutrements of their emotional and sexual lives, are just
"streamers thrown in the eyes of the charging bull," an image related to
the "beast which stamps," or to the dragon—to death devouring (220).
Susan and Jinny cannot defeat the bull of death with sex or intense emotion, either love or hate. There is no question of even distracting the beast.
We distract ourselves, while it continues to charge. Yet even if fighting
against these odds might be foolish—Woolf compares protest to pounding
a spoon on a table as often as she pictures riding noble steeds—she still
admires the spunk and dash of a Percival.

When Parzival, the medieval prototype, fails to ask the proper question
at the grail castle, the people are left grieving in the unhealed waste land.[10]
Percival likewise leaves behind "many obscure Indians, and people dying
of famine and disease, and women who have been cheated, and whipped
dogs and crying children. . .bereft" (243). Parzival, failing once, gets a
second chance. Percival, on the other hand, dies.

This longing of a whole whipped and wasted society for a once-glimpsed
grail knight to alleviate their pain modulates into the keening of the worshipers of the dead god who implore that he revive. Throughout The
Waves, a beautiful chorus calling "come" invokes Percival. The plaint

absorbs the desires of each lonely individual for a companion and finally expands into an invitation to "life." Watching the swinging doors at a restaurant, Neville begins the chant: "The door opens, but he does not come" (119). In love with Percival, Neville sounds like Isis in her lament for Osiris, as she oscillates between affirmation and despair: "O fair youth, come to thy house . . . thou shalt not part from me. . . . I see thee not."[11] Neville laments and rejoices in the same erratic pattern: "One waits and he does not come. It gets later and later. He has forgotten. He is with someone else. . . . And then the door opens. He is here." Immediately afterward, Jinny takes up the rhythm set by Neville as she beckons to men: "Rippling gold, I say to him, 'Come.' . . . And he comes; he crosses the room to where I sit, with my dress like a veil" (139–40). Finally, Neville changes the image of the lover at the door to life itself, which Percival represents: "when the door opens accept absolutely" (199). Rhoda, however, expects the opening door to admit a tiger; she suspects that life is a monster (65, 105). Also ominous, the longing for the lover to "come" mingles with the "nonsense rhyme" that returns unbidden to the idle mind: "Come away, come away, death" (259, 282). This line from Shakespeare's *Twelfth Night* continues, "And in sad cypress let me be laid; / Fly away, fly away, breath; / I am slain by a fair cruel maid."[12] The song reminds us, in the context of the other imagery for Percival, that the dying god cannot come to his sacred marriage without also accepting death from the hands of his cruel goddess, Life.

Once this godlike Percival dies, does he ever come back? In an abstract sense, he reappears in the others when each one duplicates his experience and takes on aspects of the dying god. Louis, for example, hiding among the shrubbery as a child to escape taunts, becomes identified, like a vegetation god, with nature: "I hold a stalk in my hand. I am the stalk. My roots go down to the depths of the world" (12). Jinny, whose probable formal name Virginia recalls the Virgin Goddess (and also the author, Virginia), finds Louis's hideaway. Just as Louis is perhaps discovering his sexuality for the first time—"My body is a stalk. I press the stalk. A drop oozes from the hole at the mouth and slowly, thickly, grows larger and larger"—she darts toward him, "seeing you green as a bush, like a branch, very still, Louis, with your eyes fixed. 'Is he [Louis] dead?' I thought, and kissed you" (12–13). Here Jinny plays out the scene of Isis finding the dead Osiris, reviving his body and conceiving from him. While Rhoda imitating Isis in the form of a swallow cannot awaken Percival, once he is really dead, here in childhood Jinny can still kiss Louis back into the community.

Yet no "marriage" in the world of the dying gods occurs without its sadness, and thus Jinny's kiss creates a painful jealousy in Susan. Susan trips and sprawls, spreading her anguish on the skeletal roots of a tree, as Attis is pinned to a tree. Each character in turn becomes identified with

Percival and with suffering nature. Like Louis who "is" the stalk, Susan can claim, "I am the field. . . . I am the seasons" (97–98).

Jinny also resembles the dying god when she pictures herself, through the losses and ecstasies of love, as "pierced," by antlered beasts (177). Here she approximates the pierced god, Adonis or Attis. Alternatively, she identifies with the goddess, as when she kisses Louis and, later the same day, when she hides with Bernard in an "underworld" of enclosing currant bushes, half red, half black (22). Although the red and black of the berries are both good colors, ripening and ripe, the children understand that rottenness follows ripeness, that even this apparently idyllic under-world requires death: they see the horrible side too, creatures mauled and maggoty (23).

Just as Jinny and Bernard creep into an underworld, Neville imitates the god whom he loves: "You left me. The descent into the Tube was like death. We were cut up, we were dissevered by all those faces and the hollow wind that seemed to roar down there over desert boulders" (178). If Neville descends only so far as the subway, Bernard is "pinioned" only by the hairdresser's cape, yet his melancholy surpasses the mundane circum-stances to evoke rites for dying gods: "I felt myself powerless to stop the oscillations of the cold steel. So we are cut and laid in swathes, I said; so we lie side by side on the damp meadows, withered branches and flowering" (280).

Finally, Rhoda joins the other five characters to repeat Percival's experi-ence as dying god. Unsure of her own identity throughout most of the book, she at first observes rather than plays the dying god, as when she throws the violets for Attis. In one other instance she remains an observer. Bernard calls her "the nymph of the fountain always wet" (259, 274), perhaps alluding to Cyane, the nymph of a fountain forced to witness, with horror, the abduction of the dying goddess Persephone. Cyane confronts Pluto, to no avail: "nursing silently in her heart a wound that none could heal; until entirely wasted away with weeping, she dissolved into those waters of which she had lately been the powerful spirit."[13] Similarly wasted by her awareness of death and already feeling that she has "no face" while alive (43, 130), Rhoda soon really dies, as do the gods for whom she has always mourned.

We may catch glimpses of Percival in the other characters when their own fragmentation, piercing, descent, or dissolution reflect his experience; but do we ever see *him* coming back? Does the dying god ever revive? Bernard watches constantly for a "fin," which, as Maria DiBattista indi-cates, could belong to a porpoise, a "creature traditionally associated with the journey of the newly dead through the watery wastes to that other world where they shall gain a new mode of existence."[14] Percival does return, in attenuated form, through memory: "It is strange how the dead leap out on us at street corners, or in dreams" (274). But the wraiths of memory fail to comfort us for the living person. Moreover, Bernard, apparently speaking here for Woolf, expects no literal revival. At St. Paul's he says, "I scoff at . . . the certainty, so sonorously repeated, of resurrection, of eternal life" (282).

Bernard then tests whether art might bring Percival back, through an immortal form in painting, music, or literature. This possibility has been important for artists ever since Matthew Arnold tried to substitute culture for religion. When Bernard hears of Percival's accident, he goes immediately to a gallery, in which paintings of "Venus," "pillars," and "the blue madonna streaked with tears" orient us again toward the young dying god: Adonis loved by Venus, Osiris walled in a pillar, or Christ mourned by women (157, 264). Closing in on Percival as the absent subject, the paintings bring him back in the form of "beauty." The visit to the gallery produces the one genuine moment in the book when the god revives: "Look, where he comes," Bernard triumphs before the paintings, "we are together"(156, 264).

Nevertheless, this return of Percival through art satisfies Bernard only momentarily. He muses that "Line and colours they survive, therefore," but his sentence trails off, and he yawns (158). He cannot complete the thought, possibly because *he* fails, unable to deliver the proper wording, but also because line and color cannot finally console us. Rhoda's mourning right after Bernard's recourse to the gallery casts more doubt on recovering Percival as beauty. She explicitly shuns the museum and, instead of seeing paintings hung on walls, thinks of herself as "hung with other people like a joint of meat among other joints of meat" (162). Her grisly image for the perishing physicality of our lives bluntly reminds us that no framed canvas and no wispy memory can replace Percival's unique body, now rotting. Rhoda tries attending a concert to assuage her grief, but the gesticulating performers and posing patrons strike her as ludicrous. She admits that the singer has provided sufferers with an "Ah," a cry, but she still judges that outlet for emotion squelchingly narrow. Instead of drawing solace from painting or music as forms capable of keeping the past, she will, as we saw, fling away everything.

The important question remains whether words succeed any better than the other arts in bringing Percival back. Bernard gropes toward a belief that the verbal arts—either conversational or literary—may be the only way of restoring a person and bestowing immortality. Words in the form of story, he hopes, will throw a lifeline of sequence amid jumble, a thread through incoherence. Neville also hopes to marshal words as mounts for the ride against death, attributing to words "manes and tails" (83). True to the modernist ambivalence toward language, however, Woolf matches every reverence for noble words with ridicule. Naming dents the thing named; a sentence catches only six fish out of a possible million; and the necessary words to express pain are lacking (81, 256, 263). Pain and purposelessness frequently overwhelm Bernard's "net" of words. In fact, the whole enterprise of resurrecting Percival and the past through speech falters as Bernard's doubts grow. He not only questions the adequacy of his ordered imagination to bring back the dead but wonders what is the point of continuing the cycles at all, whether natural cycles or artful ones. Day follows night, the adder sloughs its skin, Wednesday replaces Tuesday— monotonously. When Bernard goes to see Susan, pregnant, soon after Percival's death, he thinks, "It goes on; but why?" (268).

In his long summary at the end of the book, Bernard undergoes a series of crises at each of which he feels he has "died." Because he recovers from each weariness—at least temporarily—he presents again the spectacle of a dying/reviving figure, just as his new project of recapitulating most of the events we have already heard "resurrects" those events through repetition. In a mood of deep lassitude, he relinquishes, like Rhoda, his own gardens of Adonis: the emotions, plans, and self-images he has tended. He pictures himself dropping these shallow growths into water: "I could not collect myself; I could not distinguish myself; I could not help letting fall the things that had made me a minute ago eager, amused, jealous, vigilant and hosts of other things into the water. . . . Was this then, this streaming away mixed with Susan, Jinny, Neville, Rhoda, Louis, a sort of death? A new assembly of elements?" (279). Here he imagines rebirth as perhaps insisting less on his own separate identity. A worse "death," however, grips him when he loses his ability to keep fashioning his famous phrases and stories. So far alienated from any sense of personhood that he calls himself "he," Bernard records despondently, "He attempted no phrase. His fist did not form. . . . This is more truly death than the death of friends, than the death of youth. . . . A heavy body leaning on a gate. A dead man" (284–85).

Yet even from this extreme despair Bernard struggles back for a rebirth: "How then does light return to the world after the eclipse of the sun? Miraculously. Fraily. . . . Then a vapour as if earth were breathing in and out, once, twice, for the first time. Then under the dullness some one walks with a green light" (286). Who is this someone reborn with green light? In one sense it is Bernard. Although the Bernard who burbled fine phrases has died, the new one, with only "words of one syllable," like lovers or children, emerges to finish the last few paragraphs of his summary. He claims to have renounced his elaborate storytelling, as Shakespeare's Prospero abjures his magic: "I'll break my staff,/ Bury it certain fathoms in the earth/ And deeper than did ever plummet sound,/ I'll drown my book."[15] Bernard, less pretentious than Prospero, buries only match sticks, not staffs, to mark stages in his life; now he "drowns" his book only by letting it fall under a dinner table in *The Waves*.

Prospero, of course, shrewdly holds on to his art through all five acts of the play and denigrates it only when he has finished rinsing his friends in the renewing tempest. Similarly, Woolf allows Bernard to deny the power of language only after she has created a beautiful novel. If her *Waves* do not float the real Percival anywhere on their "waste of waters," they at least hint at the continuing emotional power of Percival, who remains a kind of distant shore. Because Woolf so strongly evokes him as an absent center, it is in a sense he who walks through these pages with a green light, fleetingly alive.

Can the verbal arts conjure back the people we have lost to death? Woolf answers this modernist hope: frankly, no. But she is too modest. When she comically and sadly travesties underworld as subway and harvester's sickle as barber's scissors, she reaps us a sheaf of pages that hide the hushed spirit of a joyous Percival somewhere among them.

Mann

In *Joseph and His Brothers* (1933–43), Thomas Mann extensively and explicitly recreates the legends of the dying gods. Both the narrator and Joseph become vehicles for Mann's unabashed scholarship, as they retell detailed myths and rituals for Osiris, Set, and Isis, Adonis, Tammuz, Ishtar, Astarte, and Ashtaroth, all mentioned by name. Mann gravitates toward myth in general because of his interest, learned from the romantics and from Freud, in dream and the subconscious. He leans on this predilection, however, not as a license for fantasy but rather as an excuse to redact traditional stories in a basically realistic, psychological novel.

Of all myths, Mann chooses those of the dying gods in particular for two reasons. First, these legends enable Mann to glorify art and the artist. Privileging the dying god's endless cycle as the world's most basic plot, Mann can expatiate on the artist's need for never-ending story, for opposites (indeed, for "total" experience), for irony and jest. Among these opposites, Mann focuses particularly on the male-female duality. Insisting that some vegetation deities like Ishtar and Tammuz each bore the title lord-lady, he investigates the artist's so-called feminine side. In fact, the goddess looms so importantly to determine his choice of these particular myths that I have treated Mann's fascination with her separately in chapter 8.

Second, the legends offer order and consolation for contemporary life, the cataclysmic 1930s and 1940s when he was writing *Joseph and His Brothers*. Mann can draw on the inherent optimism of these myths, but also on their goriness, as a way of coming to grips with the brutality of history. Trying to face violence, he can at the same time find a way out of what would seem to be an almost inescapable despair. Mircea Eliade locates the essential optimism of the Tammuz myth in the worshiper's ability to say, "My death is not final as his death is not final" and "I am innocent as he is innocent".[16] Although Mann does not let Joseph off scot-free without some faults to grow out of, Joseph can regard each of his downfalls, those brought on by his conceit and heedlessness and those beyond his control, as only temporary. However, as we will see, Mann faces several possible objections by making a storyteller like Joseph self-consciously imitate the dying gods. Does an ingrown love for art blind Joseph to reality after all? And if Joseph's sojourn in the "underworld" of Egypt parallels Europe's fall into the hell of Nazi rule, how can Joseph really claim innocence and maintain his blitheness?

As an artist-figure, Joseph regales his brother Benjamin with tales, and he advances his fortunes in the world solely by means of glib conversations with Mont-Kaw, Potiphar, and Pharaoh. Preferring to derive his name "Joseph" from *sefer*, meaning "book" or "writing tools," he eventually graduates to the highest office: mouthpiece to Pharaoh.[17] While constantly identifying Joseph with the series of dying gods (Osiris, Adonis, and Tammuz), Mann also consistently associates him with the Egyptian Thoth, ibis-headed, "the white ape and inventor of signs, the speaker and writer of the gods, recorder of their words and protecting deity for all those who write" (273).

Frazer ascribes the title "true of speech" to Osiris and recounts that Thoth taught Isis the "words of power" by which she brought her poisoned son Horus back to life.[18] The title and the anecdote connect two of Mann's major interests, in writing and in renewal, and imply Mann's belief that the writer does have some power to renew life. The old Ishmaelite who escorts Joseph into Egypt grumbles that "without something written you do not get through; but if you can show a potsherd or a roll and document, then they brighten up. They say, of course, that Amun is the highest, or Osiris, The Eye enthroned; but I know better, at bottom it is Thoth, the writer" (478). Through this tongue-in-cheek hierarchy, Mann elevates a god of writing to preeminent status.

Mann further identifies Thoth with the Greek Hermes, "who may be a brother of the ibis-headed or his other self" (939). Hermes displays two natures that make him the epitome of the artist for Mann. This god is a rogue, connecting him to Mann's lifelong fascination with the artist as a "confidence man."[19] Hermes steals from and deludes others with impish glee in a grand scheme of illusions. At the same time, Hermes duplicates the function of the dying gods. Although he does not suffer himself, he knows death and the underworld and how to pass through them; Thoth-Hermes is a guide of the dead (1164).

In addition to using Hermes as a connecting link between a Thoth who writes and a dying god who descends to the underworld, Mann also uses the moon as a symbol that travels easily between the two types of god, smoothing the transitions in Mann's eclectic mythology. Darkened for three nights, the moon announces the disappearance of Tammuz, as well as promising by its own pattern his eventual reemergence. The light of the moon also notoriously deceives the moongazer, and Mann borrows that light to justify his poetic "lies" (the term by which Plato designated art). Thus, it is only by "lunar syntax" or poetic license that an Eliezer in one generation blurs with an Eliezer in another. In addition, the moon in its changeableness supplies the variety that Mann needs for his story. Like Tammuz or Osiris—or Joseph in a metaphoric sense—the moon will die, be reborn, die, and be reborn over and over, each downfall and recovery offering unique twists for a seemingly inexhaustible string of tales (such as the twelve hundred ample pages of *Joseph and His Brothers*).

Like many modernists, Mann sends his artist-figure Joseph on a creative mission that is both deadly serious and playfully unimportant. Mann walks a narrow path between glorifying and mocking his Joseph as storyteller. On the one hand, the narrator approves Joseph's belief in the biblical creation by Word, because psychologically we need the defining power of words before we give attention to reality. On the other hand, the narrator finds Joseph's belief naïve: "and even today, let a thing be ever so present, it was in actual fact only actually present when man has given it life in words and called it by name. So did his pretty and well-favoured little head convince itself of the importance and wisdom of the Word" (274). If a "pretty" head can so easily "convince itself," a scraggly, mature head likely entertains doubts that words can sway people, let alone create worlds.

Yet when Mann is in the mood to praise and validate the power of speech, Joseph can actually enlarge his conception of Yahweh by chanting associated sounds. Joseph practically conjures God into being through magical and mysterious though meaning-laden syllables (39). Mann does at least nod toward the "constitutive" theory of language: the idea that symbolic forms, including language, give people the framework with which to take in the world.[20] Either the real world comes first (the purely secular world where kings conquer other kings), and propagandists make up the god stories to justify past deeds, or else humans only conceive their life's tasks at all because they can follow the script of a god's drama, which "constitutes" and determines their view of the world's possibilities. The narrator, wondering whether it is more correct to say that the god Amun has conquered the weaker gods of Asia, or simply that Pharaoh has imposed his will on tributary kings, concludes that "The thing and the image, the actual and the non-actual, formed an inextricably interwoven whole" (561). By calling the thing and the image "interwoven," Mann gives equal weight to the two views: a reality that draws people to make certain words, in order to condemn the past or to whitewash it, and words that shape reality, for good or ill, in the first place.

One way Mann elevates the artist is by comparing him to a god—not just Thoth but the Hebrew creator. The cosmic player and the individual artist blend together, to the point that Mann slyly pictures himself as a grandiose creator. In describing the Hebrew god as a farmer who sends his calf (Joseph) ahead into Egypt to make the cow (Jacob) follow after, Mann could have said "der Bauer" for "farmer," as Elaine Murdaugh notes; instead he uses the less exact term "Mann."[21] He thereby refers to himself in the same breath with the Lord.

Paralleling himself with the Hebrew god, Mann may also have identified with the Babylonian god Tammuz. I suspect he knew that "Thomas," the name of a disciple in the New Testament who became a supporting figure to the new dying god, Christ, was actually the Greek form of Tammuz, who once "occupied the central position in the sacred drama at Jerusalem."[22] If Mann knew this derivation, he surely savored the chance to imitate, under his own name Thomas, both the mythological setter of scenes and the New Testament empirically minded doubter: believer and ironist, participant and observer in one.

True to his modernist ambivalence about art, then, Mann retreats after every effort to give primacy to the word. Joseph, for example, cautions his steward, who enjoys plying the reed stylus, "Great is the writer's art! But truly I find it greater yet to live in a story" (998). When writers do sit down to compose, their most basic plot, Mann implies, is the myth of the dying deity. Yet this so orderly story in itself gives witness to the supremacy of disorderly life. The "oldest saga" to which writers repeatedly return is "the idea of a catastrophe, the invasion of destruction and wanton forces into an ordered scheme and a life bent upon self-control and a happiness conditioned by it . . . of life laughingly sweeping away the structure of art; of mastery and overpowering, and the coming of the stranger god" (718–19).

When Mann speaks of "the stranger god," he evokes the dying god Dionysus. In Euripides' play *The Bacchae* Dionysus invades Thebes as a stranger and "laughingly" sweeps away all the forms of order that the king, Pentheus, has imposed on his city and psyche. In the process of sweeping away, of course, Dionysus happens to murder Pentheus. By alluding to Dionysus, Mann opens up one of the great dilemmas of the myths of dying gods: the line between suffering for others and allowing or causing others to suffer. Dionysus's *sparagmos* might be all well and good when he submits humbly himself, but what if he inflicts his fate of being torn apart on human victims? Dionysus laughs a hyena's laugh.

Presumably, artists portray destruction because it exists; if they desire to consider life as it is, they must unflinchingly admit violence into the story, thereby creating tragedy, pathos, or absurdity. Mann insists, however, that artists also celebrate, as well as record, catastrophe, because they know that catastrophe enriches experience: as the overflowing of the Nile makes the land fertile, as the downfalls of Joseph lead to his rise, as the deaths of the deities permit their rebirth.

Nevertheless, such a conception of the fructifying overthrow entails dangerous ambiguities. The call to catastrophe sounds suspiciously like the whole romantic longing for apocalypse that George Steiner blames for rendering the intelligentsia of Europe all too passive at the signs of coming Nazi upheavals. Steiner shudderingly cities, for example, Théophile Gautier's romantic slogan, "rather barbarism than boredom."[23] Steiner interprets this nonchalance as a clue that European dissatisfaction with social structures, materialism, and philistinism had deepened into an apathy willing to see institutions swept away—along with the populations who happened to live among them. Mann's "typical" story of welcoming the stranger god does betray at least a hint of apathetic longing for dissolution.[24]

In addition to facing the accusation that he perhaps courts cataclysm heedlessly, Mann leaves himself and Joseph open to other objections against using myth in the context of Nazi Germany: objections of anti-rationalism, detachment, and paralysis in choosing and acting. By embracing myth, Mann appears to get dangerously close to the Nazis' enthusiasm for what they also called "myth," as in Alfred Rosenberg's widely read *Der Mythus des 20. Jahrhunderts*, which touted a "superior race." In fact, the National Socialists virtually instituted a religion of suffering by claiming that Germany "wants to suffer the torture that will give her a new life."[25] Is this purported self-sacrifice equivalent to saying that Osiris wants to suffer to give the plants new life? On the contrary—instead of making itself Osiris, Germany scrambled for a surrogate, which included Jews, gypsies, dissidents, and European neighbors.

Mann constantly worked to distinguish a legitimate use of the word "myth" from National Socialist irrationality and brutality. He thought that psychology would "transmute" myth for "humane ends,"[26] to provide "the resolution of our great fear and our great hate, their conversion into a different relation to the unconscious which shall be more the artist's, more ironic and yet not necessarily irreverent."[27] For Mann, conscious analysis must supplement intuition to prevent myth from decaying into Nazi anti-intellectualism. He and his myth-modeled characters do not revel in mindless "blood and guts."[28] On the contrary, Mann presents Joseph as constantly thinking, analyzing, and arranging his life. Instead of lapsing into Rosenberg's dreamy "instinct," Mann crams his book with the narrator's logic and Joseph's self-consciousness.

Another possible objection to Mann's mythologizing in the context of history is that Mann sees suffering from such detached heights of allusion-detecting and pattern-making that he fails to empathize with the sufferer. The romantic ironist to whom Mann felt most akin holds himself aloof from his "toys," above life and death.[29] T. E. Apter protests that both Mann and Joseph remain too detached, too insouciant—and for Apter Joseph even ceases then to be "mythical," which seems to mean for him "deeply felt."[30] Mann, however, does convincingly portray Joseph's fear and remorse in the pit during his first descent. Still, if Joseph feels anguish, other characters make light of it. A messenger, who sits by the well after the brothers have pulled Joseph out and sold him, tells Reuben that the present "is not to be taken quite seriously, but is only a jest and an allusion, a symbol, so that we might nudge each other and wink while we behold it" (413).

Does Mann endorse this pronouncement by the messenger, reputed to be Hermes himself, that one should "wink" at the present—maybe even at Mann's present, the 1930s and 1940s? Joseph's disappearance is no jest for Reuben, well aware of his father Jacob's impending grief. Mann depicts both Reuben's and Jacob's despair movingly. In fact, Mann "jests" in a complicated way, permeated with sadness and the awareness of life as basically monstrous. When Joseph can later wink away his brothers' guilt, he explains "jesting" to his steward:

> For lightness, my friend, flippancy, the artful jest, that is God's very best gift to man, the profoundest knowledge we have of that complex, questionable thing we call life. God gave it to humanity, that life's terribly serious face might be forced to wear a smile. My brothers rent my garment and flung me into the pit; now they are to stand before my stool—and that is life. And the question whether we are to judge the act by the result and approve the bad act because it was needed for the good result—that is life too. Life puts such questions as these and they cannot be answered with a long face. Only in lightness can the spirit of man rise above them: with a laugh at being faced with the unanswerable, perhaps he can make even God Himself, the great Unanswering, to laugh. (1056)

The sardonic lucidity and weary determination of this defiant "laughter" assure us that Joseph and Mann can, after all, empathize with suffering.

A failure to choose, between Osiris and Set, is another possible objection to Mann's use of myth. If a myth-loving person can find a purpose for both an Osiris and a Set in some universal scheme, might that observer then fail to condemn the misdeeds of Set in a real-life situation, simply because they enliven and complete an exciting drama? Suppose the mythlover sits idly by as Osiris's boar charges, excusing any idleness, "Oh, well, he *has* to be gored?"

Mann must have wrestled with this question of choice, because the irony to which he was so temperamentally drawn taught a person to hold opposing views simultaneously. In a lecture of 1939, Mann explained his use of *irony*: "In its equanimity it [has] an almost monstrous sense: the sense of *art* itself, a universal affirmation, which, as such, is also a universal negation; an all-embracing crystal clear and serene glance, which is the very glance of art itself, that is to say: a glance of the utmost freedom and calm and of an objectivity untroubled by any moralism."[31] Even in the 1930s when Mann was well aware of the Nazi blurring of opposites, he was still blithely repeating his Nietzschean, romantic dictum that the artist has to know all, experience all, even dabble in disease.[32] If the artist cultivating his irony can support any side of an issue, then Mann's ironic artist dangerously skirts one of the original meanings of *eiron*: a deceitful person who will never give a straight answer.[33]

Nevertheless, instead of concluding that artists condone opposites, Mann argues that they reconcile them. He thinks of Joseph's wit, his gift from the scribal god Thoth (the gift of writing in general), as plying between sun and moon, father and mother, the blessings of day and night (67, 1164). Joseph as mediator duplicates Thoth in himself: "For he is a guide to the world below and, with all his gay spirits, the friend of the moon and the dead. He puts in a friendly word with the upper world for the lower and with the lower world for the upper, he is a gentlemanly go-between 'twixt heaven and earth. Violence and abruptness are hateful to him and better than anyone else he knows that one can be right and yet wrong" (959). This shilly-shallying between heaven and earth looks like it might even permit a little cozying up to the devil too.[34]

Mann's philosophy of the writerly Joseph as go-between, despite its alarming appearance of tolerance to the point of condoning everything, does not after all founder in ethical relativism. Right and wrong courses do exist in *Joseph and His Brothers*. Joseph, for all his ability to see both sides, eventually has to act one way or another. It is right for him to take a social role and feed people (though Apter grumbles that Joseph rakes in profits from the grain too selfishly).[35] It is right for him to forgive his brothers. He does not, like Euripides' testy, vengeful Dionysus, coerce others to duplicate his own ordeal. Instead, he puts his brothers through a few uncomfortable moments when, falsely accused of theft, they can understand how Joseph must have felt when he pleaded with them from the pit. Their discomfort educates them, almost through psychodrama. Joseph pretends to be something he is not, a stubborn tyrant—as a boar-masked priest pretends in a ritual to be something he is not. When Joseph puts himself into the mythical role of the "black pig" Set, about to rend his brothers, he defuses any vengeful desire to torture them in reality. The brothers, formerly taking the role of Set, have now felt what it is like to be Osiris—in a game of "let's pretend" (in myth and literature) without having to die literally.

One of the "wrong" courses in *Joseph and His Brothers*—even from the viewpoint of the perpetrators, finally educated—was to have thrown

Joseph in the pit. From the viewpoint of a generous Joseph, however, that act was "right," because it enabled him to go to Egypt and provide for Israel. Actually, all Mann's "relativism" comes down to is thât, *after* the fact, declaring a crime "acceptable" forestalls vengeance and helps leave the past behind. But before the fact, or while still facing it, Joseph—at least in his finally chastened state—would know as well as anybody not to unleash the boar. Mann implies that if the boar in the form, say, of the Nazis is already unleashed, one actively works to coop it back up, meanwhile consoling oneself by looking to cyclical and cosmic patterns.

In this sense Mann reconciles the mythologist's belief that Joseph can follow a traditional path, with the existentialist's contradictory belief that no prior definitions exist and that humans must therefore mark out their own way. Joseph actively chooses to make himself a forgiver and provider; he does not just slip unconsciously into any prototype. He is especially on guard against prototypes set before him imagistically by propagandists, which is the way he interprets Mut's refashioning of him as "lover." Most important, because forgiving Set is not prominent in Osiris's myth, Joseph will *rewrite* the story. Moreover, Joseph's mythological view that Osiris *has* to go down gives him the equanimity from which he can act. His "fatalism" does not make him passive; the myths just define the rules of a game that Joseph then plays all the harder, still outmaneuvering opponents rather than capitulating to them.

Mann too, like Joseph, does act against the all-uprooting boar of National Socialism. He defiantly writes a "Jewish novel" in a period of anti-Semitism and accepts exile for his opposition.[36] He becomes an orator and pamphleteer for democracy.[37] Although Mann does not grant art the power to change reality that a committed existentialist like Jean-Paul Sartre gives it, he makes of art a galvanizing statement and an important consolation, perhaps further enabling us to act in our lives if we are saved from total despair. In a radio talk of 1952 called "The Artist and Society," Mann defends art:

If it [*art*] likes to make mankind laugh, it is still not scornful laughter that it offers but a gladness in which hate and stupidity are dissolved, a serenity that frees and unites. Born anew again and again from solitude, its effect is to unite. It is the last to harbor any illusions about its influence upon human destiny. Despiser of all that is bad, it has never yet been able to arrest the victory of evil; intent upon meaning, it has never been able to prevent the most incredible madness. It is not a power, it is only a consolation. And yet, a game of the deepest seriousness, the paradigm of all striving toward perfection, it was given to mankind from the very beginning as a companion, and from its innocence mankind will never be able to turn its guilt-saddened eye utterly away.[38]

3
Anguishing in the Underworld

Many of the ancient dying gods met death by means of a boar or a sow. Wild boars killed Adonis and Attis, whereas Set mangled Osiris during a boar hunt. Pigs were also supposed to witness Persephone's abduction into the underworld. But Frazer believed that in the oldest myths, the pig did not oppose the god as his or her enemy. Instead, following a life-death continuum, divinity became victim and victimizer by turns; periodically, the god in pig form annihilated his or her self in human form. If ancient peoples then slaughtered a pig (such as the pagan yule boar, later assimilated to Christianity), they did so not to take vengeance against the god's enemy but to reenact the sacrifice of the deity itself.[1] Normally taboo, the animal became on special occasions provider of meat for the community, as the deity repeatedly willed its death to provide for its people.

In similar imagery, goddesses who received the bodies of the dead (dying god and human alike) often went by the name of the Great Sow; these sow goddesses included Demeter, Astarte, Ceres, Freya, and Cerridwen.[2] Perhaps modeled on swine that inadvertently crush their farrow, the pig goddess was (like the pig god) terrifying but also helpful—an emblem of life, bestowing birth and death equally.

Cerridwen the Sow was another name for Morgan, queen of the dead in the Celtic paradise Avalon, or "apple land," at the end of the western seas. In Halloween games, probably attenuated forms of ancient rituals, players who bobbed for apples then "ran away to escape from the black short-tailed sow."[3] The players wanted to win by cheating death, while attempting to bite into and incorporate for themselves the apple tokens of life. For those initiated to the secrets of the goddesses of rebirth, "losing" oneself to the pig land of death would also mean finding the reassuring apple land of renewed life.

Although ancient peoples may have been able to regard the two lands as one, modern ironic authors have strictly separated them. Kafka and Beckett know some version of the dying gods facing a pig's death or inhabiting an apple land, but the images retain none of the comfort attached to ancient mythology. When Beckett places his characters in *Malone Dies* among

Druid ruins and scenes of ritualized pig butchery, the emphasis falls on repetitive, endemic, purposeless violence. Although the characters may put out to sea at the end of the book, the only "rebirth" that awaits them is the resumption of their plaintive voices by the new narrator in *The Unnamable*, who sees as little hope of personal immortality or meaning as his predecessors in Beckett's linked volumes. The dying god, halted in the underworld, thus serves Beckett as a reflexive image for the artist trapped in his hellish life and in his useless but continually renewed retellings. Kafka's dying and reviving Hunter Gracchus similarly becomes a figure of the artist, unable to live in "real" domestic life and unable to stop envying it.

Even more literally than Beckett's much reduced characters, Kafka's Gregor Samsa turns into an animal sacrificed to better a community. Although he degenerates into a timid insect, not a fierce pig, Gregor visually resembles a metamorphosed yule boar. The yule boar enclosed an apple in its mouth as its own sign of readily available rebirth. But Gregor, in a perverse twist, must carry his apples, pelted toward him, sunk inaccessibly into his back. For Kafka and Beckett, then, the apples of immortality have rotted, whereas the uprooting pigs of permanent, metaphysical senselessness are as capable as ever of goring.[4]

Kafka

In two works Franz Kafka draws on the myth of the dying god: *Die Verwandlung*, *The Metamorphosis*, written in 1912 and published in 1915, and "Der Jäger Gracchus," "The Hunter Gracchus," written in 1917 and published in 1931. (A fragment to "The Hunter Gracchus" also survives.) Some of the details of the later story recall the dying god directly, whereas Kafka's masterful novella buries the references. The author takes little comfort from a myth that taught ancient peoples to hope for eternal life.

In *The Metamorphosis*, at first Kafka seems to retain some of the links between suffering figure and beneficiary, but all reflections of the dying god turn out to be entirely ironic. Traditionally, when the god falls, both the community and nature revive. By the end of the novella, the small community of the family has indeed revived, undergoing a metamorphosis in inverse proportion to Gregor's. As he sinks, from human being to insect to dried-out corpse, his family rises, from feebleness to independence. Moreover, once Gregor has wasted away, his parents suddenly remark the mild spring weather and notice that his sister, Grete, has blossomed into a marriageable young woman. The return of spring and the possibility of human reproduction seem casually contingent on the disappearance of Gregor, in the manner of a dying god who regulates vegetable, animal, and human fertility. But if the god frequently took animal form as he willingly sacrificed himself, Gregor's animal form has degenerated. And if Gregor is admirable for assuming burdens, Kafka interferes with our admiration by showing us Gregor's passivity and pathetic self-hatred. Kafka further undercuts the tradition by showing that a cruel community is not, after all, worth the effort which the suffering figure has lavished on it.

The end of March, when Gregor succumbs, is a typical date for the demise of gods and animal victims, from Attis to Aries the ram. The Hebrews assimilated the Egyptian ram-god Ammon to the paschal lamb and sacrificed him at Passover.[5] The Jewish paschal lamb then influenced the Christian sacrificed Lamb of God. Kafka places Gregor under the sign of these figures—probably not one in particular but rather the whole class—whose suffering seems to enhance both community and nature.

The author would know of the pagan vegetation gods and their influence on Judaism from his reading about a year before he wrote *The Metamorphosis*: "Today, [I] eagerly and happily began to read the *History of the Jews* by Graetz. Because my desire for it had far outrun the reading, it was at first stranger to me than I thought, and I had to stop here and there in order by resting to allow my Jewishness to collect itself. Toward the end, however, I was already gripped by the imperfection of the first settlements in the newly conquered Canaan and the faithful handing down of the imperfections of the popular heroes. . . ."[6] Heinrich Graetz disdainfully records that Ammon wore ram's horns and that

the Canaanites worshipped the male and female deities, Baal and Astarte, who, in some cities, were designated by the names of Adonis and Baaltis. Baal was intended to be a personification of the sun, and Astarte of the moon; they did not, however, figure as luminous beings within the celestial space, but as the procreative powers of nature . . . In honor of Astarte, half-frantic youths and men mutilated themselves, and wore female attire. . . . their abominations were constantly displayed before the Israelites.[7]

Although Gregor is a sacrificial animal, he does not become a paschal lamb or even a fierce yule boar, which still have some dignity. Instead, he is only an insect: indeed, vermin, *Ungeziefer*. Ritchie Robertson summarizes how Kafka associates the word "vermin" with three types of outsider:

In the *Brief an den Vater* [*Letter to His Father*] (written in 1919), Kafka acknowledges the potential accusation that his conflict with his father was a "Kampf des Ungeziefers" ["battle between vermin"], but he also recalls that in 1911 his father described Jizchok Löwy [actor in the Yiddish theater] as an "Ungeziefer." Writing to Felice on 1 November 1912, Kafka says that only writing has given his life meaning: "Schrieb ich aber nicht, dann lag ich auch schon auf dem Boden, wert hinausgekehrt zu werden" ["But if I don't write, then I'm already prostrate on the floor, only good to be swept out"]; in *Die Verwandlung*, the servant prods Gregor's corpse with her broom and later announces that it has been "weggeschafft" ["gotten rid of, cleared away"]. These passages suggest three of the meanings Kafka associated with the image of the insect: the rebellious son, the Galician Jew (regarded with revulsion by the Prague bourgeoisie), and the artist. All three types are outcasts from conventional Western society.[8]

Although Gregor practices no art, his dumb appreciation for music endows him with aesthetic interests. In his tacit affinity to artists and Jews, Gregor, like Gracchus, seems to believe he should somehow bring light to the nations. Graetz says that one of the paschal prayers offers "thanksgiving for the light of the sun, which God had given to the whole world, and for the light of the Law, which He had given to Israel."[9] Gregor's death does seem to trigger spring, the return of the sun. But despite Gregor's surprising success in lighting the world for others, his own world dims; during his last days he cannot peer even across the street.

At first Kafka makes it look as if Gregor might retain other promising mythical characteristics; as in the case of the only partially successful light bringing, however, Kafka undercuts them. Gregor recalls an unselfish dying god in that he wills his own suffering to help the community. He gladly injures his tender mouth on the latch if opening the door will please others. He also agrees with his sister that he should "go away" to improve their lot. His considerateness and obligingness make him admirable. This toothless Gregor surpasses the other characters to the extent that he gives generously of himself, whereas the toothy lodgers, for example, aggressively demand that everyone bow to their needs. Chomping their food audibly, the carnivorous boarders rudely tear up Grete's feelings when they tire of her violin playing.

To be "human" in this story thus takes on meanings usually associated with beasts: the all-too-human lodgers trample prey in the pursuit of self-interest, and the father "hisses" at his son and attacks him. Since the gentle Gregor wants only music, companionship, and love, he does not match the ruthless version of "humanity" and is relegated to animal status. His beloved music must be a charm for beasts, his object of physical devotion—the anonymous woman in the magazine illustration—must be clothed in fur, and his very body must be classed with the six-legged creatures. The status of "animal" thus hovers ambiguously between subhuman and superhuman. The concept of animal as better than human derives both from the poor showing of the humans in the novella and perhaps from traditional reverential attitudes toward animals as forms of the dying gods.

Despite Gregor's gentleness and superiority to the lodgers, he is still not entirely admirable. Dying gods are innocent and confident. Adonis is robust, whereas Gregor is feeble. Gregor might seem more like another, more modest dying god, Christ; the servant Christ rides on a lowly ass, and an obliging Gregor appears as a lowly insect. Yet Gregor does not really resemble Christ any more than he rivals Adonis, because Gregor lacks the essential self-confidence of all the dying gods. Instead of radiating their serene humility, he scrabbles on the leather sofa in exasperated humiliation. To ask even a humble Christ who he was would elicit a prompt and assured "Son of God." Gregor, by contrast, can only identify himself as "ugly insect." Because he has internalized the prejudice and distaste heaped on him, like the apples sinking right into his back, he hates himself as much as others despise him. He can muster only enough rebellion to acquiesce in a suicidal transformation that will temporarily offend his family and spare him from going to a despised job.

Kafka may have known, as Kurt Weinberg suggests, the derivation of *Ungeziefer* from *ungezibere* and *unziver* as "the unclean animal not suited for sacrifice."[10] If Kafka did know this etymology, he underlines the irony of Gregor forced to undergo the suffering meted out to a sacrificial victim, yet without even the meager glory reserved for that creature, at least labeled "worthy to die for others." Gregor, unworthy, still dies.

Kafka also undercuts the myth of the dying god by revealing that the benefited community is as unworthy as its benefactor. In fact, the family's and lodgers' disturbing lack of compassion is worse than Gregor's distressing lack of self-confidence. Although the family complains bitterly about the disgrace caused by Gregor's unseemly metamorphosis, it has profited. His incapacity has nudged several family members to find work and has enabled them to locate a more manageable apartment. Yet this small community has hardly improved as a result of Gregor's sacrifices; instead, it has worsened. Along with her new confidence, Grete acquires a new callousness, as she vehemently insists that her brother, whom she now calls "it," should die. Along with his refurbished self-esteem, the father gets better boot soles. We already know to what brutal use he puts his boots in driving his son into his room. Kafka thus demolishes another of the givens of the myth of the dying god by showing that the community to be regenerated scarcely deserves all that effort.

Several critics see Gregor's fate, beneficial to community and nature, as hopeful. Kurt Weinberg, for example, considers Gregor's ordeal "a noble parody of Messianic passion."[11] As optimistic as Weinberg, Wilhelm Emrich believes that Gregor's eclipse "is not merely a meaningless annihilation, but a liberating realization. . . . He dies reconciled with himself and the whole world."[12] Walter Sokel, almost approaching Grete in callousness, even goes so far as to find Gregor useful but expendable, having gone "astray": "Salvation is at hand. . . through his death, his disappearance, life blooms anew—redeemed, ready to engender new life in place of the old life gone astray,"[13] Yet these three critics miss Kafka's irony. He presents Gregor as a person who must suffer a fate like that of the creaturely representatives of the dying god, without allowing him personal renewal or others' gratitude. Nor does Kafka grant us either a totally admirable model of generosity in Gregor or a community that merits the sacrifice.

"The Hunter Gracchus" tells the fantastic tale of a man who, after a fatal accident in the Black Forest, embarks on a death ship. The ship, however, does not transport him either to an afterlife or to oblivion but keeps putting into various ports, where the still living "corpse" is obliged to set up his bier and lie through his wake all over again. The story recalls motifs from folktale as well as myth. The medieval and Renaissance legend of the Wandering Jew, for example, recounts how Ahasuerus must leave wife and child to travel fitfully over the world, because he refused to let the cross-bearing Christ rest on his doorstep. Several other tales of figures all condemned to tiresome eternities became entangled, in European legend, with that of the Wandering Jew: "the curse of a deathless life has passed on the Wild Huntsman, because he desired to chase the red-deer for evermore; on the Captain of the Phantom Ship, because he vowed he would double the Cape whether God willed it or not; on the Man in the Moon, because he gathered sticks during the Sabbath rest; on the dancers of Kolbeck, because they desired to spend eternity in their mad gambols."[14] Such lore certainly lies behind Kafka's hunter. But Kafka fleshes out hints of the Wandering Jew and the Wild Huntsman in "The Hunter Gracchus" with touches that specifically recall the dying gods. Because Gracchus must climb onto his bier and lie through his wake again and again, he follows the type of the ever-living, ever-dying deity.

When Kafka draws on this ancient prototype, he changes the mood completely. The god's rebirth, affecting both nature and society, turns the leaves to green and unleashes rejoicing in the community, whereas the arrival in port of "the green Hunter Gracchus" arouses little interest from the townsfolk.[15] Gracchus's severance from the community is one of two important changes that Kafka makes in this otherwise very traditional tale. Through such alienation the author transforms the dying/reviving Gracchus into an "artist"—someone almost divine who should by his efforts bestow enlightenment and even health. Instead, ordinary citizens either ignore or misinterpret Gracchus, and he in turn both scorns and envies them.

Kafka's second change is to convert eternal rebirth into prolonged bafflement. Because Gracchus cannot die once and for all, he has that much more time to puzzle over the concealed meaning of human life: "I am forever . . . on that great stair that leads up to it ['other world']. On that infinitely wide and spacious stair I clamber about, sometimes up, sometimes down, sometimes on the right, sometimes on the left, always in motion. The hunter has turned into a butterfly" (228). Gracchus is an inheritor of the dying god whose metamorphoses keep his body returning to a chrysalis-shroud, yet whose soul flutters purposelessly each time he sets sail.

In primitive ritual, the god sometimes identifies with women; certainly women predominate in lamenting his death. Kafka knew from his reading in Graetz that the human representative of the fertility god often "wore female attire,"[16] and "a great flower-patterned woman's shawl with long fringes" covers Gracchus's limbs on the bier (229). A woman with "loosened hair" and a child at her breast attends Gracchus on board ship. Frazer says women with "streaming hair" mourn for Adonis.[17] The woman in Kafka's story also brings to Gracchus's wooden pallet "the morning drink of the land whose coast we chance to be passing," as if she were providing Gracchus the sustenance that enables him to go through yet another rebirth. Each port seems like a new incarnation, because traveling in the bark of death induces a temporary amnesia: the hunter asks a visitor's name, though he claims already to know it, "but in the first moments of returning consciousness I always forget" (228).

Doves as well as women attend Gracchus, possibly marking him again as a type of dying/reviving figure. Caroline Gordon interprets the doves that announce Gracchus as the Holy Ghost and reads the story as an elaborate Christian allegory.[18] But the "neo-Calvinist theology" that she invokes seems remote from Kafka's concerns, despite his eclectic interest in religions: "he read avidly in both Jewish and Christian writings—the Old Testament and Maimonides, but also the Gospels, St. Augustine, Pascal, Kierkegaard, Tolstoy, and the biography of Erdmuthe, wife of the founder of the Moravian Brethren."[19] The doves, however, were a mythological symbol long before the Holy Ghost evolved out of that tradition. Frazer says that doves accompany Aphrodite as her token, and Kafka's doves leave Gracchus's windowpane at which they have been pecking and fly to the woman with the loosened hair. Kafka gives an ominous twist to the behavior of these gentle creatures. When they seek entrance to Gracchus's room "as if their food were stored within," they, in fact, treat Gracchus himself as if he were their grain (226). Kafka implies that to be the bread of life, pecked or chewed, cannot be all that pleasant. Like the dying god when he is ground in a mill,[20] or simply like the writer "consumed" by his art, Gracchus faces a painful fate. His insistent and supposedly gentle doves might as well be buzzards hovering, because they remind the new arrival that his main task is to die.

While doves attend a primitive goddess, the god goes out on a fatal hunt;

here too Gracchus dies on the trail. When the Burgomaster of Riva asks him if he bears any blame, Gracchus defends himself: "I was a hunter; was there any sin in that?" (229). In the context of primitive cultures, taking an animal's life required reverence and a pact not to kill frivolously; once a hunter met these conditions, however, no primitive people would accuse him of "sin." The Burgomaster also admits that he cannot see anything wrong in Gracchus's profession, but he nevertheless reserves judgment. As is typical in Kafka's fiction, unmotivated suffering prods the innocent into a self-destructive sifting for guilt.[21]

Gracchus attributes his ability to revive—what had been the glory of the dying god—to an almost casual mistake: "a wrong turn of the wheel, a moment's absence of mind on the pilot's part, the distraction of my lovely native country, I cannot tell what it was; I only know this, that I remained on earth and that ever since my ship has sailed earthly waters" (228). Instead of affirming life and death, as did the primitive worshipers of Adonis, Kafka's world-weary Gracchus almost takes an Eastern view that it would be better to halt the round of births and deaths altogether. Yet the word "lovely" betrays his continued attachment to the earthly cycle after all.

Although Gracchus dies on a hunt, like many of the dying gods, he suffers a fall rather than an attack from a boar. Nevertheless, he does face a kind of goring. Gracchus reports that in his cabin, "On the wall opposite me is a little picture, evidently of a bushman who is aiming his spear at me and taking cover as best he can behind a beautifully painted shield" (229). This paranoiac detail conjures up a suitably primitive atmosphere to place Gracchus in the tradition of dying gods; Frazer constantly compares customs of contemporary tribesmen with rites for Adonis, Osiris, and the rest. The bushman serves to remind Gracchus that his "immortal" character is to be eternally targeted and threatened.

While the dying god's life balances threat with joys (his marriage and his integration into the community), Gracchus may start out in an affirmative mood, but his joy fades: "I had been glad to live and I was glad to die. . . . I slipped into my winding sheet like a girl into her marriage dress. I lay and waited. Then came the mishap" (229). In the primitive myths, death blends with marriage because to embrace the goddess is also to return to her womb for rebirth. Kafka, on the other hand, compares death with marriage not so much as a metaphysical hope for renewal as a kind of psychological foreboding that marriage, ending productive solitude, may bring about the death of art.

For Gracchus, while alive, always hoarded solitude. Like the legendary Wild Huntsman who follows a red deer to the exclusion of all else, he has lived only for his profession. He exclaims: "If only the chamois had not led me astray" (234). To seek this mysterious chamois suggests the pursuit of a fable, an aesthetic dream. But he simultaneously expresses his doubt that perhaps the cost of his private quest is too great, since Gracchus's life-style has left him with only a tangential, almost illicit relationship with the woman on board ship. Despite the intimacy with which she holds the drink to his lips, this woman is the boatman's wife, not his. If the chamois had not led Gracchus astray, he might not be so remote from people; but on the other hand, he used to love the wandering life. A similar ambivalence pervades Kafka's own bachelorhood, with impassioned defenses of all-absorbing artistry, punctuated by uncertain liaisons and engagements made and broken.[22]

Instead of leading a bourgeois, settled life with one woman, Gracchus travels restlessly, first across mountains, then seas; but he courts a relationship, to a wider community, with as much ambivalence as his connection to his feminine drink bearer. In the story proper, a dove tells the Burgomaster of Riva to "receive him [Gracchus] in the name of the city," but most of the inhabitants continue playing dice or sipping wine, paying no attention to Gracchus whatsoever (228). In the fragment, Gracchus's conversation with a businessman corresponds to his exchange with the Burgomaster. Both interlocutors convey the viewpoint of a solid citizen, a family man, in opposition to the artist.

This supposed opposition of bourgeois citizen (dull, philistine, but perhaps healthily closer to the physical roots of "life") and artist (attuned to hidden mysteries, but nervous and sickly) pervades much late nineteenth- and early twentieth-century European literature. Gracchus's vacillating distaste and envy for the solid citizen become especially evident in the lively fragment. Gracchus fussily corrects the businessman's vocabulary, from mundane "ship" to the more poetic "bark." When the businessman modestly excuses himself as a babbling babe in comparison with Gracchus, the hunter flashes his envy, insisting that "you who roam around outside [off the ship]" can better explain the moods of the "masters," or people in the practical, financial world who own Gracchus's bark (232). The businessman, eying this derelict with matted hair, complacently agrees, "Well, I am superior in some ways to you." At this point, Gracchus, disgruntled but still hoping to get information, harumphs, "Better, far better that you exaggerate in this direction and that you fancy yourself to be far superior" (232). Obviously Gracchus, for all his artistic knowledge about poetic terms and the aesthetically bounding chamois, cannot make up his mind whether he is truly superior or whether he is just an invalid, not fit for "real" life, with its domestic and economic cares. His perpetual "dying" may only enact his incapacity for shouldering bourgeois responsibilities.

Even though Gracchus finally dismisses the businessman as "a nonentity whom I'm filling up with wine," he still wants to establish some kind of tie with the community. The name Gracchus might suggest a wish for involvement with public affairs, if Kafka alludes to Roman reformers of that name —brothers of the nobility whose plan to redistribute public lands won popular support but incited aristocratic hatred.[23] First one brother was killed during a riot in 33 B.C.; then the younger one was similarly killed in 21 B.C. Unlike a deity dying one year and again in other incarnations, the Gracchi give no sense of hopeful reincarnation. Their mirror-image deaths result from idealism, brashness, or a failure to learn from past mistakes— not from closeness to a truly benefited community.

The Roman society of the historical Gracchi at least considered the brothers' proposals passionately, pro and con, and primitive societies eagerly awaited their dying god's mythic return, but nobody has given the Hunter Gracchus a glance. In both the story proper and the fragment, Gracchus manages to find one person to listen to him, but each listener remains skeptical. The Burgomaster Salvatore, in the main story, can, despite his hopeful name, neither save Gracchus nor be saved by him. The businessman of the fragment warns outright that life is too brief and too taken up with getting "oneself and one's family through" to fritter one's thoughts on Gracchus: "you aren't the talk of the town" (233–34). The businessman's plodding practicality infuriates Gracchus, who even insists that his visitor must be concealing what he has heard about the hunter. With this suspicion, Kafka seems both to address Europe's bad conscience about its Jews, whom nobody even hears or sees, as people, and to lament the lack of fame and especially effective place for the artist, the dreamer, the chaser of graceful and elusive deer.

The dying god by his repeated suffering gives health to the society, whereas the artist, who should stimulate and transform a community, goes unheeded. Gracchus continues to make a god's impossible sacrifices, "dying" theatrically over and over, but his efforts attach him to no one and prove only his inadequacy for "life." Whether Gracchus in this story returns, or Gregor in *The Metamorphosis* disappears, the isolation of the "savior" amounts to death in life, not the god's life in death.

Beckett

In *Malone Dies* (1951), Samuel Beckett furnishes Malone and Macmann with extensive allusions to the tradition of the dying/reviving god. Not knowing what they do nor why, these two characters, like the beheaded chickens Malone writes about, still execute a few steps recognizable as those of Frazer's human representative of the dying god. These allusions link a necessary death with a particular season, identify the dying figure with the vegetation, associate him with an Aphrodite, subject him to violent ritual, and endow him with successors who inherit his spirit—as well as his "privilege" of dying soon. Beckett recreates these requirements only to parody them. He arrests the cycle of descent and emergence at the stage of decline. The ancient gods could go to the underworld and return, but here the human representative plunges into an underworld from which he cannot redeem either himself or the land.

Beckett would know this cycle of dying god so well from Joyce's use of it in *Finnegans Wake*. Barbara Gluck shows how Beckett learned "cyclical patterns" from Joyce, while registering important differences: "And where Beckett's heroes are caught between life and death, unable to get born or to die. . .Joyce's are continually achieving both—going from birth to death to rebirth. In terms of tone, too, the two purgatories radically diverge. Joyce is joyous, celebrating Finnegan's fall because he knows he will rise (wake) again. . . . Beckett's tone, on the other hand, is grim."[24] Beckett slyly signals his intention to "redo Joyce" in the pun "rejoice," which appears in *Molloy* in conjunction with the words "Ulysses" and "wake." Molloy is describing his minimal freedom "on the black boat of Ulysses, to crawl towards the East, along the deck. . . . And from the poop, poring upon the wave, a sadly rejoicing slave, I follow with my eyes the sad and futile wake."[25] John Fletcher points out that Beckett borrows the image of the ship from the philosopher Geulinx and thinks Beckett adds Ulysses to the deck as an allusion to Dante;[26] however, I believe Beckett is mainly evoking Joyce's *Ulysses*. Just as Beckett continuousy parodies *The Odyssey* (as if to outdo *Ulysses*) throughout *Molloy*, the first part of his trilogy, in *Malone Dies*, the second part, Beckett "follows" and deflates aspects of *Finnegans Wake*, by playing so attentively on the theme of death and rebirth that serve no purpose.[27]

Malone begins his ruminations by parodying the link between the death of Frazer's priest-kings and the season of the year. Frazer speculates that people enacted the death of the god at sowing or harvest. The anthropologist then explains how they updated their old rites for purgation and regeneration to Christian holidays, mentioning Easter, St. John's Day at midsummer, All Hallow's Eve, Christmas, and Twelfth Night as holidays that betray vestiges of old rites.[28] At first Malone predicts that his demise, like the god's, will coincide with the rejuvenation of nature. He then moves on to pinpoint specific holidays after which he might die:

I shall soon be quite dead at last in spite of all. Perhaps next month. Then it will be the month of April or of May. For the year is still young, a thousand little signs tell me so. Perhaps I am wrong, perhaps I shall survive Saint John the Baptist's Day and even the Fourteenth of July, festival of freedom. Indeed I would not put it past me to pant on to the Transfiguration, not to speak of the Assumption. But I do not think so. . . . (179)

With all these dates Malone echoes Frazer's encyclopedic effect. He also manages to eke out a few extra days for himself, hoping to put off his death as he puts off the end of the sentence with delaying phrases: "dead at last in spite of all." Moreover, the ironically optimistic names of the holidays intensify the absurdity of presenting himself as a god-man: Malone will not be transfigured, he will not be assumed to heaven, he will never be free. Malone further destroys this first tenuous association with a seasonally dying god-man by promptly rejecting that figure's role as benefactor: "Let me say before I go any further that I forgive nobody. I wish them all an atrocious life and then the fires and ice of hell and in the execrable generations to come an honoured name. Enough for this evening" (180).

The traditional dying gods declined at a certain date on purpose, to usher in the new season, whereas Beckett's parodic, reluctant imitators cannot even locate the season. Malone guesses wildly that it is Easter week or high summer (208–9). He confuses night and day because of the shifting light in his room: "In a word there seems to be the light of the outer world, of those who know the sun and moon emerge at such an hour and at such another plunge again below the surface, and who rely on this, and who know that clouds are always to be expected but sooner or later always pass away, and mine" (221). His reference to those who rely on the movements of the stars and planets recalls Frazer's comments on the necessity of mapping the sky:

> But in early days the proper adjustment of the calendar is a matter of religious concern, since on it depends a knowledge of the right seasons for propitiating the deities whose favour is indispensable for the welfare of the community. No wonder, therefore, that the king, as the chief priest of the state, or as himself a god, should be liable to deposition or death at the end of an astronomical period.[29]

Malone's exercise book does actually come to him with astronomical or astrological markings, but he cannot read the ciphers and diagrams (209). In the world Beckett depicts, the chance for humans to synchronize their gestures with nature's movement or to perform life-furthering rituals correctly no longer exists.

In fact, Malone has lost touch with his proper place in the universe to such an extent that in addition to confusing the seasons, he cannot even ascertain if he is really living. He sarcastically fears he is already dead or not yet born. He constantly returns to these doubts (183, 219–20, 225–27), which force him from the role of a god, dying into rebirth, into a monstrously parodic version, that of an octagenarian fetus, birthing into death (283). Overturning everything the Frazerian dying figure stood for, Malone desperately hopes that such a "birth" into death will *not* mean "rebirth." Earlier in the trilogy, Moran similarly comes to "dread death like a regeneration" (140). As John Pilling summarizes, "only a kind of ultimate death (what Beckett calls 'fully certified death'), the end of time, offers any hope of solace, not a death from which one may awake to haunt reality again."[30]

Expecting "nothing new under the sun," the yearly recycled but unrenewed human being can find in the seasons only mechanical, not spiritual rebeginnings. Beckett echoes the tone that Eliot set in the opening lines of *The Waste Land*, "April is the cruelest month," by bitterly deriving the word May "from Maia, hell . . . goddess of increase and plenty" (234). Maia or Maya is the Hindu name for the world as it is, consisting of appearances and delusions. Beckett further echoes Eliot in subverting the pastoral tradition of Milton's Lycidas, who rose from the dead as the new vegetation arises with the spring. The two twentieth-century authors see the dead "rise" only in terms of a corpse disturbed. Eliot's narrator wonders doubtfully whether a "planted" corpse has begun to "sprout" or whether a "Dog" has dug it up. Beckett, like Eliot, debunks Lycidas in a brief allusion to the drowned who rise, while discussing the burial of a mule. The mule has already "enjoyed" a second life, of hard labor, when reprieved from the slaughterhouse:

> And Big Lambert would soon be able to plow and harrow the place where it lay, with another mule, or an old horse, or an old ox, bought at the knacker's yard, knowing that the share would not turn up the putrid flesh or be blunted by the big bones. For he knew how the dead and buried tend, contrary to what might be expected, to rise to the surface, in which they resembled the drowned. And he had made allowance for this when digging the hole. (213)

Big Lambert, even more than the fearful narrator of *The Waste Land* contemplating the intrusive Dog, presses the dead down, and he allows the mule a "reincarnation" not in its own spirit but only in a series of decrepit successors that will toil in its tracks. Beckett also evokes rebirth in the word "harrow." Christ is said to have harrowed hell to reap the souls of virtuous pagans, but Big Lambert will only save more animals from the knacker's yard, where their sufferings could have ended sooner. Although Malone knows painfully well that all living beings are approaching their end, he also knows, paradoxically, that even the slightest human project—plowing or checking his inventory, for example—often has "no end" (249). Beckett thus converts the eternal, recurrent cycles of deity into interminable, repetitious agony for animals and humans.

Because Malone cannot die quickly enough, he stops sounding like the surrogate of a deity and starts sounding more like another Frazerian character, the sibyl, who asked for immortality but forgot to ask for accompanying agelessness. Frazer describes folktale versions of the sibyl: old women who shrivel and live on in small baskets or glass bottles, gnawing one roll per year and longing for death.[31] Malone similarly pictures his restricted soul "turning in its cage as in a lantern" and calling for surcease (222).

As a result of his inability to recognize the seasons, Malone fails to receive sustenance from nature or give blessing to it in return. He and the characters he scribbles about in his notebook do not feel at home with nature emotionally, although they often blend with it physically so as to be practically indistinguishable. Frazer insists that primitive peoples imagine a spirit of vegetation simultaneously manifesting itself in theriomorphic deities, anthropomorphic ones, and a branch or corn shock. In this last case, the god literally identifies with the vegetation. Both Macmann and Malone enact this identification in ludicrous forms. Macmann, for instance, more or less *becomes* nature when he lies on the ground and rolls around in the rain (239). At the asylum he likes to wander with "a branch torn from a dead bramble" or with a hyacinth, like some King of the May with his branch or a legendary dying Hyacinth.[32] But Macmann's keepers beat him for taking even the brambles (275). When set to do garden work, he irresistibly pulls up the carrots, instead of blessing the crops, as one possessing such a closeness with nature would properly do (243).

For all his preference for the out-of-doors, Macmann displays none of the discernment or optimism belonging to the Old Man of the harvest, incarnate in the last sheaf of grain,[33] though Macmann also becomes synonymous with hay left for drying:

> And it is no doubt all the same to Macmann whether it is spring or whether it is autumn . . . he has still the whole of his old age before him, and then that kind of epilogue when it is not very clear what is happening . . . but which no doubt has its usefulness, as hay is left out to dry before being garnered. (232)

Unlike Frazer's harvest spirits, Macmann receives no assurance of human immortality by drawing an analogy between conifers or evergreen mistletoe and his own possibly renewable life: "trees must blacken even where no heart beats, though it appears that some stay green forever, for some obscure reason" (232).

This meditation on the baffling behavior of conifers, inexplicably attached to life, ensues after Macmann suddenly reappears in Malone's notebook after a long absence (229). Malone used to call Macmann "Saposcat," a near anagram for "scapegoat." According to Frazer, the scapegoat is a debased version—human or animal—of the exalted dying god or sacred king. In the French original, Macmann lands back in Malone's life with a thud—"ouf, le revoilà." He almost seems to be reincarnated, despite his doubts, down the red passage of a birth canal, a "fleuve" or river of red houses: "an equinoctial gale howls along the quays bordered by high red houses" (231).[34] Like the dying god, whose image women threw into and drew out of springs or the sea, Macmann returns to new life.[35] But he hardly rallies to new vigor.

Though confined to his room, Malone too, in the manner of his character Macmann, has a feeble memory of past gardens, associating him with a degraded version of nature as his proper setting. He seems to recall a wall-paper covered with "a writhing mass of roses, violets and other flowers in such profusion that it seemed to me I had never seen so many in the whole course of my life, nor of such beauty," but these flowers are only paper (224). If Malone now swells up to "fill a considerable part of the universe," he moves out into objects not as Adonis, immanent in nature, but only as a loner, knocking against the walls of his own head (235). The illusory roses give way to a permanent skull of bone.

Earlier in the trilogy Molloy almost mystically blends with nature:

Then I was no longer that sealed jar to which I owed my being so well preserved, but a wall gave way and I filled with roots and tame stems for example, stakes long since dead and ready for burning, the recess of night and the imminence of dawn, and then the labour of the planet rolling eager into winter, winter would rid it of these contemptible scabs. Or of that winter I was the precarious calm, the thaw of the snows which make no difference and all the horrors of it all all over again. (49)

Nevertheless, like Macmann in the rain or Malone in the flowery room, the root-filled Molloy heralds a spring that heals none of the old hurts.

Because these Adonic characters link so closely though ineffectually with seasons and vegetation, one would suspect an Aphrodite in their orbit, and, sure enough, Malone has his "Venus" (209). Unfortunately, "she" is nothing but a familiar Venus pencil. Yet he is not discouraged, making it into a kind of green fertility symbol: "I was struggling to retrieve my pencil. . . . It is a little Venus, still green no doubt, with five or six facets, pointed at both ends and so short there is just room, between them, for my thumb and the two adjacent fingers, gathered together in a little vice. I use the two points turn and turn about [first one, then the other], sucking them frequently, I love to suck" (222). Sometimes he also refers to a stick as his lover: "I used to rub myself against it saying, It's a little woman" (247).

While Malone's lover is nothing but a stick or a pencil with grotesque "breasts" to suck, Macmann's partners are even more pathetic, if possible. When Lady Pedal enters his life, the potentially vegetative "petal" of an Aphrodite has hardened to a mechanical pedal; she has nothing to do with him anyway except to include him among other inmates of the asylum in her charity project. Macmann's lover Moll is another grotesque Venus. Her earrings and a tooth, all chiseled in the form of crucifixes, strike him as aphrodisiac, like some primitive talisman (263).

Venus as pencil or mechanical pedal certainly diminishes the goddess and leaves her partner only the poor consolations of metal. On the other hand, highlighting such a trade name "Venus" lends to the pencil and the activity of writing a few meager glints of the old divine light. The god agonized and died over and over again, whereas the eternal goddess mourned and sought him, and occasionally (as in Isis's case) directly gave him new life. Here too Malone's Venus, his writing, gives him his only real life. Although he takes scant comfort in it, writing provides his reason for going on. In French he constantly refers to his "mine," his "lead," which is also his imagination to be "mined" for its riches, no matter how paltry he regards them.

As mentioned earlier, Malone alludes to another goddess, "Maia, hell, I remember that too, goddess of increase and plenty" (234). Barbara Walker has recently summarized some traits of Maia:

"Grandmother of Magic," mother of the Greeks' Enlightened One, Hermes; the western version of Maya, "Magic," mother of the Hindus' Enlightened One, Buddha. She personified the powers of transformation and physical "appearances," the same powers attributed to Maya-Kali, who made the universe by her magic. Greek writers called Maia one of the Pleiades, but also understood that she was the Great Goddess of Maytime festivals, of the renewal and rebirth of the dead. She made her son Hermes the Conductor of Souls in the underworld, just as the Hindu Maya made her masculine counterpart Ya-Ma into a Conductor of Souls and Lord of Death.[36]

If Malone is going to dredge up any mythological learning about a cosmic goddess, he will retrieve not a gracious virgin but more likely the devouring crone, who takes her offspring back into the earth. Malone belongs to her brood, though he can conduct his readers only within the hell that he perceives life to be.

Malone alludes once more to a goddess in the word "Cythera." Cythera in Crete was one of the chief cult centers of Aphrodite.[37] He speaks almost as if he could be joined with her in death, but he must immediately reproach himself for such preposterous sentiments as well as for his high-flown erudition:

But before I go I should like to find a hole in the wall behind which so much goes on, such extraordinary things, and often coloured. One last glimpse and I feel I could slip away as happy as if I were embarking for—I nearly said for Cythera, decidedly it is time for this to stop. (236–37)

Beckett's first published story, "Assumption," did contain just such inflated, romantic longings. The protagonist, an artist, vows silence but breaks it when a woman comes into his life: "Thus each night he died and was God, each night revived and was torn, torn and battered with increasing grievousness, so that he hungered to be irretrievably engulfed in the light of eternity, one with the birdless cloudless colourless skies, in infinite fulfilment."[38] He delivers "a great storm of sound" and then dies. Although Beckett soon rejected what Ruby Cohn calls the "juvenile" style of this story, he never abandoned the image of a figure repeatedly hurt and revived, who certainly no longer thinks of himself as a "God" but who still undergoes the god's ordeal.[39]

Besides recalling Aphrodite's Cythera in the preceding passage, Malone may actually be thinking of the Greek Cithaeron, sacred to the Muses and Dionysus.[40] In Euripides' play *The Bacchae*, Dionysus kills Pentheus on Mount Cithaeron by imposing on the mortal his own role as torn and dying god.[41] Though Pentheus goes willingly to Cithaeron when Dionysus promises that the king can spy on orgies there, the frenzied women turn on Pentheus and tear him apart. Malone similarly claims that he would go to his death "happy" if he could spy on some colorful scene; in fact, he does spy, immediately after the reference to Cythera, on a couple whose lovemaking he thinks looks more like painful writhings (238). Through these covert allusions, Malone recognizes himself as a much less powerful, less majestic, but just as doomed Pentheus, the coerced and unconsulted ritual substitute for the dying god.

Although Beckett traces connections between the dying figure and the season, the vegetation, and a goddess, only to show that those links have been broken, he allows one link to remain intact—that between the dying figure and violent ritual. Beckett portrays violence against animals particularly insistently and poignantly in *Malone Dies* (192, 200, 211–12, 214–15, 231). This violence takes on ritual overtones when Big Lambert looks forward to "the return of the season, the principal event of which is unquestionably the Saviour's birth, in a stable" (200). The "principal event" for Christians is the Savior's advent; however, only the stable and a regularized pig-killing time attract butcher Lambert, who goes priestlike to the kill in his Sunday suit. Pigs, which Frazer says are sacred to many of the dying deities, have their deaths associated with a season and a ritual in Beckett's world too.[42] The stuck pigs, no doubt, derive small comfort from such ceremony, but humans can extract even less consolation. The animals still fare better than Malone or Macmann, who cannot find any holiday to grace by their deaths.

Competing with the violence against animals, violence against people proceeds apace in *Malone Dies*. The vestiges of human sacrifice erupt crazily—with ritual trappings but without ritual control or meaning. At the end of the book, on Macmann's outing to an island with Druid remains and "the faint fires of the blazing gorse," Macmann's keeper, Lemuel, gratuitously kills the oarsmen, Maurice and Ernest (286–87). Frazer identifies

the golden bough itself with the mistletoe worshiped by Druids.[43] By placing Macmann's outing among Druid rocks, on "a glorious May or April
day, April more likely . . . doubtless the Easter week-end, spent by Jesus
in hell," Beckett sets up vague expectations of ritual (280). The "blazing
gorse" perhaps suggests Frazer's Easter or Beltane fires, where "the traces
of human sacrifice at them were particularly clear and unequivocal."[44]
Beckett includes the human sacrifice when the oarsmen die, but the ancient
belief that "So far as the light of the bonfire reaches, so far will a blessing
rest on the fields" has soured completely in the modern world.[45] Human
sacrifice shows up as the murder it is—not to be praised and yet hardly
even deserving special lament, so thoroughly does human murderousness
blend with the usual task of life to kill us off.

Just as they maintain skewed connections with season, nature, Venuses,
and violence, Malone and Macmann also fit into a whole series of dying
figures who, as Frazer says of the actors in periodic sacrificial rites, inherit
an abiding spirit.[46] Germaine Brée writes, "we soon begin to realize that,
from *Murphy* to *How It Is*, it is doubtless the same adventurer that goes his
way and gives birth, from book to book, to the unpredictable and inevitable book that follows."[47] John Fletcher similarly calls Malone "simultaneously the creator, and avatar" of Beckett's other characters.[48]

Beckett connects his theme of pervasive violence in the world with his
generations of narrators by having them not just succeed one another
peaceably but often kill off the preceding one; the new speakers also throt-
tle non-narrating characters. When Malone becomes too depressed by his
creature Moll's pathetic love story, he threatens that he will "kill her"; he
soon invents her death by disease (264). Malone also specifically parallels
his ability to terminate his characters' appearances on the page with
Lemuel's murders. As Malone feels himself dying at last, he watches
others—Lemuel, for instance—stopped in their tracks with him:

> he raises his hatchet on which the blood will never dry, but not
> to hit anyone, he will not hit anyone, he will not hit anyone any
> more, he will not touch anyone any more, either with it or with it
> or with it or with or
> or with it or with his hammer or with his stick or with his fist
> or in thought in dream I mean never he will never
> or with his pencil or with his stick or
> or light light I mean
> never there he will never
> never anything
> there
> any more (288)

Because Malone in his last speech substitutes "pencil" for "hatchet," he
dismally implies that "creative writing" is a misnomer. In his "destructive

writing," he mangles the emotion he tries to express with the inevitable failures of language, so that necessarily inadequate narrators stop the mouths of their predecessors in frustration:

> And if I ever stop talking it will be because there is nothing more to be said. But let us leave these morbid matters and get on with that of my demise, in two or three days if I remember rightly. Then it will be all over with the Murphys, Merciers, Molloys, Morans and Malones, unless it goes on beyond the grave. But sufficient unto the day, let us first defunge, then we'll see. How many have I killed, hitting them on the head or setting fire to them? (236)[49]

Here Malone goes on to review violent scenes, mostly from Beckett's earlier works, of the type found in Frazer. Thus if Malone guards against his own rebirth into the long confusion of life, he will accept a succession of narrators as a kind of personal corps of Kings of the Wood.

The violent narrators who "kill off" their predecessors, like the fearsome Lemuel with his hatchet, succeed to office with "a glitter of steel at the shoulder."[50] But in Beckett's world, the only priests are psychopaths; the only representatives of dying gods are pathetic substitutes such as Malone and Macmann. None of them have been able to put a stop to the renewal of suffering, neither Lemuel by swinging his weapon nor Malone by laying down his pencil. For in the context of the whole trilogy, as soon as Malone falls silent, the Unnamable starts babbling, "without their having granted me as much as a brief sick-leave among the worms, before resurrecting me" (342). New voices arise from Beckett's silences as surely as the dying gods revive. In fact, the Unnamable calls Malone a "god," but only in the sense that, like a *deus absconditus*, "he does not look at me, does not know me, wants for nothing. I alone am man [i.e., wanting] and all the rest divine" (300).

The Unnamable hears the new whisperings but would rather they cease, because the voice comes back to life only incompletely, loaded down with alien words and concepts appropriate to society, but not to the individual. To express this tyranny of "they," anonymous social members who drape themselves over him by means of their speech, the Unnamable alludes to a ceremony for flaying a victim and wearing his skin, to represent rebirth: "They loaded me down with their trappings and stoned me through the carnival. I'll sham dead now, whom they couldn't bring to life, and my monster's carapace will rot off me" (325). Frazer identifies the flayed satyr Marsyas in Phrygian mythology with the dying god Attis.[51] Rome celebrated Attis's resurrection "in the form of a carnival. It was the Festival of Joy (*Hilaria*). A universal licence prevailed. Every man might say and do what he pleased. People went about the streets in disguise. No dignity was too high or too sacred for the humblest citizen to assume with impunity."[52] Only at such a topsy-turvy carnival (which runs continuously in the modern world, Beckett implies) could the Unnamable, the humblest of the destitute, assume the sacred but hideous cast-off skin of a monster-god.

Although the violence of the old religions goes on in the Unnamable's ordeals and in Lemuel's blows, the ancient hoped-for redemptions do not follow. John Fletcher insists that Beckett's frequent motif of characters drifting out to sea at the end of a story is "a figure of the womb."[53] If so, the image is an admission of failure: the narrators have not been able to end the cycle of redundant torture that is life. Malone might be eternally dying, but only in the sense that the page freezes his last moments and offers them to generations of new readers, who perhaps reopen the book to the bleak scene with some of the same misgivings as Frazer's generations of priests returning to the grisly wood at Nemi.

4

Bowing to the Bull

The tradition of dying god in bull form influenced both Hemingway and O'Connor. These writers mimic the animal's violent rites in *The Sun Also Rises* and "Greenleaf" to reflect the violence in their world. Although the meaninglessness surrounding Hemingway's characters is largely the reuslt of World War I, with its specific historical causes, Hemingway seems to regard the violence of war (recalled for him on a much smaller scale by the bullfight) as emblematic of the usual human condition. Hemingway and O'Connor see brutality as metaphysical: life inevitably wounds us with its bull horns.

While for O'Connor the Christian god sends loving violence, for Hemingway *nada* dispenses absurd violence. Nevertheless, both authors equally choose to bow down to the bull—either because it masks the god or because it teaches an adherence to honorable codes. Most interestingly, Hemingway and O'Connor depict humans and bulls as mirror images. Instead of pitting humans, as might be expected, against an enemy bull (against death or absurdity), the authors carefully identify humans and bulls. They thereby recreate the equivalence of dying god and animal attacker noted by Frazer with such surprise.[1]

Hemingway

Ernest Hemingway subtly unifies *The Sun Also Rises* (1926) around the myth of Cybele and Attis. During Cybele's carnival Hilaria, "A universal licence prevailed. . . . People went about the streets in disguise."[2] At Hemingway's fictional Pamplona, people dance in the streets, wear costumes, and pointedly transfer their allegiance from the Christian San Fermin to Brett Ashley. Brett accepts a number of suitors, as Cybele had a series of lovers, the incarnations of Attis. Hemingway assigns Brett's suitors specific characteristics of the dying gods: the men are said to be gored, or "dead," or reawakened. In particular, Attis was castrated, and an injury received in World War I has emasculated the main character,

Jake Barnes. Moreover, the bullfighter Pedro Romero offers a killed bull's ear to Brett, as Cybele's devotees sacrificed a bull to their goddess. Insisting, as he does in other books such as *Death in the Afternoon* and *In Our Time*, that bullfighters approach their work with reverence, Hemingway underlines the ritual origins of the Spanish bullfight, which forms so large a part of *The Sun Also Rises*.

These references to the myth of Cybele and Attis help clarify Brett's and Jake's characters and Hemingway's tone and world view. Two versions of Attis's death exist: he fatally castrates himself, or a boar (perhaps Cybele, in the form of a boar) slays him. Is Brett cruel or kind? Is Jake able to salvage some sustaining value and to renew other people and himself? Or does he only flounder, remaining "emotionally sterile," as Mark Spilka has claimed?[3]

Malcolm Cowley and Philip Young sense parallels in Hemingway's work with myth and legend, but they explain them as somehow accidental. Cowley detects an atmosphere surrounding Hemingway's characters that "primitives" would recognize: hostile nature, which people can stave off only by means of compulsive custom.[4] Cowley sees Jake as a Fisher King, genitally wounded; he traces Hemingway's Parisian waste land to Eliot's poem, which Hemingway liked. Nevertheless, Cowley concludes, "I doubt very much that Hemingway bothered to look at Jessie L. Weston's book. . . . And yet when he wrote his first novel, he dealt with the same legend that Eliot had discovered by scholarship, recreating it for himself, I think, by a sort of instinct for legendary situations."[5] Philip Young also thinks of the Fisher King when he reads *The Sun Also Rises*, but, like Cowley, he refuses to grant Hemingway any conscious knowledge of legend or myth: "This may be just coincidence, though the novelist had read the poem [Eliot's *The Waste Land*]."[6]

Richard Adams in "Sunrise out of the Waste Land" corrects this view that Hemingway somehow projected myths that he did not know by means of "instinct." Adams believes that Hemingway must have read Weston's *From Ritual to Romance* because some parallels between this work and Hemingway's novel seem to him too close to be chance. He notes Brett's recourse to fortune-telling, recalling the use of Tarot cards to predict the rise and fall of the waters, and her frequent bathing, recalling ritual ablutions.[7] In fact, Hemingway bestows on Brett some of the purity that Frazer allots to a goddess: "the union of Cybele and Attis, like that of Aphrodite and Adonis, was dramatically represented at the festival, and the subsequent bath of the goddess was a ceremonial purification of the bride."[8]

Adams also points out that in *Death in the Afternoon*, Hemingway praises an 1851 book on Spain by Richard Ford, who defines "taurobolium" as the ritual drenching of an initiate in the blood of a bull.[9] Adams surmises, "It seems to me very probable that Hemingway had all or most of this material in mind [Weston's and Ford's books and Frazer's *Adonis Attis Osiris*] when he wrote *The Sun Also Rises*, and possibly more that I have not yet found."[10] By the end of his life Hemingway owned three copies of *The Golden Bough*; although the editions are from the 1940s, they at least show an interest in Frazer that could have begun earlier.[11] In the absence of definite proof as to what he read and when, Adams's conjecture that Hemingway did know some specific mythological works seems likely. I differ from Adams in revaluating Brett, whom he dismisses as "lost," and in emphasizing Attis more than the Fisher King. Weston, in fact, originates the Fisher King in Attis; she associates the taurobolium with "Attis and Kybele."[12]

Jake's injury is crucial to the interpretion of Hemingway's mythic allusions, which, in effect, bend a biblical quest back toward its primitive beginnings.[13] Jake's physical condition may determine his name, which Brett calls "a hell of a biblical name."[14] In Gen. 32:24–32, an angel (sometimes translated "a man") "touched the hollow of his thigh, and Jacob's thigh was put out of joint as he wrestled with him." The patriarch's injury sounds like Attis's castration: less serious (or else discreetly said to be so). Weston discusses thigh wounds as euphemism for castration.[15]

The angel renames Jacob "Israel" to mean he has "striven with God and with men." As the biblical Jacob wrestles, characters in *The Sun Also Rises* box and fight, and, more important, they are wrestling with the idea of God. John Clendenning, who argues whether Hemingway's characters, in general, are atheistic or agnostic, correctly emphasizes spiritual struggles, but he mistakes Hemingway's position by assuming his characters are completely bereft if they lose a Christian God.[16] Hemingway substitutes pagan gods, who mean to the characters of *The Sun Also Rises* not new literal gods in the heavens but specific values—learned from the bullfight—to be cultivated within themselves.

Some critics add insult to Jake's injury, so to speak, by inferring that physical impairment, in literature, must signal emotional inadequacy or moral bankruptcy.[17] Others, however, refute this equation, insisting either that Jake matures[18] or that he has been a caring and giving person all along.[19] Rather than impugning Jake's morals or emotions through his disability, Hemingway uses it mainly as evidence against the stupidity of war. Although Jake refrains from complaining about his handicap to the prostitute Georgette, he knows where to fix blame:

> "What's the matter with you, anyway?"
> "I got hurt in the war," I said
> "Oh, that dirty war."
> We would probably have gone on and discussed the war and agreed that it was in reality a calamity for civilization, and perhaps would have been better avoided. I was bored enough. (17)

The "calamity" of war is too obvious for Jake to feel he has to discuss it. He is not so much protesting this particular war as admitting, tacitly, that governments repeatedly funnel greed and bigotry into some foolish war or other, beyond the individual soldier's control: the likelihood of war becomes almost a metaphysical given for him. Furthermore, Jake's legacy from battle could be said to sum up the limitation and frustration that beset all mortals: casualties and unimpaired alike. The human condition mocks people—Jake seemingly more than others at the moment—in that it eventually neutralizes all efforts: everyone experiences loneliness, and everyone dies. Jake's lot, recalling that of Attis skewered against a tree, magnifies human vulnerability to emotional pain and physical decay.

In addition to indicting the war and representing loss and loneliness in general, Jake's castration associates him with the steers used to calm the bulls unloaded for bullfights. Dewey Ganzel finds the resemblance between Jake and steers not so much in sterility as in caution and control. Ganzel especially underlines the steers' function as peacemakers.[20] Jake explains the animals' role to Bill when the latter asks:

> "Do they ever gore the steers?"
> "Sure. Sometimes they go right after them and kill them."
> "Can't the steers do anything?"
> "No. They're trying to make friends."
> "What do they have them in for?"
> "To quiet down the bulls and keep them from breaking their horns against the stone walls, or goring each other."
> "Must be swell being a steer." (133).

As Brett is also aware, the steers "don't look happy" (138). Neither does Jake. But beyond his personal happiness, Jake seeks other goals. He accepts responsibility for his friends, trying to parry Mike's jabs at Cohn or going to Brett's aid with money and solace. Hemingway's implied metaphor connecting human with steer, brought out so clearly by Ganzel, also links human with god, because ancient peoples castrated the bull that represented Attis in their rites.[21]

Although Jake is the character who most obviously resembles both the castrated steers and a castrated Attis, Hemingway also compares other members of the group to steers and to bulls and, in turn, to dying gods. Mike accuses Robert Cohn of mooning around Brett: "I would have thought you'd loved being a steer, Robert. . . . They lead such a quiet life. They never say anything and they're always hanging about someone" (141). Jake claims that bulls feint with their horns, using "a left and a right just like a boxer," affiliating the boxer Robert with bulls as well as with steers (139). When Robert asks if the bulls pacified by steers will later fight well in the ring, Jake assures him, "They all know each other. . . . They're only dangerous when they're alone, or only two or three of them together" (141). Bill then adds, "Don't you ever detach me from the herd, Mike." With his comparisons to gored and goring animals, Hemingway shows that each of the characters is likely to be hurt. He excludes no one, sympathizing with Jake, Robert, Bill, and the rest, all potentially inflicting pain, all huddled together for a minimal comfort.

In addition to playing Attis indirectly through their association with bulls, characters recall the dying god in other ways. Hemingway elaborately sets up Robert, for example, as a figure suggesting vegetation, death, and revival. Though he seldom drinks, Robert gets drunk during the festival and falls asleep. Four times his companions repeat that he's "dead" (158–59). While they thereby hint rudely that they would prefer to be rid of him, they also prepare for his "epiphany":

> Two hours later Cohn appeared. He came into the front room still with the wreath of garlics around his neck. The Spaniards shouted when he came in. Cohn wiped his eyes and grinned.
> "I must have been sleeping," he said.
> "Oh, not at all," Brett said.
> "You were only dead," Bill said.
> "Aren't we going to go and have some supper?" Cohn asked.
> "Do you want to eat?"
> "Yes. Why not? I'm hungry."
> "Eat those garlics, Robert," Mike said. "I say. Do eat those garlics."
> Cohn stood there. His sleep had made him quite all right.
> "Do let's go and eat," Brett said. "I must get a bath."
> "Come on," Bill said. "Let's translate Brett to the hotel." (159)

Because Robert, draped in white garlic, obviously cannot obtain much satisfaction for his hunger from the wreath, does Hemingway imply that the ceremony at Pamplona, so much like rites for a vegetation god, can no longer console us?[22] In part, Hemingway does travesty the ancient beliefs. Robert, with his adolescent crush on Brett, his lack of humor, and his faith in romantic adventure under distant purple skies, is an ordinary human blunderer, not a god. Yet when he emerges wiping sleep from his eyes like a child and Jake pronounces him "quite all right," Hemingway allows Robert a moment of innocence and elemental simplicity that does temporarily hallow him.

Drunkenly claiming to be a "taxidermist," Bill also may establish a brief connection with a dying god. Frazer comments on straw-stuffed skins that symbolized Attis:

> if my conjecture is right, the man who represented the father-god of Phrygia [Attis] used to be slain and his stuffed skin hung on the sacred pine in order that his spirit might work for the growth of the crops, the

multiplication of animals, and the fertility of women. So at Athens an ox, which appears to have embodied the corn-spirit, was killed at an annual sacrifice, and its hide, stuffed with straw and sewn up, was afterwards set on its feet and yoked to a plough as if it were ploughing, apparently in order to represent, or rather to promote, the resurrection of the slain corn-spirit at the end of the threshing. This employment of the skins of divine animals for the purpose of ensuring the revival of the slaughtered divinity might be illustrated by other examples. Perhaps the hide of the bull which was killed to furnish the regenerating bath of blood in the rites of Attis may have been put to a similar use.[23]

Of his supposed career in taxidermy, Bill admits, "That was in another country. And besides all the animals were dead" (75). His absurd, seemingly irrelevant banter startles us into laughter, at the same time that it insinuates terrible losses. Unlike Attis, Bill can revive no one; he could not really stuff a cab horse, as he brags, nor save a live one from suffering. He has trouble just keeping himself going day after day, with his knowledge of atrocity and "Injustice everywhere," let alone making all nature fertile or worrying about arising after his funeral (71).

As Robert's companions call him "dead" during the festival and Bill lords over dead animals only, Brett accuses Count Mippipopolous of being "dead," after he advises her and Jake not to ruin wine with emotions (59, 61). To be dead in this book is to be emotionless and valueless. The reverse of "deadened" is "passionate": able to cultivate the *aficion* that lets aficionados care deeply about bullfighting and makes them try to abide by its rules in their lives. The characters choose between trying to squelch emotion, like the count, and submitting to it, even if it kills them—and emotion always hurts. Yet when Brett labels the count "dead," he denies it. Mippipopolous, despite his cherished theories, cannot prevent feeling after all. In the final tally, all the characters may harbor a little of the precious *aficion*: if not about bullfighting, at least toward each other. Jake, Brett, Bill, Pedro, Robert, Mike, and even the count all register the losses inflicted by the war, and they all reach out to other people. World War I has blasted their generation, leaving maimed souls and charred "lies" like "honor," "glory," and "patriotism" in a modern underworld. Yet they have not all lost the capacity to care about people nor the honorable courage and grace that they learn from the bullring and muster to varying degrees in their small community. For a character to resemble a dying god, therefore, does not mean to be a deadened human being but to be a suffering one.

Although Hemingway assigns Jake as the most important Attis figure, dying gods always occur in a series, and, as we have seen, Hemingway draws in Robert, Bill, and the count as exemplars. By casting them all at least fleetingly as dying gods, Hemingway achieves a sense of community.

Right after the garlic-wreathed Robert resurrects from his drunken stupor, Jake sleeps in one of the beds in Robert's room and puts on one of his coats (160). Hemingway clearly identifies Jake and Robert with each other. No matter how stupidly their crowd might try to exclude Robert or scapegoat him as somebody "different," he simply duplicates Jake and every other victim. Replacing each other in Brett's bed makes the men rivals, but Jake's sleeping in Robert's bed reveals them to be brothers after all. Because Robert, Mike, and Pedro do sleep with Brett, while Jake and (less seriously) Bill want to sleep with her, the men again look like versions of Attis, since each of his incarnations year by year mated with Cybele.

Although Hemingway casts Brett as Cybele, she is not a cruel goddess whose lovers are all "unmanned and degraded" by her.[24] Hemingway does portray her as less than perfect, but overall he treats her sympathetically. When her admirers bestow on her a "mystical penumbra," he does not mock their reverence, as Sam Baskett incorrectly infers.[25] Hemingway, like his male characters, is in some ways seriously replacing the Christian San Fermin with Brett. The *riau-riau* dancers, wearing wreaths of white garlic, enclose Brett in a circle: "Brett wanted to dance but they did not want her to. They wanted her as an image to dance around" (155). Similarly, Bill jokes that they ought to "translate" Brett to her hotel, as the statue of San Fermin is said to be "translated" from one stage of the procession to the next (159, 155). Brett might feel uncomfortable in church (208), but her nervousness does not imply that "the wench is dead," ethically, as Richard Adams claims.[26] Hemingway sees something valuable in Brett that could carry a revitalized religious meaning. Whereas early Christians replaced Cybele by building the Vatican on the site where her temple once stood,[27] Hemingway plays this mythological evolution in reverse, at least to the extent that he replaces the Christian icon of a saint with a character carrying allusions to a pagan goddess.

Every image or scene that at first seems to put Brett in a bad light turns out to clear her of cruelty. When Brett acknowledges the homage of the dancers, "walking, her head up, as though the fiesta were being staged in her honor, and she found it pleasant and amusing," the words "pleasant and amusing" in the context of bloody bullfights might sound insensitive. In addition to suspecting Brett of superficiality, readers might deem her cruel when she comments about a stained muleta, "Funny. . . How one doesn't mind the blood" (211). But Brett demonstrates *aficion* and lucidity, not callousness or empty-headedness. Hemingway makes it clear that Brett matches Jake in her ability to face the bullfight and to discern the matador's skillfulness (140). "Not minding" the blood does not mean "not feeling" the intensity, the limited triumph, and the sadness of the spectacle. When she reports that "The bull-fights are hell on one. . . . I'm limp as a rag," she is properly drained by tragedy (169).[28]

If Brett does not either ignore or gloat at the bulls, does she torture her friends, by imperception or maliciousness? Mike, tattling to Jake about Robert's complaints, protests drunkenly and bitterly:

> "Brett's not a sadist. She's just a lovely, healthy wench."
> "Are you a sadist, Brett?" I asked.
> "Hope not."
> "He said Brett was a sadist just because she has a good healthy stomach."
> "Won't be healthy long." (166)

Most critics have not judged her healthy. Carol Smith, noting that "Lady Brett has generally been considered to differ fundamentally from Hemingway's more positive portraits of women," illustrates this claim with Carlos Baker's condemnation: "Brett is not 'good' for the men she knows. Romero wants her to let her hair grow out, to become more feminine, to marry and live with him. The basic abnormality at work in Brett opposes such feminization." Although Smith excuses Brett's "abnormality" as "a brave attempt to conceal her pain and to find substitute comforts for true love," she still agrees with Baker that Brett is one of Hemingway's "bad women."[29]

Yet if Mike's definition of "sadism" comes down to a question of whether "wenching," or sharing sex, is healthy, Hemingway implies that it is, when accompanied by generosity. Sam Baskett counters Baker's charge that Brett is bad for men by citing ways, "almost maternal," she genuinely cares for them.[30] Jake admits that as long as she stayed with Pedro only a short time, "You were probably damn good for him" (241). She perhaps lies beside Jake to comfort him (55); she obviously cherishes a deep regard for him.

A detail of setting that occurs early in the book may also seem to implicate Brett in cruelty, yet the context invalidates that interpretation. Jake passes a hawker on the street selling boxer toys: "I stepped aside to avoid walking into the thread with which his girl assistant manipulated the boxers. She was standing looking away, the thread in her folded hands. The man was urging two tourists to buy" (35). Because Robert is a boxer, and he and Pedro fight over Brett, the street scene might make it appear that Brett "manipulates" the men who feel tied to her by their devotion. Yet if Brett must be identified with the "girl assistant," the hawker in turn seems to control her, as Brett is subject to the same absurd, limiting, postwar atmosphere as the other characters. The assistant's folded hands show her—and, by extension, Brett—to be passive, not active, and perhaps even vaguely holy.

Another scene that seems to indict Brett but actually exonerates her draws important metaphorical connections of Brett with both the matador and the bull. When Pedro explains in his first conversation with Brett that as a bullfighter he kills his "best friends. . . so they don't kill me," the reader might wonder if Brett too is the type to "kill" her friends (186). One parallel does hold between Brett and bullfighters, but the comparison works in her favor, as Jake reveals when he indicates the dignity of both slaying and being slain during the running of the bulls. After a man named Vicente Girones is gored, Jake and a waiter differ in their views of the event:

> "Badly cogido through the back," [the waiter] said. He put the pots down on the table and sat down in the chair at the table. "A big horn wound. All for fun. Just for fun. What do you think of that?"
> "I don't know."
> "That's it. All for fun. Fun, you understand."
> "You're not an aficionado?"
> "Me? What are bulls? Animals. Brute animals." (197)

Although the waiter is admiraby moved, Jake's question, "You're not an aficionado," implies that the waiter has missed something. Jake does not agree that the games are "for sport," "for pleasure," or that Girones dies frivolously, for nothing. The comments of the two men might apply to Brett. Does she dangle her friends and hurt them "for fun"? No. She lets herself feel for her friends because she is an aficionado, passionate, about people, the way she is a novice aficionado about bullfights. She lets herself get involved with people, which means that inevitably, not maliciously, she will hurt and be hurt. Human relations are not an either/or, kill or be killed, situation, as Pedro says of bullfighting, but rather a case of both/ and. Brett is like the matador, and she is like the bull.

Brett's identification with the bull occurs in connection with the same animal that has killed Girones. This bull later charges nobly in the ring, revealing himself to have been a worthy adversary for the dead peasant: "Boys were running toward him [the fallen bull] from all parts of the arena, making a little circle around him. They were starting to dance around the bull" (220). We have already seen how the *riau-riau* dancers circle around and honor Brett (155). By juxtaposing Brett and the bull as images to dance around, Hemingway equates them. As he compares all the men with bulls and, in turn, with the dying god, he similarly elevates Brett to the status of dying deity. He credits her with lucidity, and he sympathizes with her suffering.

Larry Grimes calls Brett "toro" in the last scene of the book, but only because he thinks Jake is "setting Brett up for the kill." According to Grimes, when Jake interrupts Brett's fantasy that they could have been happy, "he drives home a verbal sword that puts Brett and the whole of her generation away from a new life," which Jake alone can enter.[31] But

Grimes misses Hemingway's respect for Brett. He also misunderstands Hemingway's reverence for the bull, which is not killed because it is terrible or unworthy to live on with the survivor. Steven Phillips makes a similar mistake of banishing the bull to a symbolic outer darkness of evil. He assumes that the "matador's victory over the bull is our victory over the demonic, over all those passions and excesses that threaten our lives."[32] On the contrary: if the matador killed "passions," including *aficion*, he would be the one left dead, emotionally.

Grimes and Phillips mistakenly assume that the bulls have to die because they are "bad" ("demonic"), but good bulls (in the sense of "honorably brave")—along with good characters—get hurt too. If the spectators can identify with the matador as a model of courage, control, and "purity of line" (168), they can also identify with a good bull as a repository of courage and a representative of mortality.[33] The spectators will all eventually be "killed"—by death when their brief life spans run out, and they are hurt, emotionally, if they courageously open themselves to passion. When Jake sees Pedro lean to speak caressingly to the bull, as man and bull briefly "were one," Jake acknowledges that the human and animal participants are both mortal and that Pedro respects the bull, almost loves it (218–19). Loving is killing and being killed: letting a partner and oneself become susceptible to pain.

Brett does let herself be vulnerable to feeling, and that openness establishes her strength. Unlike the count, who plans to dampen all emotion, Brett does not even try. When she is beginning her affair with Pedro, she defends herself to Jake, "I've never been able to help anything. . . . I can't stop things. . . . I've got to do something I really want to do. I've lost my self-respect" (183). Although she knows that such emotional availability will cost her self-doubt, difficult decisions, and the desolation of parting, she admirably chooses to follow a genuine attraction for Pedro—for his integrity as well as for his body in tight clothes. Her attraction to Mike and Robert, which she claims not to respect, derives, by contrast, from pity—not love, but not selfishness either. She gathers strength to pursue a course of action that will hurt her more than it hurts Pedro, who actually benefits, despite Montoya's fears (241).

Admittedly, Brett has proved lacking in at least two instances. Early in the book, though she asserts, "I've never let you down," she forgets an appointment with Jake (29, 41). Worse than her muddled date book, however, is her failure to guard the ear of the bull that slew Girones: "His ear was cut by popular acclamation and given to Pedro Romero, who, in turn, gave it to Brett, who wrapped it in a handkerchief belonging to myself, and left both ear and handkerchief, along with a number of Muratti cigarette-stubs, shoved far back in the drawer of the bed-table that stood beside her bed in the Hotel Montoya, in Pamplona" (199).

But if Brett reprehensibly neglects the relic when she departs from Pamplona, by the time she makes Pedro leave her in Madrid, she has matured enough to choose, consciously, "not to be a bitch" (245). Robert Cochran even judges that "By giving Romero back to bull-fighting, his seriousness and discipline intact, Brett in effect removes the bull's ear from the bed-table drawer and restores it to its rightful place in the religious ritual of which it is a part."[34] Moreover, in the light of what such a ritual was, shoving the gift away could be defended from another angle too—less indifferently abandoning it and more actively dissociating herself from one particular magic charm rather than from the religious context of bull-fighting in general. People who tried to touch the bulls during the *encierra* to acquire fertility may originally have cut off the sacrificed bull's testicles, not ears, and buried them to "impregnate" the earth.[35] Hemingway must have known such associations with fertility rites because Jake, excluded from begetting children, is the only one of his group to sleep through most of an *encierra* (160). Because Brett refuses to have anything to do with severed parts of the bull, Hemingway attributes a kind of tact to her, further excusing her from the charge that she is a cruel Cybele who castrates her Attis.

As imperfect but admirable reflections of a noble Cybele and Attis, Brett and Jake both suffer, and they both redeem others. Jake forgives Robert and comforts Brett; she helps Pedro and her other lovers and solaces Jake. In addition to receiving homage as Cybele, Brett joins Jake to repeat Attis's experience. To be the human representative of the dying bull-god (as all the characters are potentially) means to recognize mortality and absurdity but to affirm life anyway. The couple know they will be dead soon enough, but they do not permit themselves to be dead to emotion while they live. The day of Attis's death, March 25th, is simultaneously the day of his new conception, for his rebirth on December 25th, nine months later at the winter solstice.[36] The sun *also* rises, though it has to sink repeatedly, as if to the underworld. In a letter to Max Perkins, Hemingway protested that the novel was not meant to be "a hollow or bitter satire, but a damn tragedy with the earth abiding forever as the hero."[37] Although Hemingway acutely senses the weariness in the world's recycling of life and death, of pleasure and pain, here he chooses the cycles anyway.

O'Connor

Combining humor and horror, Flannery O'Connor's story "Greenleaf" (1956) shows the terrible yet wonderful workings of grace from a Catholic viewpoint. But for all her orthodoxy, O'Connor gives to the main character, Mrs. May, the precise actions and trappings of a vegetation god. Despite the importance of Christian sacrifice to O'Connor, she recreates to a remarkable degree the kind of ordeal assigned to a fertility deity.

O'Connor learned details of pagan myths from modern popularizers, although she doubted the value of their psychologizing. She wrote in a letter of September 1955, "I have recently been reading some depth psychologists, mainly Jung, Neumann, and a Dominican, Victor White (*God and the Unconscious*). All this throws light momentarily on some of the dark places in my brain but only momentarily."[38] In "The Dying God," the last chapter of *God and the Unconscious*, White summarizes Frazer's discussion of dying gods and draws many comparisons between the "rites of Spring," as recorded in *The Golden Bough*, and Christian liturgy, gospels, and epistles. White notes that

> however [the resurrection] may be pictured or conceived, as a return from departed life as in Mesopotamia, as life issuing from only apparent death as in Egypt, as a rebirth of the individual *mystes* as at Eleusis, or as a final and definitive attainment of life in a new and immortal dimension as by St. Paul, the answer to the search of Aphrodite or Astarte or Isis or Mary Magdalene is the same. "The King is dead; long live the King" is the constant motif of the mysteries of the dying god in all their varieties and guises, elevations and debasements.[39]

"Greenleaf" reflects three aspects of such vegetation gods. First, Mrs. May dies by goring. Second, associations with the return of the fertile season abound. In fact, the proper names in the story—May, Greenleaf—announce vegetation. Mrs. May even wears fertility symbols, green "horns" and eggs in her night attire: "Green rubber curlers sprouted neatly over her forehead and her face beneath them was smooth as concrete with an egg-white paste that drew the wrinkles out while she slept."[40] In keeping with the atmosphere of a seasonal rite, Mrs. May exults, "Spring is here!" as she goes unwittingly to her death (48).

Third, O'Connor describes Mrs. May and the bull which kills her in startlingly equivalent terms. Jane Harrison suggests that "women who worshipped the bull-Dionysos wore horns" to try to identify with their god.[41] Though Mrs. May does not consciously want to hobnob with the bull in her yard in any way, O'Connor will bring about just such an identification. Frazer emphasizes that the animal which seems like the enemy of the dying god actually resembles him. The apparently destructive attacker may merit praise for furthering renewal, but, even more important, the animal *is* the god in theriomorphic form: "the pig [was] held to be an embodiment of the divine Adonis, and the analogies of Dionysus [often represented as a bull] and Demeter [represented as a sow or as a horse-headed woman] make it probable that the story of the hostility of the animal to the god was only a late misapprehension of the old view of the god as embodied in a pig."[42]

Citing Frazer, White insists that "the slayer and the slain should alike be some embodiment of divinity."[43]

In "Greenleaf" this identification of human victim and animal attacker becomes part of a whole series of fascinating "convergences." The title of the collection in which "Greenleaf" appears, *Everything That Rises Must Converge*, derives from Teilhard de Chardin; the phrase suggests a difficult spiritual movement toward divine communion and human community.[44] Mrs. May converges toward characters over whom she had mistakenly felt superior, to show their actual community; and she converges toward the bull, to intimate a godly communion. For O'Connor as much as Frazer, only "misapprehension" would see Mrs. May's murderous bull as her enemy.

In primitive ritual, human beings imitated the vegetation god by enacting his divine marriage (a king mating with a priestess, for instance) and, less appealingly, by enacting his early death. In Catholicism, the concept of *imitatio dei*, humans imitating Christ, is also important. There are several characteristics of Christ that a person might either like to or be obliged to imitate: perfection, innocence, suffering, or love and forgiveness. O'Connor's characters generally start out believing that they are perfect, innocent, and put upon. Although Mrs. May regards herself as vastly superior to the Greenleafs, she obviously falls short, first in the matter of raising sons and, more important, in the matter of religion. Seeing only slovenliness in Mrs. Greenleaf's wonderfully bizarre "prayer healing," Mrs. May fails to catch the underlying compassion:

Every day [Mrs. Greenleaf] cut all the morbid stories out of the newspaper—the accounts of women who had been raped and criminals who had escaped and children who had been burned and of train wrecks and plane crashes and the divorces of movie stars. She took these to the woods and dug a hole and buried them and then she fell on the ground over them and mumbled and groaned for an hour or so, moving her huge arms back and forth under her and out again and finally just lying down flat and, Mrs. May suspected, going to sleep in the dirt. (30)

Mrs. May is appalled. For her, "the word, Jesus, should be kept inside the church building like other words inside the bedroom. She was a good Christian woman with a large respect for religion, though she did not, of course, believe any of it was true" (31).

Snob that she is, Mrs. May does not recognize certain convergences or equalities that connect her with Mrs. Greenleaf. "May" and "Greenleaf" are related vegetable words; if they differ, the divergence is not in Mrs. May's favor. "May" is not, so to speak, greater than the summertime of full "greenleaf" but only its faint beginning. Analogously, the human potential to be a good soul has hardly budded in Mrs. May compared to the much further developed compassion in Mrs. Greenleaf. It is not her tenants, Mrs. Greenleaf and family, who are "going to sleep in the dirt," as Mrs. May insists, but she herself who sleeps on the job of holding on to faith, humility before God, and a sense of equality with others. Minutes before her death, waiting at the car, Mrs. May is still sleeping, as she thinks back to her tenants' praying: "Poor souls, she thought now, so simple. For a few seconds she dozed" (51).

Because she misses these equivalences between herself and Mrs. Greenleaf as developing souls waiting to bloom before God, other convergences come into play. First Mrs. Greenleaf blurs with the bull. Just as Mrs. May considers the Greenleafs pitifully "scrub-human," she assesses the stray animal as "Some nigger's scrub bull" (32, 25). Then, as an indecorous "disgrace," Mrs. Greenleaf seems to be an enemy—a snake or a charging animal. Startled by a cry from the still unseen prayer-healer, Mrs. May holds her snake stick aloft: "The sound was so piercing that she felt as if some violent unleashed force had broken out of the ground and was charging toward her" (31). But Mrs. Greenleaf is no snake in the garden. Instead, with her morbid newspaper clippings, she is an eccentric saint—a rudimentary, still-distorted model toward the proper worship of God. Because Mrs. May refuses to learn from Mrs. Greenleaf's example "charging" toward her, she will have to learn a considerably harsher lesson from the charge of the bull.

If the words "scrub" and "charging" make Mrs. Greenleaf and the bull converge as agents of divine instruction, Mrs. Greenleaf also converges with Mrs. May—and both then with Christ. In her prayers Mrs. Greenleaf calls out, "'Jesus, stab me in the heart!' and she fell back flat in the dirt, a huge human mound, her legs and arms spread out as if she were trying to wrap them around the earth" (31). While Mrs. Greenleaf willingly suffers in Christ, for Christ, through her compassion for the sufferings of raped women and even divorced movie stars, Mrs. May will be literally stabbed, as Christ is lanced in the side.

In O'Connor's terms, the bull's attack is neither fortuitous nor tragic. It is a chance for Mrs. May to wake up from her sleep of self-deception, to be brought to grace despite herself. Never having imitated Christ's innocence and perfection, Mrs. May will imitate his suffering, even to death. O'Connor indicates in her letters that each person must have "an acceptance of the Crucifixtion [sic], Christ's and our own."[45] As violence precedes the rebirth of spring in the old vegetation myths, violence precedes spiritual rebirth in O'Connor's view: "This notion that grace is healing omits the fact that before it heals, it cuts with the sword Christ said he came to bring."[46] Slippping into her purposely down-home style, she connects this sword with the frequently misunderstood violence in her stories: "Part of the difficulty of all this is that you write for an audience who doesn't know what grace is and don't recognize it when they see it. All my stories are about the action of grace on a character who is not very willing to support it, but most people think of these stories as hard, hopeless, brutal, etc."[47]

To some readers O'Connor's emphasis on violence sounds more American Calvinist than Roman Catholic in its "absolute denial of free will, the insistence upon the brutal, even bloody, and always catastrophic experience of faith, and the eclipsing of New Testament affirmation by Old Testament wrath."[48] But O'Connor does not deny to Mrs. May important moments of free choice, nor does she depict God as punishing Mrs. May through the bull. John Shields mistakenly believes that O'Connor portrays God gleefully blotting out an evil Mrs. May: "Both the fertility myth and Christianity demand that the evil be stricken, absolutely; for when one attempts to prevent the course of nature and God, he brings death upon himself, utter death, without hope of renewal."[49] Such vindictive annihilation could not be further from the God of her story, who is not wrathful but caring. God's acts of love—the Crucifixion, for example—only look brutal to the uninitiated.

Frederick Asals points out an important Catholic tradition of God's violent love, described by St. Augustine, whom O'Connor carefully studied. Augustine writes: "Like a bridegroom Christ went forth from his chamber, he went out with a presage of his nuptials into the field of the world. He came to the marriage bed of the cross, and there, in mounting it, he consummated his marriage. And when he perceived the sighs of the creature, he lovingly gave himself up in place of his bride, and he joined himself to the woman forever."[50] O'Connor's reading in White's book would also have informed her that "though there is not [in Christianity] the *Hierosgamos*, the sacred mating of the priest-king with the representative of the goddess, there are unmistakable resemblances to it when the flaming Paschal candle, representing Christ, is plunged into the font to the accompaniment of prayers whose references to sexual union and fertility are explicit."[51]

As vegetation rites and Augustine's vision mix imagery of violence and marriage, so does O'Connor combine these terms, and she ushers in the bull as the surprising bridegroom. The stray bull first appears as a pagan, courting deity, a Zeus, for example, in the form of a bull pursuing Europa.[52] Mrs. May spies him standing in her yard "like some patient god come down to woo her," and, at the end, the bull buries his head in her lap "like a wild tormented lover" (24, 52). But if the bull begins as pagan, divine lover, it soon becomes apparent that he embodies a form of radical love from a fully Christian God. The piece of hedge caught on the bull's horns changes from a garland, as if for Dionysian frolicking, to a "menacing prickly crown," evoking Christ's crown of thorns. Furthermore, Asals reports that for the Catholic thinker Tertullian, the bull was an appropriate type of Christ "by reason of each of his two characters,—to some fierce, as Judge; to others gentle, as Saviour; whose 'horns' were to be the extremities of the cross."[53]

After becoming oddly like God the Son, the bull goes on to merge with God the Father, through imagery that indirectly associates sky, sun, and light with the heavens, God, and enlightenment. The bull darkens the ground as the "shadow" of the sun, and then the sound of his chewing makes Mrs. May dream of the sun, "a swollen red ball, but as she stood watching it began to narrow and pale until it looked like a bullet. Then suddenly it burst through the tree line and raced down the hill toward her" (37, 47). "Bull" and "bullet" are a typical dream pun, and the image clearly unites the "charging" of Mrs. Greenleaf and the bull, both agents of a greater heavenly force racing to shock Mrs. May into awareness. As O'Connor says in a letter, "I thought Mrs. Greenleaf was a sympathetic character. She and the sun and the bull were connected and sympathetic."[54] Again linking the heavens with the bull, O'Connor describes the sky as "piercing" blue (48).

Once Mrs. May has, despite herself, imitated Christ pierced on his cross, the question remains whether she can imitate him, at least partially, in understanding and love. The ending of the story hints that she may understand the mystery of both her own death and Christ's. With the bull's horn plunged in her side, "she had the look of a person whose sight has suddenly been restored but who finds the light unbearable" (52). Horrible as her death is, the life of the body, O'Connor insists, is nothing compared to the life of the soul. Mrs. May's soul may respond with a kind of forgiveness for the bull. Her pose in death suggests someone "bent over whispering some last discovery into the animal's ear" (53). This pose of a lover crooning is presented ambiguously as either inadvertent grotesquerie or real love. Similarly, the grandmother's cry to the Misfit that "you're one of my own babies" in "A Good Man Is Hard To Find" might be either desperate cajolery or else forgiveness and recognition of kinship in sin. O'Connor clarifies her intention in a letter: "More than in the Devil I am interested in the indication of Grace, the moment when you know that Grace has been offered and accepted—such as the moment when the Grandmother realizes the Misfit is one of her own children."[55] Like the grandmother, Mrs. May, bent as if tenderly whispering, manages a Christ-like forgiveness of her tormentor.

The old vegetation myths allowed for the affinity of Dionysus and bull, Adonis and pig, showing an interdependence of victim and victimizer that Christianity often forgot in a perhaps too easy polarization of good and evil, God and devil. O'Connor shows Mrs. May and the bull converging, at the same time that Mrs. May also has the opportunity to recognize the other identities that she has missed in her false sense of superiority: equality among suffering children of God. Mrs. May and the bull are alike most obviously in that both have horns (its literal horns and her green curlers sprouting). Both die (Mr. Greenleaf shoots the bull as she dies); both are guilty (it of attacking her, she of her pride); and, paradoxically, both are innocent. The bull, a dumb beast, wears its crown of thorns that likens it to the innocent Christ, and Mrs. May too, for all her fallen nature, is potentially pure, redeemable, a possible bride of Christ ready to be pierced with the always harsh love from the divine.

5

Sacrificing to Baal

Unlike the authors in chapters 3 and 4, who by and large concentrate on metaphysical violence which cannot be helped, Faulkner, Bellow, García Márquez, and Konwicki expose social violence which human beings have stupidly and brutally imposed on each other. Although the authors seldom offer specific solutions to cultural and political ills, they at least imply that if people became aware of their delusions, they might after all change their savage environments.

Saul Bellow's essayistic short story "A Sermon by Doctor Pep" forms a good transition between metaphysical and social violence, since Bellow recognizes and laments both types. Borrowing the names of fertility deities whose worship constantly annoyed the biblical prophets, he decides to call the metaphysical threat "Moloch" and the social terror "Baal." To illustrate the violence that just *is*, Bellow points to the carnage caused even by our need to eat; to argue how people add to the pain already inherent in the world, he brings forward the shocking evidence of the French Revolution and Auschwitz, the "Baals" of recent centuries.

The authors in this chapter have no quarrel with the myth of the dying god itself. They may, in fact, admire its respect for nature, its emphasis on sexuality, or its depiction of a generous, self-sacrificing god. Nevertheless, although it might be all well and good for Baal to leap nobly from the sky, in story, human beings who unwillingly fall to their death, in rites, do not revive so easily. These authors protest any ritual—which they extend to mean any habitual social custom or attitude—calling for human victims. Although they may marvel at Baal, they pity his surrogate king who has to go down too. And they condemn an even worse situation, much more common, in which the king or governor gives himself divine status but hunts for substitutes to take on the onerous part of a life as the god's representative.[1]

The spectacle of a leader who hysterically believes that Baal requires new blood, or who cynically appropriates the myth for his own purposes, without believing anything, is not new. In Euripides' *Iphigenia in Aulis*, fifth century B.C., "sacral offering is presented as political murder."[2] In the twentieth century, Faulkner, Bellow, García Márquez, and Konwicki discover Baal lurking in racial prejudice and in totalitarian governments of both the right and the left on the political spectrum. To appease such self-proclaimed supreme gods, human sacrifices still burn.

Faulkner

In *Light in August* (1932) William Faulkner sets out to tell the story of very human characters, not to recreate myths about gods. Still, when myths of dying deities can serve his purposes, he draws on his known acquaintance with Frazer's *The Golden Bough* for details.[3] Joe Christmas bears some resemblance to Attis when he is castrated and to the King of the Wood, whom Frazer derives from dying gods, when he consorts with Joanna in her grove. Robert Slabey asserts that "The life cycle and personal problems of Joe Christmas are less directly related to those of Christ than they are to the archetypal story of the dying god and his resurrection."[4] Although I agree with Slabey about the importance of the dying god, I cannot accept the strict parallels to *The Golden Bough* he discovers in every incident nor his reductive focus on the Jungian "shadow" as Joe's chief threat. Nevertheless, noticing which Frazerian scenes Faulkner does allude to, either straightforwardly or ironically, can help clarify thematic emphases in *Light in August*: affirmation of cycles of life and death, beauty of sexuality, stupidity of scapegoating.

Whereas ancient peoples might have believed that a human victim had to die in the same manner as their god to help him in his yearly ordeal, Faulkner in no way makes Joe's and Joanna's deaths necessary or helpful. To this extent he presents the ritual for a dying god ironically. Several critics who sense vegetation myths behind *Light in August* mistakenly assume that Faulkner somehow approves the deaths, as if he were clearing the accumulated dead wood of the old year, which just happens to enclose superfluous people to be carried out too. Slabey declares complacently, "Joe's execution, already discussed as a fertility rite, is also a purification ritual, the expulsion of sins and evils from the community, the execution of one who is 'tainted' or unclean, here according to racial discrimination. . . . The destruction of the old house in the flames is like a solemn cleansing ceremony; everything of the old order must be removed in preparation for the new."[5] Slabey jumps from the townspeople's discrimination to imply that Faulkner also treats Joe and Joanna as tainted and therefore expendable. When Hugh Holman underlines Christian imagery in *Light in August*, he similarly reduces the Christian dying god to the refuse of housecleaning. Joe for Holman is a Christ figure "in that he bears our common guilt, symbolized by his Negro blood, that he is denied by the world, and that he is ultimately offered as a blood sacrifice because of the 'original sin' he bears."[6] I cannot believe that Faulkner would degrade "Negro blood" to flushable guilt-solvent. Instead, Faulkner learns from Frazer here. Just as Frazer suspects that primitive folly and superstition still operate in the modern mind, Faulkner condemns as folly the bigotry that casts Joe and Joanna as human versions of the dying god.

However, if Faulkner laments the renewed rite of sacrifice imposed on humans, he also finds something admirable in the stories of the gods. He approves that part of the myth that would join Joe and Joanna in a grove— or try to; impediments from their past and from their contemporaries prevent that union. He approves Lena's timeless placidity and her sexuality. A major reason Faulkner branches out from a Christian dying god to pagan ones is to rehabilitate the pagan celebration of fertility and especially of sexuality. As half of the dying god's cyclical story was admitting death and half was defying it with the god's marriage, Faulkner alternates Joe's chronicle with the periodic account of Lena's pregnancy.

Although nowhere implying that Joe's death enables new life, Faulkner links the two in a cycle, with life accommodating natural deaths but opposing violent ones. Besides contrasting the destructive training and tracking of Christmas with Lena's care for life, Faulkner also counteracts the hatred of anything "different" that causes Joe's death by merging characters through common traits. He thus creates subtle equivalences for the reader where the characters perceive only distinctions and enemies. By making Joe and Joanna mirror each other, for example, Faulkner shows us the kinship which even they cannot grasp. He simultaneously reveals that Joanna resembles a dying deity as much as Joe does. Instead of depicting men and women or god and goddess in irremediably separate spheres, Faulkner defines the fate of the dying god as something that happens indiscriminately to both these characters named Jo, regardless of gender. He arranges other reflections and other characters who play out, unknowingly, the tasks of the dying god. R. G. Collins discovers three "competitors for the cross," but he does not really explain why the author flanks Joe with Joanna and Hightower on a common Golgotha.[7] Faulkner moves away from the Christian message of one savior and one divine son to mourn and honor many human sons and daughters—all presently suffering, all potentially saving each other.

Far from necessary sacrifices, Faulkner's human representatives of the dying god crumble only because other people undermine them. He accuses two torturers: racial prejudice (against "niggers" and against "nigger lovers") and religious fanaticism, especially a misguided hatred of sexuality. He makes it clear that prejudice kills when he has Joe think of the blade with which he will murder Joanna right after Brown (Burch) has cursed him as "niggerblooded."[8] Scorn against blacks warps Joe and goads him to lash out in turn. Faulkner directly affiliates the town's long failure and Joe's destructiveness. At first sight of smoke from the Burden house, the mill workers joke, "'My pappy says he can remember how fifty years ago folks said it ought to be burned, and with a little human fat meat to start it good.' 'Maybe your pappy slipped out there and set if afire,' a third said. They laughed" (44). In a sense, that father and the other bigots of the town have slipped out there; they must take responsibility for murdering Joanna as much as Joe does.

Faulkner also blames the suspicion against sexuality fostered by many sects of Christianity. Hightower perceives that because Christians cannot bear "pleasure, ecstasy," their religion drives them "to crucifixion of themselves and one another" (347). Such hatred of the body thwarts and kills people—figuratively and literally. Doc Hines, who preaches both white supremacy and abhorrence of the flesh, lets his own daughter die in childbirth, without a physician, as fit punishment for an illegitimate child. Hines's hideous neglect exactly reverses Hightower's aid to Lena. Faulkner arranges the two examples not just to show Hightower demonstrating the proper Christian attitude toward "sinners," pity, which Hines perverts, but, even more important, to hint that Lena has something to teach Hightower. Her easy sexuality shows up his desregard for his wife. By ignoring his wife's need to share a sex life with him, Hightower pushes her to prostitution, in which she can only despair. As when he avoids the trees whose peace used to suggest prayer to him, he has sinned against holy nature (300).

Several critics claim that Faulkner holds Calvinist views and mistrusts women. Harold Douglas and Robert Daniel insist that he subscribes to "misogyny" and a "belief, stated or implied, that sexuality is the chief sign of man's fallen nature." They add that he treats "his Temple Drakes and Joanna Burdens and Eula Varners as mantraps."[9] Robert Barth agrees: "There are few women in Yoknapatawpha County who escape the charge of 'bitchery and abomination.' Some of Faulkner's colored women, like Dilsey and Nancy Mannigoe, or one of his old women, like Granny Millard Sartoris, manage to evoke Faulkner's admiration, but these remain rare exceptions to his general judgment of the depravity of 'womanflesh.' Even an exceptional character like gentle Lena Grove is good rather through stupidity than through deliberate choice."[10]

Such evaluations of Faulkner's works could not be further from the truth, missed partly because these critics fail to recognize signs from vegetation myths. Obviously it is Doc Hines, a twisted character, not Faulkner, who levels the charge of "bitchery and abomination." For Faulkner, sexuality does not clinch our depravity or fallen nature but rather provides us our best opportunity for generosity and mystery. And, as I will try to prove later, Lena, hardly stupid, schemes very cleverly, and Joanna does not serve as a reprehensible mantrap.

The Calvinist deprecation of the flesh, an attitude that Faulkner is repudiating, has cut off both Joe and Joanna from their own bodies and from understanding others. Repulsed by his new knowledge of menstruation, Joe seeks refuge behind a line of trees: "Each one was cracked and from each crack there issued something liquid, deathcolored, and foul. He touched a tree, leaning his propped arms against it, seeing the ranked and moonlit urns. He vomited" (178). Joe labels menses foul, instead of life promising, as a result of his early disastrous experiences with the dietitian and with Hines, who convey to him his society's taboos and repressions.

Like Joe vomiting at his new knowledge about women, Horace Benbow in *Sanctuary* gags over the shrimp he fetches his wife, Belle, on Fridays. In modern European languages, Friday derives from the day of the goddess Freya (or Frigg) or Venus (*vendredi*), and the fish later associated with fasts on Friday and with Christ were originally a sexual symbol of Friday's largess.[11] Faulkner seems to know this association; from the context of *Sanctuary*, Benbow gags not because he hates fish but because he does not know how to cope with women and sexuality. In *As I Lay Dying*, the boy Vardaman repeats, "My mother is a fish." Joe Christmas, Horace, and Vardaman are all resisting a kind of "female knowledge" that Faulkner approves: most of his female characters, unlike the men who want to stamp out evil and end up obliterating good too, recognize that life and death as well as good and evil are inextricable.

Joanna still possesses a small portion of the knowledge that Faulkner regards as feminine. He portrays her as something of a wise woman dispensing advice to Negroes in her role of "combined priest and banker and trained nurse" (244). But Joanna hardly understands herself. She has the potential to be a woman of power, but her abilities have had little play because she belongs to no large, accepting community. By mentioning the grove outside her house at important points, Faulkner transforms it from part of the natural scenery into a vestige of worship. Old Testament Hebrews frequently reverted from Yahweh to a goddess, honored in groves.[12] The grove on the Burden property survives, but it is "shaggy," a product of neglect (110).

Michael Millgate connects Joanna with the goddess Diana, who inhabits the grove guarded by Frazer's King of the Wood. Giving as evidence Diana's fire-lighted festival in August, which Frazer sees behind the feast of the Assumption of Mary, Millgate infers that Faulkner is replacing the bad virgin, Joanna, with the good Holy Mother, Lena.[13] Yet Millgate mistakes both the ancient goddess's virginity, by regarding it as asexual, and the modern Joanna's sexuality, by regarding it as bad. Frazer's point was that the Holy Mother continues Diana, instead of overthrowing what she stands for; Joanna and Lena form a continuum—one thwarted, one free—rather than complete opposites. The title "virgin" for pagan goddess does not necessarily imply asexuality or barrenness but independence and renewal. If Joanna makes Joe feel like a thief, Faulkner does not impute coldness to her: "Even after a year it was as though he entered by stealth to despoil her virginity each time anew. It was as though each turn of dark saw him faced again with the necessity to despoil again that which he had already despoiled—or never had and never would" (221). Although this passage certainly states sadly enough the couple's separateness, Faulkner includes such language, I believe, to grant to Joanna some of the majesty of the goddesses—Diana, Hera, Virgin Mary, and the rest—who renewed their virginity.

When Joanna passes through "every avatar of a woman in love," the idea of incarnations, appropriate to the realm of dying and resurrected deities, shimmers briefly in the word "avatar," even though Joanna's eternal variety has deteriorated to pathetic game playing (244). But Faulkner is not condemning her sexual hunger, as many critics claim. He pities the isolation and the drummed-in fear of damnation that have suffocated her. Faulkner sympathizes with "the imperious and fierce urgency that concealed an actual despair at frustrate and irrevocable years," whereas critics have turned hostile (244). Robert Slabey blames her "sterility—physical, moral, and spiritual," and Hugh Holman dismisses her as "a destroyer rather than a victim."[14] Joanna breaks out of her imposed religious fear of the flesh better than Joe does, but she never stops hating herself. When she finally asks him to kneel for their sins, she slips back into her own despair, which lets her then categorize Joe as "sinner" and "nigger," thus victimizing him all over again.

Although these vastly destructive attitudes—racial scorn and a belief in the "sin" of sexuality—humiliate Joe and Joanna and suppress them, social prejudices do not completely mold the lives of people under their weight. This question of determinism or freedom is important because it also applies to the relation between mythological models and individuals. Hightower deplores the way the townspeople hurt "those who like them were created by the same God and were driven by them to do that which they now turn and rend them for having done it" (345). Faulkner certainly agrees with this compassionate assessment of Joe and Joanna as "driven." Yet when Hightower also claims that his hostile congregation prevents him from being a man of God, Byron quietly reminds him, "You made your choice." Hightower chooses, badly, to ignore his wife and retreat to a romantic past. He chooses, admirably but futilely, to give Joe an alibi to protect him from Grimm. And he chooses, admirably and effectively, to help deliver Lena's baby. Society might constrain and warp people, but brief moments of freedom remain available to them. Just as society does not determine every move, neither do the myths that Faulkner reveals behind his characters. When he applies the word "avatar" to Lena and Joe as well as to Joanna (5, 213, 244), he situates them to some extent as types in a timeless recurrence, but he also creates them as distinct individuals in a definite time and place.

The main mythological role that Joe and Joanna complicatedly inherit, choose, and transcend is, I am arguing, avatar of the dying god. The mob who "canvasses about for someone to crucify" fasten on Joe during their "Roman holiday," and they consider Joanna a "body that had died three years ago and had just now begun to live again" (272–73). Frazer describes the Roman Saturnalia as a period of license whose reversal of slave and master harks back to a time when shrewd kings chose beggar "kings" to die in their place, as the local helper to the dying god.[15] By evoking the crucifixion and the Roman holiday together, Faulkner expands his allusion to dying deities to include both Christian and pagan gods. Similarly, when the townsfolk claim that Joanna died three years ago, they presumably treat her fate as sealed the moment Joe arrived in Jefferson, but the number three also recalls the three-day eclipse common to many dying gods, Christ among them. The town assumes she will awaken to vengeance, whereas she actually awakened briefly from her solitude only when Joe appeared. But besides contrasting the town's false assumptions with the reader's more privileged knowledge, calling Joanna someone who died and lived again in a space of three units makes her as much a representative of the dying god as Joe is.

The manner of their deaths likewise draws them under the sign of the dying god. Frazer mentions several types of death for this figure, and Faulkner "overdetermines" Joe's and Joanna's deaths by including most of them. The death details also emphasize how much these two characters mirror each other because each experiences to some extent the distinctive ordeal of the other. As Joe is castrated, like Attis, Joanna's brother and grandfather are nearly castrated: her father hides their graves to prevent mutilation (235). Joanna's family risks becoming Attises too. Joe slashes Joanna's throat; earlier, Max strikes Joe in the face with "a short slashing blow," so that Joe anticipates Joanna's fate, on a lesser scale (205). Both are related to the castrated Attis and a beheaded deity.

Furthermore, Joe leaves Joanna's nearly decapitated body in a house that burns, recalling Frazer's "burned god." Frazer traces the burning of effigies in "balefires" to the incineration of human victims, who in turn were meant to imitate a dying god, such as Balder.[16] Faulkner reports on the column of smoke from Joanna's destroyed house with majestic and ritual-like periodicity. The fire fills Lena's first view of Jefferson: "The wagon crests the final hill and they see smoke. . . . Following [the driver's] pointing whip, she sees two columns of smoke: the one the heavy density of burning coal above a tall stack, the other a tall yellow column standing apparently from among a clump of trees some distance beyond the town"

(26). This initial doubling of the columns implicates the town in Joanna's death because the town emits the dirtier smoke.

Later Byron notes the spectacle of fire on the Burden property, where the column-pillar suggests a temple: "It seemed to him that fate, circumstance, had set a warning in the sky all day long in that pillar of yellow smoke, and he too stupid to read it" (77). Another reference takes the pillar further from shamefulness, a sign of the town's wrongdoing, and gilds it with serenity, a hint of Faulkner's regard for Joanna. The number three and the solemn repetition of "now" intone a kind of rite: "So there was nothing left to look at now but the fire; they had now been watching it for three hours. They were now used to it, accustomed to it; now it had become a permanent part of their lives as well as of their experiences, standing beneath its windless column of smoke taller than and impregnable as a monument which could be returned to at any time" (277). As this fiery temple encloses Joanna, Joe also briefly resembles the burned god. Percy Grimm yells for the fire alarm at Joe's escape, as if the prisoner were himself the fire loosed by the town (434).

In addition to doubling as dying god, Joe and Joanna mirror each other in several smaller details. They exhibit an intense privacy and a lack of softness, which signals both an admirable independence and a lamentably stifled tenderness. Each has a rabidly bigoted grandfather and a relative who is Mexican: her father's first wife Juana, for whom Joanna is loosely named, and Joe's probably Mexican father. Each to some extent welcomes death. Joanna offers Joe guns for a murder-suicide, and Joe may possibly attempt a "passive suicide" by escaping the sheriff (419). This suspicion that they court death likens them again to the dying gods in general, but Faulkner ironically changes the motivation. Dying gods go down willingly out of hope that some good will result for the community, whereas these two characters relinquish, out of despair, lives that have already been living deaths.

Faulkner creates such identities between Joe and Joanna for several reasons. He breaks down the gender segregation between god and goddess. Instead of blaming one sex or the other, he shows them both equal to the rank of dying deity, a title that largely means, unfortunately, equally subject to its depths of suffering. Faulkner, however, does grant them both its compensation in grandeur, a claim I will argue later. Through his equal treatment of the pair, Faulkner moves beyond those stereotypes he otherwise maintains when he expects—flatteringly but falsely—that women will automatically know to accept inextricable evil for the sake of the highest good: life. Furthermore, the reflections move two people together in *possibility* who in *fact* remain at odds. By associating the couple with common words or situations—fire, the name Jo, ancestry, and so on—he merges them in a community still only dreamed.

Faulkner extends this process of mirroring from Joe and Joanna into a way of linking all the characters. Lena's name Grove encompasses Joanna's grove, and the hidden "birch" in Lucas Burch belongs to both of these groves. The Joe of Joe Brown duplicates Joe Christmas, and the similarity of the sounds Burden, Burch, and Bunch lump them all in a communal "bunch." Hightower's glittery sign, "with an effect as of Christmas," advertises "Xmas cards" and insistently announces the person within that house as almost another Joe Christmas. Like Joanna, Hightower reflects Joe as a kind of dying god. His "high tower" isolates him in a self-chosen romantic fantasy that becomes also an imposed pariahdom. He climbs to a cross or stake, like Christ's or Odin's, to signal that everyone is potentially the god's substitute. "Is God a nigger too?" Joe asks as a child (362). All suffer the fate of the oppressed, and all potentially could redeem someone else, as Hightower helps Lena, Lena tutors Byron, and Byron cares for Lena. Joe also has supportive impulses: he wants to marry Bobbie and take her away from her pimp. The task of the dying god—to ache and to aid—actually falls to every member of the community.

Faulkner's most startling mirroring occurs in Hightower's vision of a wheel, a halo of faces that are mostly distinct, though it surprisingly blends Joe's and Percy's features (465–66). This blurring shows Faulkner's great pity; all are hurt, and all are hurting. Frazer believes that Attis and his attacker, a boar, like Dionysus and the bull, were originally equivalent.[17] By superimposing the faces of Joe, who resembles Attis, and Percy, his attacker, Faulkner equates victim and victimizer. In the preceding chapter, Hemingway and O'Connor also equate goring bull and dying victim. All three authors draw on Frazer's interpretation to try to accept death as part of a cycle, a "wheel." Although Faulkner strongly condemns the brutality of Joe's and Joanna's deaths, he tries, after the deeds have been done, to incorporate death into a cyclical pattern, as a means of furthering healing. Although he hardly condones Percy Grimm, Faulkner would integrate all transgressors as pitiable into the wheeling embrace of the community.

Even though he rejects the way the hate-filled mob coerces Joe and Joanna into serving as human versions of dying deities, Faulkner lets the myth also lend to these victims some of the grandeur of the gods. Largely trapped into the role, Joe and Joanna transcend it to an extent. By disdaining their tormentors and never groveling, the two outcasts snatch back at least the appearance of choice. In addition to endowing them with this tragic nobility, Faulkner dignifies them by carefully setting out Joe's incipient innocence and justice (e.g., the child desiring only sweet toothpaste and the young man obtaining money by selling the cow that is *his*) and Joanna's ability to be counselor of the grove. Faulkner makes sure we sense his reverence for their potential by covert references to the dying god and finally by an overt reference to joint "apotheosis" (465). He ennobles Joe in the scene of castration, and he pays tribute to Joanna by again mentioning her grove, connected with worship, at a crucial juncture for Byron.

The devastating scene of Joe's death does not seem to offer any redeeming feature to warrant the description of Joe's last spurt of blood as "serene" and "triumphant" (440). Faulkner shocks us with the castration, equivalent to the hideousness of race hatred. He also moves us into the brutal atmosphere of Frazer's primitive rituals when the three men accompanying Grimm embody "the savage summer sunlight" and when Grimm himself cries out in the outraged voice of a "young priest" (438–39). Grimm's first name, Percy, from the medieval Percival, brands him ironically as a devoted quester who spreads rather than cures the waste land.

How, then, in an atmosphere of such brutality and self-delusion can Joe die "triumphant"? Joe's last horrible moments and even death cannot be any worse than the torture that his whole life has been, with the dangerous Hineses and the well-meaning McEacherns of the world. Joe is serene because he escapes that trial and triumphs because the town will never forget him. The vigilantes had thought to rid Jefferson of Joe, whereas the witnesses will never be free of their memory.

Joe triumphs for another reason, by taking on, during the last chase and cornering, aspects of the dying god. Grimm sees "the fugitive's hands glint once like the flash of a heliograph as the sun struck the handcuffs," and he sees Joe leap from a cabin "with an effect as of magic, his manacled hands high and now glinting as if they were on fire" (436). In a continuation of this light imagery, Hightower falls when Joe strikes him, Joe's "raised and armed and manacled hands full of glare and glitter like lightning bolts, so that he resembled a vengeful and furious god pronouncing a doom" (438). In part Joe resembles Balder, a dying god whose soul is caught up in the lightning-struck mistletoe. Frazer describes the intervention of the lightning in the world as fertilizing, and Faulkner seems to have similar sexual imagery in mind when he pictures an ejaculatory gush of blood: "from out of the slashed garments about his hips and loins the pent black blood seemed to rush like a released breath. It seemed to rush out of his pale body like the rush of sparks from a rising rocket; upon that black blast the man seemed to rise soaring into their memories forever" (440). Christ turns water to wine for a wedding feast, whereas these "Christians" convert what should be semen to blood for a death feast. They make Joe into a lightning-attended Balder and a castrated Attis, who is still resurrected, despite their intention to eradicate him, in memory.

Moreover, that lightning bolt fecundating the earth has its effect in *Light in August* when Lena bears her son shortly before Joe dies. Joe's grief-crazed grandmother Hines calls the baby Joey, and even Lena briefly envisions Christmas as the possible father (376, 388). Faulkner could not have accomplished so easily this sense of continuity through physical generation by relying only on the Christian myth, which (except perhaps in heterodox versions) emphasizes a celibate and even asexual savior. By surrounding Joe with allusions to the sexually active Balder and Attis, Faulkner ensures that when one dying god goes down, he reappears instantly in a new incarnation.

Just as Faulkner "divinizes" Joe with the light that darts from his manacles, he vindicates and reverences Joanna by making her grove seem permanent beyond all perversions. When Byron is riding away from Jefferson, believing that he can renounce Lena, "The hill rises, cresting. . . . 'It is like the edge of nothing. Like once I passed it I would ride right off into nothing. Where trees would look like and be called by something else except trees, and men would look like and be called by something else except folks. And Byron Bunch he wouldn't even have to be or not be Byron Bunch" (401). Byron almost contemplates withdrawing from life entirely, with all its specificity, mixed-up mess, and rewards. "But then from beyond the hill crest there begins to rise that which he knows is there: the trees which are trees, the terrific and tedious distance which, being moved by blood, he must compass forever and ever between two inescapable horizons of the implacable earth" (401).

At this critical juncture of renunciation or commitment, the natural trees seem to push him to look back toward the cabin on Joanna's property where Lena is sheltering: "the plantation is broken now by random negro cabins and garden patches and dead fields erosion gutted and choked with blackjack and sassafras and persimmon and brier. But in the exact center the clump of oaks still stand" (402). Faulkner makes it seem as if the grove itself, introduced with the strong word "But," permits Byron's restorative vision and gives him the conviction that he will eventually win Lena. The spirit of Joanna lives on: her hunger for sexuality and remnant of wisdom will find their proper outlet in Byron and Lena. For as Byron looks at the grove, he spies Lucas sneaking out the back of the cabin: "a man appears as though by magic at the rear of it, already running. . . . Then a cold, hard wind seems to blow through him [Byron]. It is at once violent and peaceful, blowing hard away like chaff or trash or dead leaves all the desire and the despair and the hopelessness and the tragic and the vain imagining too. With the very blast of it he seems to feel himself rush back. . . ." (402–3). Because Faulkner will echo these words—"appears as though by magic," "blast," and "rush"—in the scenes of Joe's hiding and death, he involves Joe and his lightning at the moment of Byron's renewal (436, 440).

Joe's lightning and Joanna's grove together duplicate a central image discussed by Frazer, which is academic in *The Golden Bough*, but now revitalized by Faulkner when he infuses it with human emotion. The anthropologist begins his series of volumes with the goddess's grove, and, as he nears the conclusion, he returns to it. He at last asserts that the "golden bough" in that oak grove is the mistletoe that has absorbed the lightning of the sky and the life of the tree, linking heaven and earth.[18] By reaffirming Joe's lightning and Joanna's oak at the end of *Light in August*, Faulkner maintains a hope for ongoing life, fully sexual, nature related, and, through Byron and Lena, made more open and considerate than it could ever be through Joe and Joanna.

To reinforce the impression that he is joining Lena and Byron through the imagery of fertility myths, Faulkner adds a wonderfully comic ending in which a furniture dealer bawdily recounts to his wife how he has met the couple on the road. Byron wants to sleep with Lena, but she calmly refuses him, for the time being—apparently nixing any expectation we might have of transposing a fertility rite to Tennessee roadsides. Faulkner reverses some of our other expectations as well. Why does Lena pursue Lucas? We have probably taken for granted all along that she wants a legitimate father for her child. And why does she postpone making love to Byron? Perhaps she waits to be decently married. But no. Faulkner turns the tables on us. Lena trails Lucas and puts Byron off because she likes to travel.

This Lena is not "bovine," as Joyce Carol Oates accuses, grumbling that Faulkner makes his "mammalian" beauty stupid and reduces her to pure natural processes.[19] On the contrary, Lena calls the shots and arranges her behavior so that people stop for her and give her free rides; when she cannot ride, she will adventurously walk the rest of the way herself. Nor does she think of herself as exclusively sexual or domestic. Although she knows she will spend a good many years raising children, she does cherish an interest outside the home—seeing the world—and she has the wit to obtain her dream.

Faulkner fits this little joke on us, the at least temporary "liberation of Lena," into his larger scheme of vegetation myths. The furniture dealer punctuates his account of how Byron tries to snuggle up to Lena with bouts of making love to his wife. Faulkner cleverly combines the "thing said" (the tale of Byron's dogged desire) and the "thing done" (the furniture dealer's conjugal caresses); Jane Harrison, in fact, defines "myth" and "ritual" as the "thing said" and the "thing done," usually with reference to sex and fertility.[20] With this amusing ending, Faulkner reminds us that for those with a proper understanding of the myth of the dying god, the appropriate ritual to accompany that myth should be lovemaking, not castration and killing.

Bellow

Saul Bellow builds his wonderful little story "A Sermon by Doctor Pep" (1949) on the unlikely premise that a soapbox orator has spent the winter more or less buried in the Newberry Library in Chicago, boning up on myths of the dying gods. At the beginning of spring Pep emerges to harangue the passersby in his tangy lingo, now studded with the learned names Attis, Osiris, Christ, Baal, and Moloch. Bellow thus combines an enjoyable spoof on the neighborhood crank, realistically spewing the newest slang, with a serious meditation on the oldest myths. The author slips us a sober essay underneath the humorous character sketch of a fanatic, who apparently worries only about his audience's "digestion." Pep, in the manner of the self-help prophet extolling a yogurt diet, warns us not to think too much about death, because it "inhibits the bite and sends us to an early grave."[21] But if Pep advises us to forget death, Bellow does want to inhibit our bustling complacency, by forcing us to look at violence in nature and in society—and by forcing us to admit a moment when we might be prepared to haul a victim to the bloody altar ourselves.

The doctor parodies the myths of the gods who revive by announcing that "skid-row is thinning out as the dead-looking are resurrected off the sidewalks and sent to be gandy-walkers [seasonal railroad workers] in the little blue flowers of Montana" (59). He rants that, in the spring weather all around him, "The slaughtered Osiris gets himself together again and his scattered body comes to life; the grave-cold Redeemer rises up; the tadpole shucks the tallowy, pond-bobbing eggs and his tender feet grow scratchy, and the fat of life begins to sizzle" (61). Although Pep lulls us with thoughts of renewal, he demolishes this initial optimism with the word "sizzle," which conjures up an unpleasant end for innocent lambs and truth-singed prophets alike. Resembling Isaiah with the live coal from Yahweh opening his lips to the truth or Jeremiah with the burning word of the Lord shut in his heart, Pep too has experienced a charred central vision.[22] This view, that "in health we are in the debt of a suffering creation" (61), underlies, in fact, the myths of the dying gods because the turn of the season and the health of the community are supposed to depend on the repeated sufferings of the deities.

Pep approaches this depressing thesis of well-being predicated on pain by means of humorous examples; however, he gradually indicts more serious targets. To show how life feeds on death, he first points to relatively innocuous butterflies feasting on dead porcupines (59). The bright creatures·derive their sustenance from a putrid "necessitous drink" (63). Next Pep describes how "my old friend Dr. Julius Widig" finished a jail sentence "a lot healthier than Ponce came out of the Florida swamps" (60). But Widig's rejuvenation, like the butterfly's, depends on a substratum of suffering. While in the "hoosegow," he "kept up his noble heart by healing the jailbird venerealees" (60). Because Widig is "arrested in the first war for an open anarchist," he must have been a pacifist. By means of this oblique anecdote, Pep seems to criticize the naïveté of opposing violence with quiescence. Even the generous soul, Widig, who tries to distance himself from giving harm, actually benefits in some way through the scourges of others.

Pep then moves to the larger arena of nature and religions, which are also based on the suffering of innocent creatures. While fulminating against Easter candy, Pep manages to sneer at both the butcher shop and at Calvary: "Yes, eat the lamb made to eat. Why not? . . . Bite off the tail, the little feet, the head, and make inarticulate love with the hungry tongue and amorous teeth, learn biting love with the little pure divinity lamb" (61). A carnivore and a Christian God who requires ransom in his son's blood are, to Pep, both sadistically obscene. At this point the doctor appears to condemn the way the natural world and a major religion both rest on sacrifice, and Pep seems to divorce himself from such complicity in pain.

Yet Pep is not preaching that Chicago lunchers stop ordering their lamb stews or even that Christians tear their scale-model instruments of torture, their crucifixes, from their necks. Rather, he wants us to admit our cannibal dependency, our debt to every drop of blood that is shed—porcupine, human, or divine—to enhance our lives. At least, he begs, don't camouflage the shape of the once-living shank by chopping it into unrecognizable hamburger and hash. By pretending that the croquette is an innocent lump and not a fish, we hide "an evidence of the living and a hint of obligation to reverence and indebtedness. Is that a deep offence, the beginning of sickness? Does that make cold tallow out of the fat which should be the grease of love? I believe so . . . the true fact is that death is not further but closer to us when we are so perfunctory and unbeholden" (62–63). Sounding very much like the Micronesians determined to remember Hainuwele's sacrifice with gratitude, Pep reminds us to meet the "necessitous drink"—the blood of the beast shed for our dinner—with the "debt of labor and acknowledgement" (63).

Besides questioning the decency of the Christian God, Pep has so far advised us mainly of the violence of the biological world: the wolves (or the humans) eating the lamb and, less painfully but no less devastatingly, the lamb nibbling the plant that cannot grow in the earth once it is ingested. Pep calls this maw of nature "Moloch": "The plans of Jerusalem are open before them, but what haunts them is the eating mouth, the betrayal of mercy in their own teeth and the insubordinate part of them facing to Moloch and his capital" (64). As a Tyrian fire god still worshiped in Palestine at the time of Solomon, Moloch was a local version of the ubiquitous dying god.[23] His myth must have assigned Moloch death by fire, because his sacrificial victims were in turn burned on the altar.

Maybe we can live with Moloch after all, Pep implies, as long as we give a nod of thanks to the big fish we eat, throw the little ones back to grow up, and reverence the seed corn. But the doctor now introduces another problem. Once we have accommodated ourselves to Moloch, or the violence of disorderly nature, how do we accept the violence of supposedly orderly civilization? As he used the name of one fertility deity to suggest biological violence, Pep now borrows the name of another dying god, Baal, to represent societies built on suffering: "Remember, Baal was the lord of cultivation and humanized land, and he was the greatest danger to the desert-bred generation, in the eyes of Moses" (65). Nature might bind us in a harsh protein chain, but the "City of Man" rises by subjugation also. As capitals of Baaldom, Pep offers Paris under the Terror and Auschwitz under the Nazis. He points to the formality of French gardens and the tidiness of German kitchens as no guarantee against moral chaos and filth. In fact, "orderliness" may signal a rigid intolerance: "Beautiful Versailles and the shaped trees of Fontainebleau fed the dream of Robespierre, prepared to murder millions of his countrymen to see it real. And were the fierce moppers of Auschwitz inspired by their squared and polished home towns and the pleasant embroidery of the regulated Rhine?" (65). Too much social order and control can be as deadly as too much natural instinct and license.

Pep strongly dissociates himself from these oppressions and, apparently, from all forms of social violence. Nor will he countenance any religion that requires a Christ pierced or an Osiris torn, because Pep could never hide from himself, with distracting chocolate lambs, what it means to accept their incarnate, vulnerable lives nailed on a tree or into Set's box for one's own personal "health." Nevertheless, he finally hints that he cannot escape violence in society altogether, just as he cannot avoid eating other living things. At the end of his lecture, he turns to the Jewish Abraham as one who "knew his debt—and I can see nothing but honor in it—for the presence and continuation of life" (66). In taking this potential slayer of a son as his model, Pep recognizes Abraham's real kinship with the dying gods, along with important differences. Like the fertility deities caught in the biological world, the patriarch knows, with anguish, that he always has a knife in his hand—a way of admitting that life does feed on death. Yet with the knife obediently and unshakably ready to kill Isaac, Abraham does not plunge it. Although respecting the *myths* that show Baal, Moloch, Osiris, and Christ sacrificing themselves, Pep in effect wants to limit the *rites* that would slay new victims to the gods. The deaths meted out, the "things done," occur prodigally enough in nature.

Pep deplores human sacrifice, whether in the name of Baal, Christ on a crusade, Robespierre, or the "moppers" of Auschwitz. Nevertheless, Pep leaves his options open to pick up, with Abraham, the grim weapon again, whenever Yahweh needs strategically to adopt the very features of his enemy Baal. Although the author does not have Pep say so outright, Bellow seems tacitly to be pleading, in 1949, that the unwilling taking of human life might sometimes be necessary, in wars against Hitlers, as the young Isaacs in the ranks of both Allies and Axis go down to Baal.

García Márquez

In *The Autumn of the Patriarch* (1975), Gabriel García Márquez draws on both history and myth to portray his tyrannical protagonist. Joseph Epstein suggests that the fictional patriarch may derive from "an amalgam of Latin American dictators": Trujillo, Batista, Perón, Hernández Martinez, and Duvalier, plus "a touch or two" of Spain's Franco.[24] Seldon Rodman thinks the patriarch may be based in part on a Venezuelan ruler, Juan Vicente Gómez, whereas Regina Janes detects traces of the cult of Eva Perón, the display of Lenin, the fetish of Napoleon's hand, the long death of Salazar, the dairy farm of Somoza, and even the murder of Caesar in the Roman senate.[25]

In addition to incorporating all-too-true details of history, García Márquez draws on the myth of the dying god to magnify the patriarch. The author imagines this canny leader as himself knowing and projecting just such a myth to consolidate his power. When the patriarch gives himself out as the god-man on whose fate the well-being of his Caribbean nation depends, he reveals the ambiguity inherent in the human representative of the dying god as Frazer presents him: a perhaps self-sacrificing embodiment of god and community, a perhaps arrogant manipulator inflicting unnecessary violence on himself and—more commonly, unfortunately—on others. The patriarch tries to create the fiction that he too experiences the dying god's multiple deaths and revivals, virgin birth, responsibility for nature, identity with the community, wound in the groin, and theogamy or sacred marriage—all to enhance his own political allure. But instead of dissipating hurricanes and distributing the "salt of health," as his propaganda maintains, the patriarch engenders only disaster and death for his nation, culminating in the haunting loss of the sea itself, which he sells and replaces with lunar dust.

According to Frazer, worshipers regarded the dying god or his sacred king as totally integrated into the community. García Márquez similarly shows the patriarch's life closely bound up with the people. The author uses a "we" of the community to narrate the story; because of their belief and therefore complicity in the patriarch's mythmaking, they must take part of the blame for their oppressor's long regime.

The narrators insist that "no evidence of his death was final," granting the patriarch the aura of an eternally reviving deity.[26] He is able to observe his own "first death" through an expedient that Frazer says shrewd kings used to weasel out of the last fatal obligation of office: finding a temporary substitute who can wield the royal seal and fondle as many slave women as he wants, for a few short days.[27] The patriarch similarly hides behind his "perfect double," a man who may enjoy all the prerogatives of sovereignty, including the patriarch's concubines. But the double, Patricio Aragones, must also suffer his "presumptuous" personal identity to be forgotten, his feet flattened, and finally his life poisoned, all part of his forced impersonation of the president. Although the patriarch may not order the murder of Patricio, he foresees its eventuality and profits by it, displaying "large signs saying God Save the Magnificent who arose from the dead on the third day" (37). The blasphemous patriarch, likening himself to Christ and to other dying gods sunk to the underworld for three days, simply arises from hiding after Aragones's funeral.

Again imitating both pagan and Christian dying gods, the president claims to be born of a virgin and venerates his mother-goddess or civil saint to the point that he makes her the recipient of all his prayers, sighs, and offhand remarks. Providing a model for her son, Bendición Alvarado reputedly rises from her catafalque, like Inanna emerging from the underworld when sprinkled with the water of life. By decree of the patriarch, her corpse

> traveled month after month among the ephemeral isles of the equatorial tributaries until it got lost in a nightmare age in which gardenias had the use of reason and iguanas flew about in the darkness, the world ended, the wooden wheel ran aground on sandbanks of gold, broke, the ice melted, the salt turned liquid, the swollen body remained floating adrift in a soup of sawdust, and yet it didn't rot, quite the contrary general sir, because then we saw her open her eyes and we saw that her pupils were bright and had the color of January wolfsbane and their usual quality of lunar stones, and even the most incredulous among us had seen the glass cover of the coffin fog over from the vapor of her breath. . . . (131)

Though the president himself begins to believe the reports of his toadying servants about the recovery of his virginal mother, the worms rudely disillusion him:

> I took the crown of orange blossoms from your moldy brow where the stiff filly-mane hair had been pulled out by the roots strand by strand to be sold as relics, I pulled you out from under the damp gauze of your bridal veil and the dry residue and the difficult saltpeter sunsets of death and you weighed the same as a sun-dried gourd and you had an old trunk-bottom smell and I could sense inside of you a feverish restlessness that was like the sound of your soul and it was the scissor-slicing of the moth larvae who were chewing you up inside. (146)

Just as the supposed resurrection of this bird-woman proves false, the lie that "ever since they had found him dead the first time all things on heaven and earth had changed into things of peace general sir" clashes with the massacre of ministers caught rejoicing prematurely to have escaped the president's oppressive presence (40).

In addition to faking "rebirths," the patriarch tries to resemble the dying gods by pretending to regulate nature and secure the community. Rendered sleepless by love pangs, he orders reveille at 3:00 A.M. and pulls strings for comets and eclipses, becoming "undoer of dawn, commander of time, and repository of light" (68). He lives in a seclusion as strict as any taboo that Frazer details against seeing the sacred king,[28] "yet we knew that he was there, we knew it because the world went on, the mail was delivered, the municipal band played its retreat of silly waltzes on Saturday under the dusty palm trees and the dim street lights of the main square, and other old musicians took the places of the dead musicians in the band" (10). Not only does the patriarch maintain the familiar background of silly waltzes, but he also seems to uphold the foreground of life, as he takes the fertile green from the lighthouse, which tints his windows every thirty seconds, and reflects it back onto the people in other forms of fertility: milk dripping from his own hands and five thousand children sired onto his nation.

Even the peculiarity that his mistresses all deliver "seven-month runts" may relate the children (and their irresponsible father) to a dying god, Dionysus. Frazer writes that "the pretence [in a modern Thracian carnival] that the baby is a seven-months' child born out of wedlock and begotten by an unknown father tallies precisely with the legend that Dionysus was born prematurely in the seventh month as the offspring of an intrigue between a mortal woman and a mysterious divine father."[29] The patriarch would prefer that his country believe him divine, but five thousand premature births fail to deify him.

Although the poverty-addled populace might insist that "the only thing that gave us security on earth was the certainty that he was there . . . dedicated to the messianic happiness of thinking for us," García Márquez ruthlessly exposes how the people's abdication of independent judgment and their refusal to believe in historical agency only add to the misery (99). He constantly undercuts all the good that the patriarch claims to bestow. Even in the early days of the patriarch's reign when he personally oversees flocks and fields and prescribes "what this soil needs is a good dose of male donkey shit, it should be spread at government expense," the patriarch actually leaves behind only domestic tragedies and drought wherever he has set foot (85). The patriarch fails to realize that when "all he had to do was point at trees for them to bear fruit and at animals for them to grow and at men for them to prosper," his pointing finger inadvertently signals innocent targets to his solicitous assassins (89).

The clearest example of his legacy of woe—in contrast to propagandized weal—occurs when the patriarch declares a bogus state of plague to justify assuming the exceptional powers of martial law. So that the number of corpses hauled out will support the fiction of plague, he marks certain houses for executions. When the unburied bodies soon cause a real epidemic, the patriarch has achieved his one indubitable and ignominious success as arbiter of nature (228). In fact, his reign is marred from one end to the other by state-directed assassinations, including two thousand children killed so as not to reveal the secret of the fixed lottery and "enemies" of state, amounting to nearly "the whole human species," whose heads are crammed in bags by his slick and elusive director of terror (209).

Although the patriarch covets the glory of the dying god, he foists off what was to have been his own sacrificial death onto others. Just as he relies on Patricio Aragones to do his suffering, he disposes of General Rodrigo de Aguilar. Instead of offering himself as nourishment in a ceremonial "eating of the god," he serves up his once-trusted general "On a garnish of cauliflower and laurel leaves . . . stuffed with pine nuts and aromatic herbs" to his horrified comrades (119).[30] Another of the endlessly fighting generals, for whose actions the patriarch is ultimately responsible, rapes and kills a young man, lifting "the Adonic cadet up into the air and [impaling] him with a plainsman's lance onto the springtime tapestry of the audience room like a butterfly and no one dared take him down for three days, poor man" (56). The victim is "Adonic" because, like vegetation gods, he dies young, he is stabbed, he hangs for three days, and he has some association with spring—artificial, however, because spring is only a picture worked in cloth and in the imagination of the patriarch.

The patriarch's own vision of an Adonic death for himself, where "someone who was a son of his in the dream gave him a stab in the groin," does not teach him to accept that fate but to forestall it by liquidating the legislature and the judiciary (88–89). The only wound in the groin that the patriarch puts up with is his chronic "herniated testicle." He seems to regard it as well worth any inconvenience, because it adds to his credentials as divine man. Never really gored like Adonis, he still makes sure that his double sustains a similar hernia. Because the innocent bystanders of his country, from the cadet to Patricio, must unwillingly assume the sufferings of Adonis that he rejects, the patriarch also forfeits the god's grandeur.

Another obvious reason why the patriarch ruins his self-proclaimed apotheosis into a dying god is that he fails to love anyone except himself. His forays into his harem may seem to mark a theogamy, a divine union with direct benefits for the whole community, since "it was as if an angel had flown across the skies of the nation, voices were muffled, life came to a halt, everybody remained stone-still with a finger to his lips, not breathing, silence, the general is screwing"; but "the respite of that sacred moment" is illusory (14). He cannot distinguish which of his women he has flopped on, he ignores all but one of his "seven-month runts," and when he beds down with the one woman for whom he shows some meager affection, Leticia Nazareno, his incontinent bowels sometimes betray him. The physical mess materializes the spiritual squalor that causes him to deprive her of freedom for long years and forget her in a matter of days after her hideous death.

García Márquez epitomizes the patriarch's murderousness, lovelessness, and his gouging of the country in the loss of the sea, through "the inconceivable evil of a heart which had sold the sea to a foreign power and condemned us to live facing this limitless plain of harsh lunar dust where the bottomless sunsets pain us in our souls" (48). The author graphically pictures the sale as not just that of fishing rights or port access but as the actual removal of the sea itself "in numbered pieces to plant it far from the hurricanes in the blood-red dawns of Arizona" (229). Instead of guarding the beautiful and life-giving sea as he should, the god-man arrogantly promotes himself as a source of life; in the process his body becomes a kind of useless "sea" all by itself. The citizens find his corpse "sprouting tiny lichens and parasitic animals from the depths of the sea, especially in the armpits and the groin" and "We scraped it with fish scales to get the deep-sea shark suckers off" (11, 157; cf. 239).

The narrators refer repeatedly to the patriarch's "dreams of a solitary drowned man," as if this ethical drifter were longing for the fructifying "death by water" that T. S. Eliot's wastelanders vaguely hope for (15, 23, 177). Yet the patriarch achieves only a wastelander's loneliness and bloated stench of failure. For all his power, he cannot even "drown" as successfully as the anonymous corpse that washes ashore in García Márquez's story "The Handsomest Drowned Man in the World." That sexy, beautiful corpse, now christened Esteban, blooms anew in the dreams of the villagers, who can find springs among the stones and make flowers grow on the cliffs after his death.[31] The patriarch wants to stop the cycle of seasons at "autumn," before winter kills him, whereas this drowned peasant has modestly submitted to death, granting his grateful admirers a chance to rejuvenate their village themselves.

While depicting a twentieth-century despot who generates his own fraudulent myth of powers equal to those of the old dying/reviving gods, García Márquez steadily undermines the patriarch's pretensions that only through the leader's life and death can nature and the human community be reborn. Ironically, though, his death *does* awaken his nation. In the very first sentence we hear that "at dawn on Monday the city awoke out of its lethargy of centuries with the warm, soft breeze of a great man dead and rotting grandeur" (7). But instead of touching his country awake through the old god's eternal self-sacrifice, this ungodlike man can finally bequeath rebirth only by ending the seeming eternity of his death-dealing regime. Dead at last, he is "alien to the clamor of the frantic crowds who took to the streets singing hymns of joy at the jubilant news of his death and alien forevermore to the music of liberation and the rockets of jubilation and the bells of glory that announced to the world the good news that the unaccountable time of eternity had come to an end" (251).

Konwicki

A Minor Apocalypse (1979) is the ninth novel by Tadeusz Konwicki and his second to be published in *samizdat*, the Polish underground system for circulating dissident literature.[32] When the narrator tries to dispel his waking thoughts about death—his own mortality, his country's subjection, the planet's extinction—with "gestures of ritual," he means only his morning routine and the habit of writing, that "narcotic of the wounded individual."[33] The narrator's friends Hubert and Rysio arrive just at this point to recommend a much more primitive ritual, one that could, in fact, come straight out of Frazer's chapter on "The Burned God." The "friends" politely propose that "tonight at eight o'clock you set yourself on fire in front of the Party Central Committee building," as a protest against Soviet domination of Poland. Naturally nonplussed, the narrator puts off a direct reply. Nevertheless, he seriously considers the plan. As he walks around the city for the rest of the book, blue plastic gasoline can in hand, the suspense builds: first, whether he will go through with the terrible suggestion and, second, whether such immolation in a kind of balefire can actually do any good.

As "mysterious hierophants . . . of the last people who suffer insomnia in this sleeping country," Hubert and Rysio still link sacrifice with the well-being of the community in the same way ancient people derived the good of the group from the demise of the god or his human surrogate (44). "Your death will bring them back to life or redeem them," the friends insist (87). Moreover, Konwicki echoes several other ritual effects of the type described by Frazer: the victim can revive the plants as well as the spiritual health of the community; he may be killed when his sexual powers fail; an effigy made out of plants may be thrown into a body of water as a rain charm; and he may enact a theogamy to make the vegetation thrive. Konwicki shrewdly matches several of these "rites," which the narrator bungles through pathetically, with competing versions conducted by the state, as if the government were claiming that communism, not this single citizen, has by its institutions already ushered the divine into life.

According to Frazer, ritual death was supposed to end winter or waste, and Konwicki paints a traditional wasteland. As the narrator wakes, he hears elderly delivery women knock over some milk crates, while an armored refrigerator truck carrying food for Party Secretaries races through the milk puddles (10). Only officials enjoy plenty—at the people's expense. The impression of dearth for ordinary folks intensifies when successive workmen arrive during Hubert and Rysio's visit to warn that they will be shutting off the water and gas supply. When a worker advises the narrator to save a tubful of water, he protests, in obvious untruth, "I don't need any water" (20). He is still desperately trying to dissociate himself from the wasteland and from his delegated role in ending it, whether as grail quester releasing the waters or as Frazerian priest-king dying to ensure fertility.

In addition to depicting communist Poland as a wasteland deprived of food, warmth, and water, Konwicki wryly parodies Frazer's claim that the man-god on whom the health of the community depends is sometimes killed at the first sign that his physical powers are beginning to wane, particularly at any sign of "incapacity to satisfy the sexual passions of his wives."[34] Just as the narrator receives the ominous visit, "A sudden hailstorm rattled past the balcony, knocking a condom withering on the iron balustrade off into the abyss. Those condoms were bouquets of violets bestowed on me by my neighbors from the upper floors on their days off" (17). Because Frazer associates violets with the blood of Attis,[35] the traditional bouquets combine with the withering signs of past potency (and infertility) to hint to the reluctant narrator that it is time for his demise.

If such a failing priest-king did bow out after any indication of aging, the vegetation was supposed to rejoice. No sooner have the friends given breath to their grim plan when the house plants revive: "My jade plant was on the windowsill. Only then did I notice how much it had shot up lately and how thick its young, strong leaves had grown. It had been sickly for many years and now suddenly, without any external cause, it had surged upward, sending out a large numebr of powerful, knotty branches" (15). This minor, natural flourishing seems to promise that the narrator might successfully carry out his mandate to revive the community. Any good he could do beyond encouraging the house plants, however, remains far from proved.

As these references to waning powers, violets, and reinvigorated plants echo rites for primitive dying gods, Konwicki also alludes to Christianity's dying god when the narrator announces "one last kilometer of my Golgotha" or when he circles the "Square of the Three Crosses." Richard Lourie, in the "Translator's Note" to an earlier novel by Konwicki, notes that "Poland in its darkest century was identified by its Romantic poets as the Christ of nations. The term evoked both the fact of crucifixion and the promise of rebirth. The Polish imagination felt itself summoned both to the unpleasant cunning of survival and to exalted martyrdom."[36]

Some allusions in A Minor Apocalypse sound both Christian and pagan. The narrator, for example, goes to a river where "My sins, my pains, my shame flowed away to the distant sea like the wreaths on St. John's Day. To leap into the water forever, that would be good. But my miserable brothers want me to leap into the fire" (45). Frazer records celebrations for St. John's Day in which people burn effigies in bonfires or throw them into streams.[37] He believes that human victims at one time underwent the god's sacrifice, with effigies only gradually replacing the live offering and Christian holidays eventually taking over old pagan ceremonies. Although folk wreaths released into the Polish rivers may have come to symbolize washing away sin, in the manner of Christian baptism, Konwicki senses an older, grimmer intention of drowning the sinner—or the sinless, as long as someone suffers. The narrator derives scant comfort from the thought of rinsing away shame because he faces only the "choice" between death by water or death by fire.

The narrator must not only try to equal the old dying god according to the plan proposed by the dissidents. He also has to outdo the communist state, which has competitively set itself up as the new idol. Replacing wreaths and effigies both pagan and Christian, the government floats the slogan "we have built socialism," made out of wreaths and lit candles, down the Vistula River. But, Konwicki intimates, the state is a tattered and unreliable savior, since a bridge disaster has already mauled the letters: "seized by an eddy, the exclamation point was sinking" (73). The pretensions of the bureaucracy to be the new god, commemorated in eternal wreaths, explain why the narrator sometimes varies his self-definition from Christ to Antichrist (158, 167). As Christ he can mount the hill of Golgotha to suffer, while as Antichrist he would signal the termination of a communist millennium.

Although the narrator seems to inherit only the doubtful prerogatives of the priest-king, like the right to throw himself into the river or onto a pyre, he does get to enjoy a kind of sacred marriage between impersonators of the god and goddess. Frazer details how wily kings marked for death came up with the brilliant idea of choosing a substitute, who would, after his brief, unexpected glory, be put to death. Such a king-for-a-day might be given as many slave women as he wished.[38] The Polish underground allows the narrator—perplexed, ordinary, shoved unwillingly to the spotlight—to meet up with the "perfect woman," Nadezhda or "Hope," on his last day.

The narrator may characterize their intercourse as "a rite of magic," but Konwicki deflates such rhapsody (63). Nadezhda's mystic recognition of the narrator turns out to be more flattery than affinity: she claims to have read all the narrator's books but later waffles, "I said that? All Poles and Russians are writers" (65). The fact that the couple meet twice also recalls the periodic nature of sacred marriages, though the narrator admits that repetition in his life is more likely to signal failed earlier attempts than reassuring recurrence.

Both lovemakings are interrupted, once by a man collecting taxes on sex in a public building, and once by a telephone call from the dissidents, wanting to know what color gas can the narrator prefers for his burning. Thus Konwicki shows how mythic theogamy, transposed to the modern, faithless world, acquires new triviality to go with the continued deadliness of the god's rites.

Despite the shoddiness of their theogamies, the second meeting between Nadezhda and the narrator occurs in a primordial "enchanted garden," where they can stand waist deep in ferns "which were strewn with white, mysterious seeds left to them from the good old days when they had been trees on this earth" (174). By force of ardor the couple may temporarily seem to cause sympathetic nature to bear seed, but basically they inhabit a ruined world in which ordinary forests, let alone paradisiacal trees, have long since disappeared.

Just as the state matches St. John's Day wreaths with those of its own, it also stages parodic theogamies and opens a garden to compete with the narrator's ferns. The government offers its grotesque version of divine bride and bridegroom in a pair of Party Secretaries, Russian and Polish. The narrator glances at them all day on various televisions: the Secretaries, at different moments in the replays of a ceremony, are clasped in a hug, holding hands, or kissing each other on the mouth. The fact that the viewers have invariably turned down the sound brings out the ritual nature of these embraces, not to mention their ludicrousness and sterility. Moreover, if the narrator is supposed to burn himself near the Palace of Culture to promote fertility, the state has preceded him in fashioning fertility symbols of its own. The Palace of Culture "shone like an indecent erection against the low, cloudy sky. The first test rocket burst over the Vistula" (205). This building also appears "bleached white by searchlights and shedding its stone slabs like some gigantic fish" (215). The fish has long been a sign of life and sexuality.[39] The state's stone fish joins the "amorous" Party Secretaries to preempt the narrator's claim to give life.

Proclaiming that its divinely ordained, millennial marriage between Russia and Poland has been perfectly fruitful, the state offers as evidence a garden, which is actually a shallow paradise over a reclaimed parking lot. Right before the narrator decides what to do with that gasoline can, he wanders into the official, stunted orchard: "The army searchlights by the Palace of Culture gave off a violet glow like a flash of light that had just died out forever. We walked past currant and raspberry bushes, and mounted beds of cauliflower, carrots, and garlic. We passed trees so small there wasn't room on them for a single pigeon" (204). In these inauspicious surroundings, where the violet glow might remind him of his earlier depressing "bouquet of violets," the narrator—as the proverbial dying man seeing his life flash before his eyes—discovers all fifteen women to whom he has ever made love. The dismal atmosphere of the state's garden overshadows the earlier idyl with Nadezhda, as these women wittily trounce any hope he may nurse to rival the god who releases the springtime:

"The nerve of him."
"Blaming us."

"That's the limit."

"The hell with him."

I pulled a torch-like firebrand from the flames. A little bit for show, a little for self-defense. The wind fluttered the meager flame like a scrap of silk.

"My dears, my darlings. We have the whole night ahead of us. Remember those springs, those summers, those autumns, even those winters. The mornings, the afternoons, the evenings. The silk sheets, the mossy forests, the little rooms off the kitchen. Weigh everything fairly, and only then should your kangaroo court pass sentence on me."

"But I hardly know him," said Rena after a moment.

"And I only know him by sight," added Rysia.

"He's more smoke than fire."

"Let's drink to ourselves, girls."

"To spring."

"To the new year."

"To tomorrow." (209)

As he meets this series of women who fill the role of priestess—only partially satisfactorily in Nadezhda, wholly sardonically in these fifteen scoffers—the narrator also encounters a series of old or dying men who resemble the long line of guardian priests at Nemi. For the narrator is actually only one of a number of stubborn Poles who have resisted the government in subtle ways: "Jan, why did you kill yourself all these years?" (219). Like the guardians of the Nemian grove, these men of conscience— Hubert, the paralytic white-bearded veteran, the renegade party official, Jan in a bathtub, and Caban—show hostility to the new arrival on the killing ground. Hubert, for example, prefers a movie director to the scorned narrator as the favorite son to stand by his deathbed. The green corpse glare in Hubert's hospital room does not augur well for the green of spring, which the narrator hopes to infuse into the world by his own death.

Other clues abound that the narrator will not be able to inaugurate a new season, either natural or political. He cannot pin down the correct year, let alone distinguish equinox from solstice. He notices contradictory placards that proclaim the city is celebrating an anniversary: the thirty-fifth, fortieth, fiftieth, or sixtieth. Konwicki probably alludes to George Orwell's *1984*, in which officials rewrite history to foster a dangerous forgetting of past alternative governments and of past wrongs. By confusing the number of the present anniversary, Konwicki may also parody the primitive idea that rituals merge historical time with the original "sacred time" at the beginning of the world, abolishing intervening centuries.[40] The state abolishes only accountability, not alienating distance from a golden age. The seasons have spun erratically all day for the narrator, who wakes on an autumnal morning, registers many summery moments, but sees the snow starting to fall when he approaches the place of immolation: no spring and

Does the narrator finally decide to go through with this hideous burning? Yes. Can it do any good, personally or communally? No. Personally, he'll be dead, and he has already used up his one facetious chance for revival. Earlier in the day he feels like a new man when a surge of flirtatiousness digs him out of a hangover. Beside market stalls that look like "ancient pagan Slavic temples," he tries for a date, but his companion, intent only on buying matches for his pagan bonfire, soon dashes his briefly reawakened self:

> "Maybe we could go for a coffee, Halina," I asked. "I'm not feeling well. I had some sort of accident yesterday but I can't remember anything about it."
> "But now you've come back to life?"
> "No. I liked you right from the start. I was looking at your legs when we were walking up the escarpment.". . .
> "Old fart," Halinka [Halina] muttered, looking at me without anger. (101)

If he cannot come back to life after too much booze, he is even less likely to do so after making himself into fuel for bonfire.

Nor can he take comfort, personally, from the thought of a hero's adulation from his fellow dissidents, who will probably ferret out base motives. A man who trails him around, hoping to write up a sensational newspaper story about suicide, mocks the narrator's artistic career: "You want to take your own life because you've had no success" (223). Assuming similar motives for protest (pique or vanity), someone accuses the character "Konwicki" in the fictionalized autobiography *The Polish Complex*: "Your cunning is that of a minister of police, a great provocateur who wants to die on the cross. Your cunning is vile, elusive, exalted, dripping with sincerity, a foul sentimental attempt at sanctity aspiring to the tragic."[41]

As for aiding the community, the "sanctimonious" deeds in either book—from refusing a state-sponsored book contract to burning oneself alive—do not topple the government. From the very first pages of *A Minor Apocalypse*, the Polish authorities and the Polish resistance blur: the narrator's friends, not the secret police, present the gasoline can. If dissidents cannot effectively change anything, they just further the suffering begun by the totalitarian system. But despite his lack of effect on the regime or even on the underground, whose members will probably sneer at his vanity rather than applaud his heroism, the narrator lights his match. Without effective ritual, he still makes the fruitless gesture. He does so for the sake of a modicum of self-respect, doubt-laden but precious. The dying god and individual surrogates go down, but only the secular, corporate state reasserts itself.

6
Trafficking with Tezcatlipoca

Like the authors in chapter 5, these artists recognize the danger of kow-towing to an imposter god, but the emphasis shifts away from the still patent falsity of the heroes onto a modicum of truth in them. Conrad, Forster, and Coppola condemn a political manipulation of myth by colonizers from Latin America to India to Vietnam. But after exposing false gods, the artists suddenly salvage something valuable about them. Conrad's Nostromo "triumphs" in a way that saves his tarnished title "incorruptible" from complete irony. To Forster, serenading an unworthy Mrs. Moore in an afternoon's street procession is still safer than glorifying Britannia. Coppola's Colonel Kurtz at least admits his hollowness, whereas the more obedient officers in the film *Apocalypse Now* delude themselves about their own ability to carry out "horrors."

Tezcatlipoca, the Aztec god to whom Conrad alludes in *Nostromo*, was known as a trickster, who flashed his ambiguous messages—part lure, part revelation—from a smoky mirror attached to his ankle where a foot had been amputated. Trafficking with the phantasm of a dying god, whether aggrandizement of oneself or adulation of another, is dangerous; neverthe-less, something can be learned even from illusory deifications. Conrad, Forster, and Coppola participate in a philosophical tradition of the inescap-able "lie," a necessarily fictional code enabling people to act in the world. This chapter, which expands the meaning of "fictions" to include public and private world views, is thus related to chapter 2 on reflexive literary fictions.

Conrad

Joseph Conrad's *Nostromo* (1904) shows definite signs of influence from an Aztec myth of a dying god. Conrad sets the novel in Latin America, and in addition to the factual histories and travelogues he is known to have consulted, he has apparently picked up information about the mythological lore of that area.[1] Although Quetzalcoatl serves as the main dying / reviving deity in the Toltec-Aztec pantheon, Quetzalcoatl's "twin," Tezcatlipoca, suffers a similar fate; it is the yearly death of a human representative of Tezcatlipoca that Conrad most closely imitates in *Nostromo*.

Conrad may well have discovered an account of Tezcatlipoca's rites in William H. Prescott's *History of the Conquest of Mexico*. T. McAlindon has shown that Conrad did indeed study Prescott.[2] Prescott chooses just this feast of Tezcatlipoca as the one ritual he will recount in detail to illustrate Aztec religious practices.[3] This historian cites Bernardino de Sahagún, a sixteenth-century Spanish friar, whose careful records on Aztec beliefs began to become available only in the nineteenth century. Conrad may have sought out Sahagún's writings too, which were translated into English and French, though he could have gleaned the main points of Tezcatlipoca's worship from Prescott.[4]

Conrad carefully evokes and decidedly modifies Tezcatlipoca's feast, showing how an ancient story of a dying deity can still inform a twentieth-century novel of disillusionment. Although the characters may repeat specific gestures of the ritual, those gestures no longer serve any purpose. At the point when ancient initiates gained enlightenment, Conrad's characters despairingly shed their previous beliefs and acquire nothing to replace them. Why would Conrad still use myth as a structural underpinning? On the one hand, the Aztec stories and rites provide him with a paradigm for the self-delusion and cruelty that afflict his modern European characters in Costaguana at least as much as these traits ever characterized indigenous peoples. On the other hand, Conrad may be drawn to myth as a version of the "saving lie" that he both scorned and envied in so many of his works. Just as Jim in *Lord Jim*, Kurtz's Intended in *Heart of Darkness*, and the "Western-ers" in *Under Western Eyes* hold to ridiculous illusions that may yet permit them to avoid the paralysis of more lucid characters, so Nostromo and Decoud, implicitly likened to Tezcatlipoca's representative, excite others' adoration in an ambiguous combination of dangerous sham and helpful inspiration.

Conrad has Nostromo and Decoud imitate Tezcatlipoca at a number of points. The Aztecs chose a human impersonator of their god to idolize for a year, feting him with song, dance, flowers, and costly ornaments. Toward the end of his dubiously privileged reign, they gave him four women as wives, named for the principal goddesses. He rowed out to an island, where all abandoned him. Breaking his flutes on the steps of the temple, he went willingly to his death. Priests offered his heart to the sun to regenerate it and all life. Sahagún notes with surprise the similarities between this victim sacrificed for the sake of the community and Christ, Son of Man, as redeemer.[5] Conrad likewise mixes biblical and pagan references, but he leans more heavily on the Aztec mythology.

Conrad models Nostromo on the Aztec victim called "our lord" to the extent that *nostro uomo*, "our man," enjoys the worship of the common people, only to find that their praise requires his danger and death. (Although the Italian word *nostromo* means "boatswain," Conrad certainly intended to pun on "our man."[6]) After receiving the love of four named women (among an anonymous throng), Nostromo rows to an island, where a man who has always protected him, Viola, kills him. The belief of the populace that Nostromo may be a savior intensifies throughout his career. From an indispensable worker, "one in a thousand," Nostromo rises to absolutely solitary and risky heights. Dr. Monygham, grasping some hope of protecting his beloved Mrs. Gould, elevates Nostromo to his final apotheosis: "You, to speak plainly, are the only man. . . . It is in your power to save this town and—everybody. . . ."[7] The word "regeneration" begins to multiply, as Conrad teases the reader with a counterfeit rejuvenation for the country that may yet include some surprisingly real triumphs.

Nostromo also parallels Tezcatlipoca's human substitute in that he belongs to a whole series of dying men, of which Martin Decoud is the most important. Decoud, abandoned on the same island where Viola later shoots Nostromo, dies "from solitude": without other people, he cannot distract himself from his own basic emptiness. He performs his last tasks "as if accomplishing some sort of rite" (558). Because he plans to commit suicide, he goes willingly, like the Aztec man, to his demise. He rows out toward the setting sun and, after waiting through a sleepless night, shoots himself in the chest across from the rising sun, as if offering it his heart. Like the Aztec darling adorned with costly articles, Decoud has draped his body with four silver ingots, but only so that he will sink to the bottom of the gulf. Furthermore, the imagery surrounding Nostromo's return to the site of Decoud's last vigil explicitly transforms Nostromo into a reincarnated Decoud. Similarly, after the Aztec who had lived as Tezcatlipoca for a year was put to death, the god was believed to come to life again immediately in a new impersonator.

Tezcatlipoca's feast may originally have symbolized for the Aztecs the equanimity that would enable people to value full sensual life and then death as equally necessary parts of a cycle. The god-man first learned his exquisite flute playing, then broke his flutes one by one, because he knew he could take up his life, relinquish it, and take it again in an endless series of incarnations. Laurette Séjourné thinks that the rite was originally a figurative story, teaching people how they could break too-close ties to the passing moment, when they should really be praising and moving on to the whole endless series of moments in eternity. For Séjourné, the Aztecs hideously warped a beautiful Toltec metaphor for killing off worldly attachments into a literal killing of a real human being.[8]

Whether Séjourné is right that a later concrete enactment ruined an abstract symbol, or whether the violence came first and politically motivated priests tacked on the fine interpretation afterward to justify it, the shocking discrepancy between pampering a man and then stabbing him remains the central paradox of Tezcatlipoca's feast. For Conrad also, our man Nostromo bluntly discovers that he (and all of us) live only to die. Nostromo feels particularly betrayed that his fine reputation has led him into a "desperate affair" where neither his own sure hands nor his good judgment can affect the inscrutable workings of fate. Both Nostromo and Decoud are initiated, one to "the disenchanted vanity which is the reward of audacious action," the other to "the disillusioned weariness which is the retribution meted out to intellectual vanity" (560–61). Learning simultaneously the puniness of all human endeavor (thought and action) and the absence of any God to supplement their weakness, Nostromo and Decoud are typically twentieth-century derelicts. The reader cannot take comfort knowing either that a transcendent power appreciates their sacrifice, or that the victims are any longer worthy to play Tezcatlipoca. Although they are better than the brutal tyrants Montero and Guzman Bento, described as "Aztec idol" and "strange god" (135, 154), Decoud and Nostromo fall far short of god-men. Decoud possesses no core of inner conviction, and the arrogance that has always tainted the "incorruptible" Nostromo worsens and finally putrefies completely into greed.

Even in details Nostromo's case parallels that of Tezcatlipoca's impersonator. The chosen Aztec must have no bodily defects, and Nostromo is "handsome, robust, and supple" (458). Sahagún says of the petted victim "there was taken the greatest care that he be taught to blow the flute, that he be able to play his whistle; and that at the same time he hold all his flowers and his smoking tube . . . he was indeed regarded as our lord. There was the assigning of lordship; he was importuned; he was sighed for; there was bowing before him; the commoners performed the earth-eating ceremony before him."[9] Nostromo rides through a festival to cheers, while a peasant, cringing at his stirrup, "begged 'his worship' insistently for employment"; meanwhile, "A red flower, flung with a good aim from somewhere in the crowd, struck the resplendent capataz on the cheek" (140–41). As the Indian played flutes, Nostromo carries a boatswain's silver whistle. The Aztec's smoking may even have inspired Nostromo's habit of cadging cigars, by means of which the author conveys both the impertinence of the capataz and the little he gets for his labors. When Nostromo accomplishes the miraculous task of bringing the railway investor Sir John over the mountains, the capitalist catches sight of Nostromo "as, from before one of the little fires burning outside the low wall of the corral, arose the figure of a man wrapped in a poncho up to the neck. . . . The man who . . . had arisen from the ground, struck a match to light a cigarette. The flame showed a bronzed, black-whiskered face, a pair of eyes gazing straight" (46–47). The fact that one of the reader's first glimpses of Nostromo is a tiny point of flame may augur the conflagration of the sun, which, in the Aztec imagery Conrad uses, will consume him.

Although the Aztec common people coddled their hero, he was not actually one of their own but a captive; Nostromo is also a foreigner, an Italian. The Aztec commanded a small group of young men for a year, as Nostromo lords over his partly cowed, partly adoring band of cargadores. The Aztecs kept their captive in the house of a guardian steward, and Viola, who practically adopts Nostromo as a son, houses him at his inn. The four Aztec women given to the condemned man also belonged to the house of the guardian; and Viola's wife, Teresa, and two daughters, Linda and Giselle, are all in love with Nostromo. Paquita, a woman of the people, is the fourth named woman who fancies him.

Although Viola does not intend to bring about his protégé's death, as the Aztec guardian planned, he does, in fact, shoot the prowling Nostromo, believing he is another youth, attempting his daughter's virtue. Nostromo has, indeed, seduced Giselle. But the Aztec executioner and victim both knew their parts clear-sightedly, whereas Nostromo's death is the result of mistaken identity, and the misdirected murder plunges old Viola into fatal grief.

Nostromo's reenactment of the feast of Tezcatlipoca actually occurs twice. He literally dies from Viola's shot when he beaches one last time on the Great Isabel Island. But his personality dies earlier, when he loses the attention and admiration that have always propped up his identity. Tezcatlipoca's devotee must have known that he would be forced to give up his lucrative post for a terrible fate; Nostromo, on the other hand, learns all of a sudden that "it was no longer open to him to ride through the streets, recognized by everyone, great and little, as he used to do every evening on his way to play monte in the posada of the Mexican Domingo; or to sit in the place of honor, listening to songs and looking at dances" (463). In order to hide his stolen silver, Nostromo has to hide himself (at first his whole person, later his secrets). To a person who gains his sense of self from reputation—the admiring gaze and the praising words of others—secrecy and silence undermine his very existence.

Although he tumbles from glorified leader to victim, like his ancient predecessor, Nostromo lacks the spirit of renunciation that was supposed to characterize the Aztec captive breaking his flutes one by one: "he went up of his own free will, to where he was to die. As he was taken up a step, as he passed one (step), there he broke, he shattered his flute, his whistle, etc."[10] Actually, Nostromo has previously displayed just this renunciatory nonchalance toward objects of the sense world (while still hankering for praise from that world), when he cuts off his silver buttons one by one to favor a girlfriend (143). But now when he feels his reputation neglected, he renounces his own incorruptibility. Convincing himself that everyone has betrayed him, he enslaves himself to the Goulds' silver as his due. Instead of perceiving spiritual meaning, Nostromo loses it. He has, in effect, died. Christ's pronouncement "It is finished," which Nostromo detects in an owl's cry, applies as much to his own giving up the ghost as to the feared death of Teresa (468), and he happens to hear this death knell in Tezcatlipoca's bird of ill omen.

In a key passage of the book, Nostromo is described as reborn. After losing his incorruptibility, he stands up in green grass; Conrad makes it seem as if Nostromo has personally produced the vegetative splendor all around him. He has passed through "blood," and the personified elements, embracing, have even provided a little "lovemaking" to precede the new birth. In the sequence "blood," "born," and "green," Nostromo duplicates the dying god's experience:

> At last the conflagration of sea and sky, lying embraced and asleep in a flaming contact upon the edge of the world, went out. The red sparks in the water vanished, together with the stain of blood in the black mantle draping the sombre head of the Placid Gulf. . . . Nostromo woke up from a fourteen-hours' sleep and arose full length from his lair in the long grass. He stood knee-deep among the whispering undulations of the green blades, with the lost air of a man just born into the world. Handsome, robust, and supple, he threw back his head . . . as natural and free from evil in the moment of waking as a magnificent and unconscious wild beast. Then, in the sudden steadied glance fixed upon nothing from under a forced frown, appeared the man. (457–58)

While Nostromo resembles the dying god, he simultaneously sums up the quintessential human being in a Christian world view, through his frowning remembrance of sin.

Dr. Monygham reinforces our perception of Nostromo as a man reborn when he thinks of "Nostromo's return to life" (479). Similarly, "the night beset Giorgio Viola and his dead wife with its obscurity and silence that seemed invincible till the capataz de cargadores, returning from the dead, put them to flight with the sputter and flare of a match"—perhaps a hint that the final burning is still to come (524). Far from the same Nostromo, this man is a different incarnation entirely. Nostromo announces bitterly that "You will find the capataz no more" (487), and he even goes by a new name, Captain Fidanza, actually his own name before the nickname Nostromo stuck. Because he now lies that Gould's silver is lost, the implication of "fidelity" in his name is entirely ironic.

Conrad describes this reborn Nostromo as if the capataz were reincarnating Decoud. A few pages after the following lines about Nostromo we learn that Decoud had sat in the same boat at sunset and that his body is now submerged in the gulf:

> the capataz of the cargadores resembled a drowned corpse come up from the bottom to idle away the sunset hour in a small boat. . . . And now,

with the means of gaining the Great Isabel thrown thus in his way at the
earliest possible moment, his excitement had departed, as when the soul
takes flight, leaving the body inert upon an earth it knows no more. . . .
Then slowly, without a limb having stirred, without a twitch of muscle or
quiver of an eyelash, an expression, a living expression, came upon the
still features, deep thought crept into the empty stare—as if an outcast
soul, a quiet, brooding soul, finding that untenanted body in his way,
had come in stealthily to take possession. (550– 52)

Such a brooding soul seeking Nostromo's body suggests either an abstract
spirit of greed, or Decoud himself. When the newly animated Nostromo
reaches the shore, he takes up the exact pose of Decoud's sunset vigil, at the
same time of day, in the same ravine—hinting that he will have to endure
Decoud's sacrifice too (560). Perhaps one clue as to just how insistently
Conrad thought of the myth of the dying god while working on *Nostromo*—
and how wearily he put himself in line with Nostromo and Decoud as one
who had to suffer in an underworld—appears in a letter Conrad wrote in
June 1904: "I am not myself and shall not be myself till I am born again after
Nostromo is finished."[11]

Like Nostromo who dies twice—once in his personality, once in his
body—Decoud feels already dead in the lighter: "He had the strangest
sensation of his soul having just returned into his body from the circumam-
bient darkness" (290). The events leading up to his literal death strikingly
resemble Tezcatlipoca's feast. Decoud is a dandy, like that god's pet, who
"fasted . . . [and] went with his face smoke-black," as Sahagún says.[12]
When Decoud writes to his sister in the silence after a skirmish, "the
candle-light fell upon a face that was grimy and scratched. His rosy lips were
blackened with heat, the smoke of gunpowder"; he records, "I am very
hungry" (254–55).

The day of the gunfight turns out to be the third of May, later commemorated by the citizens in a trivial way with Très de Mayo coffee, as Sahagún
reports that it was the fifth month when Tezcatlipoca's impersonator rowed
himself to an island and let a priest tear out his heart to offer to the sun.[13]
Once Decoud rows himself to his island, he feels completely abandoned by
people and mocked by the natural setting: "Taking up the oars slowly, he
pulled away from the cliff of the Great Isabel, that stood behind him warm
with sunshine, as if with the heat of life, bathed in a rich light from head to
foot as if in a radiance of hope and joy. He pulled straight towards the setting
sun" (559). He waits all night for the sun to rise, then dies adorned with
silver, "without having heard the cord of silence snap aloud in the solitude of
the Placid Gulf, whose glittering surface remained untroubled by the fall of
his body. . . swallowed up in the immense indifference of things" (560).
Though he does, in effect, offer his heart to the sun, as if to add his energy to
its own difficult descent and reemergence, Conrad makes it clear that no

transcendent force receives his gift because neither nature, nor the presiding Isabel, nor any other deity pays the slightest attention.

When Nostromo discovers that four ingots are missing, we hear that the sun immolates itself, hardly needing help, however, from any human being: "In the face of the open gulf, the sun, clear, unclouded, unaltered, plunged into the waters in a grave and untroubled mystery of self-immolation consummated far from all mortal eyes, with an infinite majesty of silence and peace" (553). Similarly, a bloody and burning but unconcerned sun attends Nostromo's own last days, deepening toward total conflagration as he lies about which sister he loves: "The dusk of purple and red enveloped him too—close, soft, profound, as no more than fifty yards from that spot it had gathered evening after evening about the self-destructive passion of Don Martin Decoud's utter skepticism, flaming up to death in solitude" (600).

The dismal succession of Tezcatlipoca's impersonators, reborn immediately into the body of another youth, who represented the god until he in his turn died the following year, appears not only in Decoud and Nostromo but in a whole series of sacrifices. Nostromo resents that he is as neglected as the corpse of Hirsh, strung up and shot. Dr. Monygham is almost a hanged man, as far as receiving the rope around his neck. Gould is ready to blow himself to bits with his mine. Moreover, Conrad gives Nostromo the name Gian' (Giovanni) Battista, John the Baptist, whose beheading formed a sacrifice repeatable in Christ's death, as Decoud's death anticipates Nostromo's. Both Nostromo and Decoud utter Christ's relinquishing line "it is finished," "it is done" (468, 560). This multiplication of sufferers seems to suggest for Conrad that the whole human race must line up as victims of death. The tone of the novel echoes Prescott's somber comment on the festival of Tezcatlipoca: "The tragic story of this prisoner was expounded by the priests as the type of human destiny, which, brilliant in its commencement, too often closes in sorrow and disaster."[14]

Nostromo includes not only this series of dying god figures but also hints of the corresponding goddesses. Conrad suggests goddesses in several ways. First, the islands called the Three Isabels witness Decoud's and Nostromo's deaths. They are impersonal presiding spirits, and their name of a European imperial power insinuates the cruelty of colonization, what Conrad calls "material interests" (571). In addition, Conrad portrays three powerful women, Emilia Gould, Linda Viola, and Antonia Avellanos, who variously inspire their men to a supreme sacrifice, frighten them with their passion, or receive their last confession.

Conrad specifically links Emilia with a European mythological figure: "Mrs. Gould had out her own carriage, with two white mules, to drive them down to the harbor, whence the *Ceres* was to carry them off into the Olympus of plutocrats" (74). In Roman mythology, Ceres, Juno, and Proserpina divided earth, sky, and underworld among themselves; in some ways

Emilia, Linda, and Antonia oversee these provinces. As keeper of the lighthouse on the Great Isabel, Linda enters the tower as if it were a "shrine" and lights up the night sky (616). She may share her role as star of heaven, charting Nostromo's course, with her mother, Teresa, whose harsh words Nostromo takes uncomfortably as prophecy. To Nostromo, mother and daughter seem to call for his downfall, whereas to the doctor they both tend an enormous, unreasonable fire of love for the capataz.

Like Proserpina, Antonia maintains her allegiance to a dead man, Decoud, as her Pluto. In his last days, Decoud imagines her greater than life-size, almost divine: "gigantic and lovely like an allegorical statue, looking on with scornful eyes at his weakness" (556). He acts as if Antonia, like Teresa, were taking on the destructive aspect of a goddess, indifferently receiving all corpses back into her body. Yet in reality Antonia hardly scorns Decoud; she remains as devoted to him as Linda to Nostromo. Captain Mitchell admiringly points out Antonia's tribute to her fiancé:

> a marble medallion in the wall, in the antique style, representing a veiled woman with her hands clasped loosely over her knees, commemorates that unfortunate young gentleman who sailed out with Nostromo on that fatal night, sir. See, "To the memory of Martin Decoud, his betrothed Antonia Avellanos." Frank, simple, noble. There you have that lady, sir, as she is. An exceptional woman. Those who thought she would give way to despair were mistaken, sir. She has been blamed in many quarters for not having taken the veil. It was expected of her. But Dona Antonia is not the stuff they make nuns of (534).

Veiled like a goddess of the mystery religions rather than like a nun, Antonia retains the goddess's title "virgin" but with her full sensuality. Robert Andreach in his book on Conrad and Ford Madox Ford, *The Slain and Resurrected God*, claims specifically that Conrad does not draw on any pagan Great Mother because his female characters are all Beatrices.[15] But this exclusion of non-Christian sources does not correspond to the way Conrad magnifies and reveres the sensual and intellectual power of the women.

As Linda and Antonia may preside over sky and underworld, Emilia rules an earthly domain. In addition to her link with the agricultural Ceres, Emilia fosters the San Tomé mine, which reaches down into the ground. As she sees it, the mine exists to regenerate a backward land. To wear the green insignia of the mine supposedly protects a man from army recruiters and from likely death (107, 533). Unfortunately, just as the old myths predicated life on death, more fertile green always seems to require more blood after all, from an individual and from the whole community. Although Charles Gould, dubbed the "King of Sulaco," may find his surrogate for the sacred king's ordeal in the person of Nostromo, the people have to endure periodic revolutions with no substitutes to relieve them.

The altarpiece at the San Tomé chapel appropriately shows a "Resurrection, the gray slab of the tombstone balanced on one corner, a figure soaring upward, long-limbed and livid, in an oval of pallid light, and a helmeted brown legionary smitten down, right across the bituminous foreground. 'This picture, my children, [is] *muy linda e maravillosa* [very pretty and marvelous],' Father Roman would say" (114). The pictured Resurrection, whether of Christ or a pagan dying/reviving deity, makes, in fact, a fitting emblem for Conrad's book. Soldiers smitten in the hellish civil wars line the foreground, and Nostromo and Decoud, haloed by their lovers, soar into local legend. Whether any of these sacrifices regenerate the country and the soul remains an open question. The phrase *muy linda* at least escorts the character Linda to the death scene, as the goddess always accompanies the dying god. Women, then, inherit only the sad job of guarding the body in the tomb.

Emilia, consigned like Linda to the role of helpless spectator despite her exalted status as goddess incarnate, oversees the mine as a "paradise of snakes" (116). Conrad's most masterful stroke in his portrayal of Emilia is to make her humanly aware of the inhuman burden of a goddess who must watch equally over life and over death. As the Aztec Ciuacoatl, "snake-woman," wore a necklace of severed hands and hearts, Emilia comes to realize that the mine contributes as much to the destruction of the country as to its well-being.[16] Dr. Monygham predicts, "There is no peace and rest in the development of material interests . . . it is founded on expediency, and is inhuman . . . the time approaches when all that the Gould Concession stands for shall weigh as heavily upon the people as the barbarism, cruelty, and misrule of a few years back" (571). Only a deity could regard such prospects with serenity—or perhaps divinity equals callous indifference, Conrad implies. The humanly compassionate Emilia, unlike such deities after all, does not want Nostromo's gift of confession or anything further to do with money, preferring to try to tear off her undetachable necklace of silver-inspired sacrifices.

When we consider both the hollow vanity of Nostromo and the dehumanizing effects of "material interests," the entire imagery of Nostromo as a god sacrificing himself to renew the community sounds preposterous. Yet Decoud's unlikely brainchild, the Occidental Republic, actually comes into existence and thrives; we do hear of a "regenerated Sulaco" now enjoying its "second youth" (530, 563). Although still largely ironic, because Conrad warns us that the new country's materialism can only spawn future injustices, the improvements in the standard of living and temporary peace are real, the direct result of Nostromo's daring ride for reinforcements.

The tin god Nostromo triumphs in yet another way, by commanding Linda's undying devotion. When the capataz first starts to row to the lighthouse to visit the two sisters—and especially to check on his silver—Dr. Monygham offers one of the clearest formulations yet for Nostromo as dying god: "that fellow has some continuity and force. Nothing will put an end to him" (572). Monygham's prophecy of immortality comes true as Linda vows her remembrance:

> Dr. Monygham, pulling round in the police-galley, heard the name pass over his head. It was another of Nostromo's successes, the greatest, the most enviable, the most sinister of all. In that true cry of love and grief that seemed to ring aloud from Punta Mala to Azuera and away to the bright line of the horizon, overhung by a big white cloud shining like a mass of solid silver, the genius of the magnificent capataz de cargadores dominated the dark gulf containing his conquests of treasure and love. (631)

The doctor calls the triumph "sinister" because Linda's enormous love expends itself on Nostromo's shoddiness. Yet, like the saving "lie" in *Heart of Darkness*, the sham of Nostromo's worth at least inspires Linda's "true" cry. Similarly, the empty Decoud's Occidental Republic—like the "Western" obstinacy in maintaining untenable belief and action in Conrad's *Under Western Eyes*—is a delusion that *works*. In other words, dogged "Westerners," whom Conrad pities for their ignorance but also grudgingly admires for their ability to act despite the futility of all action, have managed to create for themselves an efficacious myth. Although the sun neither notices our deaths nor requires our sacrifices, we need at least to pretend a belief in a heavenly radiance or a phantom horseman Nostromo to enable our rebirths or keep us from suicide.

Forster

In *A Passage to India* (1924), E. M. Forster synthesizes his knowledge of Western dying gods with his personal observation of Hindu and Moslem worship and of "primitive" fertility rites in India. To Forster, the temporary or serial god of fertility becomes an important common element relating the supposedly incompatible European, Hindu, and Moslem protagonists.

The narrator in *A Passage to India* seems to dismiss the dying gods as quaint fairy tales: "In Europe life retreats out of the cold, and exquisite fireside myths have resulted—Balder, Persephone—but here the retreat is from the source of life, the treacherous sun, and no poetry adorns it because disillusionment cannot be beautiful."[17] But in a climactic scene from the third section, "Temple," a reminder of the dying gods suddenly emerges in the form of "baskets of ten-day corn." The singers at the festival for Krishna's birth are preparing to throw God away, God himself, (not that God can be thrown) into the storm. Thus was He thrown year after year, and were others thrown—little images of Ganpati, baskets of ten-day corn, tiny tazias after Mohurram—scapegoats, husks, emblems of passage; a passage not easy, not now, not here, not to be apprehended except when it is unattainable: the God to be thrown was an emblem of that. (314)

The Hindus toss out a model of Krishna's birthplace, along with images of Ganpati (Ganesha), the elephant-headed god of prosperity invoked before the worship of most other gods. Unexpectedly, Moslem pilgrims also put in an appearance, heaving model tombs (tazia) into the water to commemorate Husain's death. And squeezed in among the ritual paraphernalia for Hindu and Moslem, the pagan baskets of ten-day corn coincide with Frazer's description of gardens of Adonis, despite the slight difference in number of days for growth:

These were baskets or pots filled with earth, in which wheat, barley, lettuces, fennel, and various kinds of flowers were sown and tended for eight days, chiefly or exclusively by women. Fostered by the sun's heat, the plants shot up rapidly, but having no root they withered as rapidly away, and at the end of eight days were carried out with the images of the dead Adonis, and flung with them into the sea or into springs.[18]

Why has Forster introduced these gardens of Adonis at a crucial moment? In form and effect, the baskets serve as common denominator for everything else in the list. The common form is to throw something valuable into the water; the common effect is to admit the sad transience of everything one loves, while longing for union anyway and for the new birth that might be drawn from the water's amniotic largess. The two Indian religious groups represented in the novel might eye one another suspiciously, but Forster senses the affinity between the Hindu celebrating in Gokul Ashtami the return and departure of Krishna and the Moslem celebrating in Mohurram the martyrdom and saving presence of Husain. Balder and Persephone might have quailed in the heat, but in India's rainy season Krishna and Husain replace them.

In fact, Forster highlights certain aspects of Krishna's and Husain's legends so that we see parallels with vegetation myths. The new heroes, like the old, still suffer terribly and rejoice utterly, the keynotes of the dying god. They undergo all the pain there is to endure in human existence, not hiding behind godhead or sainthood, and thus give an honest rendering, larger than life but clearer, of our world. Yet, despite their suffering, they also celebrate life unreservedly. They do not withdraw from the world into either nihilism or nirvana. Instead, they devote themselves to life through *bhakti*, the mystic Hindu "way of love," and through Sufism, the mystic Moslem "way of love," which Forster chooses to interweave with the Shiite festival Mohurram.

Altogether Forster creates six versions in *A Passage to India* of the dying god. Krishna serves as the main Hindu representative, while the floating manikin of a Hindu Rajah echoes Krishna in the secular world. Husain provides the main Moslem figure, and the saint revered in separate Shrines of the Head and of the Body parallels Husain in a briefer example. Furthermore, Forster makes both Aziz and Mrs. Moore, ironically yet seriously, incarnate the dying gods on a human level, as Frazer insists that people attempted to do in order to give the gods energy for repeating their tasks. Neither Aziz nor Mrs. Moore, of course, intends to imitate a dying god, since it is the author who arranges the parallels for the reader's benefit.

The religious ceremonies Forster depicts do not just add local color to the novel. I will argue that he consciously knows that Gokul Ashtami, Mohurram, and the offerings at the double shrine have preserved vestiges of vegetation rites. I will also argue that Forster is particularly attracted to three aspects of such rites: death, rebirth through water, and sacred marriage. He finds in these aspects convenient images for his most important themes. He can evoke the dismemberment suffered by some dying gods to mirror his theme of communities scattered and friends sundered from one another. He also evokes the flinging of the god's image into water, with water simultaneously figuring sad dissolution and exuberant rebirth. Finally, Forster focuses on Hindu and Moslem legends in which marriages occur: Krishna's many couplings and the marriages in the stories of Husain and the saint. Unlike the bachelor Jehovah, these Eastern gods and saints enjoy "sacred marriages," as Middle Eastern vegetation gods do.

Marriage becomes a central image in *A Passage to India*, corresponding to Forster's theme of "making connections." His desire to mend broken relations ranges over several levels: from individuals never quite touching, to nations at odds, to human beings calling for an unknown god. Therefore when Forster recasts a Krishna and a Husain as dying gods, he appreciates them for sanctioning, without the usual European inhibitions, *what should be*—marriage, both sensual and spiritual—and he also values them for admitting, without cushioning, *what is*—scattering, divorce, and death.

G. K. Das surmises, "Although there is not much evidence of any strong influence of Frazer on him, there are in Forster's thinking several distinct echoes which prompt a comparison. . . . Frazer seems the stimulus behind the tripartite division of the novel corresponding to the cycle of the Indian seasons, as well as the presence of the water ceremonies, the dying king, and the ritualistic sacrifice of gods and 'scapegoats' in the final section."[19] Forster himself reports that he "only glanced at Frazer."[20] Yet what he "glanced at" in Frazer surely included the section on dying and reviving gods, since Forster's personal experience of the Krishna rites made him think explicitly of Adonis. After witnessing Gokul Ashtami in Dewas, India, in 1921, Forster writes in a letter, "As to the explanation of this, as apart from what one was told by the pious, I know too little to conjecture, but was reminded of the Adonis Festival, where the god is born, dies, and is carried to the water, all in a short time." Forster may also have witnessed Indians sowing the baskets with corn: right afterward in this letter he mentions a popular festival, "really the worship of the spirit of vegetation," occurring at the same time as the court's Gokul Ashtami.[21] Both the popular vegetation festival and the court's Krishna ceremonies make Forster think of Adonis.

Forster could have connected Krishna with Adonis in several ways. Like Adonis cohabiting with Venus, Krishna experiences erotic pleasures. But he does not live blissfully forever. Instead, like Adonis participating in the hunt and wounded by a boar, Krishna is pierced by a hunter's arrow. Both Adonis and Krishna, though available for further incarnations, cannot escape pain and periodic death. Finally, as women fling the image of Adonis into the water, worshipers throw the model village of Krishna, and, in his story, women predominate, the milkmaids thronging forward first to devote themselves to him.

Krishna as playful child and youthful seducer, Krishna as mature king who dies by an arrow, and Krishna as teacher in the *Bhagavad Gita* are originally three separate legends, later combined. Forster did know all three traditions. In addition to the parallel with Adonis's gardens that Forster could actually see at the Gokul Ashtami celebration for the playful Krishna, Forster knew the other details about Krishna's life, strikingly like Adonis's, from his reading of E. O. Martin's *The Gods of India*, which Forster reviewed in 1914.

The Hindu fashioners of Krishna's stories definitely sympathize with bodily passion, showing a Krishna who pities the milkmaids and who "goes beneath a tree and rests on beds of tender leaves, with his head cushioned on a herdsboy's thigh." (Forster quotes this latter description from the *Bhagavad Purana*.[22] The Krishna who attracted Forster thus could be interpreted as representing homosexual as well as heterosexual love.) Some commentators have wondered how Forster, who valued individuality, could have admired Hinduism, which to these critics means nonsexual asceticism and annihilation of "self" in union with the oversoul.[23] Yet Hinduism includes many sects, not just the ascetic Vedanta philosophy.[24] In Krishna worship, the individual, far from annihilated, is strengthened, when Krishna multiplies his image everywhere: all his lovers believe he holds them alone. Although Martin, Forster's source, bristles at Krishna's "debauchery" and "immorality,"[25] Forster could find relief from English prudery in Krishna's frank expression of unlimited sexuality (he embraces thousands), so different from England's hesitation about heterosexual love and outright horror at Forster's own sexual preferences. In his review of *Gods of India*, he warns that Martin's "wholesale condemnation" of Krishna is "monstrous."[26]

While Forster could appreciate, on the literal level of Krishna's stories, Hinduism's view of sexuality (more tolerant than Christianity's), he could also take an interest in the symbolic dimension of *bhakti*. E. B. Havell explains in *The Ideals of Indian Art* (1911): "As a religious cult *bhakti* finds artistic expression in modern Hindu art in subjects relating to the love of Radha for Krishna, where Krishna is the Indian Orpheus, drawing all creation to listen to the divine music of his flute, and where Radha's passionate devotion is the symbol of the soul's yearning for God."[27] Forster credits Havell's book with "opening an epoch" for him.[28] When the worshipers in *A Passage to India* chant their beautiful "Radhakrishna Krishnaradha" refrain (311), fusing Krishna and his favorite milkmaid into one fleeting being, Forster calls up his main theme, the desire to make connections. He finds in *bhakti* yet another expression of the longing for marriage—for sexual union and for divine comfort—that he approves in Walt Whitman's poem:

> Passage to India! / Lo, soul, see'st thou not God's purpose from the first? / The earth to be spanned, connected by network, / The races, neighbors, to marry and be given in marriage. . . . Then . . . all these hearts as of fretted children shall be soothed, / All affection shall be fully responded to, the secret shall be told, / All these separations and gaps shall be taken up and hook'd and link'd together, / The whole earth, this cold, impassive, voiceless earth, shall be completely justified.[29]

Whitman would marry everyone to everything, on a universal and phantasmagoric scale, the way the Adonis Festival, which came to Forster's mind at Krishna's services, would mate Adonis and Venus, priest-king and priestess-queen, bull and cow, ordinary men and women, rain and crop, on a gamut from natural to supernatural. The human race is still far from implementing Whitman's dream; in fact, one reason why Forster may withhold the facts about what really happened to Adela in the cave is to reinforce the sad knowledge that we have not yet arrived at the time when "the secret shall be told." Forster implicitly contrasts the poet's vision of "total" union with the false political union of the British empire, a reality that maintains itself by exploiting divisions instead of healing them.

Even Adonis does not luxuriate forever in his "sacred marriage"; he also dies "in a short time," as Forster recalls at the disposal of the ten-day baskets.[30] Likewise the myth of Krishna, for all its pleasures and pranks, recognizes the sadness in existence. This darker awareness, along with its exuberance, gives the myth credibility with Forster. He could be "on nearer nodding terms with Krishna than with any other god," as he later said, not because of a literal belief in an actually existing Krishna, but because the poetic narratives about Krishna were intellectually compatible with his own thought: life-affirming but not escapist.[31] Krishna might embrace his milkmaids, but most of the time they cannot find him. As Godbole comments, Krishna "neglects to come" (80). Forster knew very well that, far from embracing, Moslem and Hindu fight over pepul trees, English and Indian clash over sovereignty, and nations deteriorate into a world war.

But the Krishna stories can keep pace in tone and vision with the worst the world has to offer. Martin retells several grim events in Krishna's life from the *Vishnu Purana*. Forster seems to have gleaned here a few plot details for *A Passage to India* as well as the mood ensuring that Krishna goes down to defeat, like a dying god. As an example of a possible influence on plot, a picnic led by Krishna sours when "the destructive flame of dissension was kindled among them [Krishna's progeny] by mutual collision," the way Aziz's picnic ends in accusations, arrest, dissension.[32] As Martin recounts, an enraged Krishna aims a few killing missiles himself. In the *Bhagavad Gita* (part of the *Mahabharata*) he oversees the war between two armies, which finally decimate each other.[33] Accordng to Martin, citing the *Vishnu Purana*, Krishna retreats to meditate, but while seated cross-legged, a hunter accidentally hits an arrow into the sole of Krishna's foot. Forgiving the hunter, Krishna dies painfully, though as an avatar or incarnation of Vishnu, his living substance can be gathered for further divine displays.

Martin quotes a scholar surprised to find Krishna skirmishing with the rest and then actually dying himself:

> Notwithstanding the amiable character . . . there is something sad and even cruel at the basis of the legend. It is in a smiling mood that he presides over all these acts of destruction, that he sees the end of his people approaching and prepares to meet it. . . . Though less fierce than Siva, Vishnu [and, by extension, his avatar Krishna] is nevertheless, on one side of his character, an inexorable god; he too is that Time which devours everything.[34]

While Forster can let down his inhibitions by identifying with Krishna's joys, he can also square his lucidity about the world's muddle with Krishna's honest vision of sadness. Benjamin Walker even labels Krishna's story "tragic," like those of Achilles and the dying god: "The drunken brawl, the general slaughter, the hero slain by an arrow piercing his one vulnerable spot, the city engulfed, the 'twilight of an era,' are well-known in early European literature. The notion of the dying god is widespread in the Near East. All these themes are found nowhere else in Indian mythology."[35] Walker reaches his bold conclusion, that Krishna actually belongs to the group of dying gods, through scholarly comparison, whereas Forster intuits Krishna's kinship with Adonis during his attendance at Gokul Ashtami. And Forster's reading of Martin's work could have corroborated for him that in legend the god himself goes down, not just his images that a curtain or a wave eclipses, as Krishna agrees to accept the ultimate losses with the ultimate sweets.

The second Hindu "relative" of the dying god besides Krishna is the Rajah in whose palace the fictional Gokul Ashtami ceremony originates. So as not to spoil the festivities, Aziz has been instructed to conceal the Rajah's death, which occurs shortly after Krishna's enacted birth. When Aziz and Ralph Moore are rowing on the lake to view the Hindus consign Krishna to the depths, a mysterious, shining-robed king suddenly floats out of the darkness. The vision disconcerts Aziz even when he realizes that they have discovered a monument to the late Rajah's father: "[Aziz] had heard of the image—made to imitate life at enormous expense—but he had never chanced to see it before. . . . There was only one spot from which it could be seen, and Ralph had directed him to it. Hastily he pulled away, feeling that his companion was not so much a visitor as a guide" (313). Although the Rajah has not literally been reborn, the confusion of Krishna coming, Rajah dying, Krishna going, Rajah reappearing sets the rhythm for Aziz's own renewal of friendship.

Important as these two instances of Hindu surrogates for the dying god are, Forster democratically matches them with two Moslem examples. The Mohurram procession that forms a background all through Aziz's trial in "Caves" corresponds to Gokul Ashtami in "Temple," and the briefer mention of the saint with two shrines parallels the briefer role of the Rajah's epiphany.

Mohurram commemorates the martyrdom of several spiritual leaders, especially Mohammed's grandson Husain. Shiite Moslems mourn his death with passion plays and processions. The tone of the festival combines moods: "the deepest grief does not exclude a part being played by comic figures."[36] Forster mocks the slapstick but also revels in it, as the merriment of Gokul Ashtami both baffled and attracted him. Fielding perceives only the ludicrous side of Mohurram; he thinks that a tazia looks "more like a crinoline than the tomb of the grandson of the Prophet, done to death at Kerbela. Excited children were pasting coloured paper over its ribs" (192). But Forster also detects the very real grief for Husain and transfers it to Aziz. As June Levine notes, Husain's martyrdom has a "thematic echo" in Aziz's near martyrdom, the remembrance of old wrongs resounding into "outrage and compassion for an innocent prisoner."[37]

Ellin Horowitz goes on to compare Husain to a dying god: "Although Mohurram commemorates the death and not the resurrection of a historical hero, it has borrowed from fertility ritual the concept of the sacrificial god. Hussein dies yearly so that his followers might win salvation in his name."[38] Jessie Weston in 1920 also mentions "Muharram" in conjunction with the dying gods, as does Jane Harrison in 1921.[39] Such associations with a dying god are not just impressionistic. The *Encyclopaedia of Islam* (1913) tracks down similarities of Mohurram with older practices:

> It is possible that ancient rites of earlier mythological festivals like the Tammuz and Adonis cults have survived in the subsidiary plays which in India have been adapted by some Sunnis and even Hindus; the banners for the procession, a large staff, the hand of Husain which was cut off, have thus their ancient prototypes. That the significance of the sacred properties has altered is shown by the fact that among the Shi'i Tatars the *tabut* [tazia] is called "the marriage house of Kasim." In many places there are accompanying rites with water, which were originally indigenous; the throwing of the *tabut* into water among the Indian Shi'is may be due to Hindu influence.[40]

Because Forster lists the tazias along with the ten-day baskets of corn, I believe that he consciously associates Husain as well as Krishna with Adonis. He can thus show that both Krishna worship and Shiism have compassion on a central figure done to death by violence, creating an atmosphere of sympathy for Aziz unjustly accused. Whether Forster knew that anyone referred to a tazia as a "marriage house," he may have known that one of the most popular dramas at Mohurram stages the death of a young bridegroom, Husain's son.[41] Like Krishna's frequent desertion of his milk-maids, a Moslem wedding spoiled takes realistic account of the actual relations between potential partners, England and India, and therefore between Fielding and Aziz, whose friendship must be postponed.

The second Moslem version of the dying god after Husain is the decapitated saint mentioned at the end of the book (295–97). Aziz's garden happens to enclose the Shrine of the Body, and the meeting between Aziz and Fielding after a two-year estrangement takes place in the Shrine of the Head. The saint's story adheres to two requirements of the dying god: he dies dismembered, and his marriage rite recurs year after year. Although Forster does not recreate any overt marriage rite, it exists in what I believe to be a source for Forster's saint, in Martin's *Gods of India*; marriage as the goal of the saint's worship remains implicit in Forster's more elliptical evocation. Martin's account makes Forster's implicit references to marriage clearer.

With his head and body distributed to separate shrines, the saint resembles Osiris scattered in fourteen pieces by Set, or Dionysus chopped up by the Titans. He also resembles the hero Orpheus, whose cult probably derives from Dionysus's.[42] When the Maenads tear the Greek musician limb from limb, his head goes on singing as it floats away. If Krishna with his flute is the Hindu Orpheus (as Forster read in Havell), this saint with his head under his arm, sauntering to his mother's house, is a kind of Moslem Orpheus. Forster again provides echoes between Hindusim and Islam, as if hoping to reconcile the antagonistic faiths. Thematically, the separation of a head from its shoulders is as unnatural as the estrangement of Aziz from Fielding.

Forster reports that "Shrines of the Head and of the Body were shown at Dhar. The architecture of the Shrine of the Head was suggested by a building on a hill near Bihar."[43] In addition to deriving details of place from actual travels, he appears to have drawn details of story from *The Gods of India*. Martin describes a Mohammedan "saint," Ghazi Miyan or Sayyid Salar Masaud, warrior against the Hindus, now unexpectedly revered by more Hindus than Moslems.[44] Similarly, Forster's saint is "worshipped by the few Mohammedans who live near, and by Hindus also" (296). This example of enmity giving way to common worship undoubtedly appealed to Forster, though Martin grants the Hindus only resignation, not reconciliation. Martin adds that a stone slab with the image of the sun on it lies by the edge of a tank, next to the battlefield where Ghazi Miyan died. The warrior's head rests on this image whose "material" worship he vowed to destroy in favor of the "spiritual sun."[45] Martin does not specify if that head remains attached to the rest of the corpse, but his wording suggests it is severed. Like Ghazi Miyan disturbed at picturing the sun as a deity, Aziz at first scorns the shrine as "idolatrous," but he gets used to its "crop of lamps and flowers" (296).

Martin further explains that Ghazi Miyan's marriage is reenacted in his chief ceremony, where pilgrims carry toy beds on top of bundles of clothing and pots. Then women pour water from jars into a reservoir, where the diseased can bathe their foreheads or even their whole bodies, praying, "Saint, send the wave to us."[46] For Forster's saint we do not see any pilgrimage, but Aziz's dunking in the Mau tank cures him finally of his resentments; in a refreshing collaboration of religions, Krishna's servitor with the tray seems to start the wave that collides with the boats carrying Aziz and the British visitors (315).

The rites for Krishna recall the Adonis Festival to Forster, and Mohurram preserves aspects of the cults for Tammuz in the tazias. In addition, Forster knows from Martin how Ghazi Miyan's marriage evokes the vegetation gods. Martin speculates that the observances for Ghazi Miyan's marriage "may also be a continuation of the ancient marriage of the Earth and the Sun, celebrated to promote fertility of the crops."[47] Forster likewise pictures "earth and sky leant toward one another, about to clash in ecstasy," just when Fielding and Aziz will soon make up their differences (306). But Forster is concerned not so much that crops should grow better as that loneliness should end. If he does not mention marriage for his fictional saint, a mood of longing nevertheless hovers over his shrines, as Forster continues the marriage imagery of fertilizing waters. The Shrine of the Head where the meeting with Fielding takes place overlooks the Shrine of the Body in Aziz's garden, echoing Aziz's earlier assertion that an ablution tank at his mosque overlooks and feeds a pool in Fielding's garden (71). Even if Aziz's assertion about the mosque as source is wrong, his fanciful verson of water flowing uphill and the arrangement of the two shrines both imply that the waters of friendship should flow reciprocally from one man to the other, as the soothing rains fall from sky to earth.

Because Aziz leads a disastrous picnic like Krishna, and suffers a form of martyrdom like Husain and the saint, and because those religious figures resemble Adonis and Tammuz, Forster also pushes Aziz into some of the footsteps of the dying gods. Aziz imitates them in suffering, longing, and renewal. Eclipsed through his experience in a cave, which turns to a prison, as a Tammuz or a Christ is entombed in a cavern, Aziz is finally drawn out and reinstated.[48] Prison shatters him, like the gods dismembered, and his resulting suspicions eventually separate him from his friend Fielding. Nevertheless, like the gods renewed, he at least partially reintegrates himself with Fielding and Adela Quested after his unexpected dip in the lake, releasing his resentments. Although he has seethed for years against Adela's delusion that made her accuse him, he suddenly focuses on her recovery of sense: "As I fell into our largest Mau tank under circumstances our other friends will relate, I thought how brave Miss Quested was" (317).

These "circumstances" are particularly interesting in the light of vegetation myths. When the two English boats collide, Stella, unbalanced, flings herself against Aziz and capsizes herself, him, Fielding, and Ralph into the shallow water: "The oars, the sacred tray, the letters of Ronny and Adela, broke loose and floated confusedly. Artillery was fired, drums beaten, the elephants trumpeted, and drowning all an immense peal of thunder, unaccompanied by lighting, cracked like a mallet on the dome" (315). Although critics sometimes speak of this dunking as a "baptism,"[49] it becomes so only in the sense in which Joseph Campbell explains baptism as a "variant of the sacred marriage": "The popular interpretation of baptism is that it 'washes away original sin,' with emphasis rather on the cleansing than on the rebirth idea. This is a secondary interpretation. Or if the traditional birth image is remembered, nothing is said of an antecedent marriage." Campell sees the baptismal water as a representation of amniotic fluid. He discovers the "antecedent marriage" preceding rebirth in the Catholic ceremony for blessing the baptismal font at Easter. The priest repeatedly dips a lighted paschal candle, which Campbell interprets as a phallic sign, into the font, "female water spiritually fructified with the male fire of the Holy Ghost."[50]

Forster similarly emphasizes the need for the antecedent marriage. He uses water as both a female and a male symbol, representing the water that "breaks" before birth, and semen; despite these variations, water is always associated with sexuality. Aziz emerges from the water-womb as a new man, but he also courts sacred "marriages," symbolic but still sensually portrayed, with Mrs. Moore and Fielding. He claims to love Mrs. Moore, and their association breeds Aziz's forgiveness of Adela; this joining could also propagate a better understanding between East and West than present politics allow. Forster delicately hints at their "intercourse" by showing Mrs. Moore move out of the shadow toward Aziz, "keeping the ablution tank between them," where the ablution tank offers the same receptivity as the baptismal font (20). When Aziz hears "Radhakrishna" alternating with "Esmiss Esmoor," the latter "syllables of salvation" couple the Miss and the Moor, by echoing Aziz-and-Moore in the same way that the Hindu chant links the god with the milkmaid and announces their union (314). Similarly, Aziz "marries" Fielding by imagining water from his mosque inseminating Fielding's garden: Forster grants them at least symbolic homosexual union. When the two men ride their horses together, which rear against each other, they hear "after a silence—myriads of kisses around them as the earth drew the water in" (319).

If Forster brings in both heterosexual and homosexual love through his imagery, he in fact beautifully "marries" everyone to everything else in the grand capsizing. The water douses Stella, Aziz, Ralph, and Fielding all together. Aziz accepts Ralph, Fielding recovers a friend in Aziz, and Stella virtually embraces Aziz too. Moreover, she can, afterward, respond to her husband more readily, once she has herself enacted the parting of the font: Fielding had regretted that Stella did not want sex as much as he, but after their release through the soaking, their marriage is "blessed." Apparently the marriage is newly blessed not so much with a child (they already have one, according to Ronny's letter), as with new enjoyment (319). One might say that by precipitating all into the lake Stella Moore becomes again "Stella Maris," Star of the Sea, not as the epithet fell for a time to the Virgin Mary, but as it adorned its original owners, the sexually active goddesses "Isis, Ishtar, Aphrodite, Venus, Mari-Anna."[51] Similarly, Stella's mother, Mrs. Moore, precipitated the action of the whole novel by stepping into the mosque.

Such a glorious universal wedding of Stella, Fielding, Aziz, Ralph, earth, and puddles deserves the paeans from beating drums and trumpeting elephants! As if in answer to Eliot's *The Waste Land* two years earlier, in which the thunder in Indian words announces but does not quite loose its rain over a "prison" and a "boat" in the last stanzas, Forster's peal of thunder here accompanies a downpour. Yet Forster is as aware as Eliot that the earth will parch again, that Adonis will be gored, that Fielding and

Aziz must part. But at least the cycle, no longer arrested in what Eliot presents as permanent modern sterility, moves for Forster.

As the old myths balanced a goddess with a god, Forster is careful to develop Mrs. Moore as an ironic dying god (disappointing but still somehow satisfying) to the same extent that he casts Aziz in that role. She receives exuberant apotheosis and then resurrection as she "reincarnates" in Adela. When Aziz's supporters chant their ludicrous, wonderful praise to "Esmiss Esmoor," they elevate her into a minor Hindu goddess (225). Alarming to Ronny, multiple tombs spring up, and legends flourish: "an Englishman had killed his mother for trying to save an Indian's life" or "Sometimes it was a cow that had been killed—or a crocodile with the tusks of a boar had crawled out of the Ganges" (256). Killing a revered Indian cow would be as bad as killing a mother, or killing mother India—which the English have in a sense been attempting. The fanciful rumor of the crocodile is also revealing, bringing back all the ambiguity that attends the dying god. Is it good or bad that a boar kills Adonis, since his death marks new growth? Is it good or bad that her death sets the crocodiles crawling? In the context of Indian mythology, a boar in the Ganges might be comforting, because Vishnu, the same god who takes human form as Krishna, once adopted the form of a boar to dive into a universal flood and bring the earth up from the depths on his supporting tusks.[52]

This fantastic crocodile also echoes the other crocodiles in the Ganges, which eat the dead bodies disposed there. Ronny reports this gruesome fact as Adela and Mrs. Moore watch a radiance below: "It belonged neither to water nor to moonlight, but stood like a luminous sheaf upon the fields of darkness" (32). The young people choose to laugh at Mrs. Moore's "gentle creeps" when she shivers, "What a terrible river! what a wonderful river!" Yet her broad vision then, able to recognize the good things of life (represented in a Frazerian image of plenty, a sheaf) and the bad, both in one glance, already qualifies her as that Hindu "goddess" she becomes.

A British official, Mr. McBryde, who has no notion that "the gods contribute to the great gods, and they to the philosophic Brahm" (257), can only mock such superstition, but Forster perceives the profundity along with the idiocy of adding Esmiss Esmoor to the pantheon. In the most esoteric Hinduism, all the gods, including both Krishna and Vishnu, are openly admitted to be only the mind's projections and approximations, stepping stones toward the unimaginable Absolute, Brahman. Thus in his review of *The Gods of India*, Forster specifies an important reason why the worshipers throw Krishna into the dissolving water:

Krishna and Shiva slither into the void. Nothing is more remarkable than the way in which Hinduism will suddenly dethrone its highest conceptions, nor is anything more natural, because it is athirst for the inconceiv-

able. Whatever can be stated must be temporary. "The gods and goddesses," writes Mr. Martin, "are largely self-condemned," and so, in a very
profound sense, they are. They are steps toward the eternal. To a Protes-
tant, such an arrangement seems scandalous.[53]

Why shouldn't Mrs. Moore be such a stepping stone? Calling her a goddess
is a way of loving people, of finding the divine in everyone. A Hindu like
Godbole knows very well that all gods "reside in the human breast" (to
borrow Blake's phrase): he knows that he must call Krishna for Mrs. Moore,
and, even more significant, that *he* as Krishna must respond by generating
love.

Like a dying god, Mrs. Moore grows larger than life, and she maintains a
mysterious presence after her death. Aziz fancies that she appears in court,
and he refuses to believe the news that she has died (253, 255). Her assertion
that Aziz is innocent, nonchalantly thrown out, takes life in Adela when the
young woman finally clears Aziz at the trial (233). As if Mrs. Moore had
reincarnated in Adela, the crowds confuse the two women, addressing
Adela as Mrs. Moore and garlanding her like some fertility queen. Mrs.
Moore has, in effect, performed a bit of unlikely marrying: reconciling the
Moslem mob, at least temporarily, with their most hated adversary, the
British, in the person of Adela.

Ellin Horowitz observes interestingly that Forster even has Mrs. Moore
die at sea, so that "like the vegetation god her body is cast on the water."[54]
Yet Horowitz mistakes Forster's purpose in associating Mrs. Moore with the
dying god. First Horowitz misinterprets Mrs. Moore's negative apathy as
positive detachment: "With the mystical experience in the cave, resembling
the state of Nirvana, Mrs. Moore is transformed into a kind of sacrificial
god."[55] The Buddha may well have required a person to sacrifice her
desires, but Nirvana requires no "sacrificial god." Second, Horowitz converts a dying son god into a kind of sop for an angry father god: "Just as the
Christian community is joined and revitalized in partaking of the body and
the blood of the sacrificial god, so Mrs. Moore after death becomes merged
with (or influences) the major characters, creating a union out of conflict and
bringing the rain of Part III. . . . The English rape of India finds symbolic
atonement in the death of an Englishwoman to save an Indian accused of
raping an Englishwoman."[56] James McConkey similarly exacts an eye for an
eye and insists on tarring all sufferers as evil, almost blaming Mrs. Moore for
not achieving a Wordsworthian oneness with nature: Mrs. Moore "must die
through spiritual exhaustion—and this is achieved in the cave and not in her
actual death on the sea—in order that a new birth, a new growth, may be
achieved . . . *must die*—for the earth has become alien to man; the God, the
order, the unity, which had been perceived through that earth must perforce
be discovered again."[57]

Yet there is an important difference between Forster's recognition that suffering *does* exist, and Horowitz's and McConkey's easy requirement that it *must* exist. Horowitz welcomes suffering in a mood altogether too sanguine, indeed, sanguinary: "Forster has drawn upon the cyclic pattern of fertility ritual as an objective correlative for his vision of conflict, political and spiritual, and the life-giving nature of conflict itself," as if Forster were glad about an English and Indian clash because of all the "life" that would supposedly come out of bigotry and political subjection.[58] On the contrary, Forster does not approve conflict and suffering in themselves, as if they were invigorating exercises. Instead, he firmly rejects any "homage to pain":

[Forster] is out of sympathy with Eliot's adherence to the Buddhist (as well as the Christian) belief in the relation between action and suffering— ". . . action is suffering / And suffering action"; "Our only health is the disease . . . to be restored, our sickness must grow worse." Commenting on the Eliot of "Little Gidding" he remarked: "How I dislike his homage to pain! . . . It is here that Eliot becomes unsatisfactory as a seer, as Coventry does as a shrine."[59]

But after shunning a kind of masochism he detects in Buddhism and Christianity, Forster can still find validity in the violence and suffering he encounters in the legends of Krishna, Husain, the saint of the two shrines, and Adonis. To Forster these figures do not add to the pain of existence but rather admit and accept the pain that cannot be avoided. In fact, after his reference to the baskets of ten-day corn, Forster had originally written in the manuscript, "Why this sacrifice at the heart of creation? To ask this question is to be sensible, but none who asks it will make passage to India."[60] He implies that life depends on a sad round of deaths, but he refuses to devalue fleshly life because of its harsh necessities. Forster possibly omits the line because "sacrifice" *is* too close to "propitiation," or because sadness (rather than sacrifice) and passing beyond sadness emerge so clearly in Forster's discreet allusions to dying gods.

Aziz and Mrs. Moore can serve as dying gods because they both suffer and they both fitfully reach out toward the marriages that Forster envisions. Yet both are limited. They hardly attain divine stature, as Aziz lapses into peevishness and Mrs. Moore into a disappointing apathy. She misses her chance for heroism when she refuses to testify to Aziz's good character in court and even flunks the chance to counsel Adela to recant. These failures, however, make up one of Forster's most gracious gestures. He casts his characters as dying gods but refrains from manufacturing unbelievable saints. Instead, he sees the divine in the human more as potentiality than fact, a call for us to love each other despite our failings.

If the grand religious figures behind Mrs. Moore and Aziz admit loss and loneliness, both also go on snatching their brief moments of love, before the lover evades their grasp like water evaporating. Forster's vision of love encompasses everything from a lowly herdsboy, perhaps homosexually wishing to feel Krishna pillowed on his lap, to the soul struggling for union with God. Forster extensively uses marriage imagery to represent not only human passion but divine communion for all three major religions in the book, Hinduism, Islam, and Christianity. Those traveling Krishna's path of *bhakti* hope to reach God through love. Sufis believe in union of human and God through *Ishq*, or love.[61] Aziz quotes a poem by the Sufi Ghalib: "Less explicit than the call to Krishna, it voiced our loneliness neverthe-less, our isolation, our need for the Friend who never comes yet is not entirely disproved" (106). Significantly, while Aziz knows that "the Friend" is "a Persian expression for God" (227), Ghalib's poem leaves Aziz "thinking about women again" (106). Mysticism expresses divine love through sensual metaphor but sometimes sanctions real earthly love as a step to the divine, and Forster insists on moving from one level to the other and back without restrictions.

To keep to his dominant imagery of marriage when he speaks of the Judeo-Christian God, he alludes to Psalm 19:5, in which the Lord strides through nature like a bridegroom, an image that draws on vegetation gods.[62] But like the elusive Persian Friend or the straying Krishna, Jeho-vah, who should rise sunlike as a "bridegroom coming out of his cham-ber," lies back impotently. He loses his "virtue," a word whose etymology in *vir*, "man," Forster insists on:

> But at the supreme moment, when night should have died and day lived, nothing occurred. It was as if virtue had failed in the celestial fount. . . . Why, when the chamber was prepared, did the bridegroom not enter with trumpets and shawms, as humanity expects? The sun rose without splendour. He was presently observed trailing yellowish behind the trees, or against insipid sky, and touching the bodies already at work in the fields. (137)

Important as our usually frustrated human cravings for the divine are to Forster, he can parody even the loftiest call to Krishna or Husain or Jeho-vah or the Friend. Right after Godbole sings to an absent Krishna (80), Ronny commands a servant named Krishna who "had not turned up" (97), and a few pages later Aziz "called to Hassan to clear up, but Hassan, who was testing his wages by ringing them on the step of the verandah, found it possible not to hear him; heard and didn't hear, just as Aziz had called and hadn't called" (101). While Husain is the central martyr honored at Mohur-ram, tazias also represent his brother Hassan, so that Aziz travesties the call of the Mohurram worshipers in his command to the servant. Whether servant, saint, or god, our heart's desire both hears and does not hear: he almost appears not to exist—except at exquisite, fleeting moments.

Poking fun at his most serious desires for human friend and divine Friend by means of the scenes with servants, Forster emulates the God who can "play practical jokes upon Himself, draw chairs away from beneath His own posteriors, set His own turbans on fire, and steal His own petticoats when He bathes" (289). Forster's ability to perceive call, coming, and eclipse, perfect marriage and perfunctory death, all as elaborate parts of a cosmic game (sometimes in bad taste but sometimes tender), makes Forster almost unique among modern authors who allude to dying gods. Few have seen them as funny. Forster recognizes the dying gods as poignant, terrible, but able to provoke real, joyous laughter if (in the words of a comically misprinted sign) "God si love" (285).

The myths of the dying gods that Forster stations so understatedly but firmly behind Hindu ceremonies, Moslem ceremonies, and Moslem and English characters represent both a willingness to suffer, if necessary, whatever pain is already inherent in existence, and an unquenchable will to rejoice, despite all the sadness: whether threat of crocodile, bother of eye flies, or disappointment in a Mrs. Moore who fails to support Aziz in court. Moreover, dying gods as the common denominator connecting Hindu, Moslem, and English reveal unexpected unities and potential. Dying gods thus serve to deny the assumed differences—political, religious, and sexual—through which both British imperial power and British moral dictates about sexuality operated in Forster's day.

Coppola

The film *Apocalypse Now* (1979) draws heavily on literary sources. Director Francis Ford Coppola, who coauthored the script with John Milius, most obviously borrows from Joseph Conrad's *Heart of Darkness*. As Conrad's Marlow follows a river in Africa to find a mysterious Kurtz, a European colonizer who has reverted to "primitivism," Coppola's Army Special Forces Captain Willard searches upriver during the Vietnam war for a renegade Colonel Kurtz. The U.S. Army has assigned Willard to "terminate" Kurtz after the colonel takes the war into his own hands, carries out his own executions, and sets himself up as an idol to Cambodian villagers.

Besides *Heart of Darkness*, Coppola alludes to other literary predecessors. The camera obligingly pans over Colonel Kurtz's book shelves to display the colonel's favorites: *Holy Bible*, Frazer's *The Golden Bough*, Weston's *From Ritual to Romance*. Frazer's human representative of the dying god, who willingly undergoes the god's violent death in order to bequeath some good to the community, appears in an ambiguous version in Kurtz. An early reviewer explains that Colonel Kurtz, like Frazer's divine kings, would rather die before sickness impairs his powers.[63] But there is more to Coppola's parallels with Frazer than the colonel's desire to preempt the ravages of malaria.

With his heavily ironic comparisons to dying gods, Coppola elaborately links renegade and government brutality. By mocking Colonel Kurtz's claim to be a god, Coppola simultaneously condemns the United States for its arrogant war in Vietnam. The so-called sane conduct of war exactly mirrors every "insane" act of Colonel Kurtz. Official camouflage paint duplicates Kurtz's magic paint. Nevertheless, after Coppola indicates that Kurtz and the official agents of the government conducting the war are equally unworthy of their godlike life and death powers, Coppola distinguishes between the two butchers, army and Kurtz, to make Kurtz slightly superior. When he consciously permits the captain to assassinate him in the same way that the dying god willingly goes down, the colonel actually does bequeath one small but important "good" to the community: honesty.

The director prepares us to perceive Kurtz's pretensions to godhead by means of several scenes with cows, bulls, or beef. First, the camera juxtaposes a priest saying mass against a helicopter transporting a cow tied to a rope. Just as the priest intones, "our father in heaven," we see something in those heavens. At that point we may conclude that a dangling animal substitutes ironically for the Lord, a ludicrous travesty. But when Coppola instructs us through the view of the book shelf to brush up on Frazer, the bull becomes less a jarring "new" replacement for a god and more a dignified old replacement for one.

Frazer's dying gods are likely to incarnate themselves simultaneously in human and animal form. The dying god Dionysus in particular took the form of a bull when the Titans tore him apart.[64] Colonel Kurtz, with his assumption of godly prerogatives, dies at the same moment that his followers sacrifice a bull. The camera eerily alternates between the Cambodian's machete slicing into the animal's neck, in slow motion, and the captain's machete slicing into Kurtz. Frazer's equation of animal and human forms of a god thus corroborates the inference of Kurtz's claim to "divinity," which the viewer also senses from a juxtaposition of scenes: helicoptered cow with the priest's mass and sacrificed bull with the captain's assassination of Kurtz.

This imagery of the bull-god appears in another important scene, the supper when Willard receives his assignment. The officer who labels Kurtz crazy and evil, while reserving to himself all reason and right, pointedly eats beef, over which the camera lingers with an ulterior motive that we cannot yet fathom. Frazer, though, informs us that eating a slain ox meant eating the bull-god, which in turn meant partaking of the nature of the god.[65] When all the men at the table help themselves to the meat whose animal donor we see slaughtered at the end of the film, they eucharistically partake of the nature of Kurtz. The viewer can comprehend this point just by acquaintance with the Christian communion, but knowing Frazer helps, because the primitive roots of the eucharist have generally been forgotten. By the time we understand that the rampaging Kurtz is a bull-god, we know, in retrospect, that these eaters, ingesting Kurtz's animal sign, participate in the insanity of war. Moreover, the close-up lens escorts the viewer uncomfortably near to the table, thereby asking us if we too have the same capacity to brutalize.

Putting himself in the same camp as the other beef-eaters, Kilgore holds a grotesque Texas barbeque after he has blasted a village. The atmosphere of a picnic affronts the gravity of death, while the carnivorous chomping reveals Kilgore's allegiance to the bull-god Kurtz. Kilgore thinks that he contrasts with Kurtz, but the imagery betrays him.

Several other details besides bulls reinforce the allusions to dying gods. In one celebrated scene, Kilgore pilots a bombing mission while a tape recording in the aircraft belts out Wagner's "Ride of the Valkyries." In the twentieth century, after the Nazis' use of Wagner in their propaganda, we can hardly hear this music without being reminded of Nazi atrocities. Playing the bombastic tape punctures the inflated claim of Kilgore and his government to police the world. Furthermore, because in Germanic mythology the Valkyries rode into battle selecting soldiers who would die, Kilgore unwittingly fills his helicopter with voices that announce only doom: the loss of individual soldiers and the failure of the whole U.S. engagement in Vietnam.

The Valkyries wanted the ghosts of valiant warriors in the first place to swell the ranks that would fight on the side of the gods against the giants at the end of time. The gods kept touting this wholehearted preparedness for war, even though all their oracles clearly predicted that no defense buildup could prevent the "twilight of the gods" in their mutual slaughter with the ice giants. Although the Germanic gods Odin and Thor, corrupted through violence and greed, were expected to die only once at the "twilight," the god Balder—whose goodness made him an early casualty—was supposed to return out of the underworld to start a new society after the seemingly final cataclysm.[66] "Ride of the Valkyries" makes us wonder whether Willard, emerging at the end from his experience of the war's hell, can be a Balder, or whether he will remain part of the reigning corrupt hierarchy.

Even the gruesome severed head that Colonel Kurtz deposits in the captain's lap does not just rattle the moviegoer gratuitously but suggests another Frazerian motif. Like John the Baptist's head brought in on a platter, this grisly offering announces the future death of a claimant to divinity. Like the vegetation gods, dying one year only to repeat the ordeal another year, John the Baptist dies to announce yet another agony, Christ's. In *Apocalypse Now*, the head dumped on the captain's lap so repulses him that he cries out, "Christ," in anguish—and in explanation. With the Bible and *The Golden Bough* side by side, Coppola focuses, as does Frazer, on similarities between Christ who died and arose once (but with a predecessor, John) and the gods of primitive cultures who died and revived repeatedly. The motif of "head on a platter" helps signal Kurtz's self-inflation to the position of Christ and any dying god. The head also signals a series of forerunners and successors: the unwillingly beheaded Chef, the willingly dying Kurtz, and perhaps the captain as successor.

In what sense can Willard assume Kurtz's role as dying god? Is this repetition good or bad? The captain, slinking down hallways with his machete, recalls Frazer's opening scene of sacred king stalking sacred king "with a glitter of steel at the shoulder."[67] Because the assassin whom Frazer discusses takes over the role of divine king, Colonel Kurtz's death becomes a ceremony of succession, a kind of "passing of the mantle." The metaphoric mantle enfolds nothing: first one "hollow man," Kurtz, and now another, Willard. (Colonel Kurtz recites from T. S. Eliot's poem "The Hollow Men"; Eliot pays homage to Conrad in the epigraph to that poem: "Mistah Kurtz—he dead.") Certainly Willard has revealed a core as hollow as Kurtz's when he cold-bloodedly shoots a wounded woman so that caring for her will not slow down his mission to rid the world of an uncaring Kurtz.

We already know that Willard faces his greatest enemy internally; at the beginning of the film, when the flashback narration shows him debating his new mission, he gets drunk and slugs his own reflection in a mirror. Nevertheless, as in Tezcatlipoca's mirror that reveals truth by its distortions, Willard begins to see himself most clearly once he has destroyed his shiny official image as "unquestioning special agent," by putting himself into the shattering experience of a trip upriver to Kurtz.

At the end of that voyage of self-discovery, Willard may inherit more than Kurtz's emptiness. Kurtz contains a small nugget of truth that prevents him from being completely hollow and permits him to bequeath to the community—including Willard and the audience—a few small benefits, just as Frazer's primitive god died to bestow some good. By mirroring the official war-makers all along (same war paint, strut, and taste for bulls), Colonel Kurtz exposes, writ large, what people have projected as their highest goal and good—which is what gods have always done. Furthermore, Colonel Kurtz demonstrates one real (not ironic) godly virtue, honesty. Unlike the officers who eat their beef hypocritically, not admitting the craziness and evil of their own acts of war, Colonel Kurtz at least admits that he is a worshiper of brute force.

Conrad's Marlow, appalled as he is by Kurtz's collection of heads on stakes, grudgingly admires his ability to speak the truth. When Conrad's Kurtz dies with the words "the horror" on his lips, he confesses that he himself is horrible, along with head-hunting tribes and the European colonizers who are their equally murderous successors. Marlow prefers Kurtz's truth-telling to European lying, which sentimentalizes the colonial enterprise—a failure that Marlow himself shares when he sentimentally lies to Kurtz's fiancée, claiming that her betrothed's last words were her name. Coppola also prefers Kurtz's honesty to the government's gloss of "pacification" or "a just war." Colonel Kurtz's ability to admit the possibility of evil confers a glimmer of godlike dignity.

Now that we and the captain have seen the degradation of the government and potentially of ourselves, presumably we will not resign ourselves to it. The captain inherits the mantle from Kurtz, but he does not just sling it around his shoulders, though Kurtz's followers are quite willing to bow down to him in turn. With his own murders behind him, of the wounded woman and of other official targets, the captain knows very well that he mirrors Kurtz. Yet he walks out of the jungle. His action pleads that despite our sinister potential, we can also walk away.

7

Celebrating Sexuality with Isis

One of the most important reasons why modern authors return so readily and persistently to vegetation myths is that fertility gods and goddesses frankly enjoyed their sexuality. Jehovah, by contrast, spurned any goddess, and his priests and prophets seemed, to some interpreters, either to condemn sex outright or to tolerate it only grudgingly.

Lawrence and Faulkner draw on vegetation myths in part to praise sexuality. A failure to understand which myths they use and how they transform them has led to a few misreadings. By placing Faulkner too exclusively in a Christian tradition rather than a mixed, pagan-Christian one, some critics have mistakenly assumed that he judges sexuality "the chief sign of man's fallen nature."[1] Although Lawrence proclaims himself a "priest of love," he modifies the myths of Quetzalcoatl, Osiris, and Adonis in such a way as to endow the corresponding goddesses with less power and control (in their sexual lives and other ways) than one might assume. The new versions of the myths created by Lawrence also have political implications that link him to the interests of the authors in chapters 5 and 6.

Lawrence

D. H. Lawrence uses the dying gods as metaphors for individuals or whole civilizations in need of rebirth. According to Lawrence's diagnosis, the West has been mortally undermined by too much abstract thinking, moneygrubbing in mechanical environments, and slandering of sex by Christianity. Moreover, Lawrence concludes that intellect, used to produce technology for World War I, has only made the world deadlier. William Troy suspects that Lawrence may even have cast himself as a contemporary dying god, suffering because of his benighted peers and attempting to revive his moribund society.[2] In any case, Lawrence does gravitate to the mystery religions to express the devastation that both he and Europe feel during the war: "My heart is quartered into a thousand fragments, and I shall never have the energy to collect the bits—like Osiris—or Isis."[3]

Lawrence depends on the myths of the dying gods for plot, detail, and meaning in a cluster of late works: *The Plumed Serpent*, "The Woman Who Rode Away," *Lady Chatterley's Lover*, *The Man Who Died*, "The Risen Lord," "The Flying Fish," and *Apocalypse*. He focuses on Quetzalcoatl, Osiris, Adonis, and Jesus (whose story he always combines with that of a pagan dying god). Usually, the death of a god symbolizes for Lawrence an internal, personal change: the death of old beliefs followed by rebirth into a new, fuller life. He also proposes how he would reactivate myth in a social realm; for example, in *The Plumed Serpent* the "men of Quetzalcoatl" are trying to construct a new society. Lawrence sometimes gives up on reform to imagine the outright elimination of whole groups of people—assertive women, blue-eyed whites, all Europeans. In his temporary, belligerent moods, Lawrence shockingly converts the death of the god into longed-for, human deaths. Although he expends his fury on the page and not at the barricades, and although he probably still wants us to interpret his cataclysms as symbols for painful psychological growth, he alarmingly depicts the violence as literal.

Whether he is pursuing his psychological or his cultural programs, Lawrence frequently casts his female characters—Kate, the woman who rode away, Connie—as dying gods. Although he may simultaneously compare them to eternal goddesses, he makes sure they enact the function of the god too, the one who dies. Lawrence assigns the women what he thinks of as first billing (the role of Osiris rather than Isis) for two reasons. He vests extra hope in women to revitalize the world, particularly by their sexual energy. But at other times Lawrence is not so flattering. Because he feels that women have agitated too much for intellectual and political rights, he puts female characters into his otherwise revered role of dying god almost as if to ensure their eclipse, with only subdued women allowed to imitate the deity's return.

Inspired by visits to Mexico and New Mexico and by wide reading, Lawrence adopted Quetzalcoatl as the explicitly named, presiding deity in *The Plumed Serpent* (1926). William York Tindall documents Lawrence's foraging in the works of James Frazer, Edward Tylor, and Jane Harrison; William Prescott's *Conquest of Mexico* and several other histories and travelogues; *Anales del Museo Nacional*; Lewis Spence's *Gods of Mexico*; and especially Zelia Nuttall's *Fundamental Principles of Old and New World Civilization*.[4] Quetzalcoatl, the plumed serpent, was a peaceable Toltec deity whose worship the invading Aztecs distorted but preserved in an uneasy relationship with their own deities: Tezcatlipoca, a trickster god pictured as alternating in power with Quetzalcoatl, and Huitzilopochtli, god of war. Lawrence makes a few changes in the Mexican myths. He ignores Tezcatlipoca as Quetzalcoatl's main partner and teams the feathered serpent instead with Huitzilopochtli. L. D. Clark observes that one of

Lawrence's sources, Nuttall, derives the war-god's name from both "hummingbird" and "resuscitated," so that Lawrence may have grouped the two feathered gods because both of them possessed the ability to revive.[5]

The legends of Quetzalcoatl offer contradictory explanations for his periodic departure. Lewis Spence traces Quetzalcoatl's origin to a "Man of the Sun, who has quitted his abode for a season for the purpose of inculcating in mankind those arts which represent the first steps in civilisation, who fulfils his mission, and who, at a late period, is displaced by the deities of an invading race."[6] Quetzalcoatl is said to have sailed away on a raft of serpents or immolated himself on a pyre or in a volcano, with his heart streaming up to become the morning star. The times when the morning star is invisible correspond to Quetzalcoatl's confinement in the underworld. Or, as an old man, a Toltec king Quetzalcoatl is supposed to have received some advice and a drink from the harbinger of a new Aztec culture, Tezcatlipoca, to ease his death: "You must go . . . where another old man awaits thee. He and thou shall speak together, and on thy return thou shalt be as a youth."[7] This passage from Spence may have inspired the conversation that Lawrence creates between a newly awakened Quetzalcoatl and an old and tired Jesus. Apparently Quetzalcoatl either follows the predictable cycles of the stars, to help nature, or else he heralds unpredictable cultural changes: "Whether Quetzalcoatl was rejected by men in their folly, or left the earth in obedience to the demands of a universal cycle, or was forced to leave because of his own weakness, is also unclear."[8]

Lawrence borrows Spence's idea of Quetzalcoatl as civilizer. He brings back Quetzalcoatl into an institutionalized religion to represent the need for overhauling all Western civilization. Second, he focuses on Quetzalcoatl's status as both bird and serpent to signal the reconciliation of mind and body that Lawrence sees as the central ingredient of that cultural rejuvenation. Third, Lawrence draws on Quetzalcoatl's shorter, star-linked disappearances to individualize the fate of the dying god in his characters—sketchily in Ramón but especially in Kate.

The Plumed Serpent is most successful—psychologically convincing and dramatically gripping—when it depicts Kate's "death" and rebirth as she enacts on a personal level the fate of a dying god. She expresses how deadened she felt in Europe by echoing Christ's line, "It is finished."[9] She often feels benumbed or dead in Mexico too but gradually realizes she might have to "die before dying," might have to take on the weight of an experience she first resents as oppressive, in order to sink back toward the natural roots in sexuality which she has lost (270).

Obviously Lawrence means us to see a symbolic death only, as Kate sloughs off erroneous beliefs. Yet he gets uncomfortably close to requiring real blood. Only after the attack on Ramón, when her wounded friend looks like a corpse and she herself has shed the blood of an attacker to save Ramón, does she exhibit "the face of one waking from the dead, curiously dipped in death, with a tenderness far more new and vulnerable than a child's" (343). Clark calls this scene "a descent into hell for both her and Ramón" and notes that "In the fight Ramón becomes a dying and resurrected god, sacrificed, since this is an Aztec land, not on a cross but with a knife."[10] When Kate comments, "Wonderful how people heal," Cipriano replies, "Yes. We did [apparently a misprint for "die"] very easily. But we also come quickly back to life" (338).

Despite this brief shift to Ramón as dying god during the attack, Kate serves as the main human representative. Following the death of her old self—possessive, abrasive, power-hungry—she needs to let a new self be born: softer, more intuitive, more aware of nature. A row boat takes her across a white, "spermy" lake in which votive pots have been thrown. After this conjunction of male and female symbols, the boat deposits her, presumably in embryo, on the farther shore (102). Her servant calls her "niña," child, meant to be mockery, but also a sign of newness and growth.

Kate matures slowly into the knowledge of Quetzalcoatl: the insight that spirit infuses nature rather than transcending it (as in the Judeo-Christian tradition) or disappearing altogether (as in modern scientific doubt). The book ends inconclusively, leaving us uncertain whether she will remain in Mexico or return to "rational" England. Her admiration for a newborn foal near the end of the novel tempts us to conclude that she, like the animal, has indeed just been born, into her new faith (447). By concentrating on the long gestation, on her doubts and ironic comments, Lawrence makes *The Plumed Serpent* suspenseful. Kate's gestation is more convincing than the sudden birth of the Quetzalcoatl religion, fully formed, in the second half of the book.

For in addition to putting Kate in the role of Quetzalcoatl, Lawrence makes this god the symbol of a larger cultural change. Because Christianity, Lawrence thinks, has validated only the intellect, while de-emphasizing the physical earth and the life of the body, he is ready to dismiss the institution in favor of Mexico's old gods, now updated. He renders this changing of the guard concretely and even tenderly by imagining a conversation in which Quetzalcoatl addresses Jesus as "brother" and invites him to retire "behind the sun" for a refreshing sleep. Quetzalcoatl in turn will "roll back the stone" for a new stint as culture-giver. Ramón strips the Christian icons from a church, rows them to an island, and burns them in a scene of surprisingly effective pathos. The island sacrifice possibly draws on the same rites for Tezcatlipoca that Conrad uses in *Nostromo*; elsewhere in *The Plumed Serpent* Lawrence mentions youths "plumped and perfumed," as they were for Tezcatlipoca's sacrifice (125). Lawrence's youths, through lack of self-awareness, let themselves be led to the slaughter (imposed by a materialistic society) of their more spiritual selves.

In Lawrence's rather simplistic view, Europe has developed its "head," whereas Mexico has favored "belly, breast, and loins" (398, 455). But in decrying European rationalism, Lawrence is not just advocating a new irrationalism. As much as he envies the American Indians their living religion, he admits, "I can't cluster at the drum any more."[11] Although it looks in *The Plumed Serpent* as if he is reverting to a contrived primitivism, with war paint, feathers, naked dancers, drums, and salutes, he cautions even here that the world cannot go back to some supposed unconscious bliss (153). Instead, he wants to combine thinker and natural man, "the sinking of both beings, into a new being" (455).

In a familiar romantic vein, Lawrence blends contraries as carefully as Blake mixed Reason and Energy and Nietzsche paired Apollo and Dionysus. Lawrence approves Quetzalcoatl's status as Morning Star because the star stands poised between opposites, night and day (101, 195). The god's name combines quetzal bird and serpent, again incorporating opposites in those animals' habitats of heaven and earth, standing for spirit and blood in Lawrence's scheme. In fact, inclusiveness and dynamic change come to characterize dying gods for Lawrence: "The morning-star was always a god, from the time when gods began. But when the cult of dying and reborn gods started all over the world, about 600 B.C., he became symbolic of the new god, because he rules in the twilight."[12]

Although Ramón's Quetzalcoatl-religion hallows both head and loins, the emphasis falls naturally on what Lawrence feels to be the neglected half of life, sexuality. Bringing the divine back really means preaching Lawrence's special credo of sex: "the clue to all living and to all moving on into new living lay in the vivid blood-relation between man and woman" (436). Mexicans might engage in sex more often, he thinks, but if they subjugate another person in a guilt-ridden atmosphere, the effect is just "suicide" (433). So people on both sides of the Atlantic have to be reborn into Lawrence's religion of "impersonal" sex. Couples will no longer covet a possessive togetherness, perpetually confessing and analyzing and talking out all thoughts. Instead, recognizing privacy and indeed an inevitable gulf between them, they meet in an "innermost belief" as well as in sex (298).

How will Ramón inculcate this new religion? People need to go back to their "roots" in sex, and they need a "Word" to awaken them (86). Lawrence here displays a typical nineteenth- and twentieth-century ambivalence toward speech. On the one hand, students of the "better" life should renounce words entirely (446) by looking at the stars or jumping into bed. On the other hand, he expects a Word, spoken by Ramón or, one suspects, by himself through literature, to renew all humanity. From the viewpoint of the late twentieth century, however, instituting his religion of a dying god entails several dangers: elitism, militarism, and sexism.

If spiritually lethargic materialists need a Word to wake them up, they may need an elite orator to speak it (148). Lawrence tries to deflect any accusations of egotism or tyranny on the part of the leader by having Ramón claim that his power derives not from a personal self but from "beyond" him or from a divine "middle" (80). Ramón further insists that worshipers of Quetzalcoatl do not set themselves up as "lords of men" but as "lords of themselves" (272). Still, despite their protestations and their adopted peasant clothes, both Ramón and Cipriano seem to me disturbingly to enjoy their power over others. Although Kate may need to suppress her unpalatable pride in hereditary aristocracy, an unpleasant misanthropy also taints Ramón's meritocracy. This emphasis on the few and even on the one, a Redeemer, has to be reckoned as a real danger of looking to a single human embodiment of a dying deity to save us, instead of interpreting the dying god as a representative of all mortals. With hindsight, Ramón's salute, his raised right hand, looks all too much like "Heil Hitler."

Two elements of the plot have led critics to accuse Lawrence of a "relish for cruelty": Cipriano's gorily realized execution of Ramón's attackers and especially Cipriano's shadowy but more devastating wars to spread Ramón's religion.[13] When Lawrence first encountered Aztec religion, he blamed the Aztecs for their many bloody sacrifices of slaves. In *Mornings in Mexico*, for example, he recoils from Aztec gods and goddesses, a grudging, "unlovely and unlovable lot," who "suck the smoking heart greedily with insatiable appetite."[14] In *The Plumed Serpent* he similarly calls the Aztecs' need for the blood of victims their "misinterpretation," an Aztec perversion of the earlier, gentler Toltec religion of Quetzalcoatl (135). Yet elsewhere in *The Plumed Serprent* he can accept the need for "the blood-unison of man, which made blood-sacrifice so potent a factor of life," without explaining just how far this blood-sacrifice should go (457).

Many critics think Lawrence goes too far in Cipriano's generalship. Frank Waters judges that the "Aztec vulgarization of Quetzalcoatl is what Lawrence fictionally restored to Mexico in *The Plumed Serpent*."[15] Graham Hough accuses Lawrence of "quasi-Fascist deifications of discipline."[16] Noting that Lawrence always connected social turmoil with a coming millennium, Scott Sanders admits that Lawrence entertained passing hopes from contradictory revolutions, briefly championing Mussolini's blackshirts and red-scarved communists alike.[17] Sanders adds, however, that facts soon disillusioned Lawrence. Tindall confronts Lawrence's bullying most directly: "His yearning for authority and obedience, his hatred of socialists, Catholics, and international financiers, his national religions with their pagan rites, his propaganda, symbols, and storm troopers, his attitude toward women and laborers, his desire to think with his blood, and the other ways in which he anticipated Hitler appear to justify those who have regarded Lawrence as a proto-fascist."[18] Yet Tindall finally defends Lawrence by claiming that Lawrence "wanted to destroy machines and money, not to control them. He desired a world without factories, capitalists, and proletariat, a world in which, as he called the turns, theosophists would dance tenderly about a sacred cow."[19] Nevertheless, if Tindall can defend Lawrence personally, we again have to reckon up a potential danger when Lawrence kowtows to a single representative of the dying god. Instead of concentrating on the god's sacrifice and what that means psychologically, Cipriano kills anyone who will not recognize his god or adhere to his program.

When "men would be men," as Lawrence dreams, the music starts sounding "almost martial" (383). Lawrence imagines an outlet for human aggressiveness in single combat. Yet Cipriano's care to avoid "trench and cannon" sounds decidedly naive (402). If the cults of Quetzalcoatl and Huitzilopochtli stir up the ranks to think they have to prove their manliness in combat, how can Cipriano possibly guarantee that his war will remain polite arm wrestling? In fact, Lawrence shows that Cipriano's war does expand, far beyond honorably pitting two willing combatants, into out-and-out civil war.

Ramón claims that he hates "will" and shuns "imposing" a religion, but when President Montes declares Quetzalcoatl the national god and outlaws dissenters, with Cipriano's troops to back him up, Ramón has, despite his best sentiments, entered the arena of clashing wills. Lawrence does not pursue the possibly tragic implications: if Ramón had feared to err on the side of the ravisher once he refuses to be further ravished (298), can the outbreak of war be traced to the inevitable working out of a tragic flaw in himself or his whole agenda, intending good but producing evil? Because Lawrence ends the book with Kate's dilemma, he abandons the equally fascinating denouement of Ramón's predicament. By focusing on Kate's personal problems, Lawrence also avoids speculating about the problems of civil war and tyranny for the country as a whole.

After he wrote *The Plumed Serpent*, Lawrence discards both the glorification of one elitist ruler and the martial spirit that might accompany his reign. In a letter to Witter Bynner in March, 1928, Lawrence revises his opinion:

The hero is obsolete, and the leader of men is a back number. . . . We're sort of sick of all forms of militarism and militantism, and *Miles* is a name no more, for a man. On the whole I agree with you, the leader-cum-follower relationship is a bore. And the new religion will be some sort of tenderness, sensitive, between men and men and men and women, and not the one up one down, lead on I follow, *ich dien* sort of business.[20]

Yet as Ross Parmenter observes, Lawrence never entirely renounces his hopes for a savior, returning to the ideal in *Apocalypse*: "one man is a leader, a master. It is inevitable. Accept it . . . give it homage, then there is a great joy, an uplifting, and a potency passed from the powerful to the less powerful."[21]

In addition to requiring an unsavory militarism, Lawrence's religion of the dying god looks sexist to modern readers. He defines a man as a "column of blood, with a voice in it" and a woman as a "valley of blood," with no mention of a voice for her (446, 457). Lawrence anticipates this possible objection by showing that Kate resents the omission and asks if the new religion would keep women mute (342). Cipriano equivocates that he could not keep a woman ignorant if she were not already stupid (226), yet Kate wonders in exasperation if the Quetzalcoatl-religion might require *her* as sacrifice (369). She definitely has to renounce assertive selfhood, but, in the rhetoric at least, so does her male partner: neither sex would own a "separate star" (425). Nevertheless, when Lawrence redefines what looks like "will" in Cipriano as simply "wish," he fails to convince us of Cipriano's humility (430).

In practice Cipriano and Ramón manage to keep more "self" and "stardom" than their female partners, simply because the men pursue an additional life outside their marriages. Furthermore, Lawrence's imagery retains a sexist tinge. To call the husband the arrow, phallic, and the wife the bow might seem anatomically natural, but the image has the advantage for Lawrence of allowing motion to the man while keeping the woman stationary, settled at home (426). At the services for Quetzalcoatl, Ramón forbids the men to kneel abjectly, as in Christianity; women, however, cannot similarly stand and in fact "crouch" (344, 372). Lawrence's notorious antipathy toward female orgasm—certainly surprising from a "priest of love"—is not just dislike for an "Aphrodite of the foam" who dares move in lovemaking but dislike for a "feline" woman who will "break the contact, and roam alone in a sense of power" (463, 480). The man, on the other hand, can certainly move, both in lovemaking and in roaming to work in the world. The passive, all-loving Teresa claims that if Kate had given her former husband her soul instead of hoarding it (along with, presumably, her private gratification) in her "purse," he would not have followed abstract politics in Ireland and hence would not have died (452). Yet Lawrence does not seem to notice that Teresa cannot keep Ramón from roaming away from their marriage toward abstract politics in Mexico.

When Lawrence keeps to his patriarchal ideal in *The Plumed Serpent* and his following works, he participates in "a general upsurge in male insecurity" after World War I: "By the 1920s, Lawrence had become convinced that a feminist revolution had actually occurred, and had gone badly wrong. He believed that the dominant ideology of the post-war world was feminine—not, however, a true femininity of instinct and feeling, but a perverted femininity of will and idealism—and that a masculine renaissance was necessary to restore the balance."[22] Thus, if Lawrence pictures women as devouring goddesses, he gallantly takes the blame onto the shoulders of all men who have neglected nature: "Oh, the moon could soothe us and heal us like a cool great Artemis between her arms. But we have lost her, in our stupidity we ignore her, and angry she stares down on us and whips us with nervous whips. Oh, beware of the angry Artemis of the night heavens, beware of the spite of Cybele, beware of the vindictiveness of horned Astarte."[23] It never occurs to Lawrence to assign any of the bitterness he senses in women to frustration at being excluded from jobs or from the political and artistic utterance of the "Word." Instead, to him they suffer only from the lack of a stronger, sexually fulfilling man. What "cocksure women" really want is to "lay eggs," that is, stay home with the children; Lawrence's Cybele could never be satisfied having "laid a vote" or even an "ink-bottle" of talent.[24]

Still, in his fiction Lawrence is not always so simplistic as these comments suggest. Almost despite himself, Lawrence does give some recognition to active women in *The Plumed Serpent*. Even the self-effacing Teresa manages a hacienda better than her brothers, and she admits that, as the practical Cipriano complements the more mystical Ramón, "some women must be soldiers in their spirit" (476). She obviously disapproves of a soldierly Kate; however, because Lawrence makes the always searching and resisting Irishwoman so interesting, he tacitly acknowledges the appeal of an active, fighting woman, and perhaps a talking or writing one too.

Although Lawrence carefully nurtures his European Kate's slow reform in *The Plumed Serpent*, at times he so despairs of Europe that he is ready to give up trying to put a fragmented Osiris back together again and just sweep out the pieces. In "The Woman Who Rode Away," written in the summer of 1924, between Parts I and II of *The Plumed Serpent*, Lawrence tells how a white woman in Mexico rides away from her husband and two children to an Indian tribe, hoping to "see their houses and know their gods."[25] As the woman camps out on the cold ground, "She was not sure that she had not heard, during the night, a great crash at the centre of herself, which was the crash of her own death. Or else it was a crash at the centre of the earth, and meant something big and mysterious" (W, 54). Although such a crash might at first sound like the emotional letdown that Kate experiences, followed by the "death" of her old self as she sloughs off her prejudices, here "death" is, horrifyingly, no longer symbolic. Dreamy from an herbal potion and drunk as well on Lawrence's philosophy of communion with nature, the unnamed woman languorously lets herself be pampered toward sacrifice.

Lawrence clearly casts her in the role of the human being who, Frazer thought, imitated the dying deity to help him along. This thirty-three-year-old woman, at the age of the Christian dying god, also corresponds to an Indian dying god. She offers her heart to the knife on "the shortest day of the year," as if she could thereby encourage the failing sun to be reborn (W, 88). The tribe wants "the sheep to have twin lambs," throwing in the aims of a Frazerian fertility ritual for good measure (W, 82). Actually, the Indians have complained that white people, far more than the winter season, have stolen the sun and the moon. With their visitor dead, the Indians hope they will be able to tempt sun and moon to lend their power once again to a vanquished race.

Unfortunately, the theories of these fictional Indians about the retreat of the heavenly bodies resemble the diagnosis of Lawrence, who also accused Europeans of angering the cosmos.[26] Because the story ends as the knife is about to fall, the narrator does not have to commit himself whether the tribe members feel universal power streaming back into their drab lives as the guest's blood flows out. Patently, one isolated sacrifice is not going to reverse the tides of culture. Could Lawrence ever have entertained the hope that more widespread murder might help?

To clarify some of the personal resentments that fueled Lawrence's apocalyptic fury, it is useful to set this story next to Forsters's *A Passage to India*, which Lawrence was reading as he wrote his own story. On 23 July 1924, Lawrence wrote in a letter, "Am reading *A Passage to India*. It's good, but makes one wish a bomb would fall and end everything. Life is more interesting in its undercurrents than in its obvious; and E. M. does see people, people and nothing but people ad nauseam." On 3 October 1924, Lawrence wrote, to another correspondent, "I agree Forster doesn't 'understand' his Hindu. And India to him is just negative: because he doesn't go down to the root to meet it. But the *Passage to India* interested me very much. At least the repudiation of our white bunk is genuine, sincere, and pretty thorough, it seems to me. Negative, yes. But King Charles *must* have his head off. Homage to the headsman."[27] John Beer adds that Lawrence made the first comment before he had finished the book and that he later admitted Forster as "about the best of my contemporaries in England."[28]

In both "The Woman Who Rode Away" and *A Passage to India*, significant events take place in a cave. Lawrence borrows Forster's language for a weirdly beautiful passage: "They had brought her a little female dog, which she called Flora. And once, in the trance of her senses, she felt she *heard* the little dog conceive, in her tiny womb, and begin to be complex, with young. And another day she could hear the vast sound of the earth going round, like some immense arrow-string booming" (W, 74). The odd word "booming" for a bow recalls the "boum" of the Marabar caves. Presumably, to hear the earth booming is to catch the "undercurrents" of life at its roots, which Forster's Mrs. Moore, Lawrence implies, has misinterpreted as nothingness.

Although Forster is well aware of his characters' limitations, he pities them; Lawrence, on the other hand, displays only impatience. One can imagine him growling at Mrs. Moore's irritability, at Aziz's evasiveness, and particularly at Miss Quested's sexual uncertainties or Fielding and Stella's marital difficulties. Annoyed by these characters—and by most of repressed Europe, one might say—Lawrence approves when Forster seems to chop off a king's head to overthrow a society. When Forster stabs with only satiric barbs, Lawrence in this story can picture a real flint knife in action. Lawrence might reproach Forster for making us feel like blowing everything up, for focusing on the failings instead of the possibilities of life, yet Lawrence himself in "The Woman Who Rode Away" concentrates on the clean sweep: "You with blue eyes, you are the messengers from the faraway, you cannot stay, and now it is time for you to go back" (W, 81). This language echoes the invitation of Quetzalcoatl to Jesus in *The Plumed Serpent* to "go back" for a refreshing sleep; however, the gods could effect their bloodless coups in a brotherly, tender exchange, whereas this "go back" hostilely euphemizes "death to all blue-eyed people." Lawrence's Indians turn into prototypical Hitlers; the prejudices are reversed but just as cruel.

Yet Lawrence may be railing not against Western civilization in general but against one specific aspect of it—the assertiveness and/or sexual aloofness of women. Because the moon will supposedly come back "like a woman who ceases to be angry in her house" (W, 79), the whole story at times seems to reduce to a domestic crisis. Lawrence allows his full resentment against independent women to blossom:

> In the strange towering symbols on the heads of the changeless, absorbed [Indian] women she seemed to read once more the *Mene Mene Tekel Upharsin*. Her kind of womanhood, intensely personal and individual, was to be obliterated again, and the great primeval symbols were to tower once more over the fallen individual independence of woman. The sharpness and the quivering nervous consciousness of the highly-bred white woman was to be destroyed again, womanhood was to be cast once more into the great stream of impersonal sex and impersonal passion. (W, 75)

When King Belshazzar saw the handwriting on the wall, the biblical Daniel interpreted the phrase beginning *Mene Mene* to mean that the king's days were numbered.[29] The prophet was right: somebody slew the king that night. Lawrence's woman who rode away has as little time left to reform.

What really happened to Miss Quested and this anonymous woman in their caves? Where Forster keeps a discreet silence, Lawrence goes ahead and evokes a symbolic rape: "When the red sun was about to sink, he would shine full through the shaft of ice deep into the hollow of the cave, to the innermost" (W, 89). Lawrence could have found in one of Lewis

Spence's books precedents for the sacrifice of naked women in Mexican ritual,[30] but Lawrence makes up one particular brutality: he confounds the entry of the phallic ray from the male sun ("he") with the stabbing that immediately follows. The language almost seems to suggest that if the Miss Questeds of the world, the blue-eyed people, have sexual desires that they don't know how to express, well, rape and murder them.

On the other hand, Lawrence might betray not just an exasperated desire to be rid of these unreformable women altogether but also a weary longing to give up all effort himself. When the woman who rode away feels her mind go pleasantly numb and her senses diffuse into the harmony of the sky, her awareness diffuses, ominously, like blood (W, 78). This "exquisite sense of bleeding out into the higher beauty" prefigures her death; in addition, Lawrence may be wondering if the only real way to achieve cosmic "oneness" is to die. Such an image may have prompted William Troy's blunt assertion that Lawrence belongs to the "celebrants of the tomb."[31] At times Lawrence consciously recognizes and pushes away such longings. In the late, fragmentary story "The Flying Fish," the main character, Gethin, "lost between the two days, the fatal greater day of the Indians, the fussy, busy lesser day of the white people," dreams, "Beautiful it is to be dead!" Lawrence has Gethin fight against any relaxation into death, however, apparently aware that such willingness to do away with oneself or with everything arises only from "the despair that comes when the lesser day hems in the greater."[32]

Gethin watches the flying fish as an image for himself. The fish is driven by fear to leap into the air of normal "getting ahead," but it "dives again into the great peace of the deeper day, and under the belly of death, passes into his own."[33] "Under the belly of death" suggests again the cycle of the dying god; Lawrence may have thought of it because of his own recent recovery from near fatal illness.[34] He seems to hope not so much for personal immortality as for a fuller life, without "hurrying," even after his acute reminder that death can touch him.

Eventually Lawrence retreats from a violent apocalypse applied to the whole of society, where he can indifferently watch the single individual— the woman who rode away or himself—physically go down in the general rout. By his last book, *Apocalypse* (1932), Lawrence locates that cataclysm back in the individual psyche, now to be renewed, not discarded:

This cosmic calamity no doubt corresponds to the original final death of the initiate, when his very spirit is stripped off him and he knows death indeed, yet still keeps the final flame-point of life, down in Hades. . . . Then the final flame-point of the eternal self of a man emerges from hell, and at the very instant of extinction becomes a new whole cloven flame of a new-bodied man with golden thighs and a face of glory.[35]

In fact, as he imagines this personal and symbolic reenactment of the fate of the dying god, Lawrence speculates that the biblical Book of Revelation must have developed from an original "pagan work, probably the description of the 'secret' ritual of initiation into one of the pagan Mysteries, Artemis, Cybele, even Orphic."[36] When Jewish and then Christian apocalyptists rewrote the lesson, they converted the destruction from symbolic to literal and from personal to worldwide, inviting only pain and waste and betraying their own vindictiveness, a "maniacal anti-life."[37] Lawrence declares he would gladly trade the New Jerusalem, that inorganic "jeweller's paradise," for the now-obscured pagan record of initiation.[38]

Actually, Lawrence had just undertaken to compose two such guidebooks to personal rebirth, *Lady Chatterley's Lover* (1928) and *The Man Who Died* (1929). In the first, Lawrence retains the image of the figure who dies to bring about some good, but, unlike the easy disposal of the protagonist in "The Woman Who Rode Away," Connie's "death" is figurative, more like Kate's initiation. Lawrence makes Connie a "sacrifice,"[39] but then at the last moment he whisks away all danger to assure us that only her "shame" dies. During lovemaking with Mellors, Connie "really thought she was dying: yet a poignant, marvellous death . . . the shame died . . . at last it was roused up and routed by the phallic hunt of the man" (LC, 289). With the word "hunt," Mellors becomes a kind of Set, who attacked Osiris while boar hunting. But, as John Humma observes, when this intrusive Mellors, bearing a supposedly phallic gun, first breaks up Connie and Clifford's safe tête-à-tête, he wears reassuring green, signaling that Connie experiences her demise solely for the sake of new life.[40] Walking in the "wind of March," she has consciously anticipated her conversion: "Ye must be born again! I believe in the resurrection of the body! Except a grain of wheat fall into the earth and die, it shall by no means bring forth. I too will emerge and see the sun!" (LC, 95). Here Connie combines her role as pagan dying god with the language of the New Testament,[41] as Lawrence will again combine the images of a pagan dying god and Christ in *The Man Who Died*.

Connie's relinquishment of an old self, concerned with mental relations only, is an innocuous enough version of initiatory "extinction." Yet juxtaposed to the ordeal of the woman who rode away, Connie's sacrifice acquires disturbing resonances. When Mellors shoots a "pussy" early in the novel, offending his willful, bratty daughter (named, improbably, Connie), the scene suggests that Mellors attacks the older Connie's female self-will (LC, 66). The slang implications of female genitalia for "pussy" and for the "con" of Connie also leave the unpleasant impression that Lawrence is again gibing at "Aphrodite of the foam." When the gamekeeper violently and resentfully destroys a female poaching on his pleasurable turf, he resembles the male ray piercing the cave, as the knife eliminates the person.

Although Mellors and Connie behave with convincing tenderness and realistic hesitation, the imagery of the hunt corrupts dying deity into scapegoat.

In *The Man Who Died* Lawrence is again composing a guidebook to a new self, incorporating his most explicit and extensive references to dying gods: the Osiris-Isis legend here overlays and "corrects" the Jesus-Magdalene story. Although never named, a character obviously modeled on Christ has been incompletely crucified and left for dead in a tomb. He emerges but, disillusioned, he hardly wants to be revived. Nevertheless, he allows a peasant, who owns a tethered cock, to care for him. By the end of Part I the convalescent buys and releases the cock, as he has released his old pretensions. He no longer forces others to sacrifice themselves or to praise him for his gifts. In Part II he meets a woman, a priestess of Isis, who completes his reeducation and revival by making love with him.

Why would Lawrence focus in *The Man Who Died* on Isis and Osiris rather than the other vegetation gods to develop his Christ? In a draft of Part II, Lawrence writes, "This is Isis lore, which Isis women forever will understand and only they. Aphrodite knows it not: for her the Atys, the Adonis of the afterwards is that which she has lost. And the Marys do not know it, none of the four Marys. For they never found the lost male clue to their risen man, their risen God. But Isis knew, long ago, and Isis women know today."[42] Fortunately Lawrence omits these lines, which solicit "Isis women" in the ludicrously unctuous style of modern advertising. But the same motivation for Isis holds true in the completed story. Obviously Lawrence has fastened on a detail unique to the Egyptian version of the dying god: Isis's search for the scattered parts of Osiris's body. She and her companions find everything but the phallus, but Isis then refashions one for him to bring him back to his new life as king of the underworld. For Lawrence, Isis's task parallels his own interest in integrating all aspects of a person and particularly in rehabilitating sexuality.

As in *Lady Chatterley's Lover*, Lawrence accomplishes a disturbing death of female assertiveness in *The Man Who Died*, but indirectly, through the scene in which the priestess and the stranger observe from opposite hills an encounter between two adolescent slaves, a boy and a girl.[43] Although much of the novella shouts its didactic message that Christ should seek at-one-ment with a woman rather than atonement for sin (M, 207), this scene hints its meaning in a quieter and therefore more challenging (if not necessarily more acceptable) evocativeness.

The slaves are preparing pigeons for an evening meal: "The youth pierced the throat of a blue, live bird, and let the drops of blood fall into the heaving sea, with curious concentration. They were performing some sacrifice, or working some incantation" (M, 186). But when a black and white pigeon "like a ghost escape[s] over the low dark sea," the frustration and anger of the male slave interrupt his participation in ritual. In a petulant rage, he first beats and then rapes his companion. The priestess, who is observing the scene from the hillside, turns away with a scornful dismissal: "Slaves!"

The encounter of the two adolescents prefigures the lovemaking of the priestess and the convalescent, yet it does so by first offering to the two virgin adults a "wrong" version of sexual exchange. Not only does the boy use violence but he also displays "blind, frightened frenzy" and "cringing," while the girl shows only sullenness (M, 187). Moreover, the two birds suggest other qualities besides anger and shame that the adults will have to sacrifice before they can come together in exemplary intercourse. First, the black and white pigeon that is said to escape "like a ghost" represents for the convalescent, who has emerged from the tomb in a white linen shroud and now stands in a blowing dark-gray cloak, that aspect of his former desires which he needs to dismiss. As an escaped bird himself (already identified with the escaped cock), he has to "kill off" his ghostly parts: his pretensions to otherworldliness and transcendence that must disappear like a rejected holy ghost.

If the black-and-white pigeon shows the convalescent the etherealness that he must send back to heaven so he can live reverently with earth, the stabbed blue bird represents for the watching priestess the aspect of femaleness she must avoid. The unusual color blue for a pigeon suggests that Lawrence has some specific reference in mind. The "lady of Isis," who wears a yellow mantle and a white tunic, contrasts with Lawrence's Madeleine (Mary Magdalene), who wears a blue mantle and a yellow robe when she meets the convalescent after his "resurrection" (M, 173). The two women share yellow, as they share womanhood; however, blue (also the traditional color of the Virgin Mary) sets Madeleine apart from Isis.

Because the slaves pierce a blue bird, they "kill off" the ways in which Madeleine differs from Isis. Lawrence characterizes Madeleine as an always greedy woman, who wants to "give" too much, forcing her self-sacrifice onto Christ as a compulsion to gratitude (M, 175). But it is not only the reformed Madeleine, the abstaining, idealized woman, whom Lawrence is criticizing. He also objects that when Madeleine led the life of a prostitute, she greedily "took" too much. For all her free sexuality that might seem to make her kin to Isis, Madeleine hoards her own pleasure. Because she has the audacity to enjoy her own sexuality, instead of making the man's pleasure the primary objective, the Madeleine-tendency in women has to be stabbed out of existence, with the blue sacrificial animal standing in for a female dying god in this rite.

I should point out that Lawrence dislikes "giving too much" and assertiveness in men as much as he despises these traits in women: the priestess of Isis shies away from the "golden brief day-suns" of men like Anthony or the "eagle-like rapacity" of a Caesar, preferring the "violet-dark sun that has died and risen and makes no show" (M, 189). To eliminate bossiness in his ideal man, Lawrence approves the convalescent's passage through a radically violent death and rebirth. Yet when Lawrence also pierces a blue bird to eradicate a similar bossiness in women, as he raises the knife over the blue-eyed woman in "The Woman Who Rode Away," the attack on women seems more spiteful, perhaps fearful of a greater social role for women and not just of unpleasant arrogance as it could appear in either sex.

In an essay called "The Risen Lord," written about the same time as *The Man Who Died*, Lawrence explains how he is reinterpreting Christ to conform more to the old dying gods. He puts the myths in a social context, using them to characterize three possible "image-divisions" or outlooks following World War I:

> We have the old and the elderly, who never were exposed to the guns, still fatuously maintaining that man is the Christ-child and woman the infallible safeguard from all evil and all danger. It is fatuous, because it absolutely didn't work. Then we have the men of middle age, who were all tortured and virtually put to death by the war. They accept Christ Crucified as their image, are essentially womanless, and take the great cry: *Consummatum est!—it is finished!*—as their last word. . . . The young came into life, and found everthing finished. Everywhere the empty crosses, everywhere the closed tombs, everywhere the manless, bitter or over-assertive women, everywhere the closed grey disillusion of Christ Crucified, dead, and buried, those grey empty days between Good Friday and Easter.[44]

In his middle group, Lawrence seems to be thinking of men like Hemingway, who wrote about castrated Attises and "men without women" (a title of a book by Hemingway). But Lawrence insists that the young, waiting for the Risen Lord, want to go beyond the despair imposed by the war. Searching for symbolism to express his longing for renewal, Lawrence focuses on the centrality of Easter over Christmas in Catholic countries. Easter celebrates the rebirth of the adult male rather than doting over the infant Jesus still in its mother's arms: "In Sicily the women take into church the saucers of growing corn, the green blades rising tender and slim like green light, in little pools, filling round the altar. It is Adonis. It is the re-born year. It is Christ Risen. It is the Risen Lord."[45]

Lawrence, in fact, approves this Easter celebration because it duplicates the worship of the old vegetation gods, bringing fertility ritual or sexuality back into his private brand of Christianity. He offers us the Sicilian women's gardens of Adonis, their saucers of growing corn, as an appropriate image for our modern lives, which should be rooted in instinct. We should celebrate nature, though confined to the most fragile and fleeting of growths: our life spans as brief as those blades. Lawrence invokes a Risen Lord—whether Adonis, Osiris, Quetzalcoatl, or Christ—who is Every-man, a son of God not unique but divine to the same extent as all human beings, not seeking martyrdom but undergoing the suffering that is inherent in transient, greenly exquisite life.

Faulkner

Most critics of William Faulkner's *Pylon* (1935) complain either that its mythological references do not connect to one another, or that the background myths no longer provide a sustaining belief. Faulkner's allusions to death by water and by fire in T. S. Eliot's *The Waste Land* "don't cohere," Richard Adams claims, making the "mythic structural pattern" for *Pylon* "weak" and "insufficiently assimilated."[46] Walter Brylowski catalogues some Christian and Greek allusions but says Faulkner fails to integrate them with theme or plot, so that *Pylon* is his "most carelessly written novel."[47] Even Michael Millgate, who labels the book a "success," speculates that "*Pylon* may in fact have been written rather hurriedly and perhaps at relatively low intensity."[48] (He indicates haste, however, only because Faulkner ignored editors' queries on manuscript pages and galleys, a silence that could mean Faulkner already considered the lines clear enough, not necessarily that he was hurrying.) And Hyatt Waggoner, who laments that the "brilliance" of *Pylon* has "yet to be adequately appreciated," must apologize that "clarity of symbolic implication," supposedly missing in the book, is not all-important.[49]

Some critics argue that if the mythological allusions do not cohere, Faulkner intended a hodgepodge to show a deracinated modern culture, unable to piece together the tag ends of past beliefs. Such commentators usually interpret the airmen as unbelieving, machine-age automatons. But others admire the fliers. George Monteiro and Hugh Ruppersburg, for example, point out that it is a misguided character, the reporter, not Faulkner, who says that the fliers "aint human."[50] In this view, Shumann escapes the falsity of his surroundings to achieve a genuine love, perhaps even a Christ-like sacrifice that "partially redeems the guilt of all men."[51] But even those readers who admire Shumann's sacrifice cannot place Shumann and Laverne as a couple into "the context of any larger pattern suggested by the Mardi Gras season."[52] Although a "capacity for love, loyalty, and self-sacrifice" might survive in the modern world, both Christian and pagan sources for Mardi Gras are said to represent "an exhausted tradition."[53]

I would like to argue that Faulkner makes a much more extensive use of both vegetation and Christian myths than has been noted, and that he fully integrates these mythological prototypes with each other and with very human characters. In particular Faulkner skillfully and subtly draws on the Egyptian legend of Isis and Osiris as well as European folk customs of "burying the Carnival," to give *Pylon* the "organized complexity" and "clarity of symbolic implication" denied it by critics.[54] Faulkner undoubtedly found these legends and customs in Frazer's *The Golden Bough*.[55] Although Faulkner certainly did not set out to rewrite Frazerian legends, he readily returns to them to dignify the human characters and to unify his themes. Bypassing some aspects of modern Christianity that he apparently considers unviable, Faulkner goes back to pagan rites and thereby infuses his Christianity with new meaning, though not new orthodoxy. The ending of the book is positive, without being sentimental; through a recognition of inevitable pain and death, his characters affirm life.

Frazer presents Isis and Osiris as "corn" spirits, by which he means grain guardians. After Isis discovers wild wheat and barley, Osiris travels all over the world to teach the cultivation of these plants.[56] Like Isis, Laverne has an association with grain: she sports a "blob of savage mealcolored hair," "Iowacorncolored" (19, 22). After Shumann plucks her from an Iowa or Indiana cow pasture, they barnstorm all over the country. One member of their entourage, Jiggs, carries a "drill mealsack" as his only luggage. Another member of the group, Jack, holds a sack of flour so that it looks like a "child" and scatters it while he parachutes, as if his leap could fertilize field and human. He floats down "like the haunt of Yuletide" (44), recalling Frazer's "yule boar," a loaf baked in the form of a pig and scattered with the seed.[57] For Frazer the yule boar hints at the slaying of a pig or even the sacrifice of a man, as Jack's apparently auspicious fall with the flour links inextricably to Shumann's disastrous fall into the lake.

Osiris's evil brother, Set, mortally jealous of Osiris's virtue and fame, fashions a coffer into which only Osiris can fit. When all are drinking and carousing, Set induces Osiris to lie down in the box, at which point seventy-two conspirators nail down the lid and toss the coffer into the Nile.[58]

Like Set, the reporter in *Pylon* is jealous of Shumann, in this case, over Laverne. The reporter buys the drinks that contribute to Shumann's first mishap on Friday by causing the alcoholic Jiggs to neglect repairs to the plane. The reporter then obtains and refashions an unsafe airplane, which only Shumann will fly. The reporter helps redesign the plane by rigging a movable sack of sand; the sterile sand perhaps contrasts with Jack's flour. Shumann asks jestingly if the reporter is "ribbing me up in this crate" so the latter can marry Laverne (175). The race committee, like Set's seventy-two conspirators, put aside the qualifying rules, thus sealing Shumann's fate. The rickety plane procured by the reporter becomes Shumann's coffin when it falls into the water. Finally, by telling the reporter not to mourn too much, because "He aint our brother," a photographer brings to mind brotherly jealousies—and responsibilities (238).

Shumann falls into a lake, not Osiris's river, though Faulkner frequently compares a Mardi Gras float to a "Nilebarge" (77). Frazer does describe one lake ceremony in honor of Osiris, distinctive for its "nocturnal illumination,"[59] and the lake in which Shumann dies is lavishly lit up, by no fewer than three searchlights, a beacon, scattered flashlights, kerosene flames, and a row of automobile headlights (248).

The reporter, of course, does not intend to kill Shumann, as Set does Osiris. The reporter recognizes that he is jealous, even to the point of "putting the bee on" Shumann, but he would never seriously hurt him (279). He courts Laverne not by trying to get rid of Shumann but by glorifying him to please her. Because his basically good but self-serving intentions backfire, injuring the one group he has tried to help and pushing Laverne irrevocably away from him, the reporter qualifies as a tragic hero. His character is neither wholly good nor wholly bad: exasperatingly garrulous and meddlesome, but appealingly needy and generous. The book ends with the reporter shattered too, through the loss of his illusions about an affair with Laverne, as Frazer remarks that in some legends Set is torn, along with Osiris.[60]

Faulkner describes several other characters, besides Shumann, and even places, as drowning or under water. The airport, "aquatic," filters sunlight to a "quality of having been recently taken out of water and not thoroughly dried" (17, 144). The desks in the newspaper office, under green shaded bulbs, have "that quality of profound and lonely isolation of buoymarked shoals in an untravelled and forgotten sea" (203), and the Mardi Gras floats are "like an inhabited archipelago putting out to sea on a floodtide" (57).

One reason for the ubiquitous water references is to foreshadow Shumann's death by water. When the first line compares confetti to foam, the comparison announces the later importance of water in a dismal mood; the foam is dirty, evanescent, ungraspable (7, 11). A second reason for comparisons to water might be a kind of "sympathetic magic": the reporter, living on Noyades Street and jealous of Shumann, "infects" him with his own depression, his precariousness like "hanging from the edge of a swimming pool" or sinking into water (65, 184, 239). Yet the descriptions of the reporter as drowning multiply after Shumann's death, so that a third reason for such associations might be to express his regret, his desire almost to take over Shumann's role of victim rather than to live with the knowledge that he contributed to his fall (242–44).

Finally, the fourth and most potent reason for the aquatic comparisons is to provide a link between community and victim. The dying / reviving deity is occasionally interpreted as taking away a taint that resided in the community by assuming its death and sometimes its sins. With all the explicit allusions in *Pylon* to Eliot's "The Love Song of J. Alfred Prufrock," the drowning that threatens New Valois can probably best be explained by the last line of that poem, "human voices wake us, and we drown." For both Eliot and Faulkner, the failure of communication, of love, and of animating beliefs (even if just a belief in mermaids) creates a living death. The innocent Shumann, to whom belief in teamwork and experience of love *are* available, takes on the reflected aquatic light of his corrupted community.

Once Osiris falls into the water and the coffer floats downstream, Isis follows its course. Eventually the chest washes ashore, where a tree grows around it. A royal family cuts down the tree and makes it into a pillar, still containing the body of Osiris. Isis conceives their son Horus either when she lies on the floating coffer, or as she flutters in the form of a bird around the pillar.[61]

Isis as a bird fluttering around a pillar corresponds to the central visual image of *Pylon*, an airplane fluttering around a pylon. The slender phallic tower focuses the life energies that the reporter senses and envies in the group. The reporter explicitly makes the pylon masculine ("two buried pylons in the one Iowadrowsing womandrowsing pylondrowsing"[110]); and he makes the plane feminine ("Around the home pylon on one wingtip and the fabric trembling like a bride" [47]). In addition to denoting an airport tower, "pylon" also means "gateway to an Egyptian temple," a setting that would be appropriate for Isis and Osiris. The reporter is apparently aware of the Egyptian associations for the word because he claims he is writing a Sunday feature on "how the loves of Antony and Cleopatra had been prophesied all the time in Egyptian architecture only they never knew what it meant" (204). André Bleikasten says there seem to be more Egyptian mythological references than any other kind in *Pylon*, but he does not mention Isis and Osiris.[62]

Noting the importance of the pillar as a cult object in Egypt, Frazer defines Osiris as a fertility god as well as a corn spirit. The mythologist marks a transition between Victorian indignant and modern acceptant attitudes toward sexuality when he cautions, "It would be to misjudge ancient religion to denounce as lewd and profligate the emblems and ceremonies which the Egyptians employed for the purpose of giving effect to this conception of the divine power. The ends which they proposed to themselves in their rites were natural and laudable, only the means they adopted to compass them were mistaken."[63] Faulkner shows the reporter as a kind of Victorian character, repulsed yet attracted to the group's sexual arrangements. The reporter vomits when the revelations about Laverne's youthful boyfriends affront his conventions; Faulkner, however, wants us to avoid the reporter's squeamishness. Faulkner lends to another newspaperman what seems to be his own defense and approbation of the group: "You dirtymouthed bastards. Why don't you let the guy rest. Let them all rest. They were trying to do what they had to do, with what they had to do it with, the same as all of us only maybe a little better than us" (290).

After flying around the pillar, Isis, according to Frazer, extricates the body from the wood, but Set, out on a boar hunting expedition, discovers the corpse and tears it into fourteen pieces. Isis, with the help of some other gods, searches for the scattered parts. They eventually find everything except Osiris's genitals.[64]

Although Osiris himself was not attacked by a boar, Frazer speculates that Set's boar hunt links Osiris to other dying gods, Adonis and Attis, who were gored in the thigh by boars.[65] In *Pylon* Jack plays the Adonis role, when he receives a wound running the length of his leg to the thigh (164, 187). In addition, Faulkner describes Jack's and the other contestants' parachutes as "down-cupped blooms like inverted water hyacinths" (158); the Greek figure Hyacinth suffered a death much like that of Adonis.[66]

The search by Isis and by strange creatures like Anubis for Osiris's scattered remains also has echoes in *Pylon*. The boats dragging the lake for Shumann's body are described in an archaic setting: "Among them the dredge looked like something antediluvian crawled for the first time into light, roused but not alarmed by the object or creature out of the world of light and air which had plunged without warning into the watery fastness where it had been asleep" (237). An even more striking echo to Isis's search comes from the hunt by Jiggs and the reporter, after Shumann's death, for the shinbone of a horse (266–71). This bizarre scene sends Jigg into a huge pile of bones and mechanical debris; because the cars in the heap duplicate the car bodies in the "mole" or breakwater where Shumann actually hit, in a symbolic way the pair seem to be searching for him. Osiris's missing genitals correspond to what is missing in the reporter's life: sex; the fact that the reporter retrieves statuary instead of bones increases the sense of artificiality and loss surrounding him. Jiggs initiates the search by claiming that the shinbone will somehow restore—if not a whole person— at least a whole perfect boot. He does manage to find a bone and smooth the creases in his boot with it. At the same time, by locating the shin of a horse, Jiggs, frequently described as a horse-man, is made whole. That is, he becomes "curiously serene," when he pawns his prized boots to buy presents to try to comfort Laverne (273). He thus rises to an act of generosity that atones somewhat for the alcoholic neglect that first endangered Shumann; he is restored to integrity as Osiris is restored.

In addition to drawing on the story of Isis and Osiris to dignify his characters, Faulkner apparently echoes Frazer's descriptions of Mardi Gras celebrations. For instance, Frazer recounts that a personification of the Carnival, usually an effigy (but, he believes, originally a person), suffers execution, either on Shrove Tuesday or on the first day of Lent.[67] In *Pylon*, bells ring in Lent at midnight on the day Shumann dies, so that he enacts the role of the Carnival as well as that of Osiris. In Provence, according to Frazer, "a tall gaunt personage who masquerades as Lent" accompanies the effigy of the Carnival, as the tall, skeletal reporter, repeatedly likened to a corpse, attaches himself to Shumann's group.[68] The effigy of Carnival, moreover, receives a burlesque funeral oration, and the reporter writes two obituaries for Shumann that could qualify as burlesque: one exaggeratedly sentimental, one bitterly sarcastic (314–15). At Leipsic the "bastards and public women"—names some people would apply to Laverne and her son—follow the effigy to give it greater potency.[69]

In different geographic areas, Frazer continues, the Carnival meets different forms of death. Some celebrants consign him to water (paralleled in Shumann's case), some set fire to the Carnival (reflected in Lieutenant Burnham's death), and some revelers hang him. In this last case, the executioners try to pin his death on some crime, blaming the Carnival for breaking the moral code (as the reporter registers horror at Laverne's two lovers), or even, in one locale, for wearing out the citizens' shoes.[70] This ludicrous detail about the shoes may have triggered Faulkner's invention of Jiggs's obsession: Jigg's most visible regret after Shumann's death is that he has worn and creased the boots, which he would now like to sell back to the store.

Whereas Lent begins on Ash Wednesday, Faulkner moves the bells signaling (or resignaling) Lent to Saturday midnight. The action of the book covers a five-day period, Thursday through Monday. Although Thursday at first looks happy, with Shumann winning money, we learn from the Friday morning paper that Burnham's death has marred it. The loss of Shumann's plane and Jack's leg injury spoil Friday, leading up to Shumann's death on Saturday. On Monday the reporter sinks into his disillusionment, following Laverne and Jack's departure on Sunday. The end-of-the-week sequence recalls the Friday through Sunday sequence of *The Sound and the Fury* and suggests that Faulkner may be conflating Lent and Easter celebrations. Richard Adams finds this conflation exasperating and unsuccessful.[71] It seems to me, however, that Faulkner wants us to face the losses and deprivation of our usual condition, a kind of permanent Lent, while still maintaining a muted hopefulness. Laverne's departure on Sunday provides a kind of resurrection.

Although the critics mentioned earlier consider the pagan and Christian allusions in *Pylon* unrelated to each other, Frazer easily links the Christian Mardi Gras festivities and the pagan observances for Isis and Osiris by defining them both as rites that mime the life cycle of the corn spirit. Burying the effigy of the Carnival at Mardi Gras probably originated further back than Christianity, but the assimilation of this folk custom to the later religion does remind us that Christ is also a kind of dying divinity with many parallels to Osiris and Adonis. If Shumann is in some ways like Osiris, and Jack like

Adonis, the reporter is once described as Christ, when Jack asks skeptically, "Does the race committee think he is Jesus too, the same as the rest of you do?" (188). The reporter's offer of a place to stay may have provoked the gratitude that Jack exaggerates as adulation. Yet the reporter is the most bloodless of the dying gods alluded to in *Pylon*. In *The Town*, Faulkner unfavorably contrasts the "pale and desperate Galilean" with the much stronger god of love supposedly worshiped by Eula Varner.[72] Apparently Faulkner labels "pale and desperate" any attempt by Christianity to condemn sexuality. With his admiration for Eula Varner and for Laverne, Faulkner adds passion to those qualities of Christianity—compassion and self-sacrifice—which he obviously likes.

Although Christ suffered the death of the dying gods, he did not enjoy their theogamy, or divine marriage. Faulkner in a way restores the theogamy to Christianity by consistently combining his Mardi Gras imagery with allusions to Shakespeare's Antony and Cleopatra, who are larger-than-life, almost godlike figures. Not only does the reporter supposedly write a Sunday feature on these two characters, but the Mardi Gras leaves signs that may well have spilled in the wake of Cleopatra's processional: "trodden confetti pending the dawn's whitewings—spent tinseldung of Momus' Nilebarge clatterfalque" (77, 204). While John Vickery speculates that "Nilebarge clatterfalque" refers to the phrase "Cataphracht of Nilus" in Sidney's *An Apology for Poetry*,[73] Faulkner's portmanteau words, along with other aspects of his Mardi Gras, may also recall Shakespeare's Cleopatra: "The barge she sat in, like a burnish'd throne, / Burn'd on the water: the poop was beaten gold; / Purple the sails, and so perfumed that / The winds were love-sick with them."[74] The purple and gold of Cleopatra's barge suggest the "purple-and-gold bunting" for Mardi Gras (12). The ambiguity that Faulkner creates by linking Mardi Gras both with bunting, for wrapping an infant, and with a catafalque, for displaying a corpse, corresponds to the ambiguity of Cleopatra's artful barge, full of the promises of love, but also prefiguring the display of bodies in the monument at the end of the play.

Commenting on the one specific allusion in *Pylon* to *Antony and Cleopatra* (204), Bleikasten compares Antony and Cleopatra to the lovers of *The Waste Land*, but this comparison seems completely wrong.[75] Ambiguous and finally tragic, the love of Antony and Cleopatra as Shakespeare presents it is nevertheless neither automatic, as in *The Waste Land*, nor worthless for being doomed. While Shakespeare sears us with tragedy, the partially self-created loss of something valuable, Eliot chills us with farce, the loss of value itself. Here Faulkner follows Shakespeare rather than Eliot. Shumann, Laverne, and the reporter must all take responsibility for risking a plane they know to be unsafe, yet, again as in tragedy, loss goes beyond any deserved retribution for small faults to the point of destroying Shumann and scattering the group. Just as Shakespeare's Agrippa hears of Cleopatra's epiphany in the barge, "There she appeared indeed; or my reporter devised well for her," Faulkner's reporter devises a leering version of Laverne.[76] But the reporter's horror and envy of her do not coincide with Faulkner's acceptance. Shakespeare's Enobarbus must correct Agrippa's implied condemnation: "for vilest things / Become themselves in her; that the holy priests / Bless her when she is riggish."[77] Similarly, Faulkner admires Laverne precisely because she is "riggish," recognizing that her life with both Shumann and Jack is based on love and commitment, more like Frazer's "sanctified harlotry" than the shameful "prostitution" which Shumann's parents assume.[78]

With all the references in *Pylon* to Isis, Osiris, and the burying of the Carnival, descriptions of even mundane events, like cleaning the street after Mardi Gras, often sound like exotic rituals. After the authorities adjust the traffic lights for the parade, "only the middle eye on each post stared dimly and steadily yellow, the four corners of the intersection marked now by four milkcolored jets from the fireplugs and standing one beside each plug, motionless and identical, four men in white" (88). The airport as a new temple, however, offers neither milk and honey, nor revivifying water, nor grain and wine, but only the "bloodless grapes" of its lights (18). Feinman, the bankrolling idol, whose initials flash everywhere as the new Word, is hardly a fine man, presiding with his corruption over a sewage board. His disembodied agent and angel, the amplified voice of the announcer, delivers an annunciation of the fliers' birth that is flagrantly untrue, "talking of creatures imbued with motion though not with life and incomprehensible to the puny crawling painwebbed globe, incapable of suffering, wombed and born complete and instantaneous, cunning intricate and deadly, from out some blind iron batcave of the earth's prime foundation" (28). The announcer no more understands the contestants' humanity than the reporter does.

For Faulkner carefully distinguishes the fliers from their numbing surroundings. Unlike the venal race committee which serves up a death now and then to titillate the spectators, the fliers doggedly pursue hard work and dedication to group interests. Because of their essential innocence, two genuine rituals survive in the book. In contrast to the debased rituals of the airport, these beautifully evoked scenes achieve the status of purifying theogamies.

The first "sacred marriage" occurs when Laverne, learning to parachute, eases back into the airplane, straddles Shumann at the controls, and makes love to him (194). Cleanth Brooks keeps his distance from this scene, merely calling it "outré," and Millgate observes that the copulation is "so extreme, so apparently arbitrary, that [it foregoes] any possible claims to archetypal status."[79] But this scene does become archetypal by affirming life in the face of death: "[Laverne was] clinging to the inner bay strut and looking back at him with an expression that he was later to realise was not at all fear of death but on the contrary a wild and now mindless repudiation of bereavement" (194). Although Edward Guereschi discusses the incident in an essay called "Ritual and Myth in William Faulkner's *Pylon*," he expresses only outrage at a "ceremony indicative of fertility rites," imputing to the participants "mechanical responses." In fact, Guereschi is so shocked at the lovemaking that he almost chortles over Shumann's death as a just punishment for such promiscuity: "In a sense they have paid the price for their involvement with natural experience."[80] This condemnation could not be further from the overall effect of the book. Instead, Laverne reverently demonstrates her love for Shumann. Then, when she summons her courage to jump from the plane, she floats down as a sky-goddess in near-naked splendor. Landing in a throng of lusting townsmen, she also looks like an Orpheus threatened by a mob of male maenads. Faulkner escapes sentimentalizing Laverne's love when he has Shumann recognize in the faces of her would-be rapists "not rage, not even lust, but almost a counterpart of that terror and wild protest against bereavement and division which he had seen in Laverne's face" (200). Passion is a neutral force for good or ill, but Faulkner clearly approves Laverne's good expression of that force.

A second genuine ritual occurs during the reporter's test flight in Ord's plane. He achieves a kind of union not only with Laverne but with Shumann, an imaginative identity possible through the rite of flying and through the symbolism of language. He sails through the sky "with nothing to see but Shumann's feet on the rudderpedals and the movement of the aileron balancerod and nothing to feel but terrific motion—not speed and not progress—just blind furious motion like a sealed force trying to explode the monococque barrel in which he lay from the waist down on his stomach, leaving him clinging to the bodymembers in space" (216–17). As the sense of explosion provides him with a vicarious orgasm, he transcends his selfish desire for Laverne by including Shumann in his embrace also. He moves beyond his own sexuality to encompass, mystically, the bodymembers of the admired couple, Shumann and Laverne, and finally of everyone; he has already drunkenly claimed that "I [not Laverne] got two husbands now" (100) and garbled "organasm" or orgasm with "organization" (97). The "organization" of Laverne's multiple husbands expands to take in the entire human community, blessed with a sexuality epitomized in Laverne and Shumann's earlier coupling in the airplane. The reporter perhaps gains a glimpse of this larger community by submitting himself, as in a rite, to the dangers of the plane ride. Although the ride leaves him with a "skull still cloudy with the light tagends of velocity and speed like the drifting feathers of a shot bird," this prefiguration of the drifting wisps from Shumann's downed plane hardly cancels the validity of the experience (217). On the contrary, the reporter's brief feeling of union, an achieved marriage with all, becomes that much more important in the face of inevitable death.

When Isis retrieves the scattered limbs of Osiris, she breathes into them, so that Osiris lives again as king of the underworld. When Frazer's peasants bury their Carnival, they know that he will permit the return of spring. The question hovering throughout *Pylon* is whether Faulkner alludes to these myths only to undercut them, to show the modern distance from them, or whether he hints through them at any kind of "resurrection." The most obvious answer is that the book ends negatively. Shumann does not rise from the lake. His son, left with grandparents, loses not only Shumann but his mother and Jack as well. Yet in several ways Faulkner does complete the vegetation cycle of loss followed by reaffirmation.

The reporter is shattered when he learns that Laverne will leave her son with Shumann's parents. Yet partly his disappointment stems from selfishness: he still imagines rejoining Laverne someday and using his treats for the boy as the common ground between the adults. His view of her reasons for leaving her son may be one instance in which the reporter does not "devise" aright. He apparently accepts a pressman's cynical conclusion that she "dumps" this living reminder of Shumann in order to make love to Jack with fewer "ghosts," as if she and Jack could or would even want to forget Shumann (293). But other possibilities for her decision exist. The reporter does not know about the second child on the way; Laverne may not feel that she can support both children. She may also "give" the boy to his grandparents as a self-sacrificing compensation to them for the loss of their son. The puritanical grandparents, however, would prefer certain proof that the boy *is* Shumann's son and not Jack's; if Laverne does sacrifice the boy to them, they do not appreciate either her or the gift. Moreover, Faulkner allows us to see her stoical grief, whereas the reporter perceives only his own loss.

Finally, Laverne's departure with Jack restores the emphasis at the end of the book from death to life. In the vegetation myths, the goddess lived eternally, while the god died and was replaced by his reincarnated form. Jack emerges as the new Shumann. In fact, because he already shadows Shumann while the latter is alive, the two men appear all the more as versions of the same life-force. In addition, Faulkner wants us to see the men's tolerance for each other as generous. In their gruff language, Shumann considerately offers Jack the only bed (and thus the night with Laverne) to protect Jack's hurt leg. Refusing, Jack reciprocates by allowing Shumann Laverne's company before Shumann's dangerous contest the next day: "I'll sleep in a cuckold's bed but not in a pimp's [the bed belongs to the reporter]. . . . Go on. Get yourself a piece to take to hell with you tomorrow" (190). Although Jack disparages Shumann as "cuckold," he is actually bestowing on his friend the best gift he knows: sex with Laverne. When Laverne leaves on Sunday with Jack, while still clearly grieving for Shumann, Isis has breathed life into a scattered Osiris and embraced him again, thus living up to her name, *vernal*, auguring spring.

8

Maligning the Goddess: The Case against Cybele

To please the Phrygian goddess Cybele, her priests castrated themselves. The Hindu Kali squatted on Shiva's corpse and gnawed his skull. The Aztec Coatlicue wore a necklace, like Kali's, of skulls, and a skirt fringed with snakes—some say, with severed phalluses.[1] Surely the case must seem closed against these predatory, emasculating goddesses in vegetation myths.

Yet to the ancients, Kali's sacramental posture, kneeling over Shiva, meant that she was making love to him and also that she took his body back into herself to give it rebirth. Primitive peoples surmised that Cybele and Coatlicue needed blood for menstrual or placental fluids to form life. Attis freely cut himself under a pine tree; Cybele did not attack the god. In an alternate version of his story, a boar wounded Attis in the groin, tacitly including a fatal castration.

Ancient worshipers could revere Cybele or Kali as impartial creators and destroyers, presiding over the total cycle of life from birth to death to rebirth and on to death again, whereas uncomprehending Westerners who saw the garlands of skulls depicted on statues were horrified. In turn, modern authors who mistrust women—reflecting either widespread uncertainty at times of social change[2] or personal animosity for biographical reasons—often invoke a Jungian "Terrible Mother," based on the goddess assumed to be a jealous destroyer.

Thomas Mann and Bernard Malamud combine this interpretation of a vicious goddess with the tradition (from Ovid's *Metamorphoses* through Shakespeare's "Venus and Adonis") of the goddess as capricious and even silly. Joyce Carol Oates avails herself of these images of murderous capriciousness but subverts tradition: by depicting a reprehensible Attis figure, she tries to exonerate Cybele.

Mann

The presence of a powerful goddess is, I believe, a major reason why the
stories of the dying deities appealed so strongly to Thomas Mann. Unlike
the rigorously patriarchal Judeo-Christian tradition which denigrated Eve
and her descendants, the newly popularized vegetation myths served to
remind the West that at one time people had worshiped both a goddess and
a god. Moreover, in some of these myths, as Mann tells them, the goddess
and the god could change fluidly into the sex of the other. In *Joseph and
His Brothers* (1933–43) Mann has Joseph teach Benjamin that Ishtar could
grow a beard and that Tammuz could respond to the title "lady," as the
Nile deity had one female and one male breast.[3] Mann borrows this fluidity
to a certain extent for the Hebrew God, calling him both Baal and Baalat
(288). God's double-sexedness then determines a kind of androgyny attributed also to Israel, Jacob, and Joseph. Yet in rediscovering the goddess,
Mann is by no means advocating a greater role for women in his society.
He is advising a greater role for what he calls feminine traits. His favorite
male heroes arrogate these traits, acting out a basically romantic quest for
totality and actually leaving the female characters paler than ever.

Mann, of course, does not originate religious imagery in terms of gender
or sex. The Old Testament prophets, stealing a bit from the vegetation
myths they abhorred, created the metaphor of Israel as the usually wayward bride of Yahweh.[4] Christian mystics like St. Bernard of Clairvaux
and St. John of the Cross developed the image of the soul as the betrothed
of the Lord. In the primary text of Jewish mysticism, the *Zohar*, God even
receives the feminine titles "Matrona" and "Queen" in his identity as
"Community of Israel."[5] Harry Slochower adds as a probable source for
Mann that Plato also envisioned an originally hermaphroditic cosmos.[6] By
drawing on the vegetation stories of Ishtar, Astarte, Ashtaroth, and Isis
(all explicitly named in the novel), Mann reactivates and elaborates both
the platonic tradition and the esoteric Judeo-Christian sexual imagery. He
moves such imagery into the modern world, which in fact has had a craving
for duality or multiplicity ever since William Blake pronounced "The Marriage of Heaven and Hell": "Without Contraries is no progression. Attraction and Repulsion, Reason and Energy, Love and Hate, are necessary to
Human Existence."[7]

Joseph, whose youthful beauty is described as both masculine and feminine, puts an interesting twist on this revived religious imagery of gender
(262). He announces, "I and the mother are one," parodying Christ's "I and
my Father are one" (306). To contrast with Joseph, Mann makes Pharaoh an
unwitting precursor for Christ. Pharaoh's language constantly echoes New
Testament phrases, as in the last half of the following passage: "Golden
spirit is the light, father-spirit; out of the mother-depths below power strives

upward to it, to be purified in its flame and become spirit in the Father. Immaterial is God. . . . For my words are not mine, but the words of my Father who sent me, that all might become one in light and love, even as I and the Father are one" (969).[8]

This Pharaoh, whom Mann decides is the historical Amenhotep IV or Ikhnaton, can anticipate Christ by virtue of his efforts to institute monotheism; yet, interestingly, Mann evaluates Pharaoh—and, by extension, Christ—as wanting in important respects. Pharaoh "wallowed in golden immateriality and father-spirit" (916). He aspires to such transcendent and sober heights that he fails in earthiness and in a sense of irony that Mann associates with Joseph's realm of the mothers. Incidentally, Mann also portrays Pharaoh as giddy and sentimental—and then implies that these qualities are "effeminate." By dumping some of Pharaoh's less pleasing personality traits on his "womanliness," Mann inconsistently ignores Pharaoh's main characteristic, his overemphasis on father-spirit.

The trouble with such romantic lists of "necessary contraries" as father and mother, reason and energy, is that they tempt the list-maker to equate items from the pairs. In fact, when Mann reveals that God or Israel or Joseph displays "female" qualities, he uses a nineteenth-century system of equivalences: "female" feeling, physicality, and passivity as opposed to "male" intellect, spirituality, and activity or aggression. The narrator is condescendingly "touched" that Potiphar's wife, Mut-em-enet (also called Mut, an Egyptian goddess), envies Joseph's practical and intellectual life, which contrasts with her own idle one, but what intellectual production could come out of her "nature wholly occupied with feeling" (734)?[9]

Pharaoh's mother Tiy, whose managerial skills surpass her son's, looks as if she might compete in a male preserve: practical activity outside the home. But if she breaks some stereotypes of gender, Mann uses her case to perpetuate others. It turns out that she can administer the "black earth" of Egypt so well because her feminine nature is itself darker and earthier that man's. She belongs, after all, to "maternal night" (907), an inchoate, feeling-laden "mother-darkness" and "brew of mother-stuff, hated by the light and the power of the new [Father] order," as Potiphar's parents, Huia and Tuia, believe (580). Mann condemns this brother-sister pair's sacrifice of their son's masculinity to somehow "appease" father-rule, and he does not agree that father-rule "hates" mother earth. Yet Mann does agree with the distribution of terms and spheres of activity that Huia and Tuia set up: rule and spirituality belong to men, and darkness and earth to women. God incorporates Father and Mother precisely because he shows "two faces, one a man's, turned toward the daylight, and the other a woman's, looking into the darkness" (745).

Because Mann admires Tiy for putting on the "Usir beard" of the ruler, he even assigns her masculine traits (907). In fact, instead of admitting the possibility of a competent woman, Mann makes all his energetic female characters develop the secondary physical characteristics of masculinity. Tiy possesses a "deep, almost masculine voice" (934), and Rebecca, who thinks up the plan to outsmart Esau, must even sport "little black hairs on her upper lip" to retain Mann's admiration and sense of appropriate division of labor (134). When he tries to explain how Jacob could love Rachel so much, he locates the source of her loveliness (her most important quality) in "spirit and will and power, wisdom and courage in their feminine counterparts"— as if these virtues are essentially masculine accoutrements, which Rachel has managed to don (149).

Women for Mann are more emotional, earthy, and passive than men. He calls "beauty" "a passive, feminine quality, in that it awakens longing and calls out active masculine motives of admiration, desire, and courtship" (745). Because Potiphar's wife courts Joseph with the initiative of an Ishtar, she intrudes on male prerogatives, and the narrator joins Ishtar's beloved Gilgamesh and Mut's beloved Joseph in resenting an aggressive woman (748). By contrast, Joseph's bride Asenath displays a more palatable pliancy, a "tolerant acceptance of her feminine lot"—even as she fades to a cipher. She accedes to her parents' and husband's wishes "to the point of having none of her own" (1001).

Passivity in women entails giving up individuality. Potiphar even conjectures that a man might feel stifled in his allotted role, whereas "probably women have less understanding of such a feeling. For the Great Mother has granted them a more general sense in respect of their being more woman and image of the Mother, and less this or that individual woman. For instance as though you were less bound to be Mut-em-enet than I am to be Petepre because I am conditioned by the sterner father-spirit" (686). Of course, Potiphar is "conditioned" by his state of eunuch more than by the now ironically unavailable "father-spirit," and he here betrays unconscious fears that Mut may be wishing to share her sexuality as other wives do, a desire that he euphemistically words as wanting to be less "individual." Blind to her request that he send Joseph away, Potiphar may be equally blind to individuality in women. Yet Mann agrees with Potiphar that women blur to primordial roles, and to fewer of them, more easily than men do: "Now Tamar was a woman, she was *the* woman, for every woman is *the* woman, instrument of the Fall and womb of salvation, Astarte and the mother of God" (1029).

One might ask why Tamar and Mut, who consciously (though confusedly) play out the gestures of Ishtar and Isis, should be any less "individual" than Joseph, consciously playing out the opposite roles of Tammuz and Osiris. But, Mann hints, it is just Joseph's feminine side that lets him draw so heavily from myth. Mut is femininely attuned to mythical depths; Joseph is femininely attuned to mythical depths. Joseph just happens to possess masculine intellect to boot, which Mut and Tamar never could. As Joseph explains to Potiphar: "For the pattern and the tradition come from the depths which lie beneath and are what binds us, whereas the I is from God and is of the spirit, which is free. But what constitutes civilized life is that the binding and traditional depth shall fulfil itself in the freedom of God which belongs to the I; there is no human civilization without the one and without the other" (937). Since Mann has so insistently labeled spirit male, Mut's chances of possessing either spirit or an "I" are effectively diminished.

Mann's whole treatment of Potiphar's wife further reveals the author's ambivalence toward women. He claims to pity Mut's lot as "tragic" and even judges the volume in which she appears the "artistic zenith of the work" (722) because of his "humane vindication" of her (xi). While he vindicates her out of one side of his mouth, out of the other he condemns her more thoroughly than ever, by making her both sillier and more savage than her biblical antecedent. To touch up what he calls the unfair portrait in Genesis of a "lewd" woman, Mann does show Mut struggling nobly against her passion for three years, and noticing Joseph in the first place only when a meddling dwarf and an imprudently attentive Joseph provoke her to it. Yet Mann humiliates Mut by having her lisp her plea to Joseph: "Thleep with me" (769). Not content with reducing her to a child, Mann magnifies her into a dangerous bacchante. As part of his larger social purpose to denounce fascism by way of Amun's nationalistic scorn for Hebrews, Mann reserves his most virulent demagoguery for Mut (832). Far from excusing the biblical wife, Mann heaps on more charges. He has her suggest to Joseph— "sweetly," while "pouting"—that she might kill Potiphar (774).

Mann also foists off some unbelievable physiology along with this psychologically melodramatic and biblically unprecedented "sweet" murderousness when he declares that her breasts and thighs swell once she falls in love (766). Mann makes it clear that femininity in essence equals sexuality and that sexuality inevitably degenerates into witchery (765). Mut's black maid Tabubu, in a kind of Walpurgisnacht, magically invokes a bitch-goddess in terms that might be misogynist: "You that perch at home on gallows where the criminal is flayed, squeaking and squalling and slobbering as you gnaw the carrion bones! Last lust of the hanged, wet-wombed 'receiver of his erected agony" (814).

It could be argued that Tabubu's graphic corpse imagery, along with Mut's murderousness (toward Potiphar and later toward Joseph), conforms to some extent to the myths of the goddess, which, in Mann's readings, associate sex and death. Isis, for example, hovers in the shape of a carrion bird over Osiris's corpse to conceive Horus; the force of her love causes Osiris to return to life. Mann bizarrely imagines how Osiris's erection must have torn the mummy casings and then recreates the scene by suggesting that Osarsiph (Joseph), although not actually sleeping with Mut when he leaves his cloak in her hands, did experience an erection in her presence. But Mut, unlike Isis, does not bring Joseph-Osarsiph back to life in the "underworld" of Egypt; instead, as temptress, she precipitates him into the further pit of prison. Mann does not use Isis's story to celebrate the power of life over death but rather to evoke the deathly atmosphere of love. Mann may be linking this deathliness especially with heterosexual love. If not purely a typographical error, the substitution of Anubis's name for Isis's as that of the vulture arousing Osiris might signal a kind of Freudian slip eliminating the dangerous woman altogether (191). Anubis, Osiris's son by the "wrong" wife, corresponds to Ishmael, another son of a "wrong" wife, and Mann does imply that the real reason Abraham dismisses Ishmael is that he caught him "sporting" homosexually with Isaac.[10]

Mann draws the association of sex with death from the stories of two other goddesses besides Isis: Ishtar and Persephone. Taking the view that Ishtar maliciously causes the death of her young lover, Mann patterns the behavior of both Mut and Tamar on her vindictiveness. According to the Bible, Tamar's first two husbands die; Mann adds "in her arms." Although the narrator labels Judah's evaluation of Tamar—an Ishtar who slays her beloved—as "unfair," he in fact subscribes to this view by casting sly doubts: "as tradition has it, the Lord slew [them]—well, the Lord does all" (1023, 1033).

Mann does not really distinguish between Ishtar murdering and Persephone murdered: whether the woman dies or causes her lover to die, she is somehow at fault. Thus he shows little sympathy for abducted women. He dismisses Joseph's sister Dinah, raped by Sichem, as "an insignificant thing, very yielding" (113). Mann elaborately recreates Persephone's story for Joseph's marriage to Asenath, a priest's daughter who is by convention a virgin. Although her parents consent fully to the wedding, the celebrants all act as if Joseph is abducting her. The narrator, in fact, concurs that she is an "obstinate virgin" and, disturbingly, has no objections that her first son by Joseph be conceived in "blood and pain" (1008). The narrator comments complacently:

> Behind [Joseph's] back we may agree that there does exist a certain relation between death and marriage, a bridal chamber and a tomb, a murder and the abduction of a bride. It is no great strain to think of a brideroom as a god of death. And there is a likeness between the fate of a maiden, who, a veiled sacrifice, steps across the serious divide between maidenhood and wifehood, and the fate of the seed-corn buried in the darkness there to rot and then out of corruption to come back to the light as just such another seed-corn, virgin and new. (1005).

While he is busy paralleling pregnancy and corruption, the narrator, without seeming to realize it, trenchantly pictures possible social consequences of a marriage: a woman's marriage *is* her death if it means she must lose her identity in her husband's.

In summary, Mann can proclaim that "in the sex is death and in death sex" for several uncomfortably mixed sociological, psychological, and mythological reasons. First, when Jacob sees his sons born, he realizes that he himself will die one day to make room for them; sexuality, if followed by birth, reminds him of his own mortality. Second, the link could mean that love makes the lover emotionally vulnerable. Judah, for example, resents his inability to live by himself. He blames his lustfulness (and his dependency) on "Ishtar's spears," condemning women for his own out-of-control desires (1022). Third, women, sexuality, and death have historically become associated through the image of "mother earth" as grave. Unlike the Indian belief that respects Kali for devouring the corpse as well as for delivering her multitudinous brood, the Hebrew tradition scorns Eve for ushering in death. Mann draws on the old womb-tomb imagery as well as on the whole macabre tradition by which world-weary romantic poets courted death in a kind of necrophilia.[11] Finally, given the brutality of Asenath's wedding night, Mann conveys, I think, some fear and hostility toward women. When Judah instead of Joseph unexpectedly receives the blessing, Judah muses that indulging sexuality wasn't so damning after all; however, Mann seems to mean that evil itself is necessary—"hell is taken in"—and that women are still somehow hellish (1191). For modern men, romantics to Jung, to validate irrationality, fantasy, dream, and feeling, in addition to the Enlightenment's reason, might be all well and good, but to assign these imaginative elements to a so-called female side of a person still limits both women and men.

Malamud

In addition to quarrying Arthurian legend for prototypes, Bernard Malamud also crams *The Natural* (1952) with allusions to the dying god. Malamud has his baseball hero play out two roles related to vegetation myths: priest-king succeeding priest-king through victory in battle and god succeeding himself through rebirth. Critics differ in evaluating Malamud's skill in juggling these legends. Margaret Dalziel accuses Malamud of perpetrating with his multiple sources a "fashionable gimmick," whereas Earl Wasserman praises him for organizing "the rites of baseball and many of its historic episodes into the epic inherent in baseball as a measure of man."[12] More gimmick than epic, to my mind, *The Natural* matches every mundane detail and its eternally adolescent characters with a mythical precedent too thickly and obviously for my taste. Still, the book illuminates the relation between "timeless" myth, supposedly rooted in psychology, and an attitude toward women, situated at a very definite time and place, the American midcentury. Revealingly, when Malamud creates a companion for his dying god, he chooses among the mythological candidates a predatory version of the goddess.

To a large extent, of course, Malamud is aware of the immaturity of both his male protagonist and his "snappy goddesses."[13] Satirizing false goals with appealing humor, Malamud deliberately shows myth debased in American culture from a religion to a game. If the members of the Knights team played honestly and not selfishly, Malamud believes, they could be role models as valuable as their namesake, the medieval questers. Malamud likewise expects the myth of the dying/reviving god to be meaningfully reactivated when Roy finally realizes who his true goddess is. In portraying his goddesses, however, Malamud unintentionally trivializes some mythological figures along with the social targets he purposely mocks.

From a train window at the beginning of the book, Roy (le roi) Hobbs, potentially King of the Wood, sees a boy throwing a ball to a dark oak. Frazer singles out the oak as a favorite habitation for a god of vegetation.[14] Hinting that the boy is just a hallucinatory vision of himself, Roy knows that he will soon strike at (or out) the old king guarding the wood (guarding the right to the wooden bat anyway). He then defeats the Whammer, numerous bad-luck cases on the Knights team, and Bump: earlier repositories of the vital spark. Because cyclical time limits all contenders, the rookie with the promising name Youngberry will in turn eventually replace Roy.

Representing a dying god as well as a King of the Wood, Roy succeeds himself. Although already a youth when the book begins, he manages a rebirth in the first line. The vocabulary of train rides—"lower berth" and "tunnel"—somehow conjures a birth canal. Roy soon "dies" when Harriet Bird "harries" him out of active life: "The bullet cut a silver line across the water. He sought with his bare hands to catch it, but it eluded him and, to his horror, bounced into his gut. A twisted dagger of smoke drifted up from the gun barrel. Fallen on one knee he groped for the bullet, sickened as it moved, and fell over as the forest flew upward, and she, making muted noises of triumph and despair, danced on her toes around the stricken hero" (40). Like an incarnation of the god, bloodied before Cybele, Roy fades into a series of incarnations: Harriet has already targeted a football ace and an Olympic athlete. Knowing that Malamud modeled Harriet on a motiveless girl who really did shoot an athlete in 1949 does not make the fictional feather dancer seem any less contrived.[15] The odd newspaper fact and the myth of Cybele alike fuel Malamud's case against women as destroyers.

Roy is "reborn" into baseball fifteen years or almost a generation after Harriet's attack, as if he, like the reincarnating god, were somehow his own son. But a new woman again slows him down. Whereas Harriet had invited him to her bed and then calmly shot him before he could get into it, Memo Paris slithers into bed right away—but only because she mistakes him in the dark for somebody else. The name Memo might signal "memento mori" or "remember Harriet," because, in fact, she monotonously resembles that earlier dangerous woman: equally murderous and just as flighty. Memo causes Roy a series of near-deaths. She almost runs over a boy who may or may not really be in the road; Roy helpfully informs us that this boy, like the one by the train, represents himself, "his lost youth" (128). Because Roy feels guilty for accompanying this reckless woman, he falls into the little "death" of a pitching slump.

Memo inflicts two more deaths on Roy, both mimicking aspects of his encounter with Harriet. As he swooned before Harriet's silver bullet, now, after glutting himself at a feast, he struggles to Memo and collapses, perhaps because she has tried to poison him. He has at least figuratively poisoned himself by gorging on the company of the wrong kind of people. Although he winds up at a maternity hospital (one of Malamud's too-obvious symbols), he is not likely to be reborn yet, still too foolish to perceive the shallowness of Memo and forget his life with her. He deteriorates even further to the point of agreeing to lose a game purposely, for bribe money with which to lure Memo. When he finally renounces the money, Memo again duplicates Harriet by trying to shoot him (and herself). The end of the book has thus cycled back to the beginning. Although Memo does not succeed in literally killing him, he feels deadened emotionally through his contact with her—tainted by racketeering and flushed out of baseball.

Malamud is not just blaming Harriet and Memo for keeping a good man down. He also faults Roy for tagging after false grails. Robert Shulman is glad to see that the inexorable cycle of seasons and the predictable return of archetypes do not "determine" a character's responses: Malamud still assigns Roy personal responsibility.[16] Roy confronts free choices, which he then bungles. Just as the seasons do not manipulate him, neither do the women. Still, Malamud makes it look as if they do. As Richard Schickel summarizes both the movie version of *The Natural* and the book, "In Malamud's baseball world, like Malory's Arthurian one, men are ever the victims; it is women who have the power to make them betray their best selves as well as the ability to inspire them to redemptive glory."[17]

One might use this image of redemptive women to defend Malamud's portrayal of femaleness. If women seem murderous, one of them, Iris Lemon, saves Roy too. Only because she shows confidence in him does Roy succeed in climbing out of his slump and, momentarily, out of his egotism: like Babe Ruth, he hits a home run for a sick child.[18] Perhaps an Isis in Iris is at work restoring her ethically deadened Osiris. At any rate, they rush off to make love, at lakeside, but Roy cannot yet turn water into a symbol for a real rebirth. More likely he is drowning again in his own selfishness, as he insensitively "shoves her back" when she wants to say something and finally rejects her outright when he discovers that she is a grandmother (at the ripe old age of thirty-three).

Despite Iris Lemon's floral first name and nutritious-sounding last name, her fruits are too astringent for one who prefers Memo's sickeningly sweet "apples, grapes, and melons" (65). Roy cannot resist the slang for "faulty product": this Lemon of a woman has the impudence to make him feel like a grandfather. Of course, he is still the middle-aged man he was before meeting her, but without her he can pretend he's younger. Thirty-three was the Whammer's age when Roy defeated him, and it is also Christ's year of salvation. Roy sees the age as gateway to death rather than threshold into rebirth, maturity, and power. Malamud's point is that Roy has to learn to accept cycles—including failures, new beginnings, aging, death, and generation. Roy pouts instead that he is "sick up to here of new beginnings," not realizing the ominous alternative of no beginnings (133). But Hobbs, with his all too obvious name, is still hobbled from entering into his true kingship: prevented, as he thinks, by this old lady, but actually by his own imperception.

Iris, not averse to beginning all over again, saves him a second time by standing to signal confidence. Renouncing his bad decision to fix the game, he swings, too late to win the game and just in time to slam Iris with the ball. Do men hurt women just as much as women hurt men? Roy might send her on a trip to the hospital that matches his, but he never intended to hit her (as Harriet and Memo intended to hurt him). He did, however, intend to cheat—equivalent to injuring what the good woman literally "stands for." Although the book ends just as Roy finally notices that he has botched his life, we are comforted at least that he has rejected his bribe. Roy has the chance to rise again, because he has begun to accept aging and cycles. Malamud suggests that Roy will probably join Iris and their expected child, and thus continue to mature.

Despite Iris's goodness, Malamud's "snappy goddesses" fail to measure up to their ancient prototypes. Often murderous, his goddesses are also silly. Gun-toting Harriet "giggles" and sets Roy up "sweetly" (40). Although Malamud tries to make Memo at least partly sympathetic by having her mourn so long for Bump, she, like Harriet, is superficial and venal. Malamud intends to satirize materialism, but he also trivializes the mythological figure of a powerful destroyer-goddess. Memo enjoys a bookie's company and is "amused" at seeing him and Roy bet each other, as Harriet's "eyes shone" when Roy and the Whammer face off (27). Women are jealous and they like having men fight over them because it flatters their beauty. Even Iris, who is much more mature than these two, displays little substance. She is circumscribed, as might be expected, by a fifties view of woman as homemaker only; more disturbingly, however, she cannot even think rationally about why she chooses to devote her life to the daughter with whom she was abandoned. When Roy appears, she can again only intuit:

"she thought distractedly of a home, children, and him coming home every night to supper" (160). It is hard to accept Malamud's allusions to "goddesses" when the only two choices he gives are giggling, empty-headed "lovelies" or lovely, instinctively sensible but unthinking homebodies.

Malamud's attitude toward women comes out perhaps most interestingly in his imagery of birds, more complex than his other symbols. Robert Higgs and Earl Wasserman simplistically associate the bird with Jung's "terrible mother." Harriet's last name is Bird; Roy's mother, despised by him as a whore, is "that bird"; and Roy performs tasteless magic tricks with Memo like plucking a duck's egg from her bosom. Wasserman gallantly adds that Harriet gets to be "terrible" only because Roy pushes her to it: "With Roy's blindness to the communal and reproductive purpose of his vitality . . . Harriet is the psychic mother from whose dual nature Roy has evoked the destructive."[19] Higgs, on the other hand, decides that womanly birds are always bad in themselves, with no provocation from men: "while the trees stand for potency and masculinity, the birds suggest all the castrating forces of modern society. Each of the women who influences Roy is in one way or another associated with birds."[20] Higgs does not explain why women should be responsible for "all" the forces in modern society that have been construed as "castrating"—for example, the alienating effects of the assembly line.

But the mythology in which Malamud roots his story does not invariably make birds associated with women evil figures. Isis as swallow or hawk restored Osiris, and Aphrodite's attendant dove was originally a yonic symbol that evolved into the holy ghost.[21] Malamud, in fact, does allude to the holy ghost in connection with women. When the Whammer feels his power leaving him, he sees the ball as a white bird, a pigeon; when the mantle passes to Roy, a canary descends on him as if in blessing (28, 85). He has assumed a vital power, and Malamud makes clear that in some sense this is a feminine holy ghost, because he now praises Roy in feminine terms, as "the bird that lays" (114). But this valuable feminine power, later reinforced in him by Iris, is of a very specific type. Woman's strength is solely the will to be unselfish. When that canary/holy ghost descends on Roy to invest him with its female power, he grabs it in his glove so that the impact reduces the creature to a bloody mess. Wasserman says that the Whammer's ball naturally plummets "'like a dead bird,' the terrible mother having been defeated for the moment."[22] But it is not only the terrible mother whom Roy defeats. A good, lemon-yellow canary, blessing Roy, goes down too, because she *should* sacrifice herself for him. A woman's power is her ability to efface herself—no thinking except "distractedly," no hitting baseballs; if she has the audacity to pick up a stick, it will look like a gun to those who feel threatened.

Oates

Although Joyce Carol Oates relies primarily on realism to expose the meaningless lives of upwardly mobile Americans, she too is drawn to Eliot's "mythical method" in her 1979 novel *Cybele*. The ancient Phrygian goddess unexpectedly hovers over the malls, expressways, suburbs, and business lunches of a materialistic milieu—generally at a discreet distance. Oates assigns to Cybele's voice the opening chapter and most of the last one; the goddess's first-person speeches briefly interrupt the usual third-person omniscient narration only one other time, halfway through the book. The author thus frames the story with the goddess's comments in the same way that the Greek dramatist Euripides introduces the goddesses Aphrodite and Artemis onto the stage at the beginning and end of his otherwise strictly human *Hippolytus*.

Cybele's disembodied voice may deliver harsh truths, but she herself acts less vindictively than even Euripides's vengeful and petty goddesses, let alone the supposedly cruel Cybele of legend with her emasculated priests. Oates's simple, didactic message is hardly that women always hurt men, but that the loveless pursuit of sensual pleasure destroys people. Far from presenting women as terrorizing men, Oates borrows one of the most fearsome of the vegetation goddesses to speak bluntly about the pathetic failures of both sexes in a faithless, status-conscious age. Although Oates mars some of Cybele's lines with melodrama, the framing device is, in my opinion, generally effective. The goddess's presence reminds us of beliefs more substantial than the ideals of the human characters, who are devoted to a nice lawn and a quick lay. In a realistic novel that chugs along with the competent but unexciting predictability of the evening traffic patterns, Cybele, from a mystery cult, injects at least momentary pizazz. Her appearance testifies to the longevity of the vegetation deities, if a popular novelist of the late twentieth century sees fit to blazon *Cybele* from a supermarket rack.

Cybele usually plays opposite an Attis, and Oates satirically offers her main character, Edwin Locke, for this role. One of his lovers meets him at a bookstore where she is leafing through *Secrets of Lost Atlantis, UFO's: The God Who Walks Among Us*, and *Witchcraft Black and White*.[23] Although Edwin steps miraculously from behind the stacks to pay her bill, he is obviously unworthy to be the god among us. His story records the follies of a fortyish executive undergoing a banal "mid-life crisis"; he self-indulgently pursues affairs with a series of women and dies under sordid circumstances.

Yet for all his shallowness, Edwin follows some of the patterns that Frazer sets out for Attis, for other dying gods, or for their human representatives. Edwin, for example, works for Monarch Life and Auto Insurance Co., and the constant references to Monarch Life remind us that he is living out the precarious tenure of Frazer's King of the Wood, stalked by his successor. Edwin does, in fact, die in a fight with one of his women's other lovers, Valentin Rok, who has menaced him for some time. Though Rok and several neighbors chase Edwin for molesting a child and for defacing Rok's styrofoam sculpture (it is hard to tell which of the two crimes his ethically lax pursuers despise more), the actual cause of Edwin's death is probably a heart attack, rather than the King of the Wood's defeat in battle or in a moment of lowered vigilance. Over his own morals, Edwin has no vigilance.

When the attackers decide out of fear to burn his body, they shift his identification from King of the Wood to another Frazerian character, the "burned god," entitling Edwin to ritual deference: "Rok [pouring gasoline on the corpse] forces himself to act with caution, even with a certain ceremonial grace, despite the undeniable tension of the moment" (203). Although Rok momentarily steps into the role of priest, he is hardly the rock of our salvation any more than Edwin is.

Oates also alludes to straw effigies of the Old Year or of Osiris left to sprout over the winter.[24] The mother of the children who find Edwin's charred body complains, "It's just more trouble. . . . The thing could be there all year, over the winter and everything, and nobody'd know, but *you*—you guys had to go find him, didn't you!" (191). Like the planted corpse in Eliot's *Waste Land*, which the dog is likely to dig up, Edwin's body is retrieved too soon to provide any consoling signs of the renewal of life from old seed.

Edwin fails as vegetation god: his character is weak, not godlike, and his death, therefore, does no good. Attis may have permitted the new year to bloom, whereas Edwin announces the same old years warmed over. Scurrying to a domestic reconciliation which, in Oates's chronological dislocations, we already know to have fallen apart, Edwin waxes maudlin and self-congratulatory:

stopping for a quick drink at the Ram's Horn—a pleasant surprise to find it open, when nearly every other place was closed—Edwin felt oddly, wonderfully, inexplicably *pure*. Like a man convalescing from a serious illness. He was shaking and weak yet somehow chaste; even, in a way difficult to comprehend, *sacred*. . . .

Do you know, he said to the bartender, I feel *purged*, I feel new as the New Year.

Yes? said the bartender absently. He was wiping the bar with a damp rag, in quick and ever decreasing circles.

I feel as if—as if I could go around blessing people, Edwin said, tears

in his eyes frankly and unashamedly. I feel as if—well, anyway, Happy
New Year to you!
  Is it, said the bartender. (129)

The Ram's Horn has degenerated from biblical shofar to the name of a
tavern and trysting place. If Edwin lacks the perception to initiate any real
"new" years in his life, his death likewise lacks the power to jolt other
characters into awareness of their similar failings. Cybele warns on the first
page, "There are tears of grief that are tears of fury as well. But they are
not cleansing. Nor does the earth greedily soak them up" (11). The women
Edwin knows cannot grieve deeply for relationships of no substance.
Although his body is thrown among "Last autumn's leaves, dessicated
sheets of newspaper, nameless debris. . . hardy clumps of Queen Anne's
lace, buttercups, and heal-alls, growing, as if by miracle, in a few inches of
fortuitous soil," he leaves behind no hardy queens, no miracles, no healing
(203).
  As Edwin stands in for Attis, the female characters share the role of
Cybele's inheritors: by name, paraphernalia, and, most problematically,
"cruel" personality. The Cy of Cybele goes to Cynthia; the C to Cathleen.
As Cybele was represented in ancient times by a "small black stone,"[25]
Edwin meets Cathleen in a tower made of "onyx and jade and glass," and
he later gives Zanche "a darkly translucent onyx in a silver setting" (18,
171). These women, however, fail to qualify as votaries of the goddess in
more than ornament. They lack her stature. Although Oates does not
stereotype Cynthia as either the long-suffering, innocent wife or the nag-
ging wife who fails to understand Edwin, she remains pathetic, not dignified. She pitiably dresses as a hooker because a therapist stupidly counsels that the pose will win back her husband, and she kids herself that
supporting a politician best known for his "visionary" delirium tremens will
remedy her trivial life. As pathetic as Cynthia, Cathleen nurses sad fears
that Edwin won't love her because of something so irrelevant as a cyst.
And Zanche, who makes such a poor mother to Chrissie, has to stand at
the other end of the alphabet and traditional color valuation from a pure
white Blanche; Oates thus criticizes Zanche, though the author certainly
pities her too.
  With Zanche's daughter, Edwin has a disturbing, perhaps drunken vision of a hermaphrodite, reminding us that Cybele's male followers are
dressed as women. A man dressed as a woman has already accosted Edwin
at a party. Although Edwin tries to get away from this man with foam
rubber breasts, the embrace is somehow appropriate, because Edwin has
always loved nothing but superficial physical attractions in women. Like
Cybele's priests either castrated or made temporarily impotent by the ap-

plication of hemlock, Edwin has also experienced impotence with his women. Oates makes it clear that his own doubts cause his problems, not his mistresses'or his wife's domination; Edwin does not move any closer to priestly reverence through his indisposition.

Occasionally the female characters sound faintly vengeful, as when Cathleen hysterically threatens Edwin, but she offers to kill herself too (96). When Edwin calls Cynthia "murderer," he indulges only in childish self-pity (180). Concerning Cathleen's substanceless threats, Cybele observes, "Afterward, of course, he was to forget his terror. Poor man! He was to forget the clarity of his terror in that moment when he gazed upon me, without recognition" (96). Here Cybele refers to herself, the object of Edwin's gaze, as simply death.

In a lurid, overwritten passage, Cybele again becomes death incarnate. She is describing how Edwin fights aginst sleep at his desk, when he really wants only to snooze and to die away from all responsibilities. Edwin seems to penetrate into dream and death and her body, "An immense hill into which he wants to burrow . . . And the hill becomes flesh, and the flesh seems to flinch from his violence, his need, whimpering as if it were alive. . . . And then the flesh, which has parted for him, in fear of him, begins to contract. And, horribly, he is caught in me. Trapped. Swallowed alive! He screams for help. . . . I have him, I have him forever" (193–94). If Oates melodramatically churns up the familiar imagery of mother earth as "womb and tomb," the allusion to devouring crone at least saves Cybele (and her "daughters" Cynthia and Cathleen) from a charge of special womanly malice. Cybele exposes no traps set by women but rather the impartial terrors of the grave, which Edwin himself is so recklessly seeking, in his already ethically and emotionally deadened life.

9
Maligning the God: The Case against Hades

According to myth, Hades (also called Pluton, Pluto, or Dis) rapes Persephone (Proserpine or Kore) and abducts her into the underworld as his wife. Grieving and searching for her daughter, Demeter (Ceres) petitions Zeus, who has complacently permitted the rape, but the only response he gives is to boast that Persephone now has him as brother-in-law. Not until Demeter threatens sterility over the land does Zeus compromise, allowing Persephone to return for part of the year.[1]

The authors in this chapter allude to Persephone for characters who not only experience a violent initiation to literal death or sexuality but also fight against figuratively deadening patriarchy: Woolf in *To the Lighthouse*, Faulkner in *The Sound and the Fury*, and Welty in "Asphodel." My discussions about these works will modify this too neat schema; Woolf and Welty complain about women almost more than about men. Nevertheless, all three authors sympathize with Persephone as victim. As I will try to show in the conclusion, such sympathy has by no means been automatic in twentieth-century interpretations of this myth of mother and daughter.

Woolf

In *To the Lighthouse* (1927), Virginia Woolf associates Mrs. Ramsay with myths of dying deities through two images. First, Mrs. Ramsay winds a green shawl around a pig's skull.[2] Her action at least superficially suggests life against death because many dying deities—gods of the green vegetation—fought against boars. Second, Woolf visualizes Mrs. Ramsay as a Demeter accompanying the dying deity Persephone. But if allusions to green life and fertile Demeter bolster Mrs. Ramsay's attractiveness, Woolf startlingly modifies the myths of dying gods to convey her ambivalence toward this forceful character. Instead of obliterating the skull, Mrs. Ramsay's green shawl only camouflages it and in some ways seems to embrace it complicitously. Even more surprisingly, Woolf creates a radically uncon-

179

ventional Demeter. Far from protecting any daughters (including her "spiritual" daughter, Lily Briscoe), Mrs. Ramsay blithely acquiesces in Hades' abduction.

Woolf would know these myths from her extensive classical training, especially her acquaintance with the scholar Jane Harrison. Woolf is not reinventing archetypes but rather rearranging learned mythology, usually purposefully, I believe, although perhaps sometimes unconsciously. Discovering which aspects of her inherited myths Woolf changes can help clarify her attitudes toward women and marriage and toward women and artistic creation.

Mrs. Ramsay mediates between her son James, who likes looking at the pig's skull, and her daughter Cam, who fears its shadow, by hiding the skull with a shawl, while convincing James that his prize is still there. It is a "black pig," Mrs. Ramsay says, linking this treasure of the nursery with a traditional image of death. The boar was the enemy of a number of dying gods:

> For it was in the shape of a black pig that Set injured the eye of the god Horus. . . . Again, the story that Set was hunting a boar when he discovered and mangled the body of Osiris, and that this was the reason that pigs were sacrificed once a year, is clearly a modernised version of an older story that Osiris, like Adonis and Attis, was slain or mangled by a boar, or by Set in the form of a boar.[3]

Many readers, basing their interpretation on such lore, see the shawl as life overcoming death, with Mrs. Ramsay all on the side of life. Thus Joseph Blotner, who has pointed out mythical references in *To the Lighthouse*, thinks that he has adequately pigeonholed Mrs. Ramsay as a nurturing goddess: "As Mrs. Ramsay gives love, stability, and fruitfulness to those in her orbit, so the female force should always function. It serves to ameliorate or mitigate the effects of male violence, hate, and destructiveness. And should the physical embodiment of this force pay her debt to the world of shades, this is not an ever-enduring loss, for it returns through those whom it has made fruitful [Lily] and thus drawn into the rebirth pattern."[4] But Blotner oversimplifies here. He sounds like a new Mr. Ramsay by prescribing that a woman "should" always nurture those in her orbit as her rightful role in the world, whereas the book as a whole includes "fostering her own talents" or "creating art" as other possible right uses of this "female force."

Moreover, the tone of irony and deflation that so often surrounds Mrs. Ramsay certainly undermines her as an entirely nurturing embodiment of "the female force." Carolyn Heilbrun reviews the shift in critical interpretations of Mrs. Ramsay from "all good" to "less than wholly admirable" or even "as life-denying as her husband."[5] We can gauge Woolf's ambivalence toward Mrs. Ramsay when that green shawl unwinds, one fold at a time, to mark the deaths of Prue and Andrew (196, 200). The reader might plead that if further deaths win against green life after Mrs. Ramsay has died first, then no one can blame her. Yet the image does attribute the deaths to the shawl, unwinding so negligently, as if the always-possessive Mrs. Ramsay were willfully taking Prue and Andrew back into her embrace. She is still directing, weaving and winding her fates, and she silently lets her shawl be a shroud.

If Mrs. Ramsay in any sense embodies a life-force, as Blotner wants her to do, Woolf resents the whole system of life because it tolerates and requires death. Life displays as little concern over suffering as a boy cutting a square out of a fish to bait his hook, then throwing the mutilated body—"it was alive still"—back into the sea (268). To emphasize good green goddess against destructive boar is to catch only part of the story. For as James Frazer notes, the pig may not just oppose dying gods or dying goddesses but may at one time have represented these deities in animal form. More specifically, Demeter and Persephone may originally have appeared as pigs.[6] To sacrifice a pig would not so much commemorate the slaying of the god's enemy as reenact the sacrifice of a deity who equally fosters creation and destruction. Lily, however, derives a tempered consolation from this life-force that more accurately furthers both life and death.

Mrs. Ramsay tolerates and even abets death not only with her lax shawl, enshrouding and swaying "aimlessly" (200), but also in several explicit images of Persephone and Demeter. Critics who mention Demeter in *To the Lighthouse* either make Woolf's version too benevolent[7] or see the goddess as only a passing allusion.[8] Grace Stewart in *A New Mythos* correctly perceives *To the Lighthouse* as "Persephone's plea for exemption from the eternal cycle of dominance by either Pluto or Demeter." But Stewart only applies the classical story as a general frame to a whole group of novelists who, she believes, have not "specifically known" the myth.[9] On the contrary, Woolf knew myths of dying gods from her studies in the classics.[10] Beverly Schlack points out references to Ceres in *Mrs. Dalloway* and shows how Woolf's acquaintance with the classical scholar Jane Harrison and Woolf's fondness for Shelley's "Adonais" also fostered an interest in dying deities.[11]

The Persephone story treats death as a rape, and, equally disturbingly, it treats marriage as a death. Woolf taps both aspects, using the myth to signify a woman's death and to suggest a wife's submission to a possessive man. For both purposes she frequently alludes to Persephone's scattered flowers, imagery that figures prominently in classical sources such as the "Homeric Hymn to Demeter" and Ovid's *Metamorphoses*. Ovid even imagines his Proserpine focusing all her lament on her lost bouquet:

In this glade Proserpine was playing, picking violets or shining lilies. With childlike eagerness she gathered the flowers into baskets and into the folds of her gown, trying to pick more than any of her companions. Almost at one and the same time, Pluto saw her, and loved her, and bore her off—so swift is love. With wailing cries the terrified goddess called to her mother, and to her comrades, but more often to her mother. She rent and tore the upper edge of her garment, till the flowers she had gathered fell from its loosened folds: and she was so young and innocent that even this loss caused her fresh distress.[12]

Ovid's reference to jostled baskets, torn folds of a garment, and lost flowers all encode common euphemisms for violent sexual experience. Woolf uses similar images, without, however, blaming the victim, as Ovid subtly exonerates the rapist Pluto by having Proserpine rend her garment herself. The scene of Persephone's abduction appears at least three times in *To the Lighthouse* for Prue, Mrs. Ramsay, and Cam.

Most vividly, Lily pictures Prue's dying as Persephone's dropping her flowers: "[Prue] let her flowers fall from her basket, scattered and tumbled them on to the grass and, reluctantly and hesitantly, but without question or complaint—had she not the faculty of obedience to perfection?—went too. . . . They went, the three of them together, Mrs. Ramsay walking rather fast in front, as if she expected to meet someone round the corner" (299). The name "Prue," a kind of anagram for "pure," probably comes from "Prudence," though it could well be a nickname for "Proserpine." Anne Hoffman thinks the three figures are Mrs. Ramsay and two children.[13] But I believe they are Mrs. Ramsay (Demeter), Prue (Persephone), and death (Hades) because Mrs. Ramsay roams the fields of death with a "companion" even before the children die. Indeed, Lily pictures the dying Mrs. Ramsay as herself playing out the role of Persephone, "stepping with her usual quickness across fields among whose folds, purplish and soft, among whose flowers, hyacinths or lilies, she vanished. . . . For days after she had heard of her death she had seen her thus, putting her wreath to her forehead and going unquestioningly with her companion, a shade across the fields" (270).

Although Woolf usually casts Mrs. Ramsay as Demeter and the younger women as Persephone, here Mrs. Ramsay treads Persephone's path— almost as if the overzealous mother must test every route for her daughter. Mrs. Ramsay drops the same hyacinths (themselves sacred to a dying god, Hyacinthus) and the same virginal lilies that are said to be among the flowers Persephone was culling when Hades surprised her.[14] Moreover, the gesture of putting a wreath to her forehead recalls Jane Harrison's description of spring ceremonies for dying/reviving earth goddesses: "The Horae, the Seasons, a chorus of maidens, lead in the figure of Spring, the Queen of the May, and they call to Mother Earth to wake, to rise up from the earth,

flower-crowned."[15] Woolf is known to have consulted just this section of
Ancient Art in 1923–24.[16] In fact, the degree to which Harrison influenced
Woolf might be suggested by a letter Woolf wrote to the *New Statesman* in
1920, in which she culminates a list of powerful intellectual women with
Harrison's name.[17]

Like Harrison's chorus of maidens, Lily wants to call Mrs. Ramsay back
to life, but because the older woman will not come, Lily implicitly accuses
her of having abandoned family and friends at her death. Instead of picturing the dying woman fighting against her abduction into the underworld,
the painter sees her "going unquestioningly with her companion, a shade
across the fields" (270). Maria DiBattista interprets Mrs. Ramsay in this
passage as a "nature goddess," testifying to Woolf's "feminine faith" in
transfiguration.[18] But Mrs. Ramsay is not signaling regeneration, in a positive mood; she is unpleasantly conspicuous for failing to ask questions. She
should have protested, as the Homeric Persephone goes "resisting and
screaming."[19] But she strolls along willingly with her "companion," Hades
in the form of male escort, just as she has always accepted a man by her
side.

In fact, Mrs. Ramsay acquiesces to Hades as easily as she allowed
Charles Tansley to accompany her to town. Dazzled by her beauty, Tansley imagines her in preposterously romantic terms that ominously include
the same fields of flowers as her death scene:

> With stars in her eyes and veils in her hair, with cyclamen and wild
> violets—what nonsense was he thinking? She was fifty at least; she had
> eight children. Stepping through fields of flowers and taking to her breast
> buds that had broken and lambs that had fallen; with the stars in her eyes
> and the wind in her hair—He took her bag.
> "Good-bye, Elsie," she said, and they walked up the street, she hold-
> ing her parasol erect and walking as if she expected to meet some one
> round the corner, while for the first time in his life Charles Tansley felt
> an extraordinary pride; a man digging in a drain stopped digging and
> looked at her, let his arm fall down and looked at her; for the first time in
> his life Charles Tansley felt an extraordinary pride; felt the wind and the
> cyclamen and the violets for he was walking with a beautiful woman. He
> had hold of her bag. (25)

Although Tansley, all agog, is the one who doodles violets in his mind, it is
clear that Mrs. Ramsay accepts this homage to her beauty. But such adoration comes at a price. Tansley's apparently humble worship ends in a pride-
ful possessiveness. The sexual currents between them that produce the
vocabulary of erected parasols and digging in drains culminate rather
crudely in male dominance. Mrs. Ramsay may condescend to Tansley and
initially lead him, but by the end, he "had hold of her bag": the man who

controls a woman's womb controls her property and everything else about her life. It is a system that demeans both women and men, by treating them as juveniles. If a Mrs. Ramsay or a Minta learns to present herself as an eternal little girl, "even more ignorant than she was, because he liked telling her she was a fool" (148), Tansley trails along behind Mrs. Ramsay, like a boy needing her "protection" (13).

Although Mrs. Ramsay at first insists that she always carries her bag herself (20), she in fact relinquishes possession when she marries a man or even when she walks with one. Granting such control entails a kind of death, a lessening of her independence that Mrs. Ramsay gladly pays. Just as going with men means a metaphoric death of her selfhood, going with death becomes confused with the description of following a man. Thus Lily's visualization of Mrs. Ramsay "going unquestioningly with her companion" (270) to the land of death startlingly echoes the much more innocuous outing with Tansley. The sexual tension of the earlier walk sounds again faintly in "fields among whose folds, purplish and soft, among whose flowers, hyacinths or lilies, she vanished" (270). Like the torn folds of Proserpine's gown that represent her rape in Ovid's *Metamorphoses*, the folds of the fields make it seem as if Mrs. Ramsay is reexperiencing a sexual initiation as she dies. Death ravishes her, just as accepting the homage of men meant seeing a bit of herself die for them.

Because this image of Mrs. Ramsay with her "companion" occurs to Lily "days after she had heard of her death" (270)—that is, before Prue and Andrew die—Lily's later image of Prue dropping her flowers and obediently following two others (299) implies the same companion, a shadowy male Hades, along with a mother Demeter. Alarmingly, however, this Demeter fails to protest Persephone's inclusion in the promenade. On the contrary, Mrs. Ramsay leads the way. She actually sanctions this "wrong" husband, as if she were back at her old matchmaking. Now dead herself, Mrs. Ramsay might selfishly prefer Prue in her realm, but since she holds to her conviction that a woman must have a guiding man by her side, she will allow Hades to come along in a threesome. Although Hades as death takes Prue, Mrs. Ramsay seems more powerful—and more at fault—than he, at least in Lily's moods of grief and resentment.

As Woolf alludes to Persephone for both Mrs. Ramsay's and Prue's deaths, she uses this imagery of Persephone picking flowers before a male onlooker to introduce another daughter, Cam, and her proper role in the world:

And, turning to walk back the other way, up the drive, Mr. Bankes was alive to things which would not have struck him had not those sandhills revealed to him the body of his friendship [with Mr. Ramsay] lying with the red on its lips laid up in peat—for instance, Cam, the little girl,

Ramsay's youngest daughter. She was picking Sweet Alice on the bank. She was wild and fierce. She would not "give a flower to the gentleman" as the nursemaid told her. No! no! no! she would not! She clenched her fist. She stamped. And Mr. Bankes felt aged and saddened and somehow put into the wrong by her about his friendship. He must have dried and shrunk. (36)

Now, mild Mr. Bankes is hardly a rapacious Hades. Yet as he appears in this subtle and suggestive passage, he emits an underwordly taint of the grave. After personifying his decayed relationship to Mr. Ramsay as a body "with the red on its lips laid up in peat"—the mummified friendship preserving appearances yet essentially dead—he admits to a more horrifying image of *himself* as a "dried and shrunk" mummy. Although he merely wants Cam to greet him as an adoring daughter would, his need for attention and sympathy resembles the aggressive demand for pity that makes Mr. Ramsay something of a Hades. Still an independent tomboy, Cam does not want to have anything to do with Mr. Bankes. She is "wild and fierce"—"farouche," as Jane Harrison describes a late Greek version of Persephone, now differentiated from and opposed to Demeter, who is more and more concerned with "laws and civilized marriage."[20] Yet the fact that the flower which Cam picks is called by the name of a girl, "Sweet Alice,"and the fact that it is already located on a "bank" (echoing his name) intimate that she too, in a few short years, will likely be plucked and buttonholed to ornament the life of some man.

Woolf assigns Cam to an "underworld" just two pages after the shade of Mrs. Ramsay goes "unquestioningly" to death (270). Cam "wandered in imagination in that underworld of waters where the pearls stuck in clusters to white sprays, where in the green light a change came over one's entire mind and one's body shone half transparent enveloped in a green cloak" (272). The green cloak, like the green shawl, and the pearls (perhaps from *The Tempest*'s "those are pearls that were his eyes") might announce rebirth on this trip to the lighthouse. But the word "underworld" and the former "aimlessness" of the shawl warn us that Mrs. Ramsay's green might just as soon drown as renew Cam. Persephone too, according to her myth, passes through a pool on her way to the underworld, leaving her girdle floating on the surface, as Cam thins out to a cloak—all the better to warm somebody else, while growing cold oneself.

If reconciling Cam to her father and to men in general means taming and diluting her, marrying off Prue (originally as fierce as the spring) eclipses her too. The very description of the wedding suggests her effacement, by brackets and by death imagery: "The spring without a leaf to toss, bare and bright like a virgin fierce in her chastity, scornful in her purity, was laid out on fields wide-eyed and watchful and entirely careless of what was done or thought by the beholders. [Prue Ramsay, leaning on her father's arm, was given in marriage. What, people said, could have been more fitting? And they added, how beautiful she looked!]" (198). Like a bride, spring awaits fruitful seasons. Yet the ominous words "laid out" already predict a corpse. The deathly qualities of Prue's marriage not only announce her subsequent death in childbirth but even seem to inhere in the spring wedding: like Persephone, Prue seems already to have lost a part of herself. As we have seen, Woolf persistently mixes imagery for sexuality and for death, equating death with an abduction, and marriage with a stilling of the private ambitions of a woman, such as those that would give her the time to paint.

Because Mrs. Ramsay seems not to care about the deathly aspects of marrying, Lily begins to resent her as an arrogant marriage broker. Even though Lily finds Mrs. Ramsay "irresistible" and Paul and Minta's engagement enviable, she can still picture the older woman as a frightening priestess because of her single-mindedness, her occasional triviality, and, finally, her brutality: "Mrs. Ramsay, Lily felt, as she talked about the skins of vegetables, exalted that [her ovn abundance that fosters the engagement], worshipped that; held her hands over it to warm them [her own hands], to protect it, and yet, having brought it all about, somehow laughed, led her victims, Lily felt, to the altar" (153). The victims go as much to the altar of sacrifice as to the wedding altar. It is all the same to Mrs. Ramsay if a woman marries a preposterous man such as her husband or Paul Rayley with a proudly owned wash-leather bag for his faintly obscene watch (176). To Mrs. Ramsay's mind, a woman must be married, and if she is squelched and unhappy, she learns to make the best of it.

As Mrs. Ramsay's rule of necessary marriage will pair a woman with any man, skepticism about a woman's capabilities outside marriage may limit those talents, by weighing down her spirit. Again Woolf turns to the myth of Persephone-Demeter, who are identified with the corn, to express how Charles Tansley's ridicule hinders Lily's productivity: "Women can't write, women can't paint—what did that matter coming from him, since clearly it was not true to him but for some reason helpful to him, and that was why he said it? Why did her whole being bow, like corn under a wind, and erect itself again from this abasement only with a great and rather painful effort? She must make it once more" (130). Harrison records that when Demeter becomes "more and more the actual corn," Plutarch describes harvest as the "time men shear to earth Demeter's limbs."[21] Like Persephone beginning the long trek back from the underworld over again each year, Lily must resurrect her faith in herself. Not only does Tansley's scorn crush her, but her own desire to rest from constant self-assertion against ridicule threatens to kill her creativity.

The reader might suspect that such dismal views—of marriage as shearing Demeter and of life outside marriage as tiring rebeginnings to resurrect the corn—would churn up resentment against men. These views do create bitterness, but not as much as one might think. True, Cam imagines that her brother's cherished pig's head has shadow horns, assimilating a fantastically "horned" pig to other phallic gods, ram and bull and goat; a horned skull, though, associates this masculine sign with death. And James does have a famous, harsh vision of his father's phallic "beak": "James, as he stood stiff between her [Mrs. Ramsay's] knees, felt her rise in a rosy-flowered fruit tree laid with leaves and dancing boughs into which the beak of brass, the arid scimitar of his father, the egotistical man, plunged and smote, demanding sympathy" (60).

From James's viewpoint at least, the action of smiting "mercilessly" suggests the violence of rape (59). In that sense Mr. Ramsay intrudes as a Hades. Mrs. Ramsay, however, does not begrudge her gift of pity the way James does; in fact, she falls back in a kind of "post-coital bliss":[22]

> Immediately, Mrs. Ramsay seemed to fold herself together, one petal closed in another, and the whole fabric fell in exhaustion upon itself, so that she had only strength enough to move her finger, in exquisite abandonment to exhaustion, across the page of Grimm's fairy story, while there throbbed through her, like the pulse in a spring which has expanded to its full width and now gently ceases to beat, the rapture of successful creation. (60)

But if her exertion gives her pleasure, it depletes her too. For her husband to be "restored, renewed," a part of her has to die: she is "spent" until only a "shell" is left (60).

Although Mr. Ramsay as a mild Hades exasperates Woolf, Mrs. Ramsay as a collaborating Demeter baffles her much more. Even Mrs. Ramsay's name reveals her sympathies. Naturally she takes her husband's name in the days before married women considered retaining their own, but it cannot be accident that Woolf chooses a particularly male patronymic. The ram was once a powerful male god. Woolf would know from Ovid's account of Proserpine that Jupiter could be identified with the ram-god Ammon.[23] This rammish Jupiter agrees that his brother Pluto has every right to rape Proserpine; the sky god cannot understand why Ceres is not simply delighted that her daughter now has such an illustrious brother-in-law.[24]

In the context of this book, the name Ramsay suggests that the "ram says," that the male in the family lays down the law about whether one will go to the lighthouse or not. But, perhaps even more ominously, the name implies that Mrs. Ramsay does some "ram saying" of her own. She agrees to and perpetuates the patriarchy. Woolf could have named this family, with its strong mother, Ewans or Ewert or something more "feminine."

Because Mrs. Ramsay does not do much "ewe-saying," much advocacy for women's self-expression, she is aligned against Lily. The older woman might stay more or less still for Lily's painting, but she is only condescending: "she was supposed to be keeping her head as much in the same position as possible for Lily's picture. Lily's picture! Mrs. Ramsay smiled. With her little Chinese eyes and her puckered-up face, she would never marry; one could not take her painting very seriously; she was an independent little creature, and Mrs. Ramsay liked her for it; so, remembering her promise, she bent her head" (29).

If Mrs. Ramsay "likes" her distressingly unmarriageable guest slightly, certainly Lily admires Mrs. Ramsay enormously. And Lily can appreciate the glow of love and sexual attraction that Paul Rayley inspires: "for a glory it surpassed everything in her experience, and burnt year after year like a signal fire on a desert island at the edge of the sea, and one had only to say 'in love' and instantly, as happened now, up rose Paul's fire again" (262). Paul's "signal fire" connects with the lighthouse so closely associated with Mrs. Ramsay. Demeter is known for carrying blazing pine torches through nights of searching for her daughter,[25] but Mrs. Ramsay's lighthouse seems more a phallic structure than a beacon for daughters. No matter how much Lily is attracted to Paul's sexual "fire sent up in token of some celebration by savages," it looks too much like a pyre, for suttee maybe, for her to immolate herself in it (261). Although Lily loves Mrs. Ramsay, she has to cut loose from her and her requirements for marriage.

At the very end of the book, right after the boat finally reaches the lighthouse and right before Lily finishes her painting, there is another revealing reference to the flowers of Persephone. Mr. Carmichael surges up on the lawn,

> puffing slightly . . . looking like an old pagan god, shaggy, with weeds in his hair and the trident (it was only a French novel) in his hand. . . . He stood there as if he were spreading his hands over all the weakness and suffering of mankind; she thought he was surveying, tolerantly and compassionately, their final destiny. Now he has crowned the occasion, she thought, when his hand slowly fell, as if she had seen him let fall from his great height a wreath of violets and asphodels which, fluttering slowly, lay at length upon the earth. (309)

Avrom Fleishman says that Mr. Carmichael is "sanctifying the epiphany of the risen dead [Mrs. Ramsay], strewing flowers appropriate to the underworld."[26] Yet Mr. Carmichael, pointing the way for Lily, seems actually to be dismissing Mrs. Ramsay—with regret but also with firmness. Instead of holding on to her flowers, Mr. Carmichael lets Mrs. Ramsay's wreath flutter back to earth, laid to rest. Although Mr. Carmichael with his trident looks most obviously like Poseidon, the trident also belongs to Hades. Pluto opened a passage back to the underworld by striking the earth with his trident, according to Lempriere's *Classical Dictionary*, which Woolf mentions by name in *Between the Acts*.[27] But this Pluto or Hades, in the person of Mr. Carmichael, is now absolved and tolerantly benevolent. Lily will forgive the men in her world their neediness, and she will long for—but push away—the acquiescent Demeter.

This necessity of distancing herself from Mrs. Ramsay is not a solution that Lily imposes once and for all. Rather she alternately reaches toward and pushes away the older woman throughout the book. Lily finally manages both to resurrect Mrs. Ramsay and escape her clutches by means of her painting. She composes two forms on the canvas that allow her to sort out and resolve her ambivalent feelings: a purple triangle and a vertical line (which Lily sometimes thinks of as a tree).

As Mrs. Ramsay sits for her portrait in the drawing-room window, reading to her son and responding to her husband when he passes on the terrace, she casts a triangular shadow on the steps. Framed by the window and also "outlined absurdly by the gilt frame" of an "authenticated masterpiece by Michael Angelo" (48), Mrs. Ramsay becomes an art object, the familiar madonna of painting.[28] If Mrs. Ramsay incarnates the madonna, the triangle can be said to enclose the constrictive threesome of father, mother, and son: an icon that can also devalue daughters and spinsters.[29]

All is not perfect in the privileged family: "Joseph and Mary were fighting," Mrs. Ramsay jokes about the nicknamed birds outside the window (122). But Mrs. Ramsay regards the "scimitar shapes" of the birds' strokes as "exquistite," despite the pair's incompatibility, whereas Lily wants something different than the "arid scimitar of the male" (59). Lily weakens the power of the madonna icon, still attractive despite its known flaws, by creating a nonrepresentational painting:

> Taking out a pen-knife, Mr. Bankes tapped the canvas with the bone handle. What did she wish to indicate by the triangular purple shape, "just there"? he asked.
>
> It was Mrs. Ramsay reading to James, she said. She knew his objection—that no one could tell it for a human shape. But she had made no attempt at likeness, she said. For what reason had she introduced them then? he asked. Why indeed?—except that if there, in that corner, it was bright, here, in this, she felt the need of darkness. Simple, obvious, commonplace, as it was, Mr. Bankes was interested. Mother and child then—objects of universal veneration, and in this case the mother was famous for her beauty—might be reduced, he pondered, to a purple shadow without irreverence.
>
> But the picture was not of them, she said. Or, not in his sense. There were other senses too in which one might reverence them.(81)

Because Lily has "reduced" Mrs. Ramsay to a blob, she has effected a kind of humorous revenge against the beautiful and domineering woman's expectation that Lily marry: that she keep a man leaning in the window, a pen-knife posed against the canvas, a phallic sign somewhere in the composition of her own life. Yet if Lily is snubbing Mrs. Ramsay, she is also still reverencing her. The triangle suggests, on the one hand, father, mother, and son; however, it also signifies, in ancient mythology, female sexuality in itself. In *Themis*, Woolf's mentor Harrison discusses a rounded triangular grave mound called the "omphalos," often surmounted by a stele or a tree. Although omphalos came to mean navel, it was originally, according to Harrison, a symbol of the womb, as the stele or tree represented the phallus. The two signs in conjunction were meant to assure the rebirth of the soul whose body lay in the tomb.[30]

Woolf uses some of this triangle imagery to describe Mrs. Ramsay's sense of herself while alone: "All the being and the doing, expansive, glittering, vocal, evaporated; and one shrunk, with a sense of solemnity, to being oneself, a wedge-shaped core of darkness, something invisible to others" (95). This triangular wedge seems to be the essence of Mrs. Ramsay's femaleness: at first private, though for her soon subordinated to something she meets from outside, the third caressing "stroke" of the lighthouse (96).

If Mrs. Ramsay insists on a male side to the triangle, Lily converts it back to female creativity, still using the same ancient imagery of dome-shaped tombs. Instead of James at Mrs. Ramsay's knees, Lily recounts that she once sat (or would like to have sat):

with her arms around Mrs. Ramsay's knees, close as she could get . . . she imagined how in the chambers of the mind and heart of the woman who was, physically, touching her, were stood, like treasures in the tombs of kings, tablets bearing sacred inscriptions, which if one could spell them out, would teach one everything, but they would never be offered openly, never made public. . . . How then, she had asked herself, did one know one thing or another thing about people, sealed as they were? Only like a bee, drawn by some sweetness or sharpness in the air intangible to touch or taste, one haunted the dome-shaped hive, ranged the wastes of the air over the countries of the world alone, and then haunted the hives with their murmurs and their stirrings; the hives, which were people. Mrs. Ramsay rose. Lily rose. Mrs. Ramsay went. For days there hung about her, as after a dream some subtle change is felt in the person one has dreamt of, more vividly than anything she said, the sound of murmuring and, as she sat in the wicker arm-chair in the drawing-room window she wore, to Lily's eyes, an august shape; the shape of a dome. (78–80)

Among the omphalos mounds that Harrison mentions are "beehive tombs."[31] Rosenman argues that Lily has experienced "an obvious version of the regressive urge" to be reunited with mother-Demeter's hive-shaped womb.[32] But Lily will accept from Mrs. Ramsay only that much of the older woman's internal power which will inspire Lily's painting. Lily will transmute the triangle of family into the triangle of female selfhood, and she will convert the window of birth into an opening out of her artistic, not biological, creativity.

Thus in the last part of the book Lily will bring about a "rebirth" of her painting, starting it over with the same basic outline. The old problem of connecting the masses comes back to her when someone inside the house sits in a chair "so as to throw an odd-shaped triangular shadow over the step" (299). Lily's soul calls out to Mrs. Ramsay, as Harrison says mourners call for the mother earth:

> You may bring back the life of the Spring in the form of a tree or a maiden, or you may summon her to rise from the sleeping Earth . . . . Persephone, the daughter of Demeter, is carried below the Earth, and rises up again year by year. On Greek vase-paintings the scene occurs again and again. A mound of earth is represented, sometimes surmounted by a tree; out of the mound a woman's figure rises; and all about the mound are figures of dancing daemons waiting to welcome her.[33]

Lily has, in fact, often thought of adding a tree to her painting (83, 128, 154). During her repainting of the scene at the end she puts in what may be a tree, or even a lighthouse—in any case, a line.[34] Mrs. Ramsay has always closely indentified herself with both the lighthouse and a tree. She had, "unconsciously and incongruously, used the branches of the elm trees outside to help her to stabilise her position . . . insensibly approving of the dignity of the trees' stillness, and now again of the superb upward rise (like the beak of a ship up a wave) of the elm branches as the wind raised them" (169). And James had "felt her rise in a rosy-flowered fruit tree laid with leaves and dancing boughs" (60). Mrs. Ramsay identifies with these male symbols because marriage is the most important part of her self-definition.

Lily will include the line and triangle together, but she transmutes them, as she forgives both the aggressive Hades and the collaborating Demeter in her life. First, Lily forgives Mr. Ramsay, when she discovers in herself some genuine pity for him—but not at the expense of becoming a "shell." Whereas Mrs. Ramsay had felt that as his wife "She was not good enough to tie his shoe strings" (51), Lily's commonsensical solace to Mr. Ramsay results in his demonstrating proper knots while bending over *her* feet: "Three times he knotted her shoe; three times he unknotted it" (230). After this homage (albeit condescending), this mock ritual, Lily feels pity—but not enough to prevent her from ignoring him when need be and

continuing with her work. Lily forgives Mrs. Ramsay too, even as the painter reinterprets the older woman's message from biological to artistic
creativity. Instead of uniting male and female signs in a marriage, where
(in Woolf's time) the triangle had been subordinated to the line, as
Persephone to Hades, Lily will make the two forms work together equally,
in art.

Faulkner

Twice in the second section of William Faulkner's *The Sound and the
Fury* (1929) Quentin thinks of pigs rushing: "running the beast with two
backs and she blurred in the winking oars running the swine of Euboeleus running coupled within how many Caddy" and "I could hear whis-
pers secret surges smell the beating of hot blood under wild unsecret flesh
watching against red eyelids the swine untethered in pairs rushing coupled
into the sea."[35] Faulkner compresses two important allusions into these
passages, one classical, one biblical. The combined associations focus
Quentin's ambivalence toward sexuality and his longing for death.
Although several critics have mentioned the classical allusion to
Euboeleus, they have ignored the New Testament source.[36] They have
further missed the comfort that Quentin derives from his vision of pigs.

With the name Euboeleus, Faulkner evokes the story of Persephone.
According to *The Golden Bough*, people may originally have worshiped
Persephone in the form of a pig; however, when she became solely anthropomorphic, her worshipers had to invent some new reason why they threw
pigs into sacred caverns in her honor. So, Frazer conjectures, an enterpris-
ing storyteller declared that at the moment when Hades abducted
Persephone, some pigs belonging to the swineherd "Eubuleus" happened
to be browsing nearby; when a chasm opened up in the earth to let Hades
and his victim into the underworld, the pigs also fell down and disappeared. The baffled and now pigless Euboeleus could then give Demeter
some clue about Persephone's whereabouts, and, as a reward, according to
one version, Demeter revealed to him the secret of the cultivation of
corn.[37]

Faulkner also alludes to the New Testament story of the devils who enter
a herd of pigs. The gospel writers tell the story twice (Matt. 8:28–34 and
Mark 5:1–20); Matthew describes "two possessed with devils coming out
of the tombs," and Mark says that there came "out of the tombs a man
with an unclean spirit." In both New Testament accounts, when Jesus
orders the devils out of the humans, the disgruntled spirits beg for a nearby
herd of swine as an alternate abode. After Jesus gives the devils leave to
possess the pigs, "behold, the whole herd of swine ran violently down a
steep place into the sea, and perished in the waters" (Matt. 8:32). The

visual image of a swine herd running down a steep place to perish parallels Euboeleus's herd falling down a chasm into the underworld and justifies Quentin's conflation of the two allusions.

Quentin evidently remembers Euboeleus because he thinks of Caddy as Persephone. Just as Persephone's first experience of sexuality coincides with her death, so does Caddy's sexuality, Quentin thinks, lead her into a kind of death. The several references to Caddy's "dying" are ambiguous, however, depending on whether Caddy or Quentin uses the word, and on whether she "dies" with Dalton Ames and other youths or with Herbert Head. For instance, Caddy herself says, "When they touched me I died" (185) or "yes I hate him I would die for him I've already died for him I die for him over and over again every time this [heart] goes" (188). Here Caddy relies on a basically positive use of "die," suggesting both pleasure—the traditional euphemism of "little death" for orgasm—and a willing self-sacrifice and intensity of emotion. At this point when she says, "I hate him," I believe she is lying to placate Quentin. When, however, Caddy says, "I died last year I told you I had but I didn't know then what I meant . . . . But now I know I'm dead" (153), she begins a negative association of sex and death, evoking the painful time when she discovered her pregnancy and compromised her future by accepting Herbert Head.

Benjy also connects Caddy's sexuality with dying, since he persistently mixes his memories of Caddy's wedding with those of Damuddy's funeral. For both Benjy and Quentin, Caddy has died after her wedding because she is no longer close by for them. Less selfishly, they also lament— Quentin consciously and Benjy intuitively —that Herbert's vulgarity and shallowness are likely to stifle their sister. Caddy, agreeing for the sake of respectability to marry Herbert, faces a future about as bright as Persephone's when Hades sets her up in the underworld as his bride.

Faulkner clearly does not endorse Quentin's view that Caddy's discovery of sexuality diminishes her. Instead, the author deplores the narrow-mindedness of society in general and of Mrs. Compson in particular, who would force Caddy into a hellish mismatch with Herbert rather than accept an illegitimate child. Faulkner, unlike Mrs. Compson, judges Persephone less "bad" than "wronged"—and he judges Caddy less wronged by her young men than by society's preference for propriety over emotion. Even in *Sanctuary*, where references to Eleusis abound[38] and where the rape victim, Temple Drake, decides she likes sex, Faulkner condemns Temple's eventual apathy, not her temporary passion. Similarly, in *The Hamlet*, where "Ratliff's tensely comic vision of Flem's conquest of Hell is read by many commentators as the story of Persephone's abduction by Hades," Faulkner sides with a passionate Eula-Persephone against a coldly calculating Flem.[39]

Quentin bolsters his allusion to Euboeleus with several other images of

Persephone on the same page. Hades spies Persephone as, unaware of her danger, she is innocently gathering flowers in the field where he carries her off. Quentin pictures one of Caddy's lovers carrying her: "with one hand he could lift her to his shoulder and run with her" (184). Right before the Euboeleus reference a "Miss Daingerfield" speaks, perhaps recalling Persephone's dangerous field; right after it, Mrs. Bland reminisces that "Gerald's grandfather always picked his own mint before breakfast, while the dew was still on it. He wouldn't even let old Wilkie touch it do you remember Gerald but always gathered it himself and made his own julep. He was as crotchety about his julep as an old maid, measuring everything by a recipe in his head. There was only one man he ever gave that recipe to" (184). Because Persephone was called "the maid," and Demeter gave the recipe or secret for corn to Euboeleus, Mrs. Bland's metamorphosis of Persephone gathering flowers in the dew into a crotchety, old-maidish man concocting his mint julep, effectively trivializes Quentin's preoccupations and affronts him.

Although Quentin generally wants to protect Caddy in his musings about pigs, he also disapproves of her—and himself. Frazer identifies Persephone outright with the pig, and Quentin similarly sees her and her lover as animals, "the beast with two backs"(184), "swine untethered in pairs rushing coupled" (219). The vision of her as beast is "blurred," implying that the couple merge, because their silhouettes as they kiss or copulate have "blurred not with dark [but] within the other forever more." This line also subtly suggests that Quentin's eyes blur with tears as he thinks of the scene. The vision of "oar blades winking him along" (184) serves an ambiguity exactly parallel to this dualism of "blurred." "Winking" means that oars glint, as men like Gerald wink in a leer, as men like Quentin blink back tears.

Caddy as Persephone-pig becomes a symbol for all sexual beings, and Quentin has to include himself in this category. Whereas Faulkner sanctions the healthy animal lustiness of the image, Quentin cannot accept any kinship with beasts. When as a child he touches Natalie and feels a surge of mysterious sexual response, he jumps into the hog wallow—clearly identifying himself with the swine (169–70). He probably feels himself sullied most of all because, with Natalie and Caddy jealous of each other at the moment, he must believe he has betrayed one or both of them. He then magnifies his confusion about loyalties into a revulsion against beastly sexuality.

Yet if Quentin becomes a "bad" pig as he grudgingly recognizes his own sexual impulses, he actually consoles himself by means of the Euboeleus allusion: at least Euboeleus's pigs got to follow Persephone into the underworld. Again, as with Caddy's "dying," Quentin's "following" is ambiguous. If the underworld equals Caddy's sexual initiation, Quentin would like to follow her for two possible reasons. He would like to rescue Persephone, snatch Caddy back, as if her discovery of sexuality and especially her "abduction" by Head/Hades had never occurred. On the other hand, Quentin might desire to follow Caddy into the opening earth not so much to bring her back as to experience sexuality himself. As much as he fights his impulses, he is as susceptible to the sensual urgings of honeysuckle as anyone; and when Caddy says, "Poor Quentin you've never done that have you" (185), the reader, through Caddy's perceptivity, senses his longing. Faulkner admires Caddy for accepting the painful beauty of honeysuckle, while he pities Quentin for trying to avoid it.

Because of his inhibitions, Quentin cannot, after all, follow Caddy into sexuality, either to remain close to her or to establish a new closeness with someone else. Yet if he cannot follow her into the underworld in its meaning as sexuality, he will defiantly descend into the underworld in its meaning as death. Both passages about the swine introduce his recurrent talk of hell as the "clean flame" (185), a place "to isolate her out of the loud world" (220). As André Bleikasten notes, Quentin cares not so much about preserving sexual innocence, his own or Caddy's, as preserving their togetherness.[40] Quentin now ignores the fact that she has so far "died" only into a worse life, not into his protective "clean flame." Death for Quentin becomes a way of catching up with Caddy. If Euboeleus's pigs could follow Persephone into the underworld and perhaps eat from her hand there, Quentin also would like to go to the underworld to maintain his closeness with Caddy.

The New Testament allusion to the pigs reinforces these associations of sexuality and death. When Caddy responds to Quentin's anguished "how many Caddy" with "I don't know too many there was something terrible in me terrible in me," she recalls Jesus' question to the unclean spirit, "What is thy name? and he answered, saying, My name is Legion: for we are many" (Mark 5:9). While Caddy is possessed by many men, Quentin is a wild man, one of Matthew's "two possessed with devils." His sexuality—his urges and doubts—bedevils him; his grief for the waste of Caddy's beautiful emotion on Herbert and his successors bedevils Quentin even more.

Benjy also resembles the biblical tomb dwellers, since the ancient world's "possession" developed into the modern world's mental illness. Benjy ends up in the state institution, where manic-depressives, schizophrenics, and retarded Benjys all abide together. Although the biblical "crazy" man in Mark is fierce and Benjy is docile, the fact that the man in Mark is always "crying" and cries out "in a loud voice" (Mark 5:5,7) recalls Benjy's nearly constant crying and bellowing.

In some senses, Benjy also duplicates Persephone carried off in Hades's chariot. Riding in Luster's wagon, Benjy at first whimpers because he has

no flower; later he is satisfied with a single broken narcissus. Then he bel-
lows over the wrong route to the graveyard. As Ovid says in his *Metamorphoses*, Persephone innocently weeps as much for her lost flowers as
for her lost virginity.[41] The "Homeric Hymn to Demeter" even names "a
radiantly wonderful" narcissus as Persephone's chief joy, before she must
disappear beyond graves.[42] Benjy parallels Caddy in Quentin's mind as
another victim, whose life is a hell of perpetual loss.

Thus Caddy, Quentin, and Benjy form a trio of bedeviled characters
who, Quentin believes, would do just as well to hide themselves in a herd
of pigs. He has already explicitly wished to segregate the three of them
when he plans desperately, before Caddy's wedding, "we can go away you
and Benjy and me where nobody knows us" (153). He implicitly wishes to
segregate Caddy, Benjy, and himself even more radically in his image of
pigs. The biblical swine rush into the sea, as Quentin, foul from the hog
wallow of his unsorted emotions, is seeking the river, on its way to the sea:
to death and to peace. And if Caddy-Persephone is already in the underworld, perhaps he will meet with her there.

Welty

In an interview granted in 1978, Jan Nordby Gretlund asked Eudora
Welty to what extent she made conscious use of Greek and Roman mythology in her writing. "It is conscious, clearly. I've lived with mythology all
my life. It is just as close to me as the landscape. It *naturally* occurs to me
when I am writing fiction. It is not a far-out, reached for something. . . . I
still like to read folk tales from all kinds of other lands." When Gretlund
inquired if she had ever read Frazer's *The Golden Bough* or Bulfinch's *Age
of Fable*, Welty reported that she did know the one-volume edition of *The
Golden Bough*. But she cautioned, "anyone who attributes my stories to
myths very specifically and thoroughly is overshooting it. I would rather
suggest things."[43] This caution about myth in Welty's work is especially apt
when applied to "Asphodel," a story of down-to-earth realism and dream-
like grotesquerie, which appeared in *The Wide Net and Other Stories*
(1943). Critics of "Asphodel" have misinterpreted her "mythical method"
here, failing to grasp the extent and purpose of Welty's subtle allusions to
two dying gods, Adonis and Persephone, with some details apparently
from Frazer.

In brief, the story tells how three old women, town gossips, go on an
outing to the ruined homestead, Asphodel, of Mr. Don McInnis. Just the
day before, they have buried the wife of this gentleman, Miss Sabina,
whose beauty and its comeuppance in marital difficulties the old women
have obviously kept up with and relished: the worse the scandal the better.

After the trespassers have chatted for some time, a naked man appears, Mr. Don McInnis himself; some goats, a kind of surrogate for him in his reputed randiness, chase the old ladies from the property. The story ends as the picnickers, to distract the impudent goats, throw them a baked hen left from their lunch basket.

Intending to be lord and master of his household, Mister *Don* McIn*nis* perhaps conceals a god, since er-don-nis sounds like Adonis. As Frazer observes, "The name Adonis is simply the Semitic *Adon*, 'lord,' a title of honour by which his worshippers addressed him, but, through a misunderstanding, the Greeks converted it into a proper name."[44] Don's wife, though a beauty, cannot be an Aphrodite, because in the patriarchal South that Welty depicts, Miss Sabina is hardly coequal. Far from a powerful, directing goddess, she changes hands as marriageable, unconsulted property: "Miss Sabina's father came bringing Mr. Don McInnis home, and proposed the marriage to him. She was no longer young for suitors; she was instructed to submit."[45] Under such circumstances, the wedding ceremony can only reenact the rape of Persephone, after a last reference to the chaste, never married Diana, whom Sabina has no chance to emulate:

The presents were vases of gold, gold cups, statues of Diana. . . . And the bride. . . We had not forgotten it yesterday when we drew it from the chest—the stiff white gown she wore! It never made a rustle when she gave him her hand. It was spring, the flowers in the baskets were purple hyacinths and white lilies that wilted in the heat and showed their blue veins. Ladies fainted from the scent; the gentlemen were without exception drunk, and Mr. Don McInnis, with his head turning quickly from side to side, like an animal's, opened his mouth and laughed. [. . .] He had a sudden way of laughter, like a rage, that pointed his eyebrows that were yellow, and changed his face. That night he stood astride. . . astride the rooms, the guests, the flowers, the tapers, the bride and her father with his purple face. (202)

The wilting hyacinths and lilies recall Persephone's hyacinths and lilies, lost when Hades bestrides her.[46] It is the same scene that Virginia Woolf pictures for Mrs. Ramsay's passing into the realm of death, "stepping with her usual quickness across fields among whose folds, purplish and soft, among whose flowers, hyacinths or lilies, she vanished."[47] Welty reports that she read *To the Lighthouse* "lots of times."[48] In fact, "Asphodel" resembles *To the Lighthouse* in several particulars: children whose deaths are recorded almost incidentally and especially the importance of Persephone.

Because the old women bury Miss Sabina in her wedding dress, they inadvertently admit that the dress introduced her to a death. Life with a man who hails from Asphodel, the flower of death, could never be "as pastoral and blissful as the Elysian fields," Garvin Davenport's mistaken description of Don's estate.[49] Welty's fields of Asphodel are not Elysian but hellish. Sabina sinks to their dreariness as unwillingly as the souls of Penelope's suitors, who "obeyed [Hermes's] summons gibbering like bats that squeak and flutter . . . following the Deliverer down the dark paths of decay . . . [to] the meadow of asphodel, which is the dwelling-place of souls, the disembodied wraiths of men."[50] Later, when Miss Sabina learns of her husband's unfaithfulness, she refuses food, as Persephone avoids food in the underworld: "We carried things up to her—soups, birds, wines, frozen surprises, cold shapes [ice cream—or otherworldly wraiths], one after the other. She only pushed them away" (203).

Continuing to suffer humiliation after her forced marriage, Miss Sabina loses her hair. This detail corroborates Don's dual role, as he oscillates between the diabolic Hades and the apparently more innocent Adonis. (In the "Homeric Hymn to Demeter," Hades is referred to by the title "Aidoneus," so that the two stories of dying gods are also connected by a similarity in sound, Aidoneus and Adonis).[51] According to Frazer,

> In the great Phoenician sanctuary of Astarte at Byblus the death of Adonis was annually mourned, to the shrill wailing notes of the flute, with weeping, lamentation, and beating of the breast; but next day he was believed to come to life again and to ascend up to heaven in the presence of his worshippers. The disconsolate believers, left behind on earth, shaved their heads as the Egyptians did on the day of the divine bull Apis; women who could not bring themselves to sacrifice their beautiful tresses had to give themselves up to strangers on a certain day of the festival, and to dedicate to Astarte the wages of their shame.[52]

Don's philandering leaves Sabina disconsolate. Moreover, in the "choice" for women that Frazer points to between submitting to strangers or sacrificing their hair, Miss Sabina has undergone both indignities. She has slept with a stranger (albeit in matrimony), and "She wore a fine jet-black wig of great size, for she had lost her hair by some illness or violence" (204). If any reader misses these references to violence and abduction, the name Sabina, inevitably suggesting the *Rape of the Sabines*, reinforces the impression of outrage. Audrey Hodgins, who mentions the reference to the Sabines, insensitively decides that all Sabines and Sabinas should just have "yielded."[53]

This hostility to Miss Sabina in fact pervades the criticism that has been published on "Asphodel." Hodgins sees in Miss Sabina the "symbol of sterile control which would kill the spontaneity, the creativity of life in the town. . . . What follows is the rape of the post office. . . . She had tried to keep the creative power of others in rein, but finally can put the bit only in her own mouth."[54] Instead of recognizing an arranged marriage as the equivalent of rape, Hodgins foists the rape off onto Sabina. Hodgins even goes so far as to blame her "touch of destruction" for the deaths of her children, "symbolically appropriate," and, wildly, to lay to her type of "repression of sexuality" the "decline of the South . . . the fall of Greece, of Rome, or of any civilization which cuts itself off from a creative center"—as if the Mediterranean lacks an empire nowadays because those Greeks never knew how to get in touch with their bodies.[55]

If Hodgins seems extreme in her censure, John Allen rivals the perverseness of the interpretation by flatly dismissing Miss Sabina as an example of "unequivocal evil."[56] Michael Kreyling joins them in condemning the bride's supposed frigidity, a state that he labels Apollonian, as opposed to Don's Dionysian gush. When Welty describes the couple's two homesteads as two sides of a vase, Kreyling counsels blithely that "such opposites are part of the whole, and that someone who could see all sides would realize that. The sly allusion to the Grecian urn (young men in pursuit of maidens loth to be taken) is also part of an ironic pattern. The men, Sabina's father and Don McInnis, overtake and overrule Sabina in her loathing of Don. Sabina, a bride of quietude, is ravished by Don; and the world of competing opposites goes on in spite of her refusal to acknowledge it."[57] It is hard to see how Miss Sabina could acknowledge and sustain both an unwillingnes to be chattel and an enjoyment of Don's bed, as healthily "competing" sides of one personality.

While Kreyling reproaches Sabina as a too conscious Apollo (all cerebrum and no sex), Peggy Prenshaw, usually so perceptive about Welty's subtleties, mistakenly believes that Welty is blaming the "matriarchal realm" for being too unconscious: "In fact, in looking at Livvie [from another story] and Sabina, we see that whether the lover is accepted as a natural sexual partner or grudgingly endured as a needed inseminator, the relationships are similarly devoid of a humanizing consciousness."[58] Because Prenshaw wants Sabina to exercise more consciousness and Kreyling wants her to display less, we have to reject a supposedly Apollonian versus Dionysian clash, of analysis and awareness versus instinct and sex, as irrelevant to the story.

Just as critics have chided Sabina for being too cold, even though she is the one pushing away "cold shapes," readers have misinterpreted the picnickers as too timid. The three old women at first appear to duplicate Miss Sabina, but they actually diverge from her in important ways. One oldster bears the name Phoebe, a goddess of the disappearing and reappearing moon, and Welty names another Cora. Because Kore or Cora designates Persephone, one might expect the women, somehow akin through their names, to lament Miss Sabina's fate as Persephone. But for all their protests that they come "weeping and wailing" at the news of Don's infidelity, they instead feed in predatory fashion on these tidbits, hardly mourn her

death, and cluck their regret only "languidly" and "placidly" as they recount how her children died (203). Their sympathies clearly lie with Don-
Hades: "He had the wildness we all worshipped that night, since he was
not to be ours to love" (203). They can admire him so much, Welty suggests wryly, because they don't have to put up with him in reality.

Furthermore, the old women's diet betrays their continued devotion to
him. Persephone's only food in the underworld, a pomegranate seed that
Hades deceitfully slipped to her, "ensured that she would return to him."[59]
Although the Greek Persephone unwittingly ate the seed that tied her
to Hades, these ladies cannot toss their picnic pomegranates into their
mouths fast enough, indicating that they fully acquiesce in the giving over
of a woman's life to a man (201). Like Mrs. Ramsay in the eyes of Lily
Briscoe, these three indifferent Fates hustle women into marriages that
may not be all that happy just because "that's what's done"—and also
because they harbor an unquenchable weakness for men themselves.

This incorrigible capitulation and cozying up to men, a self-abasing
adoration that the women feel as strongly in old age as in youth, appears
most clearly when the ladies throw the baked hen to the goats at the end.
The women recognize that Miss Sabina would not approve: "She would
have been ashamed of us—barefooted and running. She would never have
given up the little basket we saved back" (208). The basket suggests
perhaps the gardens of Adonis, baskets or pots that in some cultures
women offer to men. Frazer says such women thereby express "the desire
of offspring," implying that the baskets might be uterine symbols.[60]
Moreover, when Frazer discusses some variants of the rites for Adonis, he
notes that "the first victims to be immolated are a white cock for the Sun
God and a black hen for the Earth Goddess; and as the feast is the marriage of these great deities the marriage service is performed over the two
fowls before they are hurried into eternity."[61] Relinquishing the hen, the
women have symbolically sacrificed something "saved back," akin to
Woolf's "room of one's own": their privacy, virginity, or, if married, any
claim to be loved individually or for themselves. They don't understand
Miss Sabina's resentment against sacrificing all three of these possibilities.

Although Welty's old women might at first seem prudishly frightened by
the naked man and the goats, their timidity is all polite veneer. These
hardy revelers laugh vivaciously—one might almost say lasciviously—in
the last lines of the story. They turn out to be "old maids" only in the sense
in which worshipers perpetually addressed the lusty Queen of Heaven as
"virgin," despite her repeated couplings with the dying and resurrected
god.

Perhaps the most startling scene in the story and Welty's most striking
reversal of the usual plot for the dying god and eternal goddess is Miss
Sabina's fit at the post office. Miss Sabina has, over the years, recovered a

measure of matriarchal power to direct the lives of the townsfolk in her eccentric old age. She still marks her distance from a fertility figure, though, by "tangling" the maypoles at her approach, whereas a mother-goddess might be expected to twine the ribbons and bless them (205). She aspires rather to be one of the great goddesses who remained single, like Artemis (Diana) or maybe Athene (Minerva). (She tries to name a daughter Minerva, but the daughter dies.) However, despite her awesome directives and divinations, the one place where dominion escapes her is the post office. Its banality clashes comically with the pretensions of a goddess, and its flies make it a realm of death, another underworld for the reenactment of her original humiliation in marriage. She arrives stomping:

> We heard her come to the end of the street, the heavy staggering figure coming to the beat of the cane. [. . .] "Give me my letter!" We told her there was none, and we went closer and tried to gather her to us. But she said, "Give me that." And she took our letters out of our hands. "Your lovers!" she said, and tore them in two. We let her do just as she would. But she was not satisfied. "Open up!" she said to the postmistress, and she beat upon the little communicating door. So the postmistress had to open up, and Miss Sabina went in to the inner part. [. . .] She threw down her stick, she advanced with her bare hands. She seized upon everything before her, and tore it to pieces. She dragged the sacks about, and the wastebaskets, and the contents she scattered like snow. Even the ink pad she flung against the wall, and it left a purple mark like a grape stain that will never wear off.
> She was possessed then, before our eyes, as she could never have been possessed. She raged, she rocked from side to side, she danced. Miss Sabina's arms moved like a harvester's in the field to destroy all that was in the little room. In her frenzy she tore all the letters to pieces, and even put bits in her mouth and appeared to eat them.
> Then she stood still in the room. She had finished. We had not yet moved when she lay toppled on the floor, her wig fallen from her head and her face awry like a mask.
> "A stroke!" That was what we said, because we did not know how to put a name to the end of her life. . . . (205–6)

Miss Sabina is defeated—by love letters: yet another sign that the old ladies hold eternal allegiance to men. All the lush vocabulary of revelry that should connote fertility instead turns sterile, because of Don's mis-use of sexual energy. In this outbreak at the post office, Sabina parodies her groom by prancing like a randy goat and eating paper the way goats do. Her rage recapitulates Don's "sudden way of laughter, like a rage" at the wedding. The grape mark that should have been wealth instead suggests a kind of bruise, the at least psychic "stain that will never wear off." As a "harvester," she should be dancing to celebrate Adonis's influence on the seasons; however, because Don reappears only after affairs, she "destroy[s] all that was in the little room." The cycle imposed on her skips harvest and moves directly from the spring wedding to comfortless "snow."

Miss Sabina charges into the "inner part" as if she were desecrating a temple to Adonis, but he is hardly injured by her fury. Soon afterward, the old ladies spy the naked man at Asphodel, a sainted Adonis who can in a way "ascend up to heaven in the presence of his worshippers," as Frazer says.[62] "'That was Mr. Don McInnis.' 'It was not,' said Irene. 'It was a vine in the wind.' Phoebe was bent over to pull a thorn from her bare foot. 'But we thought he was dead.' 'That was as much Mr. Don as this is I,' said Cora" (207). Mr. Don McInnis resurrects from the death that the townspeople have assumed, without seeming to have suffered at all, "as rude and golden as a lion" (207). But if the god Adonis revives, sustaining no damage, Welty reverses the old myths to show that the goddess is hardly eternal. Miss Sabina dies once and for all, in a banal, ugly, and undignified manner. Welty has allowed the mythical glow to play about Don-Adonis-Hades only to reveal its falsity. The grotesque rage in the post office vents the frustration of a life sacrificed to convention, a sacrifice that begins when her father and Don constrain her to unwanted marriage.

10

Conclusion

Ancient peoples planted seeds in gardens of Adonis (shallow pots or baskets) to symbolize the god's brief life: "Fostered by the sun's heat, the plants shot up rapidly, but having no root they withered as rapidly away."[1] Celebrants then threw the gardens into water, to reenact the god's dissolution but also to foretell his passage through amniotic fluid into rebirth. Characters in twentieth-century literature are still refashioning gardens of Adonis: Forster's Krishna-worshipers toss "ten-day baskets of corn" into a tank, Woolf's mourning Rhoda drops violets into a river, Konwicki's Polish government floats wreaths down the Vistula, and tins of Plumtree's Potted Meat (samples from an irreverent "godinpotty") bob along the pages of Joyce's *Ulysses* and *Finnegans Wake*.

Hearing that the traditional sowings attained "no root," we may wonder how "deeply rooted" these modern gardens of Adonis can be. That is, do writers recreate such specific scenes for purely formal reasons, as decoration or part of a structural underpinning? Or do they believe that a myth of the dying god still has some meaning? Far from purely learned display, allusions to dying gods have played a central role in the twentieth century. Here I will address the four areas of dispute set out in the introduction: relevance of the myth for reflexive statements about art, involvement or failure of the myth with regard to history, value or detriment for gender roles, and denial or affirmation of some sort of spirituality.

Reflexivity

To a surprising extent the dying god has served as a kind of "objective correlative" for several notions of reflexivity. Modern writers have drawn analogies from the dying god to art work, artist, and any conceptual lens for seeing the world—any social code or personal vision.

DYING GOD AND ART WORK
Exploiting their inheritance from all self-conscious artists and especially

from romantics and symbolists, modern writers have judged literature both glorious and worthless: capable of conjuring worlds or only of propagating lies. To express their ambivalence, several authors underline a comparison of dying god to art, by deprecating the "divine" work that they have so painstakingly made. Through the example of the temporary god, Woolf, Mann, and Beckett conclude that even the best that the world offers must not be allowed permanence, even if it *could* survive—because it is partial. Because any one statement is inadequate, like any one avatar, authors must abandon it; yet they cannot renounce speech altogether, which is then continually reborn. A major reflexive purpose in Mann's *Joseph and His Brothers*, Woolf's *The Waves*, and Beckett's trilogy is to scoff at the limitations of each individual story, yet to renew storytelling repeatedly.

Finnegans Wake also offers a version of the "dying and reviving art work." When Joyce's character ALP advises mortals how to keep from disappearing from the face of the earth, she warns, "Once you are balladproof you are unperceable to haily, icy and missilethroes." Joyce is referring to two vegetation deities, Balder and Isis, under evergreen boughs appropriate to eternal deities: holly, ivy, and mistletoe. In the Scandinavian myth of Balder, Frigg persuades all creatures and substances to spare the young god, but she neglects to enlist the lowly mistletoe. Smug in their safety, the gods then aim harmless sticks and stones at Balder for amusement. The deceiver god, Loki, lures blind Hother to throw as his missile the unpledged mistletoe, which "pierced him [Balder] through and through, and he fell down dead."[2]

Joyce implies that none of us are bulletproof, and that no one will ever revive like Balder, who is said to live in the underworld temporarily and preside over a new society at the end of time. If we confine ourselves to an uneventful, unviolent life ("balladproof") that fails to attract the saga singer, we might escape Loki's jealous piercings. Still, we will die in our beds, Joyce reminds us, so we are hardly safer for much longer anyway. If somebody sings or writes about us, however, we will be remembered and "perceived," even when we are finally pierced or have perished.

Joyce's line invites us to look lucidly at our options: "to recognize death and mortality and to live fully with that awareness is to know the only true idea of the holy [one of the resonances of "haily," along with "holly" and "hail"] available to man in this or any other century."[3] In addition to living well (and bawdily), despite an awareness of death, Joyce adds "writing" as one of the holy activities left to the twentieth century. The artist replaces the priest. But an epitaph or an episode in a book has to content us for the promise of a renewed society that the Scandinavians drew from Balder's example, and for the promise of a personal afterlife, which the Egyptians drew from the example of Isis ("icy") and Osiris.

As Joyce might be able at times to mock his book as so much balderdash, he can also funnel any doubts about the actual "holiness" of art into a kind of "hail fellow well met" cheer, a drinking song at the wake to drown out the real paltriness of words. Mann similarly takes refuge in the cosmic "jest." Woolf, on the other hand, though she too conjures all her dying gods in *The Waves* in a mood of gentle humor, registers more clearly than Joyce a real despair at the absence of her Osiris character, the death of our friends, the intermittence of our personalities, and the failed magic of even the best artist's words to protect any of these beings. More despairing, Beckett threatens to give up words altogether. Nevertheless, Joyce, Mann, Woolf, and Beckett all translate the alacrity with which an Osiris "comes a cropper," but still makes a new crop, into the determination with which the artist disdains what he or she has written but still takes a new sheet. Their pages are, metaphorically, both "crossed out" and "starred" at the same time: tentative, temporary, sketched in a typically modernist limbo between death and rebirth.

DYING GOD AND ARTIST

In addition to making an analogy from inevitably dying god to necessarily limited art work, modern authors may draw another purely literary analogy from dying god to suffering artist. Yeats, for example, sympathizes with the castrated Attis as a metaphor for the cost in neglected life which art requires of the dedicated artist. John Vickery believes, however, that Yeats is less concerned than an earlier generation of romantics with construing the artist as a maimed victim, hurt by an uncomprehending public or initiated into mysteries available only for sufferers.[4] Later writers, notably Robert Graves, also liken themselves to the dying god as a wounded benefactor of the community. This analogy to a dying deity often takes the form of artist, assumed to be male, deriving his inspiration from a goddess, assumed to be silent.

Although Graves claims that he and indeed every "great" poet write about "the Triple Muse . . . woman in her divine character, the poet's enchantress, [as] the only theme of his song," he excludes women from self-expression, unless they confine themselves to emotional outpourings: "woman is not a poet: she is either a Muse or she is nothing. This is not to say that a woman should refrain from writing poems; only, that she should write as a woman, not as if she were an honorary man."[5] She praises or rages, making herself even as predatory as a sow who "eats her farrow," but her poetry always concerns, apparently, her relation to a man. (I will develop this modern mythical exclusion of women from the realm of reason and speech in the section on gender.) Among the fiction authors discussed in this study, both Kafka and Lawrence have cast the dying god as male Artist and the goddess as silent Woman-Life, thus occasionally adopting the somewhat self-pitying and basically romantic posture of the poets.

DYING GOD AND CONCEPTUAL LENS

As an extension of this reflexive conversion of the myths, the artists in chapter 6 expose the false promise of dying gods, but then discover something useful even in the fakery. Conrad, Forster, and Coppola recognize the tawdriness, failures, or outright malevolence of the characters modeled on dying gods, but, at the last minute, they salvage something grand about the tainted figures. This insistence that impostors can inspire truths recalls the whole nineteenth- and twentieth-century philosophy of the "necessary lie": Ibsen's working illusion, Sartre's humanly constellated meaning that we arbitrarily steer by, Stevens's "necessary fiction." In modern philosophy (since Kant), art and indeed all human creations—science, history, religion—have come to be seen as limited, makeshift structures that yet provide people their only frameworks through which to experience the world. Participating in this philosophical tradition, the artists in chapter 6 know that the dying gods in their true stature do not exist; yet their lying, parodic versions manage to offer a useful image of our tentative, inevitably limited views of the world. These partial views—private visions or social codes—as long as they are constantly reexamined, can enable the characters to act.

History

Several critics have wondered whether revivers of myth in the twentieth century have broken faith with history—ignoring it, or irresponsibly calling for a vague cataclysm, or trying to return to an unrecoverable past. Philip Rahv scornfully equates a desire for "sacred repetition" with a "fear of history," a longing to go back to an idyllic past or acquiesce in an archetypal present.[6] Franco Moretti slurs T. S. Eliot and his mythical method as "totalizing," an epithet that sounds libelously like "totalitarian." Moretti blames Eliot for anti-individualism and an acceptance of cycles that presumably preclude any further effort.[7] If the tarot deck of fate already predicts everybody's personality, then individuals no longer have to struggle to change themselves. Moreover, they do not have to try to reform society either, because the same few cultural situations probably float down out of each shuffle of the cards too. Terry Eagleton similarly worries that Eliot's earlier mythical method and his later Christian piety both invite readers to cloister themselves away from protesting social ills:

The crisis of European society—global war, severe class-conflict, failing capitalist economies—might be resolved by turning one's back on history altogether and putting mythology in its place. Deep below finance capitalism lay the Fisher King, potent images of birth, death, and resurrection in which human beings might discover a common identity. Eliot accordingly published *The Waste Land* in 1922, a poem which intimates that fertility cults hold the clue to the salvation of the West. His scandalous avant-garde techniques were deployed for the most arrière-garde ends: they wrenched apart routine consciousness so as to revive in the reader a sense of common identity in the blood and guts.[8]

Although I agree with Moretti and Eagleton that the older Eliot becomes alarmingly elitist and exclusive, the poet seems to me to betray his earlier studies in myth rather than act out a latent pernicious influence in them. His later "classicism" does convey "the suspicion of progress, the hostility toward individualism and modern democracy, the insistence on hierarchy and order."[9] Particularly disturbing, his search for a European tradition begins to include anti-Semitic undertones as he longs for a society homogenous in every way.[10] *The Waste Land*, however, crammed with allusions to Frazer, escapes that rigidity because the poem "is a product of the anthropological temper which understands by comparing, which sets systems of beliefs in relation to one another, and which disallows the special claims of any single system."[11] When still imbued with world mythology, Eliot is able to link Adonis, the Buddha, and St. Augustine in an eclectic and "democratic" collaboration.

It is true that several modern writers either praised or acquiesced to fascism to a chilling degree. Frank Kermode mentions Eliot, Yeats, Pound, Wyndham Lewis, and Lawrence as part of a "correlation betwen early modernist literature and authoritarian politics."[12] Georg Lukács castigates the German intelligentsia, including Heidegger, for collaborating in Nazism.[13] Some of these men, however, were fond of myth and some were not; surely George Steiner goes too far in laying the blame for Hitler at the doorstep of myth: "The holocaust is a reflex, the more complete for being long-inhibited, of natural sensory consciousness, of instinctual polytheistic and animist needs."[14] For all the National Socialists' misuse of Nietzschean mythologizing and their promulgation of Rosenberg's "myth of the twentieth century," Rosenberg cannot be said to represent in any way an understanding of dying gods. When these intellectuals and pseudo-intellectuals failed humanity, it was not myth and "polytheism" that failed them.

I would like to address the charges against myth by Eagleton, Steiner, and the rest in two ways: by arguing in general against the idea that authors who return to myth must ignore history because myth and history are irremediably opposed, and by arguing in particular that the authors in this study have used myth to face history and to encourage action in it, not to escape it.

History and myth cannot be seen as irremediably opposed because first of all some of the formulators most closely associated with the rising historical consciousness in the nineteenth century constructed framing myths. (Although I have so far used "myth" to mean specific ancient stories rather than new visions, here I yield to the common practice of referring to any "total world view" as a "myth," but only because the old stories so frequently turn up in the new.) For example, when Hegel postulates a universal "Spirit" "realizing itself" through history, coming to partial self-knowledge and then superseding itself, he acknowledges the influence of myths of dying gods:

> while death is the issue of life, life is also the issue of death. This is a grand conception; one which the Oriental thinkers attained, and which is perhaps the highest in their metaphysics. . . . But this image is only Asiatic; oriental not occidental. Spirit—consuming the envelope of its existence—does not merely pass into another envelope, nor rise rejuvenescent from the ashes of its previous form; it comes forth exalted, glorified, a purer spirit.[15]

Ignoring for the moment Hegel's condescending tone toward "Asiatic," I find that his abstract Spirit, which has to be accepted on faith, and his belief in Progress, which hardly seems proved by the historical record, are at least as "mythic" as any traditional story that reflects the cycles of birth and death in nature.

In fact, all interpreters of history who detect a necessary *pattern* have to be seen as mythicists to some extent, whether they expect the pattern to recur the same or changed. Those who see pattern as a rhythmic repetition of the same order of being—Vico's cycles of religious, heroic, and human ages, Blake's Eden, Nietzsche's eternal return, Spengler's organicism, Berdyaev's Christian providence, and Yeats's interplay of opposites—all reveal traces of influence by myths of death and rebirth.[16] But those who conversely insist on a pattern of necessary progress through changes also draw on related millennial myths. Steiner even claims that "Marxism is the third principal mythology [with classical and Christian] to have taken root in western consciousness."[17]

A major objection against revivers of myth is that they accept a static world and will not take any steps to try to change it because its system is set. Believers in history are not, however, automatically active politically. When they are active, they often act *through* myths. Moreover, mythicists can also act for change.

Either theory or temperament may prevent believers in history from taking political action. Determinists who think that history progresses inevitably cannot, in theory, allow for any leapfrogging of preparatory stages. Marx and Engels, for example, caution that revolution cannot occur no matter how much the "idea" of revolution has been touted if the "productive forces" have not evolved to the right level and if a "revolutionary mass" has not formed; they thus seem to dampen any enthusiasts who want to intervene in the slow grinding of historical processes.[18] In practice, however, the strict determinism of Marxism has been largely set aside (see later discussion).

Observers of history who on the contrary see no necessary pattern might not act in the world for different reasons—either an unfeeling objectivity or an overwhelming sense of hopelessness. Elie Wiesel, for example, defines the historian as a dispassionate recorder.[19] But if he or she perpetually remained "neutral," with no indignation, it is hard to say what would ever motivate him or her to protest. On the other hand, some historians might hesitate to act not out of dispassion but out of despair. Historical relativity and a sense of absurdity could induce paralysis, which is often seen as a particularly "modern" syndrome.[20] One literary critic can even conduct a whole discussion of myth and history with such a loose definition of terms that he interchanges "history" with "pessimism" and "myth" with "optimism," because myth "does not end with decay."[21] Lukács finally admits that there is really no predicting who will be politically active and who, passive, according to ideology—whether lover of myth, student of history , Communist, Catholic, or whatever: "Fatalism may have its roots in pseudo-science, or in religious modes of thought. Equally, a belief in reason, in individual responsibility, may be grounded in a theological or a materialist theory of society."[22]

Although it does not necessarily follow, then, that those who distrust myth and look to history instead (whether patterned or unpatterned), will try to improve the world, there are historicists who do take an active stance in politics. Sartre, for example, modifies his Marxism outright to warn that changes do not just happen automatically: people have to make them at every step.[23] Nevertheless, those historicists who do actively intervene have not necessarily separated themselves from myth.

In fact, the syndicalist Georges Sorel formulates very clearly at the beginning of this century how a revolutionary might knowingly employ "myth," by which he means, for example, the motivating hopes of early Christians, of Luther and Calvin for the Reformation, or of the French Revolutionaries. Chillingly, although Sorel assumes that revolutions "never" turn out as expected—in fact, results are totally unpredictable— he still recommends his "general strike" as a way to "sweep away" all present social structures. "Myth" for him is a form of subliminal imagery by which to manipulate workers into believing that they will triumph, though Sorel believes they cannot receive anything like what they envision.[24]

Even if we exclude such cynical manipulators of myth, operating either from the far right or from the far left, and consider more earnest commentators like Lukács, it is not true that in their political dealings they ignore myth, equivalent to what Lukács calls the *terminus ad quem* determining the shape of both action in the world and plot in an effective literary work. It has become commonplace to align mythicists with a static world, ordered by the cosmos, and a static work, ordered by the author, versus realists, all on the side of "contingently documentary form."[25] But does the realistic novel exhibit this form? Actually, Lukács objects to Joyce's *Ulysses* not so much because Joyce imposes too much mythic order but because he renders too much real disorder, too much "contingently documentary form," criticized by Lukács as "naturalism."[26] Lukács wants "realist" authors to infuse a pattern into literature, a view of how things *ought* to be (a myth), which would in turn, he thinks, encourage readers to translate new patterns into their society.

So far I have argued that many historicists, from Hegel and Marx to Sorel and Lukács, have not really distanced themselves from myth. Now I will argue that mythicists have not avoided history. Although I will condemn some failings, by and large twentieth-century authors have used myth to understand and act in the world.

When Conrad, Forster, and Coppola portray colonialism from Latin America to India to Vietnam, they do not just borrow a vaguely historical backdrop but pursue a profound critique of "material interests," "civilizing the savages," and "pacification." Widespread social concerns including race prejudice and bigotry (Kafka and Faulkner), World War I and industrialization (Hemingway and Lawrence), World War II (Mann and Bellow), and governmental tyrannies of the right and the left (García Márquez and Konwicki) are all attacked in these books. If we add gender questions as social and political issues, then practically no author in this study is ensconced in a private ivory tower of myth.

I view only two authors in this study as having reprehensible attitudes toward history. In *The Plumed Serpent*, Lawrence's politics become frightening, but because he did not remain true to his own myth. He at first claims that Quetzalcoatl awaits recognition in everybody's heart but later swerves from this faith in individuals to elevate special leaders as better Quetzalcoatls. According to Lawrence, the leaders will be our gods and absolve us from the difficult task of plumbing our own souls to find the features of Quetzalcoatl in ourselves and gain our own strength in making political decisions. By letting Ramón and Cipriano make all the decisions, Lawrence betrays some of his own ideals. Still, Lawrence wants to improve the whole society, not just a few myth-reading recluses; he does show inner contradictions and dilemmas in Ramón and Cipriano, and leaves the book open-ended, with the protagonist, Kate, neither completely endorsing nor abandoning Ramón and Cipriano.

If Lawrence sometimes concentrates too much power in an impossibly godlike ruler, Mann sometimes tolerates "opposites" with too neutral an irony. Nevertheless, Mann defiantly writes *Joseph and His Brothers* as a "Jewish" novel and an anti-Nazi protest, accepting exile at the same time.

The author specifically answers Eagleton's fear that myth lovers lapse into mindless "blood and guts." Joseph adopts the myths of dying gods with full consciousness; he questions his inherited myths and chooses among them. If a myth does not include a gesture that he wants to make (i.e., Osiris forgiving Set), Joseph will rewrite the script himself. Overall, when these authors show that one dangerous myth needs to be rejected (i.e., Bellow throwing out Baal), they simply choose another myth (i.e., Bellow selecting Abraham as paradigm for an anguished readiness to fight), which enables them to act politically.

Gender

A major reason so many twentieth-century writers returned to vegetation myths is undeniably the powerful presence of a goddess. Ancient devotion to a goddess—either alone or on a par with a god—contrasted strikingly with the familiar Western worship of a solitary father god. In addition to enlarging conceptions of deity, the new information from anthropologists coincided with an altered relation of the sexes in society. Socially, the mythologies of the goddess reinforced new attitudes toward sexuality and gender roles.

The open references to copulation in primitive iconography and story appealed to writers influenced by the sexual revolution of the early twentieth century, providing them with imagery by which to reverence the body. Lawrence and Faulkner (chapter 7), who allude extensively to fertility ritual, depart from the prevailing Freudian interpretation of sexuality, at least in tone. Whereas Freud takes a dour view that unavoidable, all-powerful, and basically unsavory libidinal drives keep people in thrall, Lawrence and Faulkner celebrate sexuality as a positive force. They draw on Frazer's unofficial nostalgia, rather than on his official disapproval, his stated hope that superstition and license would be superseded. Still, Lawrence and Faulkner retain enough of Frazer's pessimism about "volcanic" instincts lurking just under the surface of consciousness to desentimentalize "passion," as compared to their eighteenth- and nineteenth-century literary precursors.[27]

"Sex partner" is not the only gender role that came into question in the revival of primitive mythology, although various assignments of instinct and emotion continued to dominate expectations for women. As I tried to show in chapter 8, inviting the goddess back into the literary pantheon did not always imply inviting real women into positions of greater power in their society. On the contrary, by developing the so-called feminine side of male characters, Mann and Malamud actually leave their female characters weaker than ever.

As an influential popularizer of myth (including myths of dying gods), the psychologist C. G. Jung has perpetuated several undesirable stereotypes for women, whether he was warning against the "Terrible Mother" or supposedly praising the "Great Goddess." It is important to distinguish the socially conditioned opinion among ideas that he presents as eternal psychological truths. As Demaris Wehr cautions, Jung uses quasi-religious and quasi-scientific language to "ontologize" a historically determined status quo.[28] Many of his pronouncements severely limit roles for women.

For example, Jung repeatedly equates a "mother figure" with the "unconscious" and a "father figure" with "spirit" or "intellect." In "The Mother-Archetype," Jung lavishly admires women for "transcending reason," but he basically means that they could not "descend" to reason if they tried.[29] Jung is not concerned if women cannot put *a* with *b* logically, because they leap right away to the correct answer, *c*, whereas men are still plodding along with slow analysis. Women for Jung, like poets for Plato, might be inspired, but they are still inspired *fools*, just a sob away from hysteria or madness.

Jung even believes that "Intellectual development [in women] is often accompanied by the emergence of masculine traits in general."[30] He does not mean that they will grow mustaches, I am sure—though Mann actually pictures the biblical Rebecca with dark hairs sprouting on her upper lip, apparently because she cleverly and analytically thinks up the ruse to outwit Isaac. If an intellectual woman should speak up decisively, Jung, less graphic but no less alarmed than Mann, can only evaluate her boldness and authority as in themselves "masculine." When Jung seems to suggest that men by training subordinate Eros (love) to Logos (reason and speech), he actually means that they do so by nature. Slipping from social conditioning to eternal verities, Jung confines women to the realm of emotion: "In men, Eros, the function of relationship, is usually less developed than Logos. In women, on the other hand, Eros is an expression of their true nature, while their Logos is often only a regrettable accident."[31]

In addition to assuming that women want love to be their whole life because they cannot really do anything else, Jung all too often interprets strong women in myths not as entities in their own right but as parts of a male psyche. He insists that if Brünhilde exercises power, she gets her power from Wotan, because she really symbolizes *his* will.[32] If she acts without waiting for Wotan's nod, then she is dangerous—not even as an agent unto herself, but as a sign of *his* psyche gone awry. Jung frequently reads male divinities as models for men and female divinities as the "female side" of the male personality.

Other mythicists who mistrust powerful goddesses either whittle them down to less threatening figures or condemn them. Joseph Henderson in his portion of the jointly authored *Wisdom of the Serpent* wields his Jungianism as a tool to keep women out of the job market, asserting that Reason painted as a goddess instead of a god during the French Enlightenment perverted women's proper role at home.[33] Initially surprised that Inanna, like Odysseus, could competently get all the way to the underworld on her own, Henderson finally decides that she can rightfully descend to the underworld because that murky element represents the unconscious anyway, and the unconscious is always feminine. If Inanna wants to come back to the light of day, she will need to bring a good man, Dumuzi, with her, because no woman could ever function in the male, daylit realm of spirit. Once she has latched onto her hero "who can find his way to the heavenly light and lead her to it," Inanna has to "become, like mother Isis, content to produce heroes who went their way and achieved an autonomy of the masculine. She then remained goddess of the chthonic depths of life, as her husband became God of Heaven."[34] Having declared that women are earthy and men, spiritual, Henderson has to warp mythology to prove his point: actually, Osiris became god of the underworld, not a sky god, and Inanna was queen of heaven.[35] Henderson's interpretation of Inanna's descent smacks of the American midcentury rather than the Mesopotamian third millennium B.C. More astute inheritors of myth than Henderson also promote stereotypes. Northrop Frye, for instance, still automatically links "planning and intelligence" with masculinity.[36]

Jung's polarized Great Goddess and Terrible Mother could be seen to derive to some extent from Frazer's presentation of goddesses who either search for the dead god and restore him—or else castrate and kill him in the first place. John Vickery shrewdly suggests that one of the reasons Frazer became so popular at the beginning of this century was that writers like Swinburne had already prepared the way for Frazer's ambivalent goddesses.[37] But Vickery does not examine what social factors Swinburne and Frazer may both have reflected. Sandra Gilbert does pinpoint social developments that were alarming men by the 1920s: the "effeminacy" of the decadent *fin de siècle*, "scribbling women" taking over the literary marketplace, agitation for the vote on both sides of the Atlantic, and especially the number of women working in factories and on farms during World War I.

Gilbert argues that male modernists (e.g., Joyce, Eliot, and Lawrence), yearning to get back to myth, often longed for old social hierarchies of male dominance and female submissiveness. Gilbert believes that female modernists (Woolf, Barnes, and H. D.) wanted to get behind myth to a genderless time.[38] If for Joyce "Bloom and Molly can and must be boiled down, as it were, to Ulysses and Penelope, the 'childman weary' and the 'fulfilled, recumbent' woman," must all myth, Gilbert asks provocatively, reduce to the "Truth of Gender"?[39]

Because the myths I am dealing with *are* fertility myths, gender obviously is significant, and Gilbert's charge becomes serious. It does not seem to me, however, that Inanna adventuring to the ends of the earth or Kali dancing through life and death need always be read as either passive women or ones whose only concern is sex. To do so ignores the active independence of the ancient goddesses: "when we do not know much about a religion or about a particular goddess, we claim that the religion was an effort to ensure fertility. . . . One must wonder whether, when reading of a fertility goddess or cult, the term fertility is not just a mask for ignorance."[40] Granted that we may never know exactly what ancient peoples meant by their images, the evidence of goddesses as lawgivers, warriors, hunters, and originators of language suggests a diversity that is often downplayed in the works of Jung, Erich Neumann, and other Jungian inheritors.

In answer to Gilbert, then, the revival of mythology has, in practice, frequently reinforced stereotypes; in theory, however, it need not always do so. I would like to divide the rest of this section into a more focused examination of the two types of goddesses which appear in the literary works treated in chapters 8 and 9, respectively: Cybele and other violent goddesses; and Demeter and Persephone. For both the violent and the victimized goddesses, I will identify allusions and transformations which I consider dangerous and those which I consider valuable.

VIOLENT GODDESSES

Why did some ancient peoples paradoxically include castration as part of a fertility myth? To Frazer it looked as if Cybele viciously imposed Attis's sacrifice, whereas other students of anthropology speculate that men may have devised castration or mock castration in a kind of envy of women. Joseph Campbell explains that, among Australian aborigines, circumcision and especially subincision rites (which stop short of castration but painfully approach it) attempt to create a being who claims to be both female and male in one ultrapowerful person.[41] Barbara Walker adds that "before men understood their reproductive role, they tried to 'make women' of themselves, in the hope of achieving womanlike fertility."[42] Countering the accusation that Cybele delights in torturing men, Walker notes that the more patriarchal the society, the more brutal the attacks on young males in initiation rites: Middle Eastern circumcision, Australian subincision.[43]

Jung, drawing on the Cybele myth, either inflates the "Terrible Mother" into a malicious force or confines her to doting but still destructive motherhood. Of the two versions of the story, that a boar slew Attis or that Attis castrated himself, Jung prefers the latter, interpreting that Cybele drives her son mad with smothering love. The other version actually damns the mother too, because, Jung says, the boar is obviously Cybele. Attis nailing himself to the tree represents a man who never grew up, who keeps seeking union with his mother (mother nature), subsiding back to the womb. He would do better to destroy that tree or boar and stop yearning for the infantile comfort that a mother (apparently always willing to coddle) is all too willing to provide. Young men should be like Marduk, Jung counsels, not like Attis, and slay the female dragon Tiamat, overcoming their dependence on too demanding women.[44] The whole Cybele myth reduces to advice about cutting the apron strings.

Mann, Malamud, Hemingway, and Lawrence all use this tradition of violent goddesses but with some interesting changes. Although feminists have justly twitted Hemingway for his many displays of machismo, it seems to me that in *The Sun Also Rises* he is quite evenhanded despite his direct allusions to the myth of Cybele and Attis. If Brett wears short hair and suffers a debilitating sadness, Hemingway is neither chiding her for a false "masculinity" nor dismissing her as femininely "weak."[45] Instead, he shows her to be honorably defiant and vulnerable in the same measure as the male characters, and as likely to be identified favorably with fighting bulls, which, as Hemingway knew, were one of the forms taken by the dying god Attis. Lawrence, on the other hand, occasionally switches from an identification of female characters with goddesses to an identification of female characters with dying gods out of a kind of spite. Fearful that early twentieth-century feminism had made women too bossy and cerebral, instead of encouraging their supposedly natural passivity and nonthinking sexuality, Lawrence sometimes puts his female protagonists—in "The Woman Who Rode Away," *The Plumed Serpent*, and *Lady Chatterley's Lover*—into the role of dying god, apparently just to ensure their eclipse.

VICTIMIZED GODDESSES

Psychologists, novelists, and poets in the twentieth century have interpreted the myth of Demeter and Persephone in extremely diverse ways, which often seem to warp the story considerably (as it appears in the "Homeric Hymn to Demeter," for example, or even in the somewhat more masculinely biased version in Ovid's *Metamorphoses*). For one modern group (mostly male,) Persephone and/or Demeter represents, first, a neurotic woman fearing marriage or oppressing her children; second, a healthy woman wishing for normal sexual experience, especially in a society where such longings are considered evil or "underworldly"; third, a healthy person wishing to understand and accept death; and fourth, a neurotic woman masochistically attracted to a destructive man. For another group (mostly female), Persephone and Demeter represent women thwarted by social conditions that deaden their lives. Relatively few authors pay attention to Persephone's rape per se, hushing it into a symbol of "the patriarchy" in general, death, or, somehow, healthy sex.

First, neither Demeter nor Persephone has received much respect from psychologists who name neurotic complexes after these goddesses. Jung classifies a woman who lives parasitically through her children as a "Demeter."[46] Because Hades assaults Persephone, it seems obvious that Demeter has a right to be upset; however, Jung dismisses her as a clinging mother. He similarly borrows the name "Persephone" to criticize a weak woman who fears marriage and effaces herself in her mother's shadow:

> She [the daughter] is so inexperienced, so terribly in need of help, that even the gentlest swain becomes a daring abductor, who brutally robs a loving mother of her daughter. Such a marvellous opportunity to pass himself off as a gay Lothario does not occur every day and therefore acts as a strong incentive. This was how Pluto abducted Persephone from the inconsolable Demeter. But, by a decree of the gods, he had to surrender his wife every year to his mother-in-law for the summer season. (The attentive reader will note that such legends do not come about by chance!)[47]

By assembling a cast of timid, coy, and possessive women that Jung thinks to be readily available at all time periods under any social conditions, he complacently whitewashes the crime of mythology's most famous rapist.

In fact, several mythicists influenced by Jung suffer a curious blind spot about rape as anything different from marriage. Karl Kerenyi, in *Eleusis: Archetypal Image of Mother and Daughter*, concludes, with no sense of incongruity, that "The happy marriage of the ravished maiden was the prototype of all marriages."[48] Similarly, an investigator of myth in literature, Philip Wheelwright, wonders ingenuously why rape was so central to Persephone's story and decides, "Evidently because rape symbolizes one of the most important and emotionally arresting 'passages' in human experience—the passage from the pure state of virginity through the shock of violation and attaining to the happy issue of periodic motherhood."[49] As an overly fearful, innocent young woman, Persephone must be urged to stop protesting Hades's advances.

Second, several male authors have impressed Persephone into service to carry the banner for "healthy woman desiring sexual experience." Whereas Kerenyi and Wheelwright apparently assume that no woman would seek out sexual contact unless forced to it by the requirements of procreation, Lawrence grants women a powerful sexual nature. (His notorious disregard for female orgasm contradicts, however, his thesis that an essential sexuality is characteristic of women.)[50] Despite his willful ignorance about just what women's experience was, he did assume some kind of pleasure for both sexes. If a squeamish Christian church was going to approve sex only to acquire offspring and label pleasure evil, then, Lawrence implies, he will have to join the party of the devil or Pluto. In "The Ladybird," for example, Lawrence transvalues terms, so that "hell" equals "passion," and respectable bourgeois life becomes a "white sepulchre." If the protagonist of that story is to act on her awakened impulses, she will have to join her "king in Hades," because her new physicality would not be acceptable in her old, daylit haunts.[51]

Third, occasionally readers of Persephone's story have chosen to emphasize her passage into death rather than into sexual experience—death either in response to a necessity of nature, or though a neurotic fascination with destruction. In his beautiful poem "Bavarian Gentians," Lawrence identifies with Persephone as a ploy to help him accept finally inevitable death as a fact of life. Rather than fight it when his last hour arrives, he hopes he can picture death as a lover, to welcome an unavoidable ordeal: "let me guide myself with the blue, forked torch of this flower / down the darker and darker stairs . . . even where Persephone goes, just now, from the frosted September."[52]

Fourth, the difference between accepting mortality in a dignified embrace and longing for it in a weary revulsion against life has sometimes been slight. A few authors have combined Persephone's initiation, into both sexuality and death, with the Freudian notion of dual psychic longings for eros (sexual instinct) and thanatos (death wish). Because Freud defines eros as a desire to return to a time before birth—when "the boundary between ego and object threatens to melt away"—he makes eros itself deathly, representing a loss of identity.[53] Freud can, in turn, describe the dissolution of identity at death in terms of eros, by assuming that both eros and thanatos derive from an effort to return to the womb.

When authors allude to Persephone's descent as an illustration of thanatos and eros, they usually fashion a protagonist who becomes fascinated by her own destruction. She expresses her masochism by deliberate association with a Hades-like lover or husband. Alexander Döblin, for example, in his enormous, pedantic novel *Tales of a Long Night*, has the willing victim, who at first intended to "save" Hades, pursue an extended, self-conscious identification with a neurotic Persephone.[54]

Although the transformations of Persephone and Demeter noted so far make them complicit in their initiation into death or sexuality, another group of authors (mostly but not exclusively female) recreate the goddesses as a paradigm for women whose potential has been deadened by patriarchal conditions. Susan Gubar, who claims Demeter is "the cental mythic figure for women," explains that "the myth becomes an allusive structure . . . because it articulates the pain of growing up female in a male-dominated world. . . . Male domination in sexual relationships becomes a synecdoche for a culture based on acquisition and brutality."[55]

Gubar, however, perpetuates several dangerous stereotypes through the literary transformations of Persephone and Demeter. Gubar identifies these two goddesses with "emotional responsiveness, physical spontaneity and instinctual selflessness," which circumvent "the division between self and other, the deathly division at the center of patriarchy."[56] Gubar's perceptions of "physical spontaneity" (like Annis Pratt's "green world") and "interdependence" (like the recent psychological theories of "weak ego boundaries" for women) merely validate nineteenth-century beliefs in female dependence and greater emotional attachment, while implicitly accepting a flattering view of women as naturally more at home in their bodies, more aware of ecological issues, and more concerned with the good of the whole community than men are.[57] In actuality, women and men can, unfortunately, be equally inhibited, destructive, and selfish.

Spirituality

It is often assumed that the presence of dying deities in modern literature provides only an ironic register of convictions lost. Continuing allusions, however, indicate a healthy spiritual quest that is not entirely despairing.

Writers as well as painters and sculptors became fascinated in this century with masks, myths, and rites from outside Europe at least in part for religious motives. Robert Hughes may at first attribute "primitivism" in the fine arts to nostalgia for a Noble Savage, to a languorous sensuality, and to purely formal appreciation of line, bulk, and texture. But he finally concludes that "The main value of primitive art to modernism was not formal but quasi-magical. It gave the artist what academism could not: shamanistic power, a sense of the numinous . . . for who wants to face the tedium of a wholly secular culture?"[58] Similarly, I do not believe that when Eliot announces a mythical method, he "wants the form more than the meaning, the discipline of orthodoxy more than the fullness of tradition."[59] He and his colleagues do want some meaning from the old religions, some "sense of the numinous"—an elusive term more easily defined by saying first what modern authors do *not* include by it.

They do not want an anthropomorphic god. With the exception of O'Connor, the authors in this study generally heed Nietzsche's "madman," who trumpets the "death of God." But no sooner does Nietzsche obligingly inter a Judeo-Christian god (whom he found already moribund for most of Western society) than he invites a pagan Dionysus—a dying god, in fact—to take his place. As one of the first philosophers to predict that inhabitants of an industrial age will still look for reflections of themselves in mythology, Nietzsche practically proselytizes for Dionysus, who is "stronger, more evil, deeper, and also more beautiful" than other gods.[60] Unlike Christianity, which Nietzsche thinks reviles life in an effort to "transcend" it, myths of the dying god teach *amor fati*, a love of fate—an attachment to this earthly life, no matter how difficult.

Although Nietzsche rejects Christ as a masochist who seeks pain and inhibits life, he magnifies Dionysus into a reveler who accepts inevitable pain and indulges life. The two suffering figures, Dionysus and Christ, are obviously close; Nietzsche himself sometimes lapses from celebrant to masochist, parading his disease (syphilis) as the innovator's necessary burden for the good of society. The one who "loves fate," with its innate trials, may, unfortunately, go on actually to court pain.

For example, in order to face an unpalatable and condemned violence thought to be built into the structure of the world, would-be "initiates" may believe that they have to add to that violence. This paradox extends from the Melanesian tribe which pities Hainuwele yet duplicates her sacrifice in the lovers crushed by logs, to Hemingway's bullfighters who protest death by inflicting it. In a sad travesty, *amor fati* slips from celebration into sadism as well as masochism. Indeed, the authors in the section on politics (chapter 5) condemn any foisting off of the role of dying god onto others. But when *amor fati* means combating what can be improved (in politics) and facing what cannot (mortality), the dying god can serve as a model against paralyzing despair.

Like Nietzsche, a surprising number of the authors studied here invest real emotional attachment in dying gods. Forster is "on nearer nodding terms with Krishna than with any other god."[61] To Forster, Krishna resembles Adonis, loving and dying periodically. Hemingway brings a religious awe to the bull games, which he associates, through the taurobolium, with Attis and Cybele. Lawrences reinstates Quetzalcoatl and Isis with some seriousness in his utopian schemes. Even the more orthodox writers turn to dying gods with a measure of respect: O'Connor and Mann enlist Adonis and Tammuz to reveal the biblical god better, whereas Bellow holds up Osiris to illuminate and distinguish Jesus and Abraham.

Did all these authors believe that a dying god and goddess actually reign "somewhere"? No. They are employing imaginative constructs to suggest tentative meaning, not asserting literal fact. "Meaning" does not promise heavenly sinecure for angels. It is a religious sensibility that includes awe, joy in sexuality, acceptance of death, commitment to community, and enough equanimity to act in the world without despair. These authors look for immanence, not transcendence.

In rejecting literal anthropomorphic divine beings, they bear out a prescient observation that the classicist Jane Harrison made in 1912: "it is [again] possible to have a living and vigorous religion without a theology." For Harrison, "the function of religion is to preserve the common life physical and spiritual."[62] Religions arose, she says, when people danced to discharge an emotion and to "pre-present," or rehearse, rather than "represent," what they wanted done in the world. The idea of a god crystalized from the memory of a dancer, from a magnification of oneself, who danced in a "will to live."[63] In a kind of conscious recreation of this process, the high degree of anthropomorphism in the dying god appeals to modern artists not because they believe in a literal humanlike god somewhere, but because they are searching for the godlike features in the human. One motivating force in modern art has been just this elaboration of the deity within the individual and the community, here, in this world.

Most modern authors who return to myths of dying gods do not, then, exemplify a mindless reveling in "blood and guts" but pursue a mindful meditation on what the myths imply, through deliberate allusions to traditional stories. They resort to myths of dying gods, I believe, simply to make themselves face a bleak world. They want to admit the inevitable sadness of life, but they want to love their lives at the same time. So they take as their model a Krishna or a Hainuwele. Krishna knows that his incarnation will end shortly, when an accidental arrow veers in his direction, and that even his commemorations will fade quickly, when his yearly clay images gutter back into mud and the ten-day baskets of corn dissolve in the water. Nevertheless, he dances. He multiplies himself to embrace hundreds of milkmaids and to comfort them. Similarly aware and equally compassionate, Hainuwele foresees that her people will kill her, yet she hands out her gifts in the labyrinthine dance and lets her body be food. As typical dying deities, Krishna and Hainuwele lucidly and joyously dance in a labyrinth of painful death and still longed-for rebirth.

Notes

Chapter 1. Introduction

1. Carol Cosman, Joan Keefe, and Kathleen Weaver, eds., *The Penguin Book of Women Poets* (Harmondsworth, England: Penguin Books, 1978), 45. "Adonis, Dying" is translated from the Greek by John Dillon.

2. For the origins of the myths of dying gods, see Joseph Campbell, *Occidental Mythology*, vol. 3 of *The Masks of God* (New York: Viking Press, 1964), 43.

3. Sir James Frazer, *The Golden Bough*, 2 vols. (London: Macmillan, 1890); 12 vols. (1907–15).

4. Diane Wolkstein and Samuel Noah Kramer, trans. and eds., *Inanna, Queen of Heaven and Earth: Her Stories and Hymns from Sumer* (New York: Harper & Row, 1983), 52, 60–61, 84.

5. John B. Vickery, *The Literary Impact of the Golden Bough* (Princeton: Princeton University Press, 1973), 349.

6. Joseph Campbell, *Primitive Mythology*, vol. 1 of *The Masks of God* (New York: Viking Press, 1959), 151–229.

7. Ibid., 181.

8. Malcolm Bradbury, ed., *E. M. Forster, A Passage to India: A Casebook* (New York: Macmillan, 1970), 228.

9. John J. White, *Mythology in the Modern Novel: A Study of Prefigurative Techniques* (Princeton: Princeton University Press, 1971), 15.

10. Richard F. Hardin, "'Ritual' in Recent Criticism: The Elusive Sense of Community," *PMLA* 98 (October 1983): 849.

11. Annie Dillard, *Pilgrim at Tinker Creek* (New York: Bantam Books, 1974), 178.

12. Malcolm Bradbury and James MacFarlane, eds., *Modernism 1890–1930* (New York: Penguin Books, 1976), 395.

13. Terry Eagleton, *Literary Theory: An Introduction* (Minneapolis: University of Minnesota Press, 1983), 41.

14. Simone de Beauvoir, *The Second Sex*, trans. H. M. Parshley (New York: Knopf, 1953), 147–48; Sandra M. Gilbert, "Costumes of the Mind: Transvestism as Metaphor in Modern Literature," in *Writing and Sexual Difference*, ed. Elizabeth Abel (Chicago: University of Chicago Press, 1982), 214; Angela Carter, *The Sadeian Woman and the Ideology of Pornography* (New York: Harper & Row, 1978), 5.

15. Richard Ellmann and Charles Feidelson, Jr., eds., *The Modern Tradition* (New York: Oxford University Press, 1965), 883.

16. Franklin Le Van Baumer, ed., *Main Currents of Western Thought*, 4th ed. (New Haven: Yale University Press, 1978), 611.

17. Ellmann and Feidelson, *Modern Tradition*, 621.

18. John B. Vickery, ed., *Myth and Literature: Contemporary Theory and Practice* (Lincoln: University of Nebraska Press, 1966), 49.

19. Marvin H. Pope, *Song of Songs: A New Translation with Commentary* (Garden City, N.Y.: Doubleday-Anchor, 1977), 145–53.

20. *The New Oxford Annotated Bible with the Apocrypha*, ed. Herbert G. May and Bruce M. Metzger (New York: Oxford University Press, 1973), Deut. 23:18 and n.; 2 Kings 23.

21. Isa. 17:10–11.

22. Jer. 44:19 and Ezek. 8:14.

23. 2 Kings 23:3.

24. Henry McKeating, ed., *The Books of Amos, Hosea and Micah* (London: Cambridge University Press, 1971), 73.

25. Campbell, *Primitive Mythology*, 143, 182, 418. Cf. Samuel Noah Kramer, *The Sacred Marriage Rite: Aspects of Faith, Myth, and Ritual in Ancient Sumer* (Bloomington: Indiana University Press, 1969).

26. W. F. Jackson Knight, *Many-Minded Homer* (London: George Allen and Unwin Ltd., 1968), 37.

27. Campbell, *Occidental Mythology*, 162–77; Joseph Campbell, *Creative Mythology*, vol. 4 of *The Masks of God* (New York: Viking Press, 1968), 205, 635.

28. Joseph Campbell, *The Hero with a Thousand Faces* (Princeton: Princeton University Press, 1949), 26.

29. Hardin, "'Ritual,'" 847.

30. Hazard Adams, ed. *Critical Theory Since Plato* (New York: Harcourt, Brace, Jovanovich, 1971), 1133.

31. Adams, *Critical Theory*, 1134.

32. Apuleius, *The Transformations of Lucius, Otherwise Known As The Golden Ass*, trans. Robert Graves (New York: Farrar, Straus, and Giroux, 1951), 264.

33. Jessie L. Weston, *From Ritual to Romance* (Cambridge: Cambridge University Press, 1920), 149.

34. Margaret Dalziel, ed., *Myth and the Modern Imagination* (Dunedin, New Zealand: University of Otago Press, 1967), 38.

35. Raphael Patai, *Myth and Modern Man* (Englewood Cliffs, N.J.: Prentice-Hall, 1972), 163.

36. François Rabelais, *The Histories of Gargantua and Pantagruel*, trans. J. M. Cohen (Baltimore: Penguin Books, 1955), 511.

37. Edmund Spenser, *The Faerie Queene*, ed. Thomas P. Roche, Jr. (New York: Penguin Books, 1978), 472–73.

38. William Shakespeare, *The Complete Works of William Shakespeare* (New York: Hamlyn-Spring Books, 1958), 1018, 1021, 1017, 1024.

39. Henry A. Murray, ed., *Myth and Mythmaking* (Boston: Beacon, 1960), 128.

40. David Perkins, ed., *English Romantic Writers* (New York: Harcourt, Brace, Jovanovich, 1967), 1046.

41. Murray, *Myth and Mythmaking*, 124.

42. Phyllis Rose, *Woman of Letters: A Life of Virginia Woolf* (New York: Oxford University Press, 1978), 210; B. C. Southam, *A Student's Guide to the Selected Poems of T. S. Eliot* (London: Faber and Faber, 1968), 27.

43. Adams, *Critical Theory*, 633.

44. Walt Whitman, *Leaves of Grass: The First (1855) Edition*, ed. Malcolm Cowley (New York: Penguin Books, 1976), 71–72, stanza 41 (Whitman's ellipsis).

45. Whitman, *Leaves of Grass*, 71–72, stanzas 40 and 41.

46. Adams, *Critical Theory*, 641.

47. T.S. Eliot, "Ulysses, Order and Myth" (1923), in *James Joyce: Two Decades of Criticism*, ed. Sean Givens (New York: Vanguard, 1948), 201.

48. Norman A. Jeffares, *A Commentary on the Collected Poems of W. B. Yeats* (Stanford: Stanford University Press, 1968), 284–92; Lillian Feder, *Ancient Myth in Modern Poetry* (Princeton: Princeton University Press, 1971), 195.

49. George Russell, "Attack—and Fallout," *Time*, 22 June 1981, 24.

50. Mircea Eliade, *Myth and Reality*, trans. Willard R. Trask (New York: Harper & Row, 1963), 56, 100.

Chapter 2. Tracing and Erasing the World: Tammuz as Artist

1. Virginia Woolf, *The Waves* (New York: Harcourt, Brace, Jovanovich, 1959), 136. Subsequent citations from this work are noted parenthetically in the text.

2. James G. Frazer, *The New Golden Bough*, ed. Theodor H. Gaster (New York: New American Library, 1959), 370. In subsequent references, this title will be abbreviated *NGB*.

3. Ibid., 371.

4. Ibid., 350.

5. Ibid., 386.

6. Phyllis Rose, *Woman of Letters*, 210.

7. Virginia Woolf, *A Room of One's Own* (New York: Harcourt, Brace, Jovanovich, 1957), 30.

8. Weston, *From Ritual to Romance*, 149.

9. See also Jane Ellen Harrison, *Epilegomena to the Study of Greek Religion and Themis: A Study of the Social Origins of Greek Religion* (New Hyde Park, N.Y.: University Books, 1962), xl.

10. Wolfram von Eschenbach, *Parzival*, trans. Helen M. Mustard and Charles E. Passage (New York: Random House-Vintage, 1961), 134.

11. Frazer, *NGB*, 388.

12. William Shakespeare, *Twelfth Night*, act 2, sc. 4.

13. Ovid, *Metamorphoses*, trans. Mary M. Innes (Baltimore: Penguin Books, 1955), 127.

14. Maria DiBattista, *Virginia Woolf's Major Novels: The Fables of Anon* (New Haven: Yale University Press, 1980), 156.

15. William Shakespeare, *The Tempest*, act 5, sc. 1.

16. Mircea Eliade, *The Myth of the Eternal Return, or Cosmos and History*, trans. Willard R. Trask (Princeton: Princeton University Press, 1954), 101.

17. Thomas Mann, *Joseph and His Brothers*, trans. H. T. Lowe-Porter (New York: Knopf, 1966), 56, 975. Subsequent citations from this work are noted parenthetically in the text.

18. Frazer, *NGB*, 389, 386.

19. See Mann's novel *Felix Krull, Confidence Man*.

20. Adams, *Critical Theory*, 726, 993.

21. Elaine Murdaugh, *Salvation in the Secular: The Moral Law in Thomas Mann's "Joseph und seine Brüder"* (Frankfurt, Germany: Lang, 1976), 102.

22. Barbara G. Walker, *The Woman's Encyclopedia of Myths and Secrets* (San Francisco: Harper & Row, 1983), 971.

23. George Steiner, *In Bluebeard's Castle: Some Notes towards the Redefinition of Culture* (New Haven: Yale University Press, 1971), 11.

24. See also Mann's *Death in Venice*.

25. T. E. Apter, *Thomas Mann: The Devil's Advocate* (New York: New York University Press, 1979), 146.

26. Karl Kerenyi, ed., *Mythology and Humanism: The Correspondence of Thomas Mann and Karl Kerenyi*, trans. Alexander Gelley (Ithaca: Cornell University Press, 1975), 100.

27. Thomas Mann, "Freud and the Future," in Ellmann and Feidelson, *Modern Tradition*, 590.

28. Eagleton, *Literary Theory*, 41.

29. Douglas C. Muecke, *Irony and the Ironic*, 2d ed. (New York: Methuen, 1982), 47, 49.

30. Apter, *Thomas Mann*, 97, 111.

31. Haskell Block and Herman Salinger, eds., *The Creative Vision: Modern European Writers on Their Art* (New York: Grove Press, 1960), 88.

32. Mann, "Freud and the Future," 587.

33. Muecke, *Irony*, 15.

34. See also *Doctor Faustus*, Mann's novel about the dangers of artistic cultivation of opposites.

35. Apter, *Thomas Mann*, 97.

36. Thomas Mann, *The Theme of the Joseph Novels* (Washington, D.C.: Government Publishing Office, 1943), 14.

37. Block and Salinger, *Creative Vision*, 98.

38. Ibid., 105.

Chapter 3. Anguishing in the Underworld

1. Frazer, *NGB*, 525.

2. Walker, *Woman's Encyclopedia*, 182.

3. Ibid., 50.

4. For pigs and dying gods, see also the sections on Woolf and Faulkner in chapter 9.

5. Walker, *Woman's Encyclopedia*, 75.

6. Franz Kafka, *Diaries 1910–13*, ed. Max Brod and trans. Joseph Kresh (New York: Schocken Books, 1965), 125.

7. Heinrich Graetz, *History of the Jews* (Philadelphia: Jewish Publication Society, 1891), 1:9, 54.

8. Ritchie Robertson, *Kafka: Judaism, Politics, and Literature* (Oxford: Clarendon Press, 1985), 79.

9. Graetz, *History of the Jews*, 399.

10. Franz Kafka, *The Metamorphosis*, ed. and trans. Stanley Corngold (New York: Bantam Books, 1981), 66.

11. Ibid., 95.

12. Ibid., 128.

13. Ibid., 181.

14. Sabine Baring-Gould, *Curious Myths of the Middle Ages* (London: Longmans, 1897), 29.

15. Nahum N. Glatzer, ed., *The Penguin Complete Short Stories of Franz Kafka*, trans. Willa and Edwin Muir, and Tania and James Stern (Harmondsworth, Eng-

30. Baskett, "Brett and Her Lovers," 48–49.

31. Larry E. Grimes, *The Religious Design of Hemingway's Early Fiction* (Ann Arbor: UMI, 1985), 95.

32. Steven R. Phillips, "Hemingway and the Bullfight," *Arizona Quarterly* 29 (Spring 1973): 49.

33. Frederick J. Hoffman, *The Mortal No: Death and the Modern Imagination* (Princeton: Princeton University Press, 1964), 154; Weeks, *Hemingway*, 133.

34. Cochran, "Circularity," 304.

35. DeLaet, "Man and the Bull," 128, 131.

36. Walker, *Woman's Encyclopedia*, 77.

37. Angel Capellán, *Hemingway and the Hispanic World* (Ann Arbor: UMI, 1985), 55.

38. Flannery O'Connor, *The Habit of Being*, ed. Sally Fitzgerald (New York: Vintage-Random, 1979), 103.

39. Victor White, *God and the Unconscious* (London: Harvill, 1952), 219.

40. Flannery O'Connor, *Everything That Rises Must Converge* (New York: Farrar, Straus, and Giroux, 1956), 25. Subsequent citations from this work are noted parenthetically in the text.

41. Jane Ellen Harrison, *Prolegomena to the Study of Greek Religion* (Cleveland: World, 1959), 474.

42. Frazer, *NGB*, 528.

43. White, *God*, 215.

44. O'Connor, *Habit*, 438.

45. Ibid., 124.

46. Ibid., 411.

47. Ibid., 275.

48. J. Oates Smith, "Ritual and Violence in Flannery O'Connor," *Thought* 41 (Winter 1966): 560.

49. John C. Shields, "Flannery O'Connor's 'Greenleaf' and the Myth of Europa and the Bull," *Studies in Short Fiction* 18 (Fall 1981): 431.

50. Frederick Asals, "The Mythic Dimensions of Flannery O'Connor's 'Greenleaf,'" *Studies in Short Fiction* 5 (Summer 1968): 327.

51. White, *God*, 217.

52. Shields, "Europa and the Bull," 431.

53. Asals, "Mythic Dimensions," 327.

54. O'Connor, *Habit*, 148.

55. Ibid., 367.

Chapter 5. Sacrificing to Baal

1. Frazer, *NGB*, 293.

2. Kott, *Eating of the Gods*, 220.

3. Thomas L. McHaney, "*Sanctuary* and Frazer's Slain Kings," *Mississippi Quarterly* 24 (Summer 1971): 224; Joseph Blotner, *Faulkner: A Biography* (New York: Random House, 1984), 138.

4. Robert M. Slabey, "Myth and Ritual in *Light in August*," *Texas Studies in Literature and Language* 2 (Autumn 1960): 329.

5. Slabey, "Myth and Ritual," 345.

6. C. Hugh Holman, "The Unity of Faulkner's *Light in August*," *PMLA* 73 (March 1958): 161.

7. François L. Pitavey, ed., *William Faulkner's Light in August: A Critical Casebook* (New York: Garland, 1982), 53–89.

8. William Faulkner, *Light in August* (New York: Vintage-Random House, 1972), 96. Subsequent citations from this work are noted parenthetically in the text.

9. Robert J. Barth, ed., *Religious Perspectives in Faulkner's Fiction* (Notre Dame: University of Notre Dame Press, 1972), 42, 39, 48.

10. Barth, *Religious Perspectives*, 26.

11. Walker, *Woman's Encyclopedia*, 314.

12. 1 Kings 14.

13. Michael Millgate, *The Achievement of William Faulkner* (New York: Random House, 1963), 134.

14. Slabey, "Myth and Ritual," 343; Holman, "Unity," 163.

15. Frazer, *NGB*, 644.

16. Ibid., 732.

17. Ibid., 525.

18. Ibid., 695.

19. Joyce Carol Oates, "'At Least I Have Made a Woman of Her': Images of Women in Twentieth-Century Literature," *Georgia Review* 37 (Spring 1983): 27.

20. Harrison, *Themis*, 42.

21. Saul Bellow, "A Sermon by Doctor Pep," in *The Best American Short Stories 1950* (Boston: Houghton Mifflin, 1950), 66. Subsequent citations from this work are noted parenthetically in the text.

22. Isa. 6:6; Jer. 20:9.

23. Walker, *Woman's Encyclopedia*, 667.

24. Jean C. Stine et al., eds., *Contemporary Literary Criticism* (Detroit: Gale, 1984), 27:156.

25. Stine, *Contemporary Literary Criticism* 27:157; Regina Janes, *Gabriel García Márquez: Revolutions in Wonderland* (Columbia: University of Missouri Press, 1981), 92. See also Gene H. Bell-Villada, "Pronoun Shifters, Virginia Woolf, Béla Bartók, Plebeian Forms, Real-Life Tyrants, and the Shaping of García Márquez's *Patriarch*," *Contemporary Literature* 28 (Winter 1987): 460–82.

26. Gabriel García Márquez, *The Autumn of the Patriarch*, trans. Gregory Rabassa (New York: Avon, 1976), 45. Subsequent citations from this work are noted parenthetically in the text.

27. Frazer, *NGB*, 294.

28. Ibid., 210.

29. Sir James G. Frazer, *Spirits of the Corn and Wild*, 3rd ed., vol. 5 of *The Golden Bough* (London: Macmillan, 1912), pt. 1, p. 29.

30. Frazer, *NGB*, 543.

31. Gabriel García Márquez, *Leaf Storm and Other Stories*, trans. Gregory Rabassa (New York: Avon, 1972), 153.

32. Stine, *Contemporary Literary Criticism* 28:207.

33. Tadeusz Konwicki, *A Minor Apocalypse*, trans. Richard Lourie (New York: Vintage-Random House, 1984), 8, 3. Subsequent citations from this work are noted parenthetically in the text.

34. Frazer, *NGB*, 275–76.

35. Ibid., 370.

36. Tadeusz Konwicki, *The Polish Complex*, trans. Richard Lourie (New York: Viking-Penguin, 1984), xx.

37. Frazer, *NGB*, 326, 733.
38. Ibid., 287–88.
39. Walker, *Woman's Encyclopedia*, 313.
40. Eliade, *Eternal Return*, 21.
41. Konwicki, *Polish Complex*, 93.

Chapter 6. Trafficking with Tezcatlipoca

1. Jocelyn Baines, *Joseph Conrad: A Critical Biography* (London: Weidenfeld, 1960), 295; cf. John E. Saveson, "Sources of 'Nostromo,'" *Notes and Queries* 19 (September 1972): 331–34.
2. T. McAlindon, "*Nostromo*: Conrad's Organicist Philosophy of History," *Mosaic* 15 (September 1982): 31–32.
3. William H. Prescott, *History of the Conquest of Mexico* (New York: Burt, 1843), 73–74.
4. Munro S. Edmonson, ed., *Sixteenth-Century Mexico: The Work of Sahagun* (Albuquerque: University of New Mexico, 1974), 270.
5. Bernardino de Sahagún, *Florentine Codex: General History of the Things of New Spain*, trans. Arthur Anderson and Charles E. Dibble (Sante Fe: School of American Research and University of Utah, 1981), 3:68.
6. Roger Cox, "Conrad's Nostromo as Boatswain," *Modern Language Notes* 74 (April 1959): 303–6.
7. Joseph Conrad, *Nostromo* (New York: Modern Library, 1951), 509. Subsequent citations from this work are noted parenthetically in the text.
8. Laurette Séjourné, *La Pensée des anciens mexicains* (Paris: Maspero, 1966), 34.
9. Sahagún, *Florentine Codex* 3:68.
10. Ibid., 71.
11. Claire Rosenfield, *Paradise of Snakes: An Archetypal Analysis of Conrad's Political Novels* (Chicago: University of Chicago Press, 1967), 43.
12. Sahagún *Florentine Codex* 3:69.
13. Ibid., 66, 71.
14. Prescott, *Conquest of Mexico*, 74.
15. Robert J. Andreach, *The Slain and Resurrected God: Conrad, Ford, and the Christian Tradition* (New York: New York University Press, 1970), 22.
16. Sahagún, *Florentine Codex* 2: 11–21; Prescott, *Conquest of Mexico*, 412–19.
17. E. M. Forster, *A Passage to India* (New York: Harcourt, Brace, Jovanovich, 1952), 210. Subsequent citations from this work are noted parenthetically in the text.
18. Frazer, *NGB*, 350.
19. Judith Scherer Herz and Robert K. Martin, eds., *E. M. Forster: Centenary Revaluations* (Toronto: University of Toronto Press, 1982), 248–49.
20. Robert L. Selig, "'God si Love': On an Unpublished Forster Letter and the Ironic Use of Myth in *A Passage to India*," *Journal of Modern Literature* 7 (September 1979): 473.
21. E. M. Forster, *The Hill of Devi and Other Indian Writings*, ed. Elizabeth Heine (London: Arnold, 1983), 68.
22. Forster, *Hill of Devi*, 73.
23. David Shusterman, "The Curious Case of Professor Godbole: *A Passage to*

India Re-examined," in *Perspectives on E. M. Forster's A Passage to India: A Collection of Critical Essays*, ed. V. A. Shahane (New York: Barnes and Noble, 1968), 92.

24. Michael Spencer, "Hinduism in E. M. Forster's *A Passage to India*," *Journal of Asian Studies* 27 (February 1968): 281–95.

25. E. Osborn Martin, *The Gods of India: Their History, Character, and Worship* (1914; reprint, Delhi: Varanari, Indological, 1972), 142.

26. E. M. Forster, *Albergo Empedocle and Other Writings*, ed. George H. Thomson (New York: Liveright, 1971), 222.

27. E. B. Havell, *The Ideals of Indian Art* (London: Murray, 1920), 114.

28. Wilfred Stone, *The Cave and the Mountain: A Study of E. M. Forster* (Stanford: Stanford University Press, 1966), 303.

29. Malcolm Bradbury, ed., *E. M. Forster, A Passage to India: A Casebook* (New York: Macmillan, 1970), 134.

30. Forster, *Hill of Devi*, 68.

31. E. M. Forster, "The Blue Boy," review of *The Loves of Krishna*, by W. G. Archer, *Listener* 57, 14 March 1957, 444.

32. Martin, *Gods of India*, 139.

33. See also Forster's comments on the Krishna of *The Bhagavad Gita* in "Hymn Before Action," in E. M. Forster, *Abinger Harvest* (London: Arnold, 1936).

34. Martin, *Gods of India*, 140.

35. Benjamin Walker, *The Hindu World: An Encyclopedic Survey of Hinduism* (New York: Praeger, 1968), 1:566.

36. M. Th. Houtsma et al., eds., *The Encyclopedia of Islam* (London, Luzac and Leyden: Brill, 1913), s.v. "ta'zia."

37. June Perry Levine, *Creation and Criticism: A Passage to India* (Lincoln: University of Nebraska Press, 1971), 46–47.

38. Ellin Horowitz, "The Communal Ritual and the Dying God in E. M . Forster's 'A Passage to India,'" *Criticism* 6 (Winter 1964): 80. Hussein and Husain are two spellings for the same name.

39. Weston, *From Ritual to Romance*, 9; Harrison, *Epilegomena*, xlii.

40. Houtsma, *Islam*, s.v. "ta'zia."

41. Ibid.

42. Harrison, *Prolegomena*, 455.

43. Oliver Stallybrass, ed., *A Passage to India* (London: Arnold, 1978), 366.

44. Martin, *Gods of India*, 268.

45. Ibid.

46. Ibid.

47. Ibid., 269.

48. See Louise Dauner, "What Happened in the Cave?" in Shahane, *Perspectives on Passage*, 59, on cave as womb. See also Edgar A. Austin, "Rites of Passage in *A Passage to India*," *Orient West* 9 (May–June 1964), 64–72, quoted in Frederick P. W. McDowell, ed., *E. M. Forster: An Annotated Bibliography of Writings About Him* (DeKalb: Northern Illinois University Press, 1976), 452.

49. Hélène L. Webner, "E. M. Forster's Divine Comedy," *Renascence* 23 (Winter 1971): 109.

50. Campbell, *Hero*, 249–51.

51. Walker, *Woman's Encyclopedia*, 958.

52. Martin, *Gods of India*, 112.

53. Forster, *Albergo*, 223.

54. Horowitz, "Communal Ritual," 81.

55. Ibid., 77.

56. Ibid., 80–81.

57. Bradbury, *Forster*, 158.

58. Horowitz, "Communal Ritual," 70.

59. G. K. Das and John Beer, eds., *E. M. Forster: A Human Exploration* (London: Macmillan, 1979), 210.

60. Levine, *Creation and Criticism*, 157.

61. Chaman L. Sahni, "E. M. Forster's *A Passage to India:* The Islamic Dimension," *Cahiers Victoriens et Edouardiens* 17 (April 1983): 79.

62. See also Isa. 62:5, in which God longs to be a husband to Israel.

63. John Tessitore, "The Literary Roots of 'Apocalypse Now,'" *New York Times*, 21 October 1979, D21.

64. Frazer, *NGB*, 419.

65. Ibid., 528.

66. H. R. Ellis Davidson, *Gods and Myths of the Viking Age* (New York: Bell Publishing Company, 1964), 35–38, 61.

67. Frazer, *NGB*, 32.

Chapter 7. Celebrating Sexuality with Isis

1. Barth, *Religious Perspectives*, 39.

2. William Troy, *Selected Essays*, ed. Stanley Edgar Hyman (New Brunswick, N.J.: Rutgers University Press, 1967), 122; cf. Gregory L. Lucente, *The Narrative of Realism and Myth: Verga, Lawrence, Faulkner, Pavese* (Baltimore: Johns Hopkins University Press, 1979), 123.

3. Letter of 1915, quoted in Larry V. LeDoux, "Christ and Isis: The Function of the Dying and Reviving God in *The Man Who Died*," *D. H. Lawrence Review* 5 (Summer 1972): 146.

4. William York Tindall, *D. H. Lawrence and Susan His Cow* (New York: Columbia University Press, 1939), 114.

5. L. D. Clark, *Dark Night of the Body: D. H. Lawrence's The Plumed Serpent* (Austin: University of Texas Press, 1964), 122.

6. Lewis Spence, *Myths and Legends: Mexico and Peru* (Boston: Nickerson, 1913), 81.

7. Clark, *Dark Night*, 113.

8. Ibid., 116.

9. D. H. Lawrence, *The Plumed Serpent* (New York: Vintage Books, 1959), 52. Subsequent citations from this work are noted parenthetically in the text.

10. Clark, *Dark Night*, 65–66.

11. D. H. Lawrence, *Phoenix: The Posthumous Papers of D. H. Lawrence*, ed. Edward D. McDonald (New York: Viking Press, 1936), 99.

12. D. H. Lawrence, *Apocalypse* (New York: Viking Press, 1932), 163. Lawrence's date is too recent: see Campbell, *Occidental Mythology*, 43.

13. Graham Hough, *The Dark Sun: A Study of D. H. Lawrence* (New York: Capricorn, 1956), 137.

14. D. H. Lawrence, *Mornings in Mexico* (London: Secker, 1927), 55.

15. Frank Waters, "Quetzalcoatl Versus D. H. Lawrence's *The Plumed Serpent*," *Western American Literature* 3 (Summer 1968): 112.

16. Hough, *Dark Sun*, 137.

17. Scott Sanders, *D. H. Lawrence: The World of the Major Novels* (London: Vision, 1973), 141.

18. Tindall, *D. H. Lawrence*, 174.

19. Ibid., 177–78.

20. Quoted in James C. Cowan, *D. H. Lawrence's American Journey: A Study in Literature and Myth* (Cleveland: Case Western Reserve, 1970), 121; cf. Eugene Goodheart, *The Utopian Vision of D. H. Lawrence* (Chicago: University of Chicago Press, 1963), 146.

21. Ross Parmenter, *Lawrence in Oaxaca* (Salt Lake City: Smith, 1984), 301.

22. Hilary Simpson, *D. H. Lawrence and Feminism* (DeKalb: Northern Illinois University Press, 1982), 17.

23. Lawrence, *Apocalypse*, 43–44.

24. D. H. Lawrence, *Phoenix II*, ed. Warren Roberts and Harry T. Moore (New York: Viking Press, 1959), 555; written in 1928.

25. D. H. Lawrence, *The Woman Who Rode Away and Other Stories* (New York: Knopf, 1928), 57. Subsequent citations from this work are noted parenthetically, with the letter W, in the text.

26. Lawrence, *Apocalypse*, 43–44.

27. Bradbury, *Forster*, 47.

28. Das and Beer, *Forster*, 246.

29. Dan. 5:25.

30. Spence, *Myths and Legends*, 87.

31. Troy, *Selected Essays*, 129.

32. Lawrence, *Phoenix*, 784.

33. Ibid., 786.

34. Donald Gutierrez, *Lapsing Out: Embodiments of Death and Rebirth in the Last Writings of D. H. Lawrence* (Rutherford, N.J.: Fairleigh Dickinson University Press, 1980).

35. Lawrence, *Apocalypse*, 106.

36. Ibid., 62; cf. Campbell, *Occidental Mythology*, 268–69.

37. Lawrence, *Apocalypse*, 140.

38. Ibid., 106.

39. D. H. Lawrence, *Lady Chatterley's Lover* (New York: Pocket Books, 1959), 202. Subsequent citations from this work are noted.parenthetically, with the letters LC, in the text.

40. John B. Humma, "The Interpenetrating Metaphor: Nature and Myth in *Lady Chatterley's Lover*," *PMLA* 98 (January 1983): 84.

41. John 12:24 and 1 Cor. 15:36.

42. D. H. Lawrence, *The Escaped Cock*, ed. Gerald M. Lacy (Los Angeles: Black Sparrow Press, 1973), 125.

43. D. H. Lawrence, *St. Mawr and The Man Who Died* (New York: Vintage-Random House, 1953), 186–87. Subsequent citations from this work are noted parenthetically, with the letter M, in the text.

44. Lawrence, *Phoenix II*, 572.

45. Ibid., 573.

46. Richard P. Adams, *Faulkner: Myth and Motion* (Princeton: Princeton University Press, 1968), 102.

47. Walter Brylowski, *Faulkner's Olympian Laugh: Myth in the Novels* (Detroit: Wayne State University Press, 1968), 120.

48. Millgate, *Faulkner*, 142.

49. Hyatt Waggoner, *William Faulkner: From Jefferson to the World* (Lexington: University of Kentucky Press, 1959), 121, 132.

50. William Faulkner, *Pylon* (New York: Random House, 1935), 50. Subsequent citations from this work are noted parenthetically in the text. See George Monteiro, "Bankruptcy in Time: A Reading of William Faulkner's *Pylon*," *Twentieth Century Literature* 4 (April–July 1958): 9–20, and Hugh M. Ruppersburg, *Voice and Eye in Faulkner's Fiction* (Athens: University of Georgia Press, 1983), for the view that a character, not Faulkner, scorns the fliers.

51. Donald T. Torchiana, "Faulkner's 'Pylon' and the Structure of Modernity," *Modern Fiction Studies* 3 (Winter 1957): 305; cf. John R. Marvin, "*Pylon*: The Definition of Sacrifice," *Faulkner Studies* 1 (Summer 1952): 20–23.

52. Brylowski, *Faulkner's Olympian Laugh*, 119; cf. Adams, *Faulkner*, 100.

53. Olga W. Vickery, *The Novels of William Faulkner* (Baton Rouge: Louisiana State University Press, 1964), 145-55.

54. Waggoner, *Faulkner*, 132.

55. Millgate, *Faulkner*, 133; McHaney, "*Sanctuary*," 243.

56. Frazer, *NGB*, 385.

57. Ibid., 527.

58. Ibid., 385.

59. Ibid., 398.

60. Ibid., 406.

61. Ibid., 385–86.

62. André Bleikasten, "*Pylon* ou l'enfer des signes," *Etudes anglaises* 29 (July–September 1976): 446.

63. Frazer, *NGB*, 410.

64. Ibid., 387.

65. Ibid., 529.

66. Ibid., 382.

67. Ibid., 306.

68. Ibid., 308.

69. Ibid., 314.

70. Ibid., 311.

71. Adams, *Faulkner*, 100.

72. William Faulkner, *The Town* (New York: Vintage-Random House, 1957), 212.

73. John Vickery, "William Faulkner and Sir Philip Sidney?" *Modern Language Notes* 70 (May 1955): 349–50.

74. William Shakespeare, *Antony and Cleopatra*, act 2, sc. 2.

75. Bleikasten, "*Pylon*," 446.

76. Shakespeare, *Antony and Cleopatra*, act 2, sc. 2.

77. Shakespeare, *Antony and Cleopatra*, act 2, sc. 2.

78. Frazer, *NGB*, 356.

79. Cleanth Brooks, *Toward Yoknapatawpha and Beyond* (New Haven: Yale University Press, 1978), 184; Millgate, *Faulkner*, 148.

80. Edward Guereschi, "Ritual and Myth in William Faulkner's *Pylon*," *Thoth* 3 (Spring 1962): 106–09.

Chapter 8. Maligning the Goddess: The Case against Cybele

1. Walker, *Woman's Encyclopedia*, 70, 172, 1053.

2. Gilbert, "Costumes of the Mind," 210.

3. Mann, *Joseph and His Brothers*, 305, 745. Subsequent citations from this work are noted parenthetically in the text.

4. McKeating, *Amos, Hosea and Micah*, 73.

5. Ewa Kuryluk, "Mirrors and Menstruation," *Formations* 1 (Fall 1984): 68.

6. Harry Slochower, *Thomas Mann's Joseph Story: An Interpretation* (New York: Knopf, 1938), 25–26.

7. Perkins, *English Romantic Writers*, 69.

8. John 10:30.

9. See also Inta Miske Ezergailis, *Male and Female: An Approach to Thomas Mann's Dialectic* (The Hague: Martinus Nyhoff, 1975), 170.

10. See also Slochower, *Mann's Joseph Story*, 48.

11. Mario Praz, *The Romantic Agony*, trans. Angus Davidson (Cleveland: World, 1967).

12. Dalziel, *Myth*, 46; Earl R. Wasserman, "*The Natural*: Malamud's World Ceres," *Centennial Review* 9 (1965): 439.

13. Bernard Malamud, *The Natural* (New York: Farrar, Straus, and Giroux,1952), 31. Subsequent citations from this work are noted parenthetically in the text.

14. Frazer, *NGB*, 139.

15. Wasserman, "The Natural," 439.

16. Robert Shulman, "Myth, Mr. Eliot, and the Comic Novel," *Modern Fiction Studies* 12 (Winter 1966–67): 403.

17. Richard Schickel, "Swinging for the Fences," *Time*, 14 May 1984, 91.

18. Wasserman, "*The Natural*," 439.

19. Ibid., 446–47.

20. Robert J. Higgs, *Laurel and Thorn: The Athlete in American Literature* (Lexington: University of Kentucky Press, 1981), 128.

21. Walker, *Woman's Encyclopedia*, 252–54.

22. Wasserman, "*The Natural*," 451.

23. Joyce Carol Oates, *Cybele* (Santa Barbara: Black Sparrow Press, 1979), 170. Subsequent citations from this work are noted parenthetically in the text.

24. Frazer, *NGB*, 404.

25. Ibid., 369.

Chapter 9. Maligning the God: The Case against Hades

1. See Ovid, *Metamorphoses*, 126–30; and "Homeric Hymn to Demeter," in *The Ancient Mysteries: A Sourcebook*, ed. Marvin W. Meyer (San Francisco: Harper & Row, 1987), 20–30.

2. Virginia Woolf, *To the Lighthouse* (New York: Harcourt, Brace, and World, 1955), 172. Subsequent citations from this work are noted parenthetically in the text.

3. Frazer, *NGB*, 529.

4. Joseph L. Blotner, "Mythic Patterns in *To the Lighthouse*," in Vickery, *Myth and Literature*, 255.

5. Carolyn G. Heilbrun, *Toward a Recognition of Androgyny* (New York: Knopf, 1973), 155.

6. Frazer, *NGB*, 525.

7. Blotner, "Mythic Patterns," 255; see also Anne Golomb Hoffman, "De-

meter and Poseidon: Fusion and Distance in *To the Lighthouse*," *Studies in the Novel* 16 (Summer 1984): 182–96.

8. Lee M. Whitehead, "The Shawl and the Skull: Virginia Woolf's 'Magic Mountain'," *Modern Fiction Studies* 18 (Autumn 1972): 401–15; see also Jane Lilienfeld, "'The Deceptiveness of Beauty': Mother Love and Mother Hate in *To the Lighthouse*," *Twentieth Century Literature* 23 (October 1977): 345–76.

9. Grace Stewart, *A New Mythos: The Novel of the Artist as Heroine 1877-1977* (St. Albans, Vt.: Eden, 1979), 69, 45.

10. Elaine K. Ginsberg and Laura Moss Gottlieb, eds., *Virginia Woolf: Centennial Essays* (Troy, N.Y.: Whitson, 1983), 93–109, 257–68.

11. Beverly Ann Schlack, *Continuing Presences: Virginia Woolf's Use of Literary Allusions* (University Park: Pennsylvania State University Press, 1979), 53, 74.

12. Ovid, *Metamorphoses*, 126.

13. Hoffman, "Demeter," 196.

14. Frazer, *NGB*, 382, 424.

15. Jane Ellen Harrison, *Ancient Art and Ritual* (New York: Henry Holt, 1913), 78.

16. Brenda R. Silver, *Virginia Woolf's Reading Notebooks* (Princeton: Princeton University Press, 1983), 99, 103.

17. Virginia Woolf, *The Diary of Virginia Woolf: Volume Two 1920–1924*, ed. Anne Olivier Bell (New York: Harcourt, Brace, Jovanovich, 1978), 339.

18. Ralph Freedman, *Virginia Woolf: Revaluation and Continuity* (Berkeley: University of California Press, 1980), 174.

19. Meyer, *Ancient Mysteries*, 21.

20. Harrison, *Prolegomena*, 275–76.

21. Ibid., 275.

22. Ellen Bayuk Rosenman, *The Invisible Presence: Virginia Woolf and the Mother-Daughter Relationship* (Baton Rouge: Louisiana University Press, 1986), 103.

23. Ovid, *Metamorphoses*, 125.

24. Ibid., 130.

25. Ibid., 127.

26. Avrom Fleishman, *Virginia Woolf: A Critical Reading* (Baltimore: Johns Hopkins University Press, 1975), 115.

27. J. Lempriere, *A Classical Dictionary* (New York: Duyckinck, 1825), 619. Woolf mentions this work by name in *Between the Acts* (New York: Harcourt, Brace, Jovanovich, 1969), 25.

28. Ginsberg and Gottlieb, *Woolf*, 95.

29. Rosenman, *Invisible Presence*, 103.

30. Harrison, *Themis*, 396, 402.

31. Ibid., 401.

32. Rosenman, *Invisible Presence*, 102.

33. Harrison, *Ancient Art*, 78.

34. Fleishman, *Woolf*, 134.

35. William Faulkner, *The Sound and the Fury* (New York: Vintage-Random House, 1954), 184, 219. Subsequent citations from this work are noted parenthetically in the text.

36. Richard P. Adams, "The Apprenticeship of William Faulkner," *Tulane Studies in English* 12 (1962): 151; Adams, *Faulkner*, 236; Barbara M. Cross, "*The Sound and the Fury*: The Pattern of Sacrifice," *Arizona Quarterly* 16 (Spring 1960): 14.

37. Frazer, *NGB*, 526.

38. McHaney, "*Sanctuary*," 232.

39. David Williams, *Faulkner's Women: The Myth and the Muse* (Montreal and London: McGill-Queen's University Press, 1977), 199; Karl E. Zink, "Faulkner's Garden: Woman and the Immemorial Earth," *Modern Fiction Studies* 2 (Autumn 1956): 141.

40. Arthur F. Kinney, ed., *Critical Essays on William Faulkner: The Compson Family* (Boston: G. K. Hall, 1982), 275.

41. Ovid, *Metamorphoses*, 126.

42. Meyer, *Ancient Mysteries*, 21.

43. Peggy Whitman Prenshaw, ed., *Conversations with Eudora Welty* (Jackson: University Press of Mississippi, 1984), 224.

44. Frazer, *NGB*, 342.

45. Eudora Welty, *The Collected Stories* (New York: Harcourt, Brace, Jovanovich, 1980), 202. Subsequent citations from this work are noted parenthetically in the text.

46. Frazer, *NGB*, 424.

47. Woolf, *To the Lighthouse*, 270.

48. Prenshaw, *Conversations*, 325.

49. Peggy Whitman Prenshaw, ed., *Eudora Welty: Criticial Essays* (Jackson: University Press of Mississippi, 1979), 195.

50. Homer, *The Odyssey*, trans. E. V. Rieu (Baltimore: Penguin Books, 1946), 351.

51. Meyer, *Ancient Mysteries*, 21, 255. Aidoneus (Greek) means "Unseen One" and Adonis (Semitic) means "Lord."

52. Frazer, *NGB*, 346.

53. Audrey Hodgins, "The Narrator as Ironic Device in a Short Story of Eudora Welty," *Twentieth Century Literature* 1 (January 1956): 218.

54. Hodgins, "Narrator," 216.

55. Ibid., 218.

56. Prenshaw, *Essays*, 30.

57. Michael Kreyling, *Eudora Welty's Achievement of Order* (Baton Rouge: Louisiana State University Press, 1980), 23.

58. Louis Dollarhide and Ann J. Abadie, eds., *Eudora Welty: A Form of Thanks* (Jackson: University Press of Mississippi, 1979), 61. See, though, Peggy Whitman Prenshaw's more cogent interpretation in "Persephone in Eudora Welty's 'Livvie'," *Studies in Short Fiction* 17 (Spring 1980): 149–55.

59. Frazer, *NGB*, 424.

60. Ibid., 352.

61. James G. Frazer, *Adonis Attis Osiris: Studies in the History of Oriental Religion*, 3rd ed., vol. 4 of *The Golden Bough* (London: Macmillan, 1914), 47.

62. Frazer, *NGB*, 346.

Chapter 10. Conclusion

1. Frazer, *NGB*, 350.

2. Ibid., 673. Joyce's allusion to Balder and Isis occurs in James Joyce, *Finnegans Wake* (New York: Viking Press, 1974), 616.

3. Vickery, *Literary Impact*, 423.

4. Ibid., 221; Jeffares, *Yeats*, 362.

5. Robert Graves, *The White Goddess: A Historical Grammar of Poetic Myth* (New York: Farrar, Straus, and Giroux, 1948), 388, 446.

6. Vickery, *Myth and Literature*, 111.

7. Franco Moretti, *Signs Taken for Wonders: Essays in the Sociology of Literary Forms*, trans. Susan Fischer et al. (London: Verso, 1983), 220–27.

8. Eagleton, *Literary Theory*, 41.

9. Michael H. Levenson, *A Genealogy of Modernism: A Study of English Literary Doctrine 1908–1922* (Cambridge: Cambridge University Press, 1984), 210.

10. T. S. Eliot, *After Strange Gods: A Primer of Modern Heresy* (London: Faber and Faber, 1934), 20.

11. Levenson, *Modernism*, 202.

12. Frank Kermode, *The Sense of an Ending: Studies in the Theory of Fiction* (New York: Oxford University Press, 1966), 108.

13. Georg Lukács, *The Meaning of Contemporary Realism*, trans. John and Necke Mander (London: Merlin Press, 1963), 27.

14. Steiner, *Bluebeard*, 41.

15. Ellmann and Feidelson, *Modern Tradition*, 453, 460.

16. Ibid., 455, 620.

17. George Steiner, *A Reader* (New York: Oxford University Press, 1984), 164.

18. Ellmann and Feidelson, *Modern Tradition*, 338.

19. Alan M. Olson, ed., *Myth, Symbol, and Reality* (Notre Dame: University of Notre Dame Press, 1980), 23.

20. Lee W. Gibbs and W. Taylor Stevenson, eds., *Myth and the Crisis of Historical Consciousness* (Missoula, Mont.: Scholars Press, 1975), 21.

21. John M. Warner, "Myth and History in Joyce's 'Nausicaa' Episode," *James Joyce Quarterly* 24 (Fall 1986), 20.

22. Lukács, *Contemporary Realism*, 15.

23. Baumer, *Western Thought*, 768.

24. Ibid., 634–40.

25. Bradbury and McFarlane, *Modernism*, 465.

26. Lukács, *Contemporary Realism*, 19, 34.

27. Ellmann and Feidelson, *Modern Tradition*, 531.

28. Estella Lauter and Carol Schreier Rupprecht, eds., *Feminist Archetypal Theory: Interdisciplinary Re-visions of Jungian Thought* (Knoxville: University of Tennessee Press, 1985), 23.

29. Carl G. Jung, "The Mother Archetype," in *A World of Ideas*, ed. Lee A. Jacobus (New York: St. Martin's Press, 1983), 281.

30. Jung, "Mother Archetype," 289.

31. Ellmann and Feidelson, *Modern Tradition*, 656; cf. Naomi R. Goldenberg, "A Feminist Critique of Jung," *Signs* 2 (Winter 1976), 445.

32. Carl G. Jung, *Symbols of Transformation: An Analysis of the Prelude to a Case of Schizophrenia*, trans. R. F. C. Hull, 2d ed. (Princeton: Princeton University Press, 1970), 359.

33. Joseph Henderson and Maud Oakes, *The Wisdom of the Serpent: The Myths of Death, Birth, and Resurrection* (New York: Braziller, 1963), 23.

34. Henderson and Oakes, *Serpent*, 25–27.

35. Frazer, *NGB*, 389, and Wolkstein and Kramer, *Inanna*, xvi. Inanna eventually became goddess of sky, earth, and underworld, but her name means "Queen of Heaven."

36. Northrop Frye, *The Great Code: The Bible and Literature* (New York: Har-

court, Brace, Jovanovich, 1982), 69; cf. Annis V. Pratt, "Spinning Among Fields: Jung, Frye, Lévi-Strauss," in Lauter and Rupprecht, *Feminist Archetypal Theory*, 112–15.

37. Vickery, *Literary Impact*, 35.

38. Gilbert, "Costumes of the Mind," 210.

39. Ibid., 214.

40. Charles Olson, ed., *The Book of the Goddess: Past and Present* (New York: Crossroad Publishing Company, 1983), 71.

41. Campbell, *Primitive Mythology*, 108; Marjorie W. McCune, Tucker Orbison, and Philip M. Withim, eds., *The Binding of Proteus: Perspectives on Myth and the Literary Process* (Lewisburg, Pa.: Bucknell University Press, 1980), 255.

42. Walker, *Woman's Encyclopedia*, 142.

43. Ibid., 144.

44. Jung, *Symbols of Transformation*, 423–24, 415.

45. Nagel, *Hemingway*, 132–33.

46. Jung, "Mother Archetype," 286.

47. Ibid., 288.

48. Quoted in Stewart, *New Mythos*, 46.

49. Philip Wheelwright, "Notes on Mythopoeia," *Sewanee Review* 59 (Autumn 1951): 586.

50. Lawrence, *Plumed Serpent*, 463.

51. D. H. Lawrence, *Three Novellas* (New York: Penguin Books, 1960), 35, 80.

52. D. H. Lawrence, *Last Poems*, ed. Richard Aldington and Guiseppe Orioli (New York: Viking Press, 1933), 21, 312.

53. James A. Snead, *Figures of Division: William Faulkner's Major Novels* (New York: Methuen, 1986), 107.

54. Alfred Döblin, *Tales of a Long Night*, trans. Robert and Rita Kimber (New York: Fromm, 1984).

55. Susan Gubar, "Mother, Maiden and the Marriage of Death: Women Writers and an Ancient Myth," *Women's Studies* 6 (1979): 302, 305.

56. Gubar, "Marriage of Death," 304.

57. Ibid., 311–13; cf. Lauter and Rupprecht, *Feminist Archetypal Theory*, 15, 116.

58. Robert Hughes, "Return of the Native," *Time*, 15 October 1984, 97.

59. Ellmann and Feidelson, *Modern Tradition*, 621.

60. Ibid., 557.

61. Forster, "Blue Boy," 444.

62. Harrison, *Epilegomena*, xliii, xlii.

63. Harrison, *Ancient Art*, 30.

Bibliography

General

Adams, Hazard, ed. *Critical Theory Since Plato.* New York: Harcourt, Brace, Jovanovich, 1971.

Apuleius. *The Transformations of Lucius, Otherwise Known As The Golden Ass.* Translated by Robert Graves. New York: Farrar, Straus, and Giroux, 1951.

Baring-Gould, S. *Curious Myths of the Middle Ages.* London: Longmans, 1897.

Baumer, Franklin Le Van, ed. *Main Currents of Western Thought.* 4th ed. New Haven: Yale University Press, 1978.

Beauvoir, Simone de. *The Second Sex.* Translated by H. M. Parshley. New York: Knopf, 1953.

Becker, Ernest. *The Denial of Death.* New York: Free Press, 1973.

Besterman, Theodore, comp. *A Bibliography of Sir James George Frazer.* London: Macmillan, 1934.

Block, Haskell, and Herman Salinger, eds. *The Creative Vision: Modern European Writers on Their Art.* New York: Grove Press, 1960.

Bradbury, Malcolm, and James McFarlane, eds. *Modernism 1890–1930.* New York: Penguin Books, 1976.

Brooks, Cleanth. *The Hidden God: Studies in Hemingway, Faulkner, Yeats, Eliot, and Warren.* New Haven: Yale University Press, 1963.

Budge, E. A. Wallis. *The Gods of Egypt.* 1904. 2 vols. New York: Dover, 1969.

Campbell, Joseph. *Creative Mythology.* Vol. 4 of *The Masks of God.* New York: Viking Press, 1968.

———. *The Hero with a Thousand Faces.* Princeton: Princeton University Press, 1949.

———. *Occidental Mythology.* Vol. 3 of *The Masks of God.* New York: Viking Press, 1964.

———. *Primitive Mythology.* Vol. 1 of *The Masks of God.* New York: Viking Press, 1959.

Campbell, Joseph, and Henry Morton Robinson. *A Skeleton Key to Finnegans Wake.* New York: Viking Press, 1961.

Carter, Angela.*The Sadeian Woman and the Ideology of Pornography.* New York: Harper & Row, 1978.

Cavendish, Richard, ed. *Man, Myth and Magic.* 11 vols. New York: Marshall Cavendish, 1983.

Cosman, Carol, Joan Keefe, and Kathleen Weaver, eds. *The Penguin Book of Women Poets.* Harmondsworth, England: Penguin Books, 1978.

Dalziel, Margaret, ed. *Myth and the Modern Imagination*. Dunedin, New Zealand: University of Otago Press, 1967.

Davidson, H. R. Ellis. *Gods and Myths of the Viking Age*. New York: Bell Publishing Company, 1964.

DeLaet, Sigfried J. "Man and the Bull." *Diogenes* 115 (Fall 1981): 104–32.

Dillard, Annie. *Pilgrim at Tinker Creek*. New York: Bantam Books, 1974.

Döblin, Alfred. *Tales of a Long Night*. 1966. Translated by Robert and Rita Kimber. New York: Fromm, 1984.

Eagleton, Terry. *Literary Theory: An Introduction*. Minneapolis: University of Minnesota Press, 1983.

Ehrenzweig, Anton. "The Theme of the Dying God." In *The Hidden Order of Art*, 171–256. London: Weidenfeld, 1967.

Eliade, Mircea. *Myth and Reality*. Translated by Willard R. Trask. New York: Harper & Row, 1963.

———. *The Myth of the Eternal Return, or Cosmos and History*. Translated by Willard R. Trask. Princeton: Princeton University Press, 1954.

———. *Rites and Symbols of Initiation: The Mysteries of Birth and Rebirth*. Translated by Willard R. Trask. New York: Harper & Row, 1958.

Eliot, T. S. *After Strange Gods: A Primer of Modern Heresy*. London: Faber and Faber, 1934.

———. "Ulysses, Order and Myth." 1923. In *James Joyce: Two Decades of Criticism*, edited by Sean Givens, 198–202. New York: Vanguard Press, 1948.

Ellmann, Richard, and Charles Feidelson, Jr., eds. *The Modern Tradition*. New York: Oxford University Press, 1965.

Feder, Lillian. *Ancient Myth in Modern Poetry*. Princeton: Princeton University Press, 1971.

Fisch, Harold. *A Remembered Future: A Study in Literary Mythology*. Bloomington: Indiana University Press, 1984.

Frazer, James G. *Adonis Attis Osiris: Studies in the History of Oriental Religion*. 3d ed. 2 parts. Vol. 4 of *The Golden Bough*. London: Macmillan, 1914.

———. *The Dying God*. 3d. ed. Vol. 3 of *The Golden Bough*. London: Macmillan, 1912.

———. *The Golden Bough: A Study in Magic and Religion*. Abridged ed. New York: Macmillan, 1922.

———. *The New Golden Bough*. Edited by Theodor H. Gaster. New York: New American Library, 1959.

———. *Spirits of the Corn and Wild*. 3d ed. 2 parts. Vol. 5 of *The Golden Bough*. London, Macmillan, 1912.

Frye, Northrop. *Anatomy of Criticism: Four Essays*. Princeton: Princeton University Press, 1957.

———. *The Great Code: The Bible and Literature*. New York: Harcourt, Brace, Jovanovich, 1982.

Gibbs, Lee W., and W. Taylor Stevenson, eds. *Myth and the Crisis of Historical Consciousness*. Missoula, Mont.: Scholars Press, 1975.

Gilbert, Sandra M. "Costumes of the Mind: Transvestism as Metaphor in Modern Literature." In *Writing and Sexual Difference*, edited by Elizabeth Abel, 193–219. Chicago: University of Chicago Press, 1982.

Goldenberg, Naomi R. "A Feminist Critique of Jung." *Signs* 2 (Winter 1976): 443–49.

Gould, Eric. *Mythical Intentions in Modern Literature.* Princeton: Princeton University Press, 1981.

Graves, Robert. *The Greek Myths.* 2 vols. Baltimore: Penguin Books, 1955.

————. *The White Goddess: A Historical Grammar of Poetic Myth.* New York: Farrar, Straus, and Giroux, 1948.

Gros Louis, Kenneth R. R., ed. *Literary Interpretations of Biblical Narratives.* Nashville: Abingdon Press, 1974.

Gubar, Susan. "Mother, Maiden and the Marriage of Death: Women Writers and an Ancient Myth." *Women's Studies* 6 (1979): 301–15.

Hardin, Richard F. "'Ritual' in Recent Criticism: The Elusive Sense of Community." *PMLA* 98 (Octocter 1983): 846–62.

Harrison, Jane Ellen. *Ancient Art and Ritual.* New York: Henry Holt, and London: Williams and Norgate, 1913.

————. *Epilegomena to the Study of Greek Religion.* 1921. *Themis: A Study of the Social Origins of Greek Religion.* 1st ed., 1912. 2d ed., 1927. New Hyde Park, N. Y.: University Books, 1962.

————. *Prolegomena to the Study of Greek Religion.* 1st ed., 1903. 2d ed., 1908. 3d ed., 1922. Cleveland: World, 1959.

Hastings, James, ed. *Encyclopaedia of Religion and Ethics.* New York: Scribner's, 1922.

Hays, Peter. *The Limping Hero: Grotesques in Literature.* New York: New York University Press, 1971.

Henderson, Joseph, and Maud Oakes. *The Wisdom of the Serpent: The Myths of Death, Birth, and Resurrection.* New York: George Braziller, 1963.

Herd, E. W. "Myth Criticism: Limits and Possibilities." *Mosaic* 2 (Spring 1969): 69–77.

Homer. *The Odyssey.* Translated by E. V. Rieu. Baltimore: Penguin Books, 1946.

The Homeric Hymns. Translated by Thelma Sargent. New York: W. W. Norton, 1973.

Houtsma, M. Th., et al., eds. *The Encyclopaedia of Islam.* London, Luzac and Leyden: Brill, 1913.

Hughes, Robert. "Return of the Native." *Time,* 15 October 1984, 96–97.

Jeffares, A. Norman. *A Commentary on the Collected Poems of W. B. Yeats.* Stanford: Stanford University Press, 1968.

Joyce, James. *Finnegans Wake.* New York: Viking Press, 1974.

Jung, Carl G. "The Mother Archetype." In *A World of Ideas,* edited by Lee A. Jacobus, 277–90. New York: St. Martin's, 1983.

————. *Symbols of Transformation: An Analysis of the Prelude to a Case of Schizophrenia.* Translated by R. F. C. Hull. 2d ed. Princeton: Princeton University Press, 1970.

Jung, Carl G., and Karl Kerenyi. *Essays on a Science of Mythology: The Myths of the Divine Child and the Divine Maiden.* Translated by R. F. C. Hull. New York: Harper & Row, 1949.

Kermode, Frank. *The Sense of an Ending: Studies in the Theory of Fiction.* New York: Oxford University Press, 1966.

Kirk, Geoffrey S. *Myth: Its Meaning and Functions in Ancient and Other Cultures*. Berkeley: University of California Press, 1970.

Knight, W. F. Jackson. *Many-Minded Homer*. London: George Allen and Unwin, 1968.

Kott, Jan. *The Eating of the Gods: An Interpretation of Greek Tragedy*. Translated by B. Taborski and E. Czerwinski. New York: Random House, 1970.

Kramer, Samuel Noah. *The Sacred Marriage Rite: Aspects of Faith, Myth, and Ritual in Ancient Sumer*. Bloomington: Indiana University Press, 1969.

Kuryluk, Ewa. "Mirrors and Menstruation." *Formations* 1 (Fall 1984): 64–77.

Larousse World Mythology. Edited by Pierre Grimal. 1965. Translated by Patricia Beardsworth. New York: Excalibur, 1984.

Lauter, Estella, and Carol Schreier Rupprecht, eds. *Feminist Archetypal Theory: Interdisciplinary Re-visions of Jungian Thought*. Knoxville: University of Tennessee Press, 1985.

Leeming, David Adams. *Mythology: The Voyage of the Hero*. 2d ed. New York: Harper & Row, 1981.

Levenson, Michael H. *A Genealogy of Modernism: A Study of English Literary Doctrine 1908–1922*. Cambridge: Cambridge University Press, 1984.

Lucente, Gregory L. *The Narrative of Realism and Myth: Verga, Lawrence, Faulkner, Pavese*. Baltimore: Johns Hopkins University Press, 1979.

Lukács, Georg. *The Meaning of Contemporary Realism*. Translated by John and Necke Mander. London: Merlin, 1963.

McCune, Marjorie W., Tucker Orbison, and Philip M. Withim, eds. *The Binding of Proteus: Perspectives on Myth and the Literary Process*. Lewisburg, Pa.: Bucknell University Press, 1980.

McKeating, Henry, ed. *The Books of Amos, Hosea and Micah*. London: Cambridge University Press, 1971.

Meyer, Marvin W., ed. *The Ancient Mysteries: A Sourcebook*. San Francisco: Harper & Row, 1987.

Moretti, Franco. *Signs Taken for Wonders: Essays in the Sociology of Literary Forms*. Translated by Susan Fischer et al. London: Verso, 1983.

Muecke, Douglas C. *Irony and the Ironic*. 2d ed. New York: Methuen, 1982.

Murray, Henry A., ed. *Myth and Mythmaking*. Boston: Beacon, 1960.

Mylonas, George E. *Eleusis and the Eleusinian Mysteries*. Princeton: Princeton University Press, 1961.

The New Oxford Annotated Bible with the Apocrypha. Edited by Herbert G. May and Bruce M. Metzger. New York: Oxford University Press, 1973.

Nietzsche, Friedrich. *Beyond Good and Evil*. Translated by Helen Zimmern. Vol. 12 of *The Complete Works of Friedrich Nietzsche*. 1909–11. Edited by Oscar Levy. 18 vols. New York: Russell and Russell, 1964.

Olson, Alan M., ed. *Myth, Symbol, and Reality*. Notre Dame: University of Notre Dame Press, 1980.

Olson, Charles, ed. *The Book of the Goddess: Past and Present*. New York: Crossroad Publishing Company, 1983.

O'Reilly, Robert F. "Ritual, Myth, and Symbol in Gide's *L'Immoraliste*." *Symposium* 28 (Winter 1974): 346–55.

Ostriker, Alicia. "The Thieves of Language: Women Poets and Revisionist Myth-making." *Signs* 8 (Autumn 1982): 68–90.

Ovid. *Metamorphoses*. Translated by Mary M. Innes. Baltimore: Penguin Books, 1955.

Patai, Raphael. *Myth and Modern Man*. Englewood Cliffs, N.J.: Prentice-Hall, 1972.

Perkins, David, ed. *English Romantic Writers*. New York: Harcourt, Brace, Jovanovich, 1967.

Pope, Marvin H. *Song of Songs: A New Translation with Introduction and Commentary*. Anchor Bible. Garden City: Doubleday, 1977.

Praz, Mario. *The Romantic Agony*. 1933. Translated by Angus Davidson. Cleveland: World, 1967.

Quinones, Ricardo J. *Mapping Literary Modernism: Time and Development*. Princeton: Princeton University Press, 1985.

Rabelais, François. *The Histories of Gargantua and Pantagruel*. Translated by J. M. Cohen. Baltimore: Penguin Books, 1955.

Righter, William. *Myth and Literature*. Boston: Routledge and Kegan Paul, 1975.

Russell, George. "Attack—and Fallout." *Time*, 22 June 1981, 24–28.

Ruthven, K. K. "The Savage God: Conrad and Lawrence." *Critical Quarterly* 10 (Spring–Summer 1968): 39–54.

Sacks, Peter M. *The English Elegy: Studies in the Genre from Spenser to Yeats*. Baltimore: Johns Hopkins University Press, 1985.

Sandars, N. K., trans. *The Epic of Gilgamesh*. Baltimore: Penguin Books, 1960.

Schmidt, Jöel, ed. *Dictionnaire de la mythologie grecque et romaine*. Paris: Larousse, 1965.

Séjourné, Laurette. *La Pensée des anciens mexicains*. Paris: Maspero, 1966.

Shakespeare, William. *The Complete Works of William Shakespeare*. New York: Hamlyn-Spring Books, 1958.

Shulman, Robert. "Myth, Mr. Eliot, and the Comic Novel." *Modern Fiction Studies* 12 (Winter 1966–67): 395–403.

Slote, Bernice, ed. *Myth and Symbol*. Lincoln: University of Nebraska Press, 1963.

Southam, B. C. *A Student's Guide to the Selected Poems of T. S. Eliot*. London: Faber and Faber, 1968.

Spenser, Edmund. *The Faerie Queene*. Edited by Thomas P. Roche, Jr. New York: Penguin Books, 1978.

Steiner, George. *A Reader*. New York: Oxford University Press, 1984.

———. *In Bluebeard's Castle: Some Notes towards the Redefinition of Culture*. New Haven: Yale University Press, 1971.

Stewart, Grace. *A New Mythos: The Novel of the Artist as Heroine 1877–1977*. St. Albans, Vt.: Eden, 1979.

Stine, Jean C., et al., eds. *Contemporary Literary Criticism*. 36 vols. Detroit: Gale, 1984.

Vickery, John B. *The Literary Impact of the Golden Bough*. Princeton: Princeton University Press, 1973.

———, ed. *Myth and Literature: Contemporary Theory and Practice*. Lincoln: University of Nebraska Press, 1966.

————. *Myths and Texts: Strategies of Incorporation and Displacement.* Baton Rouge: Louisiana State University Press, 1983.

————. *Robert Graves and the White Goddess.* Lincoln: University of Nebraska Press, 1972.

Walker, Barbara G. *The Woman's Encyclopedia of Myths and Secrets.* San Francisco: Harper & Row, 1983.

Warner, John M. "Myth and History in Joyce's 'Nausicaa' Episode." *James Joyce Quarterly* 24 (Fall 1986): 19–31.

Weisinger, Herbert. *The Agony and the Triumph: Papers on the Use and Abuse of Myth.* East Lansing: Michigan State University Press, 1964.

Weston, Jessie L. *From Ritual to Romance.* Cambridge: Cambridge University Press, 1920.

Wheelwright, Philip. "Notes on Mythopoeia." *Sewanee Review* 59 (Autumn 1951): 574–92.

White, John J. *Mythology in the Modern Novel: A Study of Prefigurative Techniques.* Princeton: Princeton University Press, 1971.

Whitman, Walt. *Leaves of Grass: The First (1855) Edition.* Edited by Malcolm Cowley. New York: Penguin Books, 1976.

Wolfram von Eschenbach. *Parzival.* Translated by Helen M. Mustard and Charles E. Passage. New York: Vintage-Random House, 1961.

Wolkstein, Diane, and Samuel Noah Kramer, trans. and eds. *Inanna, Queen of Heaven and Earth: Her Stories and Hymns from Sumer.* New York: Harper & Row, 1983.

Yeats, W. B. *Collected Poems.* London: Macmillan, 1950.

Zimmer, Heinrich. *The King and the Corpse: Tales of the Soul's Conquest of Evil.* Edited by Joseph Campbell. New York: Pantheon, 1948.

Beckett

Beckett, Samuel. "Assumption." In *Transition Workshop*, edited by Eugene Jolas, 41–44. New York: Vanguard Press, 1949.

————. *Malone meurt.* Paris: Minuit, 1951.

————. *Three Novels by Samuel Beckett: Molloy, Malone Dies, The Unnamable.* Translated by Patrick Bowles and Samuel Beckett. New York: Grove, 1965.

Cohn, Ruby. *Back to Beckett.* Princeton: Princeton University Press, 1973.

Fletcher, John. *Samuel Beckett's Art.* London: Chatto and Windus, 1967.

Friedman, Melvin J., ed. *Samuel Beckett Now.* 2d ed. Chicago: University of Chicago Press, 1970.

Gluck, Barbara Reich. *Beckett and Joyce: Friendship and Fiction.* Lewisburg, Pa.: Bucknell University Press, 1979.

O'Hara, J. D., ed. *Twentieth Century Interpretations of Molloy, Malone Dies, The Unnamable.* Englewood Cliffs, N. J.: Prentice-Hall, 1970.

Phillips, K. J. "Beckett's *Molloy* and *The Odyssey.*" *International Fiction Review* 11 (Winter 1984): 19–24.

Pilling, John. *Samuel Beckett.* Boston: Routledge and Kegan Paul, 1976.

Bellow

Bellow, Saul. "A Sermon by Doctor Pep." In *The Best American Short Stories 1950*, 59–66. Boston: Houghton Mifflin, 1950.

Detweiler, Robert. "Patterns of Rebirth in *Henderson the Rain King.*" *Modern Fiction Studies* 12 (Winter 1966–67): 405–14.

Conrad

Andreach, Robert J. *The Slain and Resurrected God: Conrad, Ford, and the Christian Tradition.* New York: New York University Press, 1970.

Baines, Jocelyn. *Joseph Conrad: A Critical Biography.* London: Weidenfeld, 1960.

Conrad, Joseph. *Nostromo.* New York: Modern Library, 1951.

Cox, Roger. "Conrad's Nostromo as Boatswain." *Modern Language Notes* 74 (April 1959): 303–6.

Edmonson, Munro S., ed. *Sixteenth-Century Mexico: The Work of Sahagún.* Albuquerque: University of New Mexico Press, 1974.

McAlindon, T. "*Nostromo*: Conrad's Organicist Philosophy of History." *Mosaic* 15 (September 1982): 27–41.

Prescott, William H. *History of the Conquest of Mexico: With a Preliminary View of the Ancient Mexican Civilization and the Life of the Conqueror Hernando Cortes.* New York: Burt, 1843.

Rosenfield, Claire. *Paradise of Snakes: An Archetypal Analysis of Conrad's Political Novels.* Chicago: Chicago University Press, 1967.

Sahagún, Bernardino de. *Florentine Codex: General History of the Things of New Spain.* Translated from Aztec by Arthur J. O. Anderson and Charles E. Dibble. 13 vols. Sante Fe: School of American Research and University of Utah, 1981.

Saveson, John E. "Sources of 'Nostromo.'" *Notes and Queries* 19 (September 1972): 331–34.

Sherry, Norman. *Conrad's Western World.* Cambridge: Cambridge University Press, 1971.

Coppola

Apocalypse Now. Dir. Francis Ford Coppola. Screenplay by John Milius and Francis Ford Coppola. With Marlon Brando and Martin Sheen. Production credit: Omni Zoetrope, 1979.

Tessitore, John. "The Literary Roots of 'Apocalypse Now.'" *New York Times* 21 October 1979, D21.

Faulkner

Adams, Richard P. "The Apprenticeship of William Faulkner." *Tulane Studies in English* 12 (1962): 151–52.

————. *Faulkner: Myth and Motion*. Princeton: Princeton University Press, 1968.

Barth, J. Robert, ed. *Religious Perspectives in Faulkner's Fiction*. Notre Dame: University of Notre Dame Press, 1972.

Bleikasten, André. "*Pylon* ou l'enfer des signes." *Etudes anglaises* 29 (July–September 1976): 437–47.

Blotner, Joseph. *Faulkner: A Biography*. New York: Random House, 1984.

Brooks, Cleanth. *Toward Yoknapatawpha and Beyond*. New Haven: Yale University Press, 1978.

Brylowski, Walter. *Faulkner's Olympian Laugh: Myth in the Novels*. Detroit: Wayne State University Press, 1968.

Cross, Barbara M. "*The Sound and the Fury*: The Pattern of Sacrifice." *Arizona Quarterly* 16 (Spring 1960): 5–16.

Faulkner, William. *Light in August*. New York: Vintage-Random House, 1972.

————. *Pylon*. New York: Random House, 1935.

————. *The Sound and the Fury*. New York: Vintage-Random House, 1954.

————. *The Town*. New York: Vintage-Random House, 1957.

Guereschi, Edward. "Ritual and Myth in William Faulkner's *Pylon*." *Thoth* 3 (Spring 1962): 106–109.

Hlavsa, Virginia V. "St. John and Frazer in *Light in August*: Biblical Form and Mythic Function." *Bulletin of Research in the Humanities* 83 (Spring 1980): 9–26.

Holman, C. Hugh. "The Unity of Faulkner's *Light in August*." *PMLA* 73 (March 1958): 155–66.

Kinney, Arthur F., ed. *Critical Essays on William Faulkner: The Compson Family*. Boston: G. K. Hall, 1982.

Marvin, John R. "*Pylon*: The Definition of Sacrifice." *Faulkner Studies* 1 (Summer 1952): 20–23.

McHaney, Thomas L. "*Sanctuary* and Frazer's Slain Kings." *Mississippi Quarterly* 24 (Summer 1971): 223–45.

Millgate, Michael. *The Achievement of William Faulkner*. New York: Random House, 1963.

Monteiro, George. "Bankruptcy in Time: A Reading of William Faulkner's *Pylon*." *Twentieth Century Literature* 4 (April–July 1958): 9–20.

Oates, Joyce Carol. "'At Least I Have Made a Woman of Her': Images of Women in Twentieth-Century Literature." *Georgia Review* 37 (Spring 1983): 7–30.

Phillips, K. J. "Waste Land in Faulkner's *Go Down, Moses*." *International Fiction Review* 9 (Summer 1982): 114–19.

Pitavy, François L., ed, *William Faulkner's Light in August: A Critical Casebook*. New York: Garland, 1982.

Ruppersburg, Hugh M. *Voice and Eye in Faulkner's Fiction*. Athens: University of Georgia Press, 1983.

Slabey, Robert M. "Myth and Ritual in *Light in August*." *Texas Studies in Literature and Language* 2 (Autumn 1960): 328–49.

Snead, James A. *Figures of Division: William Faulkner's Major Novels*. New York: Methuen, 1986.

Torchiana, Donald T. "Faulkner's 'Pylon' and the Structure of Modernity." *Modern Fiction Studies* 3 (Winter 1957): 291–308.

Vickery, John. "William Faulkner and Sir Philip Sidney?" *Modern Language Notes* 70 (May 1955): 349–50.

Vickery, Olga W. *The Novels of William Faulkner*. Baton Rouge: Louisiana State University Press, 1964.

Waggoner, Hyatt. *William Faulkner: From Jefferson to the World*. Lexington: University of Kentucky Press, 1959.

Williams, David. *Faulkner's Women: The Myth and the Muse*. Montreal: McGill-Queen's University Press, 1977.

Zink, Karl E. "Faulkner's Garden: Woman and the Immemorial Earth." *Modern Fiction Studies* 2 (Autumn 1956): 139–49.

Forster

Bradbury, Malcolm, ed. *E. M. Forster, A Passage to India: A Casebook*. New York: Macmillan, 1970.

Das, G. K., and John Beer, eds. *E. M. Forster: A Human Exploration*. London: Macmillan, 1979.

Forster, E. M. *Abinger Harvest*. London: Arnold, 1936.

———. *Albergo Empedocle and Other Writings*. Ed. George H. Thomson. New York: Liveright, 1971.

———. "The Blue Boy." Review of *The Loves of Krishna*, by W. G. Archer. *Listener* 57, 14 March 1957, 444.

———. *The Hill of Devi and Other Indian Writings*. Ed. Elizabeth Heine. London: Arnold, 1983.

———. *A Passage to India*. New York: Harcourt, Brace, Jovanovich, 1952.

Havell, E. B. *The Ideals of Indian Art*. 1911. London: Murray, 1920.

Herz, Judith Scherer, and Robert K. Martin, eds. *E. M. Forster: Centenary Revaluations*. Toronto: University of Toronto Press, 1982.

Horowitz, Ellin. "The Communal Ritual and the Dying God in E. M. Forster's 'A Passage to India.'" *Criticism* 6 (Winter 1964): 70–88.

Levine, June Perry. *Creation and Criticism: A Passage to India*. Lincoln: University of Nebraska Press, 1971.

Martin, E. Osborn. *The Gods of India: Their History, Character and Worship*. 1914. Delhi: Varanari, Indological, 1972.

McDowell, Frederick P. W., ed. *E. M. Forster: An Annotated Bibliography of Writings About Him*. DeKalb: Northern Illinois University Press, 1976.

Sahni, Chaman L. "E. M. Forster's *A Passage to India*: The Islamic Dimension." *Cahiers Victoriens et Edouardiens* 17 (April 1983): 73–88.

Selig, Robert L. "'God si Love': On an Unpublished Forster Letter and the Ironic Use of Myth in *A Passage to India*." *Journal of Modern Literature* 7 (September 1979): 471–87.

Shahane, V. A., ed. *Perspectives on E. M. Forster's A Passage to India: A Collection of Critical Essays*. New York: Barnes and Noble, 1968.

Spencer, Michael. "Hinduism in E. M. Forster's *A Passage to India*." *Journal of Asian Studies* 27 (February 1968): 281–95.

Stallybrass, Oliver, ed. *A Passage to India*. Abinger ed. London: Arnold, 1978.

Stone, Wilfred. *The Cave and the Mountain: A Study of E. M. Forster*. Stanford: Stanford University Press, 1966.

Walker, Benjamin. *The Hindu World: An Encyclopedic Survey of Hinduism.* 2 vols. New York: Praeger, 1968.

Webner, Hélène L. "E. M. Forster's Divine Comedy." *Renascence* 23 (Winter 1971): 98–110.

García Márquez

Bell-Villada, Gene H. "Pronoun Shifters, Virginia Woolf, Béla Bartók, Plebeian Forms, Real-Life Tyrants, and the Shaping of García Márquez's *Patriarch.*" *Contemporary Literature* 28 (Winter 1987): 460–82.

García Márquez, Gabriel. *The Autumn of the Patriarch.* Translated by Gregory Rabassa. New York: Avon Books, 1976.

———. *Leaf Storm and Other Stories.* Translated by Gregory Rabassa. New York: Avon Books, 1972.

Janes, Regina. *Gabriel García Márquez: Revolutions in Wonderland.* Columbia: University of Missouri Press, 1981.

Hemingway

Baker, Carlos, ed. *Ernest Hemingway: Critiques of Four Major Novels.* New York: Scribner's, 1962.

Baskett, Sam S. "'An Image to Dance Around': Brett and Her Lovers in *The Sun Also Rises.*" *Centennial Review* 22 (Winter 1978): 45–69.

Brasch, James D., and Joseph Sigman. *Hemingway's Library: A Composite Record.* New York: Garland, 1981.

Capellán, Angel. *Hemingway and the Hispanic World.* Ann Arbor: UMI, 1985.

Clendenning, John. "Hemingway's Gods, Dead and Alive." *Texas Studies in Literature and Language* 3 (Winter 1962): 489–502.

Cochran, Robert W. "Circularity in *The Sun Also Rises.*" *Modern Fiction Studies* 14 (Autumn 1968): 297–305.

Ford, Richard. *Gatherings from Spain.* London: Murray, 1851.

Ganzel, Dewey. "*Cabestro* and *Vaquilla*: The Symbolic Structure of *The Sun Also Rises.*" *Sewanee Review* 76 (Winter 1968): 26–48.

Grant, Sister Mary Kathryn. "The Search for Celebration in *The Sun Also Rises* and *The Great Gatsby.*" *Arizona Quarterly* 33 (Summer 1977): 181–92.

Grimes, Larry E. *The Religious Design of Hemingway's Early Fiction.* Ann Arbor: UMI, 1985.

Hemingway, Ernest. *Death in the Afternoon.* New York: Scribner's, 1932.

———. *The Sun Also Rises.* New York: Scribner's, 1954.

Hoffman, Frederick J. *The Mortal No: Death and the Modern Imagination.* Princeton: Princeton University Press, 1964.

Nagel, James, ed. *Ernest Hemingway: The Writer in Context.* Madison: University of Wisconsin Press, 1984.

Phillips, Larry W., ed. *Ernest Hemingway on Writing*. New York: Scribner's, 1984.

Phillips, Steven R. "Hemingway and the Bullfight." *Arizona Quarterly* 29 (Spring 1973): 37–56.

Reynolds, Michael S. *Hemingway's Reading 1910–1940: An Inventory*. Princeton: Princeton University Press, 1981.

Wagner, Linda, ed. *Ernest Hemingway: Five Decades of Criticism*. East Lansing: Michigan State University Press, 1974.

Weeks, Robert P., ed. *Hemingway: A Collection of Critical Essays*. Englewood Cliffs, N. J.: Prentice-Hall, 1962.

Kafka

Corngold, Stanley, ed. *The Commentators' Despair: The Interpretation of Kafka's Metamorphosis*. Port Washington, New York: Kennikat, 1973.

Glatzer, Nahum N., ed. *The Penguin Complete Short Stories of Franz Kafka*. Harmondsworth, England: Penguin Books, 1983. "Der Jäger Gracchus" translated by Willa and Edwin Muir; "Fragment zum 'Der Jäger Gracchus'" translated by Tania and James Stern.

"Gracchi, the." *The New Encyclopedia Britannica*. 15th ed. 1984.

Graetz, H. *History of the Jews*. Vol. 1. Philadelphia: Jewish Publication Society, 1891.

Gray, Ronald D., ed. *Kafka: A Collection of Critical Essays*. Englewood Cliffs, N. J.: Prentice-Hall, 1962.

Kafka, Franz. *Diaries 1910–1913*. Edited by Max Brod and translated by Joseph Kresh. New York: Schocken Books, 1965.

———. *The Metamorphosis*. Edited and translated by Stanley Corngold. New York: Bantam Books, 1981.

Kundera, Milan. "Somewhere Beyond." Translated by Jaroslav Schjebal. *Formations* 1 (Spring 1984): 122–29.

Pawel, Ernst. *The Nightmare of Reason: A Life of Franz Kafka*. New York: Farrar, Straus, and Giroux, 1984.

Robertson, Ritchie. *Kafka: Judaism, Politics, and Literature*. Oxford: Clarendon, 1985.

Spann, Meno. *Franz Kafka*. Boston: Twayne, 1976.

Konwicki

Konwicki, Tadeusz. *A Minor Apocalypse*. Translated by Richard Lourie. New York: Vintage-Random House, 1984.

———. *The Polish Complex*. 1977. Translated by Richard Lourie. New York: Viking-Penguin Books, 1984.

Lawrence

Clark, L. D. *Dark Night of the Body: D. H Lawrence's The Plumed Serpent*. Austin: University of Texas Press, 1964.

Cowan, James C. *D. H. Lawrence's American Journey: A Study in Literature and Myth*. Cleveland: Case Western Reserve, 1970.

Foster, John Burt, Jr. *Heirs to Dionysus: A Nietzschean Current in Literary Modernism*. Princeton: Princeton University Press, 1981.

Goodheart, Eugene. *The Utopian Vision of D. H. Lawrence*. Chicago: University of Chicago Press, 1963.

Gutierrez, Donald. *Lapsing Out: Embodiments of Death and Rebirth in the Last Writings of D. H. Lawrence*. Rutherford, N.J.: Fairleigh Dickinson University Press, 1980.

Hinz, Evelyn J., and John Teunissen. "Savior and Cock: Allusion and Icon in Lawrence's *The Man Who Died*." *Journal of Modern Literature* 5 (April 1976): 279–96.

Hough, Graham. *The Dark Sun: A Study of D. H. Lawrence*. New York: Capricorn, 1956.

Humma, John B. "The Interpenetrating Metaphor: Nature and Myth in *Lady Chatterley's Lover*." *PMLA* 98 (January 1983): 77–86.

Lawrence, D. H. *Apocalypse*. New York: Viking Press, 1932.

———. *The Escaped Cock*. Edited by Gerald M. Lacy. Los Angeles: Black Sparrow Press, 1973.

———. *Lady Chatterley's Lover*. New York: Pocket Books, 1959.

———. *Last Poems*. Edited by Richard Aldington and Guiseppe Orioli. New York: Viking Press, 1933.

———. *Mornings in Mexico*. London: Secker, 1927.

———. *Phoenix: The Posthumous Papers of D. H. Lawrence*. Edited by Edward D. McDonald. New York: Viking Press, 1936.

———. *Phoenix II*. Edited by Warren Roberts and Harry T. Moore. New York: Viking Press, 1959.

———. *The Plumed Serpent*. New York: Vintage Books, 1959.

———. *St. Mawr and The Man Who Died*. New York: Vintage Books, 1953.

———. *Three Novellas*. New York: Penguin, 1960.

———. *The Woman Who Rode Away and Other Stories*. New York: Knopf, 1928.

LeDoux, Larry V. "Christ and Isis: The Function of the Dying and Reviving God in *The Man Who Died*." *D. H. Lawrence Review* 5 (Summer 1972): 132–48.

Meyers, Jeffrey. "*The Plumed Serpent* and the Mexican Revolution." *Journal of Modern Literature* 4 (September 1974): 55–72.

Parmenter, Ross. *Lawrence in Oaxaca*. Salt Lake City: Smith, 1984.

Sagar, Keith. *D. H. Lawrence: A Calendar of His Works*. Manchester: Manchester University Press, 1979.

Sanders, Scott. *D. H. Lawrence: The World of the Major Novels*. London: Vision, 1973.

Simpson, Hilary. *D. H. Lawrence and Feminism*. DeKalb: Northern Illinois University Press, 1982.

Spence, Lewis. *Myths and Legends: Mexico and Peru*. Boston: Nickerson, 1913.

Tindall, William York. *D. H. Lawrence and Susan His Cow*. New York: Columbia University Press, 1939.

Troy, William. *Selected Essays*. Edited by Stanley Edgar Hyman. New Brunswick: Rutgers University Press, 1967.

Vickery, John B. "*The Plumed Serpent* and the Reviving God." *Western American Literature* 3 (Summer 1968): 103–13.

Waters, Frank. "Quetzalcoatl Versus D. H. Lawrence's *The Plumed Serpent*." *Western American Literature* 3 (Summer 1968): 103–13.

Malamud

Higgs, Robert J. *Laurel and Thorn: The Athlete in American Literature*. Lexington: University Press of Kentucky, 1981.

Malamud, Bernard. *The Natural*. New York: Farrar, Straus, and Giroux, 1952.

Schickel, Richard. "Swinging for the Fences." *Time*, 14 May 1984, 91.

Wasserman, Earl R. "*The Natural*: Malamud's World Ceres." *Centennial Review* 9 (1965): 438–60.

Mann

Apter, T. E. *Thomas Mann: The Devil's Advocate*. New York: New York University Press, 1979.

Bloch, Adèle. "The Archetypal Influences in Thomas Mann's *Joseph and His Brothers*." *The Germanic Review* 38 (March 1963): 151–56.

Campbell, Joseph. *Erotic Irony and Mythic Forms in the Art of Thomas Mann*. Bronxville N.Y.: Sarah Lawrence College, 1973.

Ezergailis, Inta Miske. *Male and Female: An Approach to Thomas Mann's Dialectic*. The Hague: Martinus Nyhoff, 1975.

Kerenyi, Karl, ed. *Mythology and Humanism: The Correspondence of Thomas Mann and Karl Kerenyi*. Translated by Alexander Gelley. Ithaca: Cornell University Press, 1975.

Lehnert, Herbert H. "Fictional Orientations in Thomas Mann's Biography." *PMLA* 88 (October 1973): 1146–61.

Mann, Thomas. "Freud and the Future." 1936. In *The Modern Tradition*, edited by Richard Ellmann and Charles Feidelson, Jr., 585–90, 672–79. New York: Oxford University Press, 1965.

———. *Joseph and His Brothers*. Translated by H. T. Lowe-Porter. New York: Knopf, 1966.

———. *The Theme of the Joseph Novels*. Washington, D.C.: Government Publishing Office, 1943.

Murdaugh, Elaine. *Salvation in the Secular: The Moral Law in Thomas Mann's "Joseph und seine Brüder."* Frankfurt: Lang, 1976.

———. "Thomas Mann and the Bitch Goddess: Rejection and Reconstruction of the Primal Mother in *Joseph and His Brothers.*" *Revue des langues vivantes* 44 (1978): 395–407.

Slochower, Harry. *Thomas Mann's Joseph Story: An Interpretation.* New York: Knopf, 1938.

Oates

Oates, Joyce Carol. *Cybele.* Santa Barbara: Black Sparrow Press, 1979.

O'Connor

Asals, Frederick. "The Mythic Dimensions of Flannery O'Connor's 'Greenleaf.'" *Studies in Short Fiction* 5 (Summer 1968): 317–30.

Getz, Lorine M. *Flannery O'Connor: Her Life, Library and Book Reviews.* New York: Mellen, 1980.

O'Connor, Flannery. *Everything That Rises Must Converge.* New York: Farrar, Straus, and Giroux, 1956.

———. *The Habit of Being.* Edited by Sally Fitzgerald. New York: Vintage-Random House, 1979.

Shields, John C. "Flannery O'Connor's 'Greenleaf' and the Myth of Europa and the Bull." *Studies in Short Fiction* 18 (Fall 1981): 421–31.

Smith, J. Oates. "Ritual and Violence in Flannery O'Connor." *Thought* 41 (Winter 1966): 545–60.

White, Victor. *God and the Unconscious.* London: Harvill, 1952.

Welty

Dollarhide, Louis, and Ann J. Abadie, eds. *Eudora Welty: A Form of Thanks.* Jackson: University Press of Mississippi, 1979.

Hodgins, Audrey. "The Narrator as Ironic Device in a Short Story of Eudora Welty." *Twentieth Century Literature* 1 (January 1956): 215–19.

Karem, Suzanne Story. "Mythology in the Works of Eudora Welty." *DAI* (University of Kentucky) 39 (1978): 3581A.

Kreyling, Michael. *Eudora Welty's Achievement of Order.* Baton Rouge: Louisiana State University Press, 1980.

Prenshaw, Peggy Whitman, ed. *Conversations with Eudora Welty.* Jackson: University Press of Mississippi, 1984.

———, ed. *Eudora Welty: Critical Essays.* Jackson: University Press of Mississippi, 1979.

———. "Persephone in Eudora Welty's 'Livvie.'" *Studies in Short Fiction* 17 (Spring 1980): 149–55.

Welty, Eudora. *The Collected Stories.* New York: Harcourt, Brace, Jovanovich, 1980.

Woolf

Blotner, Joseph L. "Mythic Patterns in *To the Lighthouse.*" In *Myth and Literature: Contemporary Theory and Practice*, edited by John B. Vickery, 243–55. Lincoln: University of Nebraska Press, 1983.

DiBattista, Maria. *Virginia Woolf's Major Novels: The Fables of Anon.* New Haven: Yale University Press, 1980.

Fleishman, Avrom. *Virginia Woolf: A Critical Reading.* Baltimore: Johns Hopkins University Press, 1975.

Freedman, Ralph, ed. *Virginia Woolf: Revaluation and Continuity.* Berkeley: University of California Press, 1980.

Ginsberg, Elaine K., and Laura Moss Gottlieb, eds. *Virginia Woolf: Centennial Essays.* Troy, N.Y.: Whitson, 1983.

Heilbrun, Carolyn G. *Toward a Recognition of Androgyny.* New York: Knopf, 1973.

Hoffman, Anne Golomb. "Demeter and Poseidon: Fusion and Distance in *To the Lighthouse.*" *Studies in the Novel* 16 (Summer 1984): 182–96.

Lempriere, J. *A Classical Dictionary.* New York: Duyckinck, 1825.

Lilienfeld, Jane. "'The Deceptiveness of Beauty': Mother Love and Mother Hate in *To the Lighthouse.*" *Twentieth Century Literature* 23 (October 1977): 345–76.

Marcus, Jane, ed. *Virginia Woolf: A Feminist Slant.* Lincoln: University of Nebraska Press, 1983.

Rose, Phyllis. "Mrs. Ramsay and Mrs. Woolf." *Women's Studies* 1 (1973): 199-216.

———. *Woman of Letters: A Life of Virginia Woolf.* New York: Oxford University Press, 1978.

Rosenman, Ellen Bayuk. *The Invisible Presence: Virginia Woolf and the Mother-Daughter Relationship.* Baton Rouge: Louisiana University Press, 1986.

Schlack, Beverly Ann. *Continuing Presences: Virginia Woolf's Use of Literary Allusions.* University Park: Pennsylvania State University Press, 1979.

Silver, Brenda R. *Virginia Woolf's Reading Notebooks.* Princeton: Princeton University Press, 1983.

Sprague, Claire, ed. *Virginia Woolf: A Collection of Critical Essays.* Englewood Cliffs, N.J.: Prentice-Hall, 1971.

Whitehead, Lee M. "The Shawl and the Skull: Virginia Woolf's 'Magic Mountain.'" *Modern Fiction Studies* 18 (Autumn 1972): 401–15.

Woolf, Virginia. *Between the Acts.* New York: Harcourt, Brace, Jovanovich, 1969.

———. *The Diary of Virginia Woolf Volume Two: 1920–1924.* Edited by Ann Olivier Bell. New York: Harcourt, Brace, Jovanovich, 1978.

———. *The Diary of Virginia Woolf Volume Four: 1931–1935.* Edited by Anne Olivier Bell. New York: Harcourt, Brace, Jovanovich, 1982.

———. *To the Lighthouse.* New York: Harcourt, Brace, and World, 1955.

———. *The Waves.* New York: Harcourt, Brace, Jovanovich, 1959.

Index